Living East

of the

Sandy

Volume 1

By Clarence E. Mershon

Published for the
East Multnomah County Pioneer Association
and
Professional Graphics Center, Inc.
17272 NE Sacremento, Portland OR 97233

Foreword

Clarence Mershon, inspired by the work of Bea Graff in compiling the stories of the early pioneers and their descendants in East Multnomah County, made a commitment some time ago to add to the information Bea and the East Multnomah County Pioneer Association had previously published. Mershon had completed some work in this regard after being asked by Bea to research and report on how the early residents made a living. After Mershon retired in 1989, he continued his interest in and activities to support the Association and also joined the Crown Point Country Historical Society.

Meetings of the Society are often devoted to story telling by "old-timers" invited to participate. On one such occasion several years ago, Alice Wand suggested that these 'stories' should be recorded, otherwise the history would be lost. Mershon determined at that meeting to undertake the task and at a subsequent meeting made the commitment alluded to above.

As a result, under the aegis of the East Multnomah County Pioneer Association, Mershon published his first book, *Corbett Now and Columbian Then*. This, his second book, contains stories of the descendants of early pioneers and those of more recent 'settlers.' Thanks to the generosity of many individuals (and recent technological advances), *Living East of the Sandy* includes numerous pictures of historical interest as well as more personal photographs of those who made this area their home. If the reader gains a better understanding of life in East Multnomah County in earlier days the author's objective has been met.

Information included herein documents how important farming was to economy of the area. Much farmland, which once provided the principal livelihood for the people, is now overgrown with trash trees or underbrush. Independent farmers, who could provide produce for a relatively short period during the year, found it impossible to compete with corporate farms, which could supply produce to chains year-round. Once a great dairying region, the area does not now have a single producing dairy farm. Commercial fishing is only a memory of a bygone era. Some logging continues, but regulations are onerous. Not a single lumber mill survives. Savor these 'stories' for they tell of a way of life that has been supplanted by historic trends that few understand, let alone have the means to change.

When Mershon found that the 'stories' he had written greatly exceeded what could be accommodated in one book, he decided to continue the work in a second volume. Chapters regarding the mills at Bridal Veil and the construction of Bonneville Dam will appear in Volume 2. Also, a second volume will provide an opportunity to add information and pictures that will make certain family 'stories' more complete. For example, the Frank/Theresa Wand family history, written by David Wand, was complete in every respect except for photos. Since pictures add much to the 'story,' David decided to locate pictures. Therefore, the Wand family section will appear in volume two. Much 'story gathering' remains to be accomplished. Mershon appreciates the cooperation of those who have shared family lore and pictures with the community.

Finally, though several individuals have scrutinized the text and pictures, some errors may be found. Please accept the author's apology for any that remain.

CONTENTS

Dedication

Micheal E. Mershon was born March 9, 1991. The first years of his life were uneventful, but happy. He lived with his parents in a small home in Gresham. Micheal was proud when he tried something new. When he first tried potato salad, he said, "I ate potato salad." He learned to play ball with his brother, Daniel, and asked everyone to play ball with him. He learned to swim, and enjoyed visiting his Aunt Elise, where he could swim in the pool. Being the youngest of two brothers, he often managed to get his mother, Robin, his father, Perry, or his Aunt Elise, Uncle Mike or Uncle Chris to pull him around in a wagon, which he loved.

When Micheal was two years of age, his parents moved to a new home in Carson, Washington. He learned to ride a bike and rode it to visit neighbors across Bear Creek Road. He was enthralled with a new pair of shoes with a blinking red light that his grandparents bought for him. His grandfather took him to a trout farm where his father, Perry, helped him catch fish. He liked Kindergarten. It helped that his mother volunteered at the school. He collected "Chevron" cars, and always asked his grandfather, "Do you need gas?"

One day when he was six, his parents took him to Bend. He came back with a shiner, explaining that he fell off the sidewalk. One time he fell while following his grandmother around and came up with a big red spot above his eye. When she commented, "You must have tripped over your own feet," he laughed and repeated, "I tripped over my own feet." Gradually, so gradual that it was hardly noticeable, similar incidents occurred more frequently. When his great grandmother, who had not seen him for several weeks, observed him later that summer, she noticed that something was wrong. She thought he ought to see a doctor.

That is when an inoperable tumor on his brain stem was found. Many people made the last few months of his life memorable. He became an active member of the 142nd Fighter Group for one day, and his father's commanding officer took him for a 'taxi' ride in an F-15. Through the *Make a Wish Foundation*, he got to meet his idol, Shaq O'Neal, of the Los Angeles Lakers. He also went to DisneyWorld in Florida. When he could no longer walk, he told his father, "I can learn to walk again." He tried, but couldn't. He was happy when he could hold his new baby brother, Kurtis - until he could no longer hold his arms up. He noticed that when other children became ill, they recovered. Micheal, too, thought that he would get well. But he didn't.

Dedicated to my Grandson

Micheal E. Mershon

March 9, 1991 – May 2, 1998

Micheal E. Mershon, soccer player. Photo courtesy of Robin Mershon.

Sergeant Bryce seats Micheal in an F-15 while Lt. Colonel Dean preps everyone involved.

Louis H. Arneson
Grace Z. (Lindsay) Arneson

Louis H. Arneson was born July 12, 1874 in Wisconsin of Arne and Ingeborg Arneson, who immigrated to the United States from Norway. Seven of the couples nine children were born in Norway while the two youngest, Ida and Louis 'Lou' were born in the United States. In 1882, the Arnesons brought five of their nine children west to San Francisco by train, then to Portland by boat. In 1883, the family settled on a farm near the community of Fairview, Oregon. Shortly after their arrival, Arne Arneson died leaving Ingeborg with two children remaining at home to raise. The family owned a few cows, and Ida and Louis would take turns turning them out to pasture in the morning and bringing them in at night. One evening Ida asked Lou to take her turn. He stopped by the shed to get a few extra shells for the shotgun, which he used to shoot gray diggers (ground squirrels) that feasted on the family's garden. After opening the shed door, he obtained four shells, stuck them in his pocket and jumped down. As he climbed down the ramp, he bent to pick up the shotgun with his left hand. There was a boom as the gun discharged and Lou fell to the ground unconscious. The open trigger had caught on something and the gun discharged into the boy's left armpit, nearly severing his arm.

Alerted by the blast, Lou's mother and sisters, Ida and Julia, who happened to be visiting, found him unconscious and carried him to the barn. Ida ran to the neighbors and asked them to go for a doctor. The family members did what could be done to stem the bleeding until the doctor arrived. Lou lost the arm and lay for weeks near death, watched and cared for night and day by his mother and sisters. Many weeks later, wane and pale, Lou walked out of the barn. Though his arm was buried in the yard, the missing limb gave him much pain. A few months later he was back in school, determined not to let the loss of his arm keep him from realizing his future plans.

Lou attended Portland Academy and obtained a teaching certificate when he was sixteen. He signed his first contract to teach at Taylor School in Corbett the 1890-91 school year for $25.00 per month. He found his duties included janitorial work and guiding about 30 students in their studies. Among his pupils were Louis Benfield and Clarence 'Monk' Deverell. According to Inga, Louis Benfield once told her, "Your father was one of the best teachers we had. He really taught us to write." Lou boarded with different families, among whom were the Rasmussens, caretakers at the Corbett Estate. They became and remained life-long friends. The teaching job at Taylor lasted only a year, but acquaintances made would be renewed at a later date. Lou also taught at Hurlburt School and mentioned having Ward Evans, Rae Perkins and Art Johnson as pupils (see "Louis and Grace Arneson," *Pioneer History*).

Early in the 1890's, Lou Arneson obtained a job at the land office in The Dalles. He married Grace Z. Lindsay, also of Wisconsin origins, April 12, 1903, in Hood River. Grace, born June 17, 1881, had earlier been a student of Lou Arneson at the Oak Grove School. The couple had three children, Louis L., b. June 18, 1909; Edith C. 'Carolyn,' b. September 15, 1910; and Inga G., b. August 29, 1913, all born in The Dalles. In 1913, the Arnesons moved to Hood River after the job at the land office ended. They moved to a 20-acre farm in the valley near Oak Grove. The farm included a house and yard, farm buildings, a garden area, a few different fruit trees, an apple orchard, a strawberry field and 'woods.' Lou built the frame house on the property himself. The children all started grade school in Hood River. The oldest of the children, Louis, died from injuries received in a bicycle accident near his home in Oak Grove at age 10. He injured his knee and died from blood poisoning October 10, 1919, within a couple days of the accident. The death caused much anguish for the family and the date became an anniversary date for a later tragedy in the family.

In 1920, the Arnesons, troubled by the loss, decided to rent the farm to relatives and moved back to The Dalles. The family stayed in The Dalles for about six years, where Carolyn and Inga continued elementary school. In 1926 Mr. Arneson purchased a store in Corbett from Sig and Xene Knighton, and the family moved there in February 1926. The store was located across the street from Rickert's Garage. It turned out to be a wooden structure with one big room in front for the store, two bedrooms with a walk-through closet between them, a kitchen, a small side room off the store and a larger side room off the kitchen. There was a 'two-holer' out back. Upon the Arnesons arrival the previous owners greeted them. According to Inga, Orval Johnson, a nephew of the owners, was sitting at a table with "an impudent grin on his freckled face." Inga minced no words regarding the situation:

Arneson's Corbett Store

Arneson's Store from CHS.

Arneson's Store (note Corbett Hardware through station bay).
Photos courtesy of Inga (Arneson) Myers.

"The only heat in the entire building was a barrel stove. It scorched you up close and you froze when any distance away from it. ...We surely pared right down to basics, farther than ever before, even on the farm. In fact, the farm was pure heaven on earth (compared to) this dump..." For weeks it rained and the east wind blew. "We didn't dress the same as 'Corbettites;' we didn't talk the same; ...we had no friends;" and it was Inga's considered opinion that "the 'Corbettites' weren't particularly interested in alleviating the situation."

3

Of course Carolyn and Inga attended Corbett schools. The grade school was a short walk beyond the Christian Church to the east and the high school was just west across the highway. By Inga's eighth-grade year, her attitude regarding her surroundings seemed to have mollified. The grade school had a new principal, George Lusby, who was "young and just married. He was good looking and a really good teacher." Also, shortly after the move to Corbett, Mr. Arneson bought Roy Anderson's store, which was just west beyond the little cottage where Lydia Ostrand lived and adjacent to Claude Woodle's Corbett Hardware. Arneson remodeled the building, adding two bedrooms, a bathroom, a garage and a partial basement. Clarence Deverell, a former student of Mr. Arneson, did much of the digging and building, exchanging labor for groceries for his family. The existing grocery and lunch businesses were moved to the new location and several new 'lines' added, including gas pumps, over-the-counter drugs, auto parts, fishing supplies, bus tickets and the Post Office. Arnesons kept the store open 24 hours a day, with Mr. Arneson taking the midnight to morning shift, Mrs. Arneson the eight to midnight shift, and both were there during the busy part of the day. Inga practiced the piano in the early morning hours, swept the floor at eight and cooked breakfast. After she started high school, the first bell sent her dashing across the highway to school in order to get there before the final bell rang.

Inga recalled a visit from Mr. and Mrs. R.P. Rasmussen and their daughter, Alice. At the time the Rasmussens owned a cabin near the Sandy River, close to Springdale, where they spent the summer.

"On the afternoon of this particular day, Mrs. Rasmussen asked me if I would like to help her find the old trail that led down the hill…to the Corbett Estate, where she and her husband had been caretakers many years before. …Mrs. Rasmussen led the way. I thought she must be wrong when she headed across a neighbor's field. We trudged through the weeds to a barbed-wire fence. …I held the wires up as Mrs. Rasmussen crawled under and I followed her into the woods. She seemed so sure of the way.

Mrs. Rasmussen, who had a Danish accent, said, 'I tink der should be a big log right about here.' We found the log within a few yards. It was rotted and covered with moss, but there it lay. In the middle was a depression, worn by many feet that crossed it in the years gone by. On we went into the woods. …The trail was al-

4

Inga Arneson

Catching the Portland Stage. Photo courtesy of Pat (Bramhall) Paget

CHS graduate, 1931.
Photo courtesy of Inga (Arneson) Myers.

most a fantasy. If you looked closely, it disappeared. If you glanced ahead, it appeared again. Finally we reached an old cabin. 'Dat vas de old vood chopper's place,' explained Mrs. Rasmussen. 'Now ve come to my hidevay.' Sure enough around the next bend in the trail was an enchanting spot. The ground was a mossy carpet extending from a bank grown thick with maidenhair fern to a mossy log with licorice fern growing over its sides. …This lovely spot was to be used during the next few years whenever I needed to be alone."

Carolyn and Inga's summers were spent in berry picking, swimming, hiking, picnicking and working at the store. Another favorite pastime was dancing. Dances were frequently held at the Grange Hall or the dance hall in Springdale. Parents served as chaperones and everyone sat down for a midnight supper, which sent all home full and happy. During the school year, people attended the plays, operettas, games and other activities associated with the schools. Inga played piano for the glee club and operettas, was a member of the girls' basketball team and attended all the boys' basketball games, no matter where they were held. Her father often took a carload of students to the games, or they took the spectator bus. Inga recalled some of her high school experiences:

"High School was no easier for me than grade school had been. (However), I worked hard and made excellent grades most of the time. …We had awful ice storms in the winter. One winter…the big boiler blew up and sent the end of it through the basement where the boys' shop class would have been if it (had) happened while school was in session.

Once in a while something funny would happen during class. One afternoon during typing class Jimmy Tanner and one of the girls decided to exchange typewriters. Instead of taking everything out of the drawers from the tables to change that way, they decided to just pull the drawers from the tables and exchange. Just then Miss Remington came in and saw what was going on. She (pointed) toward Jimmy and cried out, 'Oh, don't change your drawers. They won't fit!' Pandemonium reigned."

During her early high school years, Inga dated Gene Chamberlain. She said, "Gene was a thoroughly nice kid. He had a wonderful sense of humor and sang like an angel. He wasn't very big, but he made up for it by being such fun to be with. He was a whiz of a basketball player." Another friend was Mabel Chamberlain. Inga explained that she and Mabel took turns at church and school playing the piano. According to Inga, it was better for her to play than Mabel because Mabel sang so well. "All the Chamberlains had good voices."

On one occasion Mabel invited Inga to a slumber party. The girls had a great time and talked about forming a group that would do special things together and remain close friends. Time passed and rumors abounded about the group, the "Holy Seven." When Inga discovered she was not to be one of the "select few," she was devastated. One of the girls explained to her that it was because Inga was always the "Big I." Because she always thought so much of her friends, admiring their talents and abilities, she thought they felt the same of her. "Not so!" she realized. Though she eventually recovered from the slight, her self-confidence suffered for some time.

Inga's attitude got a boost when she and Bob Ellis started dating. She recalled this as one of the best things that ever happened in her life. She had "admired him from afar so long," she reported that she "was flattered out of her skin." They went dancing, swimming, hiking and to the movies. She mentioned "two wonderful places" where school parties

6

Mrs. Henderson's Crown Point Chalet.   Photo courtesy of Steve Lehl.

were held, the Chanticleer Inn and Moessner's Mizpah Inn. In her words, "The parties we had up there were memorable, to say the least. Pure joy!" She described Bob as "ever protective and a gentleman." They went together for two years, often double-dating with his sister, Mildred Ellis, and her boyfriend.

Inga also remembers a party held at the Crown Point Chalet, but remembers it best as the place where she worked, fixing salads and waiting on tables. The waitresses "carried huge trays and served dinners for the people who reserved it for special times. Others who worked there included Mabel Chamberlain, Doris Emily and Agnes Soderstrom. "Mrs. M.E. Henderson trained us well and would brook no nonsense. Working there was fun, anyway." Inga described the ballroom floor: "It was built of oak flooring laid on edge, which made a beautiful, smooth surface. It was really quite unique." The girls, who stayed in a dormitory room during the summer season, worked 6 days from 10:00 a.m. until 12:00 midnight. They earned $1.00 per day plus tips, which were shared with the 'salad' girl. The waitresses cleaned the dance floor, dining room, outdoor eating areas and wiped dishes after the luncheon crowd left and before the evening crowd came. The Chalet was known for its chicken dinners.

Inga Arneson remembered Owen Emily, who was in her class.

"Owen was always our top student and walked away with honors. He deserved them. He was an avid reader and had a really

Owen Emily, Valedictorian, CHS
Class of 1931. Photo courtesy of Pat
(Bramhall) Paget.

good mind. He had a wonderful sense of humor, also, and added much to the lives of all of us who knew him. Owen's dad, Roy Emily, was janitor at the grade school. He also drove the old school bus, facetiously named the 'Monkey Cage.' Roy was thin and somewhat bent with long arms and big hands. Rarely did you see him without a smile and often he could be heard telling a story or joking with someone, his husky voice a sort of half chuckle. Owen had lost a year of school so his younger brother, Gerald Emily, a year younger, was in our class, too. Gerald was built just like his dad and was a complete imp."

Inga mentioned trips on the Columbia River with fishermen, one of whom was Orlie Sworden. Sometimes Orlie would take them across the river to Reed Island for picnics and a swim. Carolyn Arneson started dating Orlie's son, Ed, while she was in high school. According to Inga, her father "didn't approve of the situation, so (the couple) met in secret... (In the fall of 1927), just before Carolyn turned seventeen, she and Ed eloped. They accompanied Ed's parents to Edmonton, Alberta, to work in the grain harvest." When the couple returned, they lived with Ed's parents at Lower Corbett.

Louis H. and Grace Arneson with granddaughter, Shirley Sworden.   Photo courtesy of Inga (Arneson) Myers.

Fill 'er Up

One of many unusual customers of the Arnesons.
                              Photo courtesy of Inga (Arneson) Myers.

Another memory related by Inga concerned Corbett's famed ice storms and east wind. One icy, windy day Vern Lucas came into the store and asked for gasoline. Grace Arneson looked out and said, "Where's your car?" "Out front," replied Vern. However, it wasn't out front, having been sent scooting across the ice by the east wind to land in front of Woodle's hardware store.

Before leaving school, Carolyn had earned enough credits to graduate and her mother pleaded with her to go through the graduation ceremony. Carolyn complied and received her diploma from CHS (CHS) in 1930. Carolyn and Ed had one child, Shirley, b. February 12, 1931. The family moved into the former store building across from Pounder's Truck Service during the 30's. Ed worked for Linde Air, a firm that sold bottled oxygen and acetylene. When Ed and Carolyn divorced in 1939, she stayed with her parents at the store. Shirley attended school at Corbett through the 8th grade. Carolyn Arneson worked at Bridal Veil during the war. She married Ben Harris and they moved to Portland to live with Lou Arneson, who had purchased a home in Ladd's Addition in July 1944. Carolyn's second child, Karen, was born September 6, 1947. Carolyn (Arneson) Harris passed away July 29, 1982.

Inga graduated from CHS in 1931. Owen Emily gave the valedictory and Inga and Agnes Soderstrom, the salutatory. Inga wore a pink chiffon dress with a short embroidered batiste jacket for graduation. Inga's Aunt Ida gave her a choice of a trip to Europe or two years of college for a graduation gift. Inga chose college. Her aunt compromised by giving her a trip to Alaska and she paid for three years of college for Inga. Inga took the trip during the final two weeks of August, which provided lasting memories of the Inside Passage. She visited Ketchikan, Juneau, Sitka, Fort Haines and Skagway. Another adventure was taking the narrow gauge train into the Yukon through the White Pass. Altogether, it was a memorable trip for Inga, an interlude before she left for college in Eugene.

After a year at the University of Oregon, Inga transferred to the Oregon Normal School in Monmouth to complete a course in teacher training. She signed her first contract to teach in Culver, 1934-35. During Christmas vacation (December 22, 1934) that school year, she and Eugene 'Gene' Myers were married. Such were the times, however, that the event had to be kept quiet. His job was in Florence, so the couple was separated the balance of that year. The next year Gene signed a contract to teach in Jefferson and Inga substituted that year. She and Gene taught

Louis Arneson

Louis Arneson holds his granddaughter, Shirley Sworden. Photos courtesy of Inga Arneson.

in a number of locations until 1941, when they went to San Francisco. After spending the summer there, they returned to Grants Pass where Gene taught the school year 1941-42. On December 7, 1941, Japanese planes bombed Pearl Harbor and the United States was at war. When the school year ended, Gene took a job at American Can in Portland, but shortly thereafter received his draft notice. Rather than waiting to be drafted, he enlisted in the Army Air Force, and was stationed at Chico, California. However, a prior back injury caused such problems that he was medically discharged.

Gene and Inga's first child, Howard Vincent 'Skip,' was born May 23, 1943. Shortly thereafter, the family discovered that Inga's mother, Grace, suffered from heart trouble. She and Lou had continued to operate the Corbett store. She died January 26, 1944. Lou Arneson wanted Gene and Inga to take over the place, but they declined. He sold the store in the summer of 1944 and moved to a home in Portland. On October 12, 1944, close to the 25th anniversary of his son's accidental death, Lou Arneson took his own life.

Gene returned to the teaching field after the war. His and Inga's second child, Barbara Lindsay, was born September 29, 1945. A third child, Kathleen Alice, was born September 10, 1953. In 1962, both Gene and Inga obtained Bachelor of Science degrees from the Oregon College of Education. They were living in The Dalles at the time. Inga Myers returned to the classroom full time in The Dalles in 1957. Gene Myers took a job in the County Assessor's office in The Dalles after completing 18 years in the classroom. He passed away August 2, 1980. Inga Myers now lives independently in her home near 12-mile corner.

Inga (Arneson) Myers

Edwin A. Arrington
Dorothy (Wenban) Arrington

Edwin A. Arrington was born in Oregon of pioneer stock August 6, 1893. The Arrington family had come across the plains in the 1860's by wagon train. The wagons were pulled by oxen, as those beasts had more stamina to withstand the hard pulling day-after-day than horses. The family first settled near Molalla, where their children were raised. When grown, the children scattered throughout the Northwest. Edwin A. Arrington's father, Edwin J., moved to Washington State, and married a young lady from Chewelah he met there. The couple had four children, Edwin A., Mabel, Warren and Lillian. In 1912, Edwin J. decided to homestead in Multnomah Basin, accompanied by his four children (See "Edwin A. Arrington," *Pioneer History*, 1st Supplement).

The family planned to settle and establish a community in Multnomah basin, hoping that a school, store and other establishments would follow. However, the area was just too remote and hard to reach by automobile, which was fast becoming the transportation mode of choice, so the family's dreams did not materialize. The Arringtons attended the Swedenborgian Church of North America, which had a parish in Portland. Edwin A. met his future wife, Dorothy Wenban, at church. She was born in Ohio, July 29, 1896, and had come to Portland with her family shortly after the turn of the century.

The couple married in April 1919, and lived in the basin for several years. Because of its remote location, supplies had to be brought in from Latourell, Bridal Veil, Corbett or other places when stocks ran low. In addition, Edwin A. sometimes had to leave home for a time to work at the Bridal Veil mill or other places in order to make a living. Edwin A. and Dorothy Arrington had four children: Jackson W. 'Jack,' b. March 28, 1920; Edith A. 'Adele,' b. June 24, 1921; Dorothy J. 'Janet,' b. January 15, 1923; and Audrey J., b. December 11, 1935. When the two oldest children reached school age, the Arringtons decided to move from the basin to a less remote area, one that would be more convenient for the youngsters to attend school. The family moved into Portland for a few months, but that was too much of a change, so the family looked for a place on Larch Mountain "closer to civilization." They located and pur-

Edwin A. Arrington's home in Multnomah Basin c1920.

Edwin and Dorothy Arrington in Multnomah Basin.

Jack, Adele and Janet Arrington.
Photos courtesy of Janet (Arrington) Lucas.

chased a farm on Brower Road (that portion of which later became a part of Larch Mountain Road when it was built during the 30's.) Jack and Adele had started school in Portland. After the family moved back to the East County area, they attended Springfield (Egypt) School. Janet also started at Springfield, but the youngsters transferred to Corbett when the schools in the area consolidated in the early 30's. Thereafter, the chil-

13

Arrington Farm on Brower Road

The Arringtons moved from the basin to a farm on Brower (now Larch Mountain) Road c1933.   Photo courtesy of Janet (Arrington) Lucas.

dren attended Corbett Grade School and graduated from CHS, Jack, in 1938, Adele, in 1939, Janet, in 1941, and Audrey, in 1953. Because they lived quite far from the farmers who hired local children during the summer, the Arrington youngsters did not often work for them. They did pick berries for Dick Ellis at times. They had plenty to do at home, feeding and caring for horses, cows, chickens, pigs and other animals. Janet also worked for Judge Languth part time during her high school years. In addition to hay and grain, the Arringtons grew berries and cucumbers. Janet remembers George Shelley picking up the cucumbers by truck, but does not know who bought them. In addition to the farm, Mr. Arrington worked at various jobs in the area. He was a mail carrier for the Corbett Station for a time. During the late 30's, he worked for the WPA, the State Parks Department and various other jobs. During World War II, he worked for a furniture store in Portland. After the war, he worked for the Multnomah County Road Department.

After completing high school, Jack enlisted in the Oregon National Guard, 41st Division. Activated prior to the attack on Pearl Harbor, he was sent to the European Theater after training and saw action in France. He married Eileen Miller of Elma, Washington in 1941, and had a stepson and two other children, Janice and Mike. Adele married Charles B.

14

Janet Arrington, CHS graduate, 1941.

Rear: Chuck Willis, Adele (Arrington) Willis, Janet (Arrington) Lucas, Audrey Arrington, Clarence Lucas, Gertrude LaRue, Blanche Rimes, Carroll Rimes, Edith Evans, Fred Kaiser, Mildred Kaiser, Edwin A. Arrington. Front: Aunt Carrie holding Cheryl Lucas, Kirk Kaiser, Grandmother Edith Wenbam, Jim Rimes and Greg Lucas.

Photos courtesy of Janet (Arrington) Lucus.

Willis and moved to Portland. She has three children, William, Larry and Dian. Janet married Clarence W. Lucas February 28, 1942, and they made their home in Springdale. They have three children (see "Vern Lucas"). Audrey started college at Oregon State, then transferred to the Oregon College of Education at Monmouth, graduating in 1957. She taught for a time, but quit to raise a family. She married David Clark and they have three children, Eric, Gwen and Sean. Dorothy (Wenban) Arrington passed away September 5, 1956. Edwin A. Arrington died December 15, 1973. *Janet Lucas*

Louie Baker
Clara (Kerslake) Baker

Louie Baker moved to Springdale with his family in 1908. Louie had brought a load of household goods by wagon via the Columbia River, landing at Lower Corbett early in January. A winter storm hit about the time that he arrived at the new place, and the Kerslake family invited him to stay with them until the storm abated. His future wife, Clara Kerslake, was twelve years of age at the time. Louie worked for the Kerslakes during the time his family lived in the area. According to Clara, she and Louie became better acquainted as "he was around a lot." When his family moved back to Friend, Oregon (near Dufur), Louie and Clara corresponded, but saw each other rather infrequently.

Louie was drafted into the Army during World War I, and saw action in France. He suffered lung damage from the effects of poison gas, which thereafter caused health problems for him. After the armistice was signed, Louis remained overseas for nearly a year before returning home. A mishap involving his brother kept him from visiting Clara Kerslake on his way to Friend. Though discouraged by events, Louie took a job in the wheat fields and visited Clara that Christmas. She returned with him to Eastern Oregon. Jointly, they decided they did not wish to live in Eastern Oregon.

In January, Louie loaded his belongings onto a wagon and left for Springdale. The trip took three bitterly cold days over steep and narrow roads before he arrived at the Kerslake home. Soon Louie's parents joined him and settled in Cottrell. Louie courted Clara, walking to see her every Sunday. Land that veterans could homestead opened in the Aims area so Louie filed for 120 acres at $2.50 per acre. The purchase required a $50.00 down payment with the balance due within three years. Though Jessie Kerslake became ill at about this time, love prevailed and the couple married March 26, 1921 (see "Allan B. Kerslake," {this volume}, and "Louie and Clara {Kerslake} Baker," *Pioneer History*).

Because of her mother's illness, Clara often rode a horse to reach her parents' home so that she could help. On the return trip, she carried groceries or other needed supplies obtained in Springdale. Water for household use at the homestead was obtained from a spring and carried to the

Equipped for Muddy Roads

Louie Baker (L) with Allan B. Kerslake.

Cameron Hogg Crew c1923

Workers pose on the locomotive of the mill train. Photos courtesy of the Kerslake Family.

Cameron Hogg Mill c1923

Louis Baker (in overalls) is standing on the log boom, left.

Photo courtesy of the Kerslake family.

A Newborn Son

From left: Clara Hyerstay, Clara Baker (holding Allan), and Jessie Kerslake.

Photo courtesy of the Kerslake family.

house. In May 1922, a fire that started at the former Thomas Mill site caused some excitement as it swept across the road to the Baker place. Men fought the fire, which crowned into the trees, but no serious damage resulted. Another fire swept the area in 1924, started by men attempting to burn brush. To keep the fire from engulfing the house, wet sacks were placed around nearby snags and kept wet.

By April 1924 the Bakers had saved enough money to pay the balance due for the homestead. About this time Louie decided to forgo the job at the Cameron and Hogg Sawmill and make a living off the land. They had two cows and sold milk at the mill for 9-cents per quart. They had a thousand chickens and sold eggs to neighbors and to Art Groce at his Springdale store. They sold vegetables to neighbors and raised beef for sale. After buying a cream separator, Louie sold cream to the creamery and fed the milk to calves and pigs. The 'pig' business ended when the couple found it was not profitable. But from this time on, income from the various family enterprises was sufficient to support Louie and Clara's growing family. Later, wood and timber sale income would add to the family's resources.

Four children were born to Louie and Clara: Allan, b. January 21, 1922; James 'Jim,' b. January 16, 1924; Catherine (Dunlap), b. June 24, 1926; and Marilou (Bowman), b. August 27, 1929. Catherine is the only one of the children born at home in Aims. In 1934, Mr. and Mrs. Baker took Louie Anderson, age seven, into their home. His mother had passed away, and he had been passed from place to place before settling with the Bakers. He became ill in 1938, and died suddenly after being ill just 12 days. Jim Baker had appendicitis in 1931. He had been working for Harvey Crook and came home ill. The next morning he was still very sick, so Dr. Botkin, who had a summer place close by, was consulted. He informed the Bakers that Jim was seriously ill and needed to be hospitalized quickly. He was rushed to Portland Sanitarium and operated on by Dr. Ripley. His appendix burst as they removed it, which was a serious complication in those days before antibiotics. Fortunately, after spending 16 days in the hospital with around the clock care, he recovered enough to be sent home to convalesce and eventually recovered completely.

Carolyn Baker came into the Baker family at age two and lived as a family member until she was grown. After the youngsters were in school, the Aims School Board decided to transport students by bus. Louie pur-

Jim Baker

Waiting

Jim Baker, USN, WWII.

L to R: Ardis (Mershon) Baker, Catherine Baker and Lorraine Bridges.   Photos courtesy of Ross Johnson.

chased a Ford truck and modified it to carry them. He took the high school kids to the top of Buck Creek Hill to meet the Corbett bus and hauled the grade school kids to Aims. The Baker children attended Aims Grade School until February 1944, when the District consolidated with Bull Run (Clackamas County portion) or Corbett (Multnomah County portion). Allan had the same teacher for eight years at Aims Grade School. After the consolidation, Marilou completed her final year at Corbett Grade School. Each of the youngsters graduated from CHS: Allan in 1939, Jim in 1940, Catherine in 1943, Marilou, in 1947 and Carolyn in 1961. After the consolidation, the Baker youngsters still in school rode the bus that their father drove from Aims to Corbett, taking children from the far (southern) reaches of Multnomah County and picking up students along Gordon Creek Road, Rickert Road, Littlepage Road and Pounder Grade on its way to school. The Bakers, as students, established enviable records at the high school. Two, Allan and Catherine, were recognized by the faculty, who selected them as recipients of the P.J. Mulkey Citizenship Cup because of their achievement, spirit and exemplary behavior.

The depression years created hardships for everyone. The Bakers got into the wood business when a businessman from Portland wanted 1000 cords of wood. Louie hired cutters and a neighbor to haul the wood. However, the deal fell through and the neighbor wanted to sell his truck, so Louie bought it. Thereafter he was in the wood business for good. With some help from Art Groce, more cutters were hired and wood delivered to Portland for $5.00 per cord. According to Clara, some of the

Family and Friends in Aims

Front, L to R: Allan 'Pete' Mershon, Ardis (Mershon) Baker, Carol Mershon, Virginia Pomante, Doris Gravett, Mary Anderson, Marilou Baker. 2nd Row: ?, ?, Jeanette Crook, Tom Pomante, Bill Mershon, John Kerslake, Jean Kerslake, George Crook. 3rd Row: Lawrence Johnston, Elsie Johnston, Rosie Johnston,?,?, Alice Kerslake, Clara Baker holding ?, Richard Kerslake, Claude Urbach, Marjorie Urbach, Grace Urbach, Dorothy (Kerslake) Pomante holding Barbara Pomante. Photo courtesy of Ross Johnson.

woodcutters who worked for them were very interesting folk. One time a car with two couples and some small children pulled into their drive. The girls, age 16 and 18, were married to cousins and had three younger siblings with them. They were desperate for work, so the Bakers put them up in their garage. The boys started cutting wood the next day. Years later one of the couples visited to reminisce about those difficult depression days.

After graduating from high school, Allan worked on the family farm and wood lot. The wood business had grown so Allan cut and hauled cordwood to Gresham and Portland. In September 1942, Allan joined the Army Air Force. After completing basic and advanced training, he was sent to Australia where he worked rebuilding airplane engines. When the war ended, he was sent to Japan to serve in the Army of Occupation. He was discharged from the Army on Christmas Day, 1945, with the rank of Staff Sergeant.

When he returned home, Allan, with his brother, Jim, and brother-in-law, Frank Dunlap, started building up a dairy herd, which Mr. Louis Baker had long envisioned. They cleared more land to add acreage for pasture and for other crops. For several years the Bakers delivered fresh

21

milk to customers in Aims, along Gordon Creek Road and other points. They also raised strawberries, which were sold to the cannery in Gresham. The Bakers operated the dairy until 1965.

In addition to the farm, the Bakers logged portions of their own land and also logged for others. They logged for Publisher's Paper Company from 1966 to 1988, when Publishers sold their holdings to Longview Fiber. Since 1988, they have logged for that company. When Jim and Frank retired in 1989, Allan's son, Tim, joined the business, which now operates as Baker and Son Logging. Allan's daughter, Judi, also works in the operation, driving a dump truck.

Ruth M. Spencer was born in Wasco, Oregon, September 12, 1929. She attended grade school in Wasco and after her family moved to The Dalles, she attended junior and senior high school there. She happened to be visiting her sister, Idabelle, in Aims in the spring of 1947. Idabelle and her husband, Harry, had been invited to dinner at Jim and Ardis Baker's home, and Ruth went along. Allan Baker had stopped in to see Ardis and Jim's new baby, Pat, and met Ruth. Allan asked Ruth to go to a softball game at Blue Lake Park with him, which was their first date. They were married August 17, 1947, in Gresham.

Allan and Ruth had 4 children: Norma E., b. June 4, 1948; Judi E., b. September 18, 1950; Marsha E., b. November 21, 1952; and Timothy A., b. October 10, 1957. All attended school in Corbett, Norma graduating from CHS in 1966, Judi in 1968, Marsha in 1971 and Timothy in 1975. Norma attended Cascade College and completed work for her degree and teaching credentials at Westmont College in California. Judi attended the University of Oregon MHCC. Marsha earned an Associates Accounting degree at MHCC and Tim also attended MHCC.

After her children had grown, Ruth started working at Woodland Park Hospital in the cafeteria. When a colleague suggested urged her to get further training, she enrolled at Portland Community College in its dietician-training program. She completed requirements to become a certified dietician and was subsequently promoted to that position at Woodland Park. She worked for the hospital for more than 20 years before retiring in 1991. Ruth has a sideline business making wedding cakes, which provides her with an outlet for her creative talents.

Ruth and Allan have always taken an active part in community affairs. They have served the East Multnomah County Pioneer Association for many years in various offices, and are regularly called upon at the annual reunion. Allan served on the Corbett Board of Education for 13 years and was among the individuals who played an active role in preventing the consolidation of Corbett School District with Reynolds School District in the spring of 1970. Corbett voters rejected the merger with 260 in favor versus 430 opposed. Allan, Jim, Catherine and Marilou, together with their spouses, are recognized in this community for their willingness to be involved in those activities that make East Multnomah County a more viable, positive community. Allan, Jim, and others in the family have been active volunteers with the Corbett Fire Department. They are caring individuals blessed with the spirit of giving unto others. Allan and his partners are also known for the manner in which they conducted their business. In 1995, Allan was named Oregon Forester of the Year.

Norma Baker taught at Corbett High School after graduating from Westmont College. She is now teaching music at Franklin High School in Portland. She has an adopted daughter, Caitlin, who attends Reynolds Middle School. They live in Troutdale. Judi married Tom Hoffman, and has two children, Aaron and Joel. Aaron graduated from Wheaton College in Illinois, and is teaching at Stayton High School. He married Amy Smith, and the couple now lives in Stayton. Marsha married Rich Huff and they have two children. Lindsi attends CHS and Nathan is a student at Corbett Grade. Marsha has worked for American Data Processing in ADP Dealer Services for more than 15 years. Timothy married Debbie Walmer. They have four children, Josh, who attends CHS, Carrie, who is at the Corbett Middle School, Allan, who attends Corbett Grade School and Laura, an infant (1998).

Catherine went to work at the U.S. Weather Bureau at Crown Point for two years. When that facility closed she worked at the Troutdale Station until December 1947. Catherine married Frank R. Dunlap, who was a shipmate of her brother, James, in the Navy. Frank was born in Ohio June 26, 1926. The couple married December 13, 1946, in Gresham. Frank worked in the Reynolds Metals plant for a short time before entering a partnership with the Baker brothers in the logging business. Catherine did the bookkeeping for the family business over the years. For years she also kept books from her home for the Big 8 Lumber Company.

After Catherine and Frank married they built a small home close to her parents' home in Aims. As their family grew, they added to the structure six times. They had two birth children, Christine, b. January 25, 1951, and Sarah, b. June 4, 1953, before starting to adopt other youngsters. Desiree, b. August 9, 1955, in Oakland, California, was adopted at age 10; Lori, b. May 13, 1957, in Hutchinson, Kansas, was adopted at age 8; Sandra, b. August 31, 1962, in Portland, was adopted at age 7; Marc, b. March 2, 1966, in Klamath Falls, Oregon, was adopted at age 3; Edmund, b. March 27, 1966 in Portland, was adopted at age 10; Ben, b. October 25, 1966, in Portland, was adopted at age 4; and Tami, b. February 2, 1967, in Portland, was adopted at age 21 months. One set of children came with an elderly set of grandparents for whom the Dunlaps also made a home for about ten years during the 70's. Catherine reports, "We've had little time for hobbies." Christine, Sarah, Marc, Ben and Tami Dunlap attended Corbett schools twelve years. The other Dunlap children attended grade school in Corbett from the time of their adoption and each of the youngsters graduated from CHS, Christine in 1969, Sarah in 1971, Desiree in 1973, Lori in 1975, Sandra in 1981, Edmund in 1984, Marc in 1984, Ben in 1985 and Tami in 1985. Catherine states, "We have been active in the (Aims) church and raised kids. We have nine grandchildren, a great adventure with the Lord, lots of fun and (feel) very blessed." Clara Baker, who celebrated her 100th birthday June 22, 1998, lived with Frank and Catherine the last years of her life. She died September 13, 1998, which happened to be the day of the East Multnomah County Pioneer Association meeting for 1998.

Jim Baker joined the U.S. Navy in 1943. On June 6, 1944 (D-day, Normandy) he married Ardis Mershon, who was born in Portland, Oregon June 2, 1924. Ardis, daughter of Ernest 'Mac' and Magdaleine (Pulliam) Mershon, graduated from CHS in 1942. Her mother was also a CHS graduate, class of 1920. Soon after the couple married, Jim was dispatched to the Pacific Theater of war, where his ship participated in the Battle of Okinawa. The invasion fleet came under attack by Kamikaze aircraft, which inflicted terrible damage to several ships in the fleet. Jim's ship, a LCS 13, escaped unscathed. Jim served in the Navy until January 1946.

Upon his return, Jim worked at the aluminum plant in Troutdale for about a year. According to an article in the February 7, 1947 issue of the Cardinal, "Jim Baker and his brother-in-law Frank Dunlap have quit their

Clara Baker and Her Children

L to R: Carolyn, Allan, Marilou, Clara Baker, Catherine and Jim.
Photos '61 Cohimore (exerpt) and Jim Baker.

jobs at the aluminum plant to go into partnership with Allan Baker in the logging business. The logging is to be done on the Baker holdings in Aims. The logs are to be cut into lumber by the Big 8 Mill in Aims." He and Ardis settled in a home they built on property given to them by Jim's parents, part of the family homestead. The Baker Brothers also farmed, and hired local youngsters to pick berries, including Colleen and Carroll Innes, Richard and Sandra Childers and others. They also sold milk, which was delivered fresh to customers in the area.

Jim and Ardis Baker had two daughters, Patricia 'Pat,' b. April 17, 1947, and Linda, b. March 30, 1951. Both attended Corbett schools. Pat graduated from CHS in 1965 (a third generation graduate of that school). She then attended Eastern Oregon College in LaGrande, from which she graduated in 1969. Pat married Rick Lucas of Seaside. They had two boys, Jeffrey 'Jeff,' b. September 17, 1971 and James 'Jamie,' b. March 26, 1973 (both born in Stuttgart, Germany). Both attended Corbett Schools, graduating in 1989 and 1991, respectively, from CHS. Thus they are fourth generation graduates of CHS (Magdaleine Mershon, Ardis (Mershon) Baker, Pat (Baker) Lucas, Jeff and Jamie Lucas). Jeff is a Navy SEAL and Jamie is a fireman/paramedic with the Hoodland Fire Department.

Linda graduated from Corbett High School in 1969. She married Larry Traxler of Sandy. They have three boys, Peter, b. January 13, 1977

25

and twins Rob and Sam, b. August 30, 1978. The three boys all graduated from Corbett High School, adding to the number of fourth generation family members to graduate from Columbian/Corbett. Pete and Sam volunteer for the Corbett Fire Department and work for Crown Point Towing. Rob is self-employed in the logging business.

Marilou Baker married Ralph Bowman in Gresham August 12, 1949. Ralph was born in Cross Plains, Texas August 19, 1926. He came to East Multnomah County with his parents in September 1943, and the family lived on Ellis Road. After their marriage, the couple lived in Aims on Hogg Mill Road. They have three children, Douglas, b. August 20, 1952, Rebecca, b. November 9, 1954 and Clair, b. October 11, 1957. The children completed their elementary and secondary education at Corbett schools. Marilou kept in touch as she drove the school bus from Aims to Corbett and return for 28 years until her retirement from that endeavor, but she continues her work as a behind-the-wheel instructor for Corbett School District. Ralph worked as a fitter and welder building heavy equipment.

Of their children, Douglas graduated from Corbett High School in 1970, attended Portland State University and is now a schoolteacher. He is married to Kathy Knudson, who also teaches. They have three children, Corrie, Kelly and Christy. Rebecca 'Becky' graduated from Corbett in 1972, attended Linfield College and Oregon Health Sciences University and is a registered nurse at Kaiser Hospital. She is married to Rick Christensen, who had two girls, Kimberly and Brandi, and they have two birth children, twins Kyle and Kelsie. Clair graduated from Corbett High in 1975, attended Mt. Hood Community College and is a medical secretary. She married Dale Moore and had two children, Ian and Molly. Clair is now married to David Brooks.

Carolyn (Baker) Osborn now lives in North Bend, OR. She has two sons, James and Andrew. *The Baker Family*

26

Harley Bates
Hazel (Lucas) Bates

Harley Bates was born in Alton, Kansas, March 6, 1889. He was brought when about six months old to Oregon (see "Sutliff Bates," *Pioneer History*). Harley grew up on the place his father purchased on what is now Bell Grade. Sutliff Bates and his son-in-law, Grant Bell, divided the approximate 100 acres the two families purchased, Sutliff taking the northern half, and Grant taking the southern half. A coin toss determined the outcome, but interestedly enough, each participant thought they got the best of the deal: Grant, because his half had a good spring, and Sutliff, because his was the higher, more scenic piece. The two families lived in tents on the property the first winter (1889-90).

When Harley started school, he walked from his home through the woods to attend Taylor School (later Corbett). As was often the practice in those days, he quit school after completing grade four. Harley Bates married Hazel Lucas on November 21, 1911. Hazel, a daughter of Thomas and Sarah Lucas, was born October 3, 1893, and grew up on the place in Springdale (see "Thomas Lucas," *Pioneer History*). This property was located on the West Side of Lucas Road near its intersection with the Columbia River Highway. After the marriage, the Bates lived in the home Harley had built on Bell Grade just east of its intersection with the highway. This place was later sold to the Babbitt family. When Harley's father died in 1915, the Bates moved to the home place on Bell Grade. The Bates had five children: Arlene, b. July 26, 1917; Gordon, b. February 7, 1919; Floyd, b. September 3, 1921; June, b. February 4, 1925; and Harley (Ronald), b. August 23, 1934.

Arlene died in 1924 at age six from complications resulting from pneumonia. The other children all attended Springdale Grade School, but Ronald finished at Corbett Grade after completing his first school year at Springdale. While the Bates children were growing up, they worked for neighboring farmers, planting cabbage and other crops, picking berries and performing other similar tasks. Of course they picked cucumbers for their father and helped with the farm work at home. Since Mr. Bates had a truck, it was used to haul the cucumbers to Libby McNeil and Libby off Powell in SE Portland. Harley Bates owned a "New Idea" cabbage planter, which other farmers were able to use. June or another

Sutliff Bates Family, c 1889

The Bates

L to R, Rear: Anna, Alta, Etta, Front: Orilla (holding Harley), Frank and Sutliff Bates.

Harley and Hazel Bates. Photos courtesy of Ron Bates.

of the Bates children sort of "went with" the planter. Consequently, June remembers planting cabbage for many other farmers besides her father. She was paid $.25 per hour for her work on the machine. Since she planted with her left hand, her help was welcomed. One time June was planting cabbage for John Burbee when one of his horses balked. After a few choice expletives, Mr. Burbee got off the planter, walked up to the recalcitrant animal and jabbed it with a long nail he held in his fist. The team immediately took off, with June and her co-worker still sitting on the planter. They had quite a ride, but suffered no injuries. June says she was always somewhat reluctant to work for Mr. Burbee after that. Also, the police dogs that roamed his property created some apprehension for potential visitors. When "greeted" by these canines, a caller often decided that the reason for the visit was not that urgent.

In addition to farming, Harley Bates built several houses in the area. He started in the garage business with Fred Salzman in Springdale, but apparently decided the business was not for him as he sold out to Fred shortly after the opening. After he returned to the home place, he built a house in Corbett, located across from where the fire hall is now (1997)

Harley Bates' Buzzsaw

Used by Harley Bates to cut cordwood.   Photo courtesy of Ron Bates.

located. After this place was finished, the Bates moved there to live for a time, renting the farm during the interim. This house was later sold to Frank Bell. The family then returned to the farm on Bell Grade. Later, Harley purchased the Kincaid Place, which was adjacent to his property, and which extended his property boundary to Mershon Road on the east close to its intersection with the highway. Harley built a house on this property at the upper end of Bell Grade, and rented it to Miss Maude Sherman, who lived there during much of her teaching career at Corbett Grade School (teaching 1st Grade). He built still another house off Mershon Road, across from Dewey Carpenter's place. That house too, was rented to others. Mrs. Bates was a homemaker who enjoyed gardening and crafts, such as quilt making. She also kept busy rearing her children.

During the depression, the Bates family grew cucumbers, among other crops, probably because there was usually a market for this "cash crop." Early in the 30's, the Conrad Price family came to the Bates' farm looking for work. Harley fixed a place in his garage for the family to live, and they worked for him that year. The Prices had six children: Anna, Bertha, Ronald, Harry, Elsie and Richard. After working that summer and fall, the family found a place to rent on Woodard Road. Though Anna and Bertha were out of school, the younger siblings attended school at Corbett, and the family subsequently did very well. June remembers Harry as being "a brilliant student." Sometimes the Bates farm help camped in an orchard-like area near the old Kincaid house off Mershon Road. (The

Bates Children c1940

Gordon, June, Floyd; Ron in front.
Photo courtesy of Ron Bates.

government doesn't permit such practices now (1997).) June said she always wanted to camp out with the help, but her folks would not permit this. In addition to cucumbers, the Bates family raised grain, cabbage, cauliflower, carrots, potatoes and hay. Each year, Lloyd Trickey brought his thrashing machine to the place, and thrashed their grain. Orland Zeek also came each summer to bale their hay. While the Bates didn't have cattle, they did have a milk cow, work horses, pigs and chickens. Each year Martin Nelson would come to butcher the hogs. Sometimes, John Burbee would help with this chore.

Mr. Bates had quite a business cutting wood for many of his neighbors. He attached a buzz saw to the back of a small truck, and used it to cut up cordwood. He also drove school bus for the Corbett School District. In the mid-30's, Mr. Bates decided to quit farming and to rent his cropland to other farmers. One of the first tenants was the Takeuchi family that planted the entire farm to brussel sprouts. This was a fairly new

Original Bates Home, c 1909

L to R, Sutliff, Frank, Harley and Orilla Bates.

Bates Home After Remodeling

The Bates home after it was remodeled.   Photos courtesy of Ron Bates.

crop to the area, and it did very well in the local soil. The Matsuba family also rented the ground for one year. When the Japanese were sent to "relocation camps" in May 1942, Mr. Bates stored some of the Matsuba's personal property for which the family expressed its gratitude many years later. Another year he rented the land to the Roy Malcolm, who planted the entire acreage to gladiolas. June thought the farm was extraordinarily beautiful that year. MB McKay, who lived across Mershon Road, also rented the place to grow certified seed potatoes.

The four Bates children who lived to adulthood attended CHS in Corbett. Gordon, who graduated in 1937, served in the Army Air Force during World War II, including time in England and several months in France after the invasion June 6, 1944. After the war, he married Mary Louise Cadmun, and worked for the Standard Register Company, principally in California. Gordon and Mary have two children, Sheryl and Randall, and now live in Costa Mesa, California. Floyd, who graduated in 1939, worked in the shipyards at Bremerton during World War II. After the war, he worked for Barnard Cadillac, Portland, in the body and fender department. Later, he worked as an insurance adjuster for the Allstate Insurance Company. He married Dorothy Conn (CHS, 1941), and they have four children: Dennis, Judy, Linda and Kathy. Floyd and Dorothy now live in SE Portland.

June graduated from CHS in 1943 after which she worked as a secretary for various firms, such as Amfac and Mt. Hood Mortgage. She met Ridgley "Ridge" Law at work. Ridge and June married May 5, 1945. Ridge Law, who served in the U.S. Merchant Marine during World War II, opened Ridge's Hardware and Millwork after the war, and operated that business until his son, Gary, took over the business when Ridge retired. The February 19, 1947 issue of the CHS *Cardinal* contained the following information:

> "Three hundred and ten cold storage lockers are being installed at Springdale by Mr. R. Law. The lockers range in size from six cubic feet to thirteen cubic feet and are priced from six dollars to thirteen dollars…Anyone who wishes may sign up for a locker at the home of Mr. Law. The lockers are open for inspection, and some will be available for use by the first of next month."

For many years the Laws lived in a house on the Columbia River Highway opposite Groce's store, which they rented from June's Aunt Alta (Bates) Crowston. When they remodeled the house, they found newspapers and other material from the late 1880's in the walls. Tiring of renting, Ridge and June built a house on Northway Road, which they started in 1961 and completed in 1963. They built it in their "spare" time, working nights and those days the store was closed. June and Ridge raised three children: Gary, Ridge's son by a previous marriage, b. Sep-

Ridge Law Family, c1959

L to R, Ridge, Gary, Becky, Lynne and June Law.
Photo courtesy of June Law.

tember 24, 1939; Lynne, b. July 28, 1947, who now lives in Eugene; and Rebecca, b. January 14, 1951, who lives in Vancouver, Washington.

Gary Law graduated from Corbett High School in 1957. He attended Portland State University, majoring in mathematics. After completing college, he student taught in Parkrose at the Junior High School. In 1964 he returned to CHS as a teacher to replace Burns Clark for the remainder of the 63-64 school year. He married Barbara Rose, who graduated from CHS in 1959. The couple has a daughter, Bethany, and a son, Andy. Lynne graduated from Corbett High School in 1965 and Rebecca in 1969. Ridge died February 17, 1997, at age 81. June continues to live in the house located on Northway Road.

Harley (Ronald) Bates, b. August 23, 1934, graduated from CHS in 1952. He attended Lewis and Clark College, graduating in 1956, and entered the banking business soon thereafter. He married Margaret Buyalos April 24, 1959. After working for Benjamin Franklin Sav'
and Loan, Ronald worked with the founder of Oregon Trail Sa'
Loan when it opened for business in Gresham, and serve
tive capacity with that organization for many years
contraction of the late 70's and early 80's, Oreg
the federal government to combine with a similar in

became a real estate broker, consultant, and property appraiser. He also serves in an advisory position with Warner Pacific College as the Director of Planned Giving. He and Margaret have three sons, Harley, who lives in Troutdale, Kevin, who lives in Portland, and Jason, who lives in Troutdale.

Harley Bates (Sr.) died of a heart attack March 5, 1959. The original Sutliff Bates place, plus the acreage added in later years, has been retained by the Bates family, belonging now to Harley and Hazel Bates' heirs, Gordon, Floyd, June and Ronald. Therefore, the property has been in the family for more than 100 years.   *June (Bates) Law*

'Tansy' Control

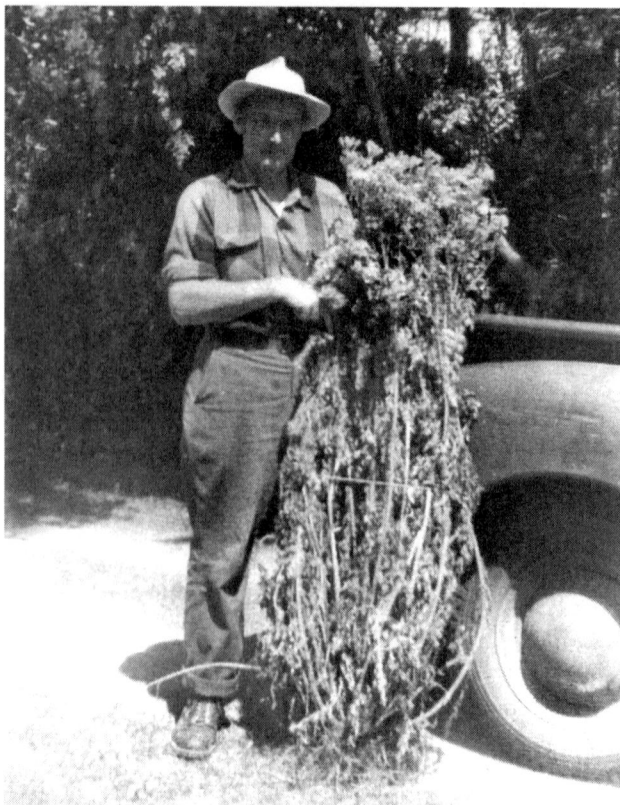

Harley Bates helps with the tansy control program.
Photo courtesy of Ron Bates.

Crystal (Pounder) Bayley

Crystal Pounder was born September 1, 1912, the fifth surviving child (one child died in infancy) of James 'Jim' and Minnie (Crozier) Pounder. Her parents owned an 80-acre farm located at the junction of Knieriem Road with Littlepage Road. The Pounder children attended school at the old Hurlburt Grade School located near what is now the junction of Gordon Creek Road with Hurlburt Road. Crystal's memories of Hurlburt Grade School are instructive:

> "(The school was) a one-room building with a bell in belfry that the boys and girls liked to have the opportunity to ring. There were two cloakrooms - one for the girls and one for the boys. The coats and caps were supposed to be hung on pegs with the boots underneath if (one) had shoes there. Blackboards were usually all around the room. Superintendent Alderson had all of (the students) go to the board, gave us problems and (tried to) embarrass us. We hated to see him coming. I think the teachers dreaded his visits, too. The teacher's desk was up on a platform except when there was a program. The desks were lined up with the largest desks in the back and a recitation bench in front. There was always a picture of President Washington and (often one of) President Lincoln. The American flag was up front."

Crystal's brothers, Earl, Cecil and Albert, and Earl's son, Stanley, all learned how to work on the farm. In 1912 when the cement-block house was built, Cecil got a start in carpenter work. In his spare time he built a dresser for his mother. Mr. Pounder had an implement house built and furnished it with tools that were needed. He said, "Cecil's learning, but it's costing me money!" According to Crystal, "Papa always watched the markets carefully. If a crop became popular with other growers, he would plant much less of that crop." He reduced his cauliflower acreage in the mid-20's for that reason. Jim Pounder had dairy cattle and hogs, and grew cabbage, cauliflower and potatoes as well as crops for the livestock, including hay, grain, corn, rye and vetch. In addition to family members, Mr. Pounder always hired help. For example, Howard Winters worked for Mr. Pounder in the late 20's and early 30's. Howard always expressed his appreciation for the opportunity that Mr. Pounder gave him to learn how to work and how to operate farm machinery.

Crystal Pounder

Crystal as a student at CHS. Photo courtesy of Donna Monoske.

Crystal said that her father utilized farm machinery as much as possible. For example, he had a 'New Idea' cabbage planter and a potato planter before many other farmers. He also purchased a tractor-driven thrashing machine. Crystal recounted how her older brother, Albert, competently operated the thrasher when he was just sixteen years of age. She rode the cabbage and potato planters, which were pulled by horses. She also drove the team when hay was lifted into the barn by a hayfork. In addition to the crops there were cows to milk, pigs to feed and other farm chores. In November 1921, a big ice storm hit the area, causing much damage. According to Crystal, the ice was "more than a foot thick in some places."

Cecil Pounder started a construction business when he left home. He became active in the building trade and built several structures in the area. One structure of note is the lodge he completed in 1926 near Bridal Veil Falls, which is now operated as a Bed and Breakfast by Laurel (Brown) Slater. Later he operated an airport and a flying service. He became a franchised 'Byrd' aircraft distributor. The 2nd son, Earl, was helping Cecil at the flying service one day in 1931 and was killed in a plane crash while accompanying a student pilot on a training flight. Earl's son, Stanley J. Pounder, founded Pounder Realty and established a very successful real estate business in the Portland area. Crystal's older sister, Elizabeth, married and later she and her husband entered the ministry with the Salvation Army. Their Church of God missions took them to many states and eventually to Central America. After retirement, they lived in Gresham (See "James and Minnie (Crozier) Pounder," *Pioneer History*).

As mentioned, Crystal attended Hurlburt Grade School, from which she graduated in 1926. She enrolled at CHS, which she attended four years, graduating in 1930. She then attended Oregon Normal School in Monmouth, and completed the two-year program to gain a teaching certificate. After becoming certified, she obtained a teaching position at Brower Grade School for the school year 32-33. She was paid $90.00 per month, which, considering the times, was a good salary. At the end of that year, Brower School District consolidated with Corbett, so Crystal was out of a job.

Crystal went to Colorado to be with her sister, Elizabeth, who was expecting a child. She spent some time with her sister's family and then went to Spokane, Washington to work for her brother, Cecil, who had moved there and established an insurance business. In 1937, Elizabeth and her husband had moved to a church in North Dakota. Elizabeth called Crystal with a message that a teacher was needed at the school in town. Crystal traveled there, took the job and stayed for three years. She then returned to Oregon and taught two years in Wallowa before returning to her parents' home in 1942.

Crystal married Harry R. Bayley May 30, 1942. Harry had been working for her father, which is how the couple met. After the marriage, she taught in Sandy, Oregon. They had a son, Billy Keith, who was born February 14, 1944, while they lived in Springdale. Crystal wanted to take care of him when he was a baby, so she did not teach that year. When she resumed her teaching career, she obtained a position in Troutdale. She taught at Troutdale Grade School for 29 years. Crystal (Pounder) Bayley retired in 1976, which ended a 36-year teaching career. Of the 36 years, 33 were spent in Oregon schools and 3 in North Dakota.

Billy Keith married Joyce Collins in 1967. Joyce had a son, Michael, by a previous marriage and the couple had one birth son, Timothy. Michael Bayley now lives in Orient and Timothy lives in Kent, Washington. He owns and operates three 'Papa Murphy' stores in Kent. Billy Keith Bayley died in October 1987. Crystal Bayley now lives in a retirement community in Gresham. She is active in church and community affairs, particularly the Crown Point Historical Society. She recently worked on a research project concerning East Multnomah County Schools (some of which is included herewith). (See "Albert Pounder," this volume, for more information about his life.)   *Crystal (Pounder) Bayley*

Benjamin Bennett
Alice C. (Peerboom) Bennett

The Bennetts moved to Oregon in 1936, settling in Albany on River Road. They purchased the Latourell Villa towards the end of World War II, opening the restaurant on V-J (Victory over Japan) Day, September 2, 1945. In order to open, family and friends pooled their meat ration coupons to get hamburger for the opening. Mrs. Bennett made a pot of beans, cooking them in the basement furnace. Opening day the restaurant ran out of food by 12:30 p.m., which cut short the opening day ceremony. When the Bennetts moved to Latourell, they had two children, Dean, b. March 29, 1932 and Patricia 'Pat,' b. March 25, 1935, both born in North Dakota. Both were in grade school at the time of the move, and started attending Corbett Grade School.

When the restaurant opened traffic was so heavy on the Columbia River Highway that Pat remarked, "To get from one side of the road (the restaurant) to the curio shop took easily (a) 10 minute wait before there was a break." Pat learned to cook in the restaurant, and her favorite dish was French toast. One day her brother, Dean, asked his mother to cook breakfast because Pat had served him French toast 234 consecutive days. The restaurant's specialty was salmon steak. It came with a fruit cup, salad, peas, potatoes, homemade pie and coffee, all for $1.25. Pat stated that when she started waiting on tables and had to give the customer a check, she ran back into the kitchen because she couldn't understand why a customer had to pay for the meal! During Pat and Dean's high school years they would have parties at the Villa, play the jukebox and have a great time. When it came time for the party to end her father would flash the lights, serve cocoa and the party was over.

In 1949 the culvert of a small side creek to the east became plugged and resulted in a huge portion of the highway washing out. The Latourell Villa sign teetered on the edge of the abyss. However, the Highway Department repaired the damage and, according to Pat, "One wouldn't have known that there had ever been a wash out." The curio shop was rebuilt and the Villa reopened for business. Latourell Villa was a busy place until the freeway opened when business dropped off dramatically. Mr. Bennett had lobbied the Highway Commission for an exit at Latourell to no avail, and the family soon decided the restaurant had to close. The

Latourell Villa

Latourell Villa, formerly Maffet's Villa, Columbia River Highway near Latourell Falls.
Photo courtesy of Steve Lehl.

Bennetts sold 40 acres, including 32 acres on the falls side of the highway, the 8 acres on which the restaurant was located, the restaurant and the curio shop to the State of Oregon for $8,000.00. In 1959, the state or Oregon razed the restaurant and the curio shop and added the land to Talbot State Park.

After graduating from CHS, Dean Bennett attended Santa Monica Community College and the University of Southern California. Pat attended Seattle University, the College of Great Falls and the University of North Dakota. She holds Associates of Arts, Bachelor of Science, Master of Science and Ph.D. degrees. She married Bruce Well February 11, 1956, and had two children, Bruce and Barbara. Bruce is an opthamologist practicing in Los Angeles and has two children, Layla and Joseph. Barbara earned a Bachelor of Science Degree in corrections and is married to a Corrections Counselor who works at Eastern Oregon State Prison in Ontario, Oregon. She works as a certified dental technician and has two children, Austin and Lee. Pat married William Castellini December 17, 1994, and currently lives in Baton Rouge, Louisiana.

Pat Bennett

39

Charles A. Berney
Laura (Mueller) Berney

Charles 'Charlie' Berney came to the United States with his brother, Jim Berney, in June 1883. The family eventually settled along the Columbia River near Roosevelt. Charles purchased a ranch of several thousand acres near Bickleton, Washington. He married Laura Mueller December 11, 1896. In 1907, the Berneys moved to the 'hill' for two reasons: to be close to a school that his children could attend and to be close to a church that the family could attend. He purchased 120 acres south of Haines (now Ogden) Road west of Ogden Road and east of Seidl Road. The Berneys had six children: Lovell, b. November 1, 1897; Louis, b. 1900; Blanche, b. 1901; Ida E., b. January 28, 1905; Ruth, b. 1912; and Lucille, b. 1914. The older children were born while the family lived in Bickleton, but Ruth and Lucille were born after the move to the 'hill.' The Berneys farmed and built up a dairy herd as the principal income-producing endeavor. Not too long after purchasing the property, the Berneys sold a 20-acre parcel along what is now Seidl Road to a Mr. Byze.

Lovell Berney attended Pleasant View Grade School. During his era, education for boys often ended with elementary school, after which one was expected to work on the farm. Lovell married Arlie G. Kincaid September 8, 1927, in Springdale. Arlie had graduated from CHS in 1923. The couple first lived at the Salzman place located on Salzman Road, which they farmed for several years. The couple had four children, two of whom were born at Corbett: Robert 'Bob,' b. June 21, 1929 and Donald E., b. August 16, 1932. Janice L., b. July 1, 1941 and Lovell N. 'Norm,' b. March 2, 1945 came after the move from Corbett. Bob recalled an incident when his father and a bachelor neighbor, Mr. Byze, found a bee tree and brought it to the yard. As they removed the honey, the bees were swarming about, and Bob was stung. Mr. Byze thought that was funny and started laughing. However, Arlie Berney didn't think it was funny, and she ran Mr. Byze off the place.

In addition to dairy cows, the Berneys grew row crops such as cauliflower, cabbage and beans. During the depression (1933), as Bob recalls family lore, his father took a load of cauliflower into Portland. When he returned in the evening, the load was intact - not a crate having been sold. The hardships occasioned by the depression and the fact that Donald had a reoccurring problem with pneumonia (which caused a doctor to recommend a warmer climate) prompted the family to make a change. The Berneys located a dairy farm in Canby, and the family moved there in 1934. The children completed their elementary and secondary school years in Canby and Hubbard.

In the 50's, Arlie (Kincaid) Berney returned to school and completed a master's program in education at Portland State College, with plans to teach. In addition to the dairy, Lovell Berney worked as a milk tester for Clackamas County. Of the children, Robert worked for Crown Zellerbach for seventeen years before going into the construction trade. He has three children, Carol, a teacher, Robert, an engineer, and Patricia, a caregiver. Bob Berney now lives in West Linn with his wife, Hilda (Durtchi). Donald Berney became a pastor after graduating from college. He married Linda L. Hunt the couple also had three children, Donald, Darren and Desha. Janice Berney married Lloyd A. Danielson and has two children, Kimberlee and Cheryl. Janice works for US West in the payroll department as a data systems specialist. Norman Berney taught at Clackamas Junior College and now serves as the Director of Community Affairs for the school. He is married with two children. Lovell Berney passed away June 11, 1984 and Arlie (Kincaid) Berney died January 9, 1990.

Louis Berney's story is similar to Lovell's with regard to schooling. In 1926 he married Margaret Smith and they purchased a farm (26+ acres) on the south side of Mershon Road just below Mike Rogers' place, which was at the top of the long hill about 3/4 mile from the Columbia River Highway. The Berneys kept dairy cattle, and also grew berries and vegetables, including cucumbers. Louie rented the Crowston Place, at the end of Mutch Road off Woodard Road (and on the bluff above the Sandy River across from Viking Park), where he grew various crops, but principally, strawberries. He hired neighbor children to pick berries for him, including Wauneta Davis, George Mershon, Clarence Mershon and the Letsinger kids, among others. The Berneys had three children, Richard 'Dick,' b. April 13, 1929, Juanita, b. October 13, 1933 and Jack, b. October 8, 1939. Dick always finished his strawberry crates by placing the strawberries on top with the stems down, making his berries look especially attractive. No other person took the time to do this, and his crates probably sold more quickly.

During WWII, Louie Berney took care of the Uyetake farm for that family while they were interned in a 'relocation camp,' sent there by the

Louie Berney   **Arlie (Kincaid) Berney**   **Ruth Berney**

Louie Berney
(CHS ex-'20)
Cohimore Photo

Arlie Berney didn't ap-
preciate humor at her
child's expense!
Cohimore Photo

Ruth Berney at CHS. Photo
courtesy of Belle (Campbell)
Evans.

U.S. Government. In 1949, the Berneys moved to a sheep ranch in the
Roseburg area that was originally homesteaded by the Smith (Mrs.
Berney's) family. Juanita and Jack completed their schooling there. Dick
Berney passed away from lung cancer in October 1996.

Blanche Berney attended Pleasant View Grade School and CHS. She
completed the prerequisites necessary to enroll in the School of Nursing,
University of Oregon, from which she graduated. She married Henry
Morgan of Portland August 11, 1927. The couple had four children, Jack,
Don, Dale and Donna and resided in Portland all their married life. Henry
and Blanche Morgan owned the Physicians and Hospital Supply Company in Portland.

Ida Elise Berney completed her elementary years at Pleasant View
Grade School. She attended CHS for two years, then completed a busi-
ness course at Behnke-Walker Business College. Ida married Edward
'Ed' Klinski October 24, 1925 (see "Edward W. Klinski").

Ruth Berney attended Pleasant View Grade School until it closed
when the District consolidated with Corbett in 1923. Thereafter she attended school at Corbett, graduating from CHS in 1931. An article ap-
pearing in the January 31, 1934 *Cardinal*, concerned Ruth: "We sin-
cerely feel the loss of Ruth Alta (Berney) Luscher…Ruth Berney was
Secretary-Treasurer of the student body at Columbian High during her
senior year. Her work was always very efficiently and promptly handled.
Ruth could always be depended upon when she was a member of any

committee appointed for student body affairs. She was an excellent student, well liked by her teachers, and much of her interests were centered in the Brethren congregation in Springdale. She will always be lovingly remembered by the many friends which she made during the time she lived in the vicinity of Corbett and Springdale." Ruth passed away in January of 1934 from tuberculosis.

Lucille Berney's school experience is similar to that of her sister, Ruth, except she graduated from CHS in 1932. She then attended and completed the teacher-training program at the Oregon Normal School in Monmouth and taught school in Manning, Banks and Fairview. She married George Fehrenbacher June 15, 1942, and the couple purchased a 20-acre farm on Seidl Road from Mr. Byze, who had earlier purchased that parcel from her father. Later this place was sold and Lucille and George moved to a ranch in Central Oregon. The couple had two children. When they retired from ranching, they purchased a home in Prineville, where Lucille now makes her home. George Fehrenbacher passed away in 1992.

A November 20, 1946 issue of the *Cardinal* reported: "A surprise birthday dinner was held last Sunday for Mr. Charles Berney to honor him on his 83rd birthday. Mr. Berney is the father of Mrs. Edward Klinski, Mrs. George Fehrenbacher, Mr. Louis Berney, all of Troutdale, and Mrs. Henry Morgan of Portland and Lovell Berney of Hubbard. All were present except Lovell. Charles Berney and his wife celebrate their Golden wedding anniversary on December 11, 1946." When the Berney place was sub-divided, the Knopfs purchased a portion of it and the balance was sold to John and Arlene Seidl. Later the Seidls sold that portion to Mr. Calcagno, who currently farms it.

The Lovell Berney Family, Barbara (Klinski) Wells

Edward A. Berney
Lou E. (Ponath) Berney

Edward 'Ted' Berney was born in Portland, Oregon August 12, 1908, the second of three birth children born to James Amedeé Berney and Clara (Maurer) Berney. The two others were: Grace, b. March 16, 1904, in Arlington, Oregon, and Raymond 'Ray,' b. August 9, 1910 in Spokane, Washington. The Berneys also raised a neighbor's son, Paul Bosshardt, b. June 21, 1900 in the Sundale area, whose mother died when he was an infant. James 'Jim' Berney owned a sheep ranch south of Bickleton, Washington along the Columbia River (across from Arlington) comprised of seven sections (5120 acres). In 1909, he decided to purchase a 70-acre place in Springdale (see "James Berney and Clara Maurer Berney," *Pioneer History*). His brother, Charles, had moved to a farm east of Troutdale in 1907 (see "Charles Berney"). In 1911, Jim and Clara Berney moved their family to Springdale. At the Sundale, Washington ranch, there were no churches and schools were miles away. In Springdale, both needs were met. Mr. Berney continued to operate the sheep ranch and lived there much of the year. The family commuted between the ranch and the Springdale farm, traveling by riverboat or railroad and later, by car.

When it was time for Paul Bosshardt to start school, he was sent to stay with his Uncle Charles in Troutdale. Paul attended school at Pleasant View his first school years. After the family moved he attended Springdale, graduating in 1915. After graduating from grade school, Paul returned to the sheep ranch to work (his choice). Ted's older sister, Grace, attended Springdale Grade School starting in 1911. She completed 8 years there, then attended CHS, graduating in 1922, completing all requirements in three years. After graduating, she was accepted into the nurses training program at Good Samaritan Hospital, and enrolled at that institution.

Ted attended Springdale Grade School from 1915 to 1923. He describes the school:

"Most of the grade schools in this area were about the same, with an entry room containing a pail of water and a dipper. Later, we each had our own tin cups that we hung on a nail. On each side of the entry (were hooks to) hang our coats. In the front (of the

44

The Berney Family

From L: Paul Bosshardt, Ted (in front), Ray (behind) and Grace Berney.

Clara Berney with her sons, Ted (left) and Ray.   Photos courtesy of Ted Berney.

classroom) was a raised platform where the teacher had her desk. The seats were arranged in such a way that the older pupils sat in large desks in the back...then the seats tapered for the smaller children who occupied the front seats. All the classes...were called forward to recite as the teacher called upon each class. Sometimes it was difficult for teachers...On one occasion, the teacher and the pupils were outside jumping rope. Somehow the teacher was close to a tree and the pupils tied her to it and left her. The teacher finally freed herself and walked to Mr. Christensen's house and resigned. Such were some days at school."

"The Christmas program at the Springdale Grade School was also special. Nearly all the community would come to the one room school. A large tree was decorated and the many candles were so pretty. There was a special program and then each child in the community would get a present. It seemed that each person received a bag of hard candy. Things were simple then, but enjoyed by all. The one room school is gone, but we have many memories of our school days."

Berney Home c1918　　　　　　**Ted Berney**

Ray (L) and Ted Berney use a snow drift to enter their second floor bedroom.
Photo courtesy of Ted Berney.

Ted Berney at CHS. '25 Cohimore photo (exerpt) courtesy of Ann (Reeves) Steers.

Ted enrolled at CHS as a freshman in 1923, the year that the new high school building opened to students. The staff included G.N. McKay (Principal), Joy Crockett, Pauline Rickli, Robert Hamill and Joseph Finley. Mr. Hamill was the first boys' basketball coach while Miss Crockett coached girls' basketball. During Ted's junior year, CHS defeated Gresham High in basketball for the first time by a score of 16-13 (in overtime). His senior year the team duplicated the feat, defeating Gresham by a score of 12-11. Opponents during this era included: Beaverton, Cascade Locks, Dayton, Gresham, Hill Military, Milwaukie, Newberg, Parkrose and Sandy. Similarly to Columbian students in subsequent years, these first students of Miss Crockett (later Mrs. Perry) praised her for her rapport with students. Ted states: "We all thought highly of Mrs. Perry who helped us all so much. She always encouraged us to do our best." At Mrs. Perry's 90th birthday party, four members of Columbian's first basketball team of 1923 were present: Ted Berney, Gaylord Davies, Roy Pulliam and Ray Wilson. Ted Berney graduated from CHS in 1927.

Ray Wilson attended Springdale Grade School eight years, but decided to attend Benson Tech rather than CHS. He wanted to play football, a sport not offered at Corbett. Ray had to get up early in order to catch the streetcar in Troutdale to make it to school on time. He did this for his first two years of high school, but his parents permitted him to buy a car his junior year and he was able to drive back and forth. Ray excelled at football and wrestling at Benson, earning athletic scholar-

46

ships at both Oregon Agricultural College and Pacific University upon his graduation from Benson in 1930. He chose Pacific and completed two years there before transferring to Washington State College in Pullman.

Jim Berney continued to operate the ranch in Washington during the years his youngsters were in school. The entire family spent summers on the ranch and there was plenty of work to keep everyone occupied. Lambing, which started around March 1, and shearing, which came later in the spring, had been completed by the time school was out. If the season was favorable there would be approximately 3000 ewes and lambs to care for. About mid-April the sheep were trailed to an intermediate range northwest of Goldendale, Washington. The prime, fat lambs were sold at Goldendale before the final trek to the summer range on the slopes of Mt. Adams.

The herder and helpers left the interim camp around the end of June. The Forest Service tallied the flock at Guler and the first stop was generally Dead Horse Meadows. Thereafter the Forest Service informed the herder when and where to move the flock. Paul, Ted and Ray participated in these annual drives, both to and from Mt. Adams. One year Mr. Berney decided to ship about fifty-head of sheep to Springdale by boat with Ted and Ray assisting. The sheep were herded to Roosevelt, about 7 miles from the ranch. When the boat arrived around midnight, the Berneys herded their charges aboard. Ted and Ray were allowed to stay in the wheelhouse on the down river trip. The ship's cook fed them and Ted remembered the gingerbread treat they received. The sheep were unloaded at Lower Corbett and Mr. Berney and the boys herded them to the Springdale farm. As Ted says, "that was quite an experience for two small boys."

After graduating from high school, Ted worked at the ranch year round for several years. His good friend and high school basketball teammate, Ray Wilson, would occasionally come to the ranch to go hunting. Paul, Ted and Ray (Berney) all worked with Mr. Berney and the ranch crew during these early depression years of the 30's. In 1931, the Springdale farm became the setting for Grace Berney's wedding to Bud Thompson. Hal Babbitt, another classmate and friend of Ted, built an arbor in the yard for the event. Grace chose two close friends of hers as bridesmaids, Lou Ella Ponath and Harriet Boughman. After the wedding Ted and Ray escorted these two young ladies back to Good Samaritan

Hospital. That is how Ted came to meet his future bride, Lou Ponath. Lou was born August 14, 1908 in Bladen, Nebraska. Her father, a minister, moved quite a lot, and the family lived in Livingston, Montana when Lou left to attend the Good Samaritan Nursing School. The couple wed in Portland at the Trinity Episcopal Church May 12, 1935. Their first home was on the sheep ranch.

Mrs. Clara Berney had previously returned to the ranch to live and the Springdale farm was in the hands of tenants. The depression created problems for sheep ranchers as well as other farmers. As the impact of the depression deepened, Mr. Berney optimistically expected each season to be better than the one just experienced, but the situation did not greatly improve. Though 1936 was a better year than some prior years, Jim Berney, because of failing health, decided he must sell the ranch. The sale was completed in November 1936. The Berneys took property in Medford and Eugene in exchange. The property in Medford was a fruit orchard, to which Ted and Lou moved. Ray and his wife, Hazel, moved to Eugene, where they managed the Cabin City Auto Court and Log Cabin Café, obtained in the transaction. Since there was a residence connected to the Eugene property, Mr. and Mrs. Jim Berney moved there.

Paul Bosshardt returned to the Springdale place. Shortly thereafter he married Agnes Hurt, daughter of William 'Bill' Hurt. After he and Agnes married, they moved to the Ross Place east of Corbett where they operated a dairy and grew vegetables. He also worked at the Palmer Mill for a time before moving to Eugene. He and Agnes had two children, Edward and Betty.

After graduating from the Nursing School at Good Samaritan Hospital in 1928, Grace worked as a registered nurse. As mentioned, she married Bud Thompson in 1931, and they had three children, Joan, Bernie and Carol. Bud passed away in 1978. Grace now resides in Portland.

After working the Medford ranch for two years, Ted and Lou were told that the Springdale farm was vacant. They decided to return there in April 1938. The move was accomplished in a borrowed truck loaded with all their possessions plus 'Sport,' an Australian Shepherd puppy that sat in the front seat beside Ted on the trip to Springdale. Ted unloaded their belongings and returned to Eagle Point to get his family. At the time of the move, Ted and Lou had one son, James 'Jim', b. December 31, 1937, in Medford. After the trip, the family found the home and other buildings, which had been rented, in disrepair. They were also faced

48

Berney Farm

Looking south, the Berney home (center), the barn (right) and other outbuildings.

Looking east from the Berney's farm. Note Canzler Hill in the background (center right).   Photos courtesy of Ted Berney.

with the necessity of making a living. Nearby neighbors, Gib and Alice Bates, were very helpful during this period. Ted's brother, Ray, helped with repairing the buildings. Ted managed to purchase a tractor with necessary implements from Bill Hessel in Gresham for $825.00, using his Dodge pickup for the down payment of $400.00.

After repairing the house, buildings and fences, and making other changes, Ted and Lou purchased five registered Holsteins from Bert Evers and started their dairy herd. The herd gradually increased until they were

Ted and Lou Berney

Lou stands on a guard rail to 'gain' on Ted.

Ted and Lou Berney's Family

Rear from L: Jim, Barbara and Ted Jr. Front: Ted Sr. and Lou (Ponath) Berney.

Photos courtesy of Ted Berney

milking about twenty-five cows. A couple of parcels totaling 23 acres had been added to the original 70 acres. In addition to the dairy herd, the Berneys raised vegetable crops, chiefly cabbage and cauliflower. Ted and Lou had two more children: Edward A. 'Ted' Jr., b. October 28, 1940 and Barbara M. (Goertz), b. August 29, 1942. The Berneys continued operating a dairy until 1956 when Ted went to work for Willamette Iron and Steel in Portland. After selling the dairy herd, the Berneys ran about 40 or 50 beef cattle on the place. The three Berney children followed in their father's footsteps, attending Springdale Grade and CHS, Jim graduating in 1955, Ted in 1958, and Barbara in 1960. Barbara's two girls, Aimeé and Holly Goertz, also graduated from CHS, the third generation in Ted and Lou's family to do so. Of more recent years, Ted states, "Cattle went to depression level prices in 1995 and 1996." Mr. and Mrs. Berney continue to live at their home in Springdale.

After leaving Washington State, Ray also worked at the ranch. In 1936, he married Hazel Cardwell, whom he had met at a Christian camp gathering in Virginia. The couple adopted four children, Linda, David, Robert and Ray Jr. As mentioned, after the sale of the ranch Ray assumed management of the Cabin City Auto Court and Log Cabin Café in Eugene. His parents lived in a house on the property. His father, Jim Berney, suffered a cerebral hemorrhage and died in October of 1938. He is buried in the Douglas Pioneer Cemetery in Troutdale. Ray sold the Auto Court and built the Eugene Motel. In subsequent years he became a hotel and motel property developer and operator, and eventually built up a chain of establishments on the West Coast. He became the President and Chief Executive Officer of the Pacific Hosts chain, which owned and/or operated approximately thirty hotels and motels from the Surfer Motor Lodge in San Diego to the Market Bowl and Marco Polo in Seattle. He built one large complex, the Surfrider Motor Hotel in LaJolla, California specifically for his three surviving children, Linda, Robert and Ray Jr., to own and operate. (David was killed in a tragic accident in Brookings, Oregon in 1950.) Ray Berney passed away December 18, 1991. His wife, Hazel, preceded him in death, passing away in May 1970.

Mrs. Clara Berney lived with her daughter, Grace, after the death of her husband. She died in Portland in January 1942. She is buried beside her husband, James A. Berney, in the Douglas Pioneer Cemetery in Troutdale, Oregon.   *'Ted' Berney*

Springdale Grade School c1942

Springdale Grade School, World War II scrap drive.

Photo courtesy of Sandy Cartisser.

51

Charles Bramhall
Alma (Graham) Bramhall

The Bramhall Place was located on Woodard Road, and their 54-acre farm extended south and west to Mutch Road. Charles 'Charlie' and Alma Bramhall purchased the place from Alma's parents, Robert and Anna (Pellett) Graham. Charlie was the son of Eleazar Bramhall, who came to Oregon in 1883 at the behest of his son, Allison. He settled in Aims shortly thereafter. Eleazar was active in founding the community of Aims. He built a mill there that initially used waterpower (later steam). He established and operated a store and the Aims post office for many years. The family history has been published previously by the East Multnomah County Pioneer Association (see "Eleazar S. Bramhall," and "The Descendants of Eleazar Smith Bramhall," *Pioneer History*).

Eleazar and Martha Bramhall had ten children. The first four, John, Allison, Elona and Jane, were born in Iowa. William, Maud, Nellie, Joseph, Charles and Harry were born in Kansas. When the family settled in Aims, the boys had the entire Bull Run watershed as fishing grounds. The family picked huckleberries on the slopes of Larch Mountain and wild blackberries on Walker Prairie. Since the family's history has been documented, it shall not be duplicated here. However, Dorothy Larson, granddaughter of Harry Bramhall and great-granddaughter of Eleazar and Martha, found family pictures of the Bramhall Mill in Aims, which are published here as part of the community's historical record.

Alma's parents, Robert and Anna (Pellett) Graham came to Oregon in 1885. Early in the 1890's, the couple had a home built in the Pleasant View area. Robert Graham became involved in the work of transporting (driving) log or timber 'rafts' by water to a place where the material could be shipped to market. On January 1, 1902, while driving log rafts on the Molalla River, Robert Graham lost his life when, trying to clear a log jam, he fell into the torrent and drowned. Besides his widow, he left three children, Hattie, b. October 11, 1881, Alma, b. June 2, 1885 and Archie, b. 1887. Another son, Robert, b. 1889, had died in his childhood years. Hattie married Harry Carter, and had three children: Henry, Leonard and Myrtle. Leonard, who graduated from CHS in 1925, was killed in France during WW II, where his remains lie in a cemetery in Lorraine Province, France. Myrtle graduated from CHS in 1928 after which she

Bramhall Mill

The mill and yard of the Bramhall Aims Mill.

Circular Head Rig

Top and bottom saws reduced gigantic trees to useable lumber.

Photos courtesy of Dorothy Larson.

Robert Graham **Anna A. Graham**

Robert Graham father of Hattie, Alma, Henry and Robert and Anna (Pellett) Graham, their mother.   Photos courtesy of Pat (Bramhall) Paget.

married Carl Lindell. She had two daughters and lived in Gresham. Archie died of typhoid fever in 1910 while on a trip to Michigan with his mother. Tragedy struck the family hard that year as Henry died in a logging accident at Castle Rock, Washington (see "Robert Graham," *Pioneer History*).

Later Hattie married Fred Keisel and had two more children, Elda, b. November 18, 1918 and Robert W. 'Bob,' b. January 27, 1922. The couple lived on Smith Road on the place Hattie had purchased from Peter Vande-Kerkhover and Leonardes de-Witte. Elda married John Boggs and moved to Alexandria, Virginia. Bob Keisel graduated from Benson, spent time in Alaska working on construction, joined the Air Force during WW II and remained in the service until 1948. He married Wanda Lassiter, and the couple lived in California and other locales for several years. They had three children, Karen, Ronald and Steven. Bob returned to East County where he became a partner with Marion Kirkham and Albert Soderstrom in KASO plastics (see "Descendants of Fred and Hattie Carter Keisel," *Pioneer History*).

Graham Children

Hattie [left] and Alma Graham.
Photo courtesy of Pat Paget.

After Robert Graham's death, Charlie and Alma Bramhall moved to the property on Woodard Road to help Anna Graham with the farm. Later, they purchased the farm from her. During these years Charlie became Road Supervisor for Multnomah County. In this position, he took an active role in the construction of the Columbia River Highway. He happened to be on the truck hauling gravel from the Baker Pit on Stark that plunged off the Nielsen Bridge to the Sandy River below, leaving him with a broken arm that did not heal properly. Later, after the new CHS opened at its present location, he became its janitor. During the summer months he worked as a forest ranger in the Mt. Hood National Forest stationed at Eagle Creek. In the summer of 1931, a lightning strike caused a power line to fall, which started a fire. Charlie didn't know the cause of the problem and while walking through the brush, touched the line and was electrocuted. The 1931-32 *Cohimore* was dedicated to his memory (see "Charles Bramhall," *Pioneer History*).

Mrs. Alma Bramhall will always be remembered by the children who attended Corbett Grade School because of her excellent meals, especially her bread rolls, which children could take almost without limit. The Bramhalls had two sons, Lloyd and Kenneth. Lloyd was an early pilot, and would often fly with Cecil Pounder over the Corbett area, which provided a thrilling and unique experience (in those days) for the kids below.

The Charlie Bramhall Family

From L, Charles, Lloyd, Alma (Graham) and Kenneth Bramhall. Photo courtesy of Rosetta (Henkle) Heitzman .

The Bramhall Home

The Bramhall home on Woodard Road built by the Grahams.
Photo courtesy of Pat (Bramhall) Paget.

Picking Up Potatoes

Lloyd Bramhall picking up potatoes on the Bramhall place.
Photo courtesy of Pat (Bramhall) Paget.

The Bramhall Place was rented to Tatsuzo Nakishimada before WWII. The family was forced to leave in May, 1942 when the local families of Japanese extraction were sent to 'relocation' camps by the United States government. When the Nakashimadas left, Howard Winters rented the Bramhall place and purchased the farm machinery and crops in the ground from the Nakashimadas. Howard has farmed the Bramhall Place continuously since that time and purchased the property in 1945.

After graduating from CHS in 1924, Lloyd Bramhall married Doris Emily, daughter of Roy Emily (see "Descendants of Roy Emily and Jessie Morgan Emily," *Pioneer History*, Volume II). Lloyd and Doris had two daughters, Patricia and Beverly. When the Bramhalls took over the store in Springdale, both started school at Springdale Grade, where Pat completed grade 4 and Beverly, grade 2. The family lived in the store. Just before World War II commenced, Lloyd and Doris Bramhall moved to Reedville (near Beaverton) to operate another store. Bill and Shirley Mishey took over the Springdale store. Patricia and Beverly then attended school in Reedville. Patricia graduated from Hillsboro High, but Beverly completed high school at CHS, graduating in 1948. Her mother had returned to the Emily home in Corbett to care for Mrs. Emily, who was ill.

Lloyd Bramhall sold the Reedville store shortly after he had obtained a job driving bus for Oregon Motor Stages. Later he went to work as a driver for Union Pacific Stages (later Greyhound), driving the Portland to Pendleton route. In the early 50's he and his brother, Kenneth, took over the Salem Dad's Root Beer franchise, but the venture did not work

Bramhall's Springdale Store

Bramhall's store, [formerly Atkisson's], located between Northway Road and Lucas Road on the Columbia River Highway.

Lloyd Bramhall Family

Rear, Lloyd and Doris Bramhall; front, Pat and Beverly Bramhall.   Photos courtesy of Pat (Bramhall) Paget.

out for them. He returned to the Portland area and purchased a laundromat in Beaverton, a relatively new business at the time. Due to some investments in U-Haul rentals that worked out well, Lloyd Bramhall retired at age 57. In fact, Pat and Beverly continue to receive checks (in 1999) from these investments. Lloyd Bramhall died May 29, 1974; Doris (Emily) Bramhall passed away November 6, 1985.

Kenneth Bramhall married LaVerne Edwards, and lived on Woodard Road close to where it intersects with Ogden (just south). Kenneth drove stage (bus) for Greyhound Lines). He also worked in the refrigeration business. Kenneth and LaVerne had two children, Donald and Cheryl. Kenneth Bramhall passed away April 2, 1971.

Pat (Bramhall) Paget

Bridal Veil Lodge

Bridal Veil Lodge built by Cecil Pounder, now operated by Laurel Slater as a 'Bed and Breakfast.'   Photo courtesy of Steve Lehl.

Meredyth Brown
Dorothy (Began) Brown

Meredyth Brown lived close to Bridal Veil in a home across from what is now the state park at Bridal Veil Falls. He attended CHS, from which he graduated in 1933. He worked for a time at the Bridal Veil Mill, then attended the University of Washington. He completed about two years before enlisting in the U.S. Army in 1941. He was posted to an ordinance outfit and was transferred to several stateside forts before being sent to England where his outfit helped prepare for the D-Day landing of June 6, 1944. He remained in England until the war in Europe ended May 8, 1945. He was in the states on his way to being re-deployed in the Pacific when the war ended.

Meredyth Brown married Dorothy Began in 1942. They have two daughters, Janet, b. July 11, 1949, and Laurel, b. October 26, 1955. The family lived at Bridal Veil in the former Bridal Veil Lodge until the early 60's when they moved to Milwaukie. The Lodge was built by Cecil Pounder, and is considered one of the historic buildings in the Gorge. When the Browns moved, they retained ownership of the Lodge. Laurel (Brown) Slater now operates a 'bed and breakfast' business in the 'Lodge,' the Brown's former residence.

Joseph A. Bucher
Elma (Wyss) Bucher

Joseph Bucher came to the United States from Switzerland in 1919, together with two of his sisters and several other people. He worked as a logger until he broke his leg, which ended his career in the woods. He started working at various dairy farms as a milker. He saved money to start his own dairy in the Rockwood area where he met his future bride, Elma Bertha Wyss. Her parents owned a farm located at 163rd and NE Halsey. The couple married June 30, 1926 in Portland, Oregon.

Joseph and Elma leased the Fred Luscher place near Bridal Veil in the late 20's, and that is where their first daughter, Carol, b. February 22, 1929, was born. They had five more children, Lillian, b. August 23, 1930; JoAnne, b. March 13, 1934; Conida E., b. July 19, 1938; Joseph Jr., b. September 28, 1942; and Susan, b. January 3, 1946. In 1930, the Buchers leased a farm in Dodson and started a dairy there with eight cows. Joseph had initiated a milk route to serve customers in Bridal Veil and Coopey Falls, and he continued to serve them from the dairy in Dodson. When an influx of workers came to the area to construct Bonneville Dam, his route expanded eastward to that area. In 1941, the Buchers purchased the farm they had been leasing and expanded their herd to approximately 70 cows. They sold dairy products from Bridal Veil to Cascade Locks on the Oregon side of the Columbia River, and from Prindle to Home Valley on the Washington side.

During World War II, the family sold their milk to the Mayflower Farmers' Coop in Portland. After the war they went back to selling milk, predominantly in gallon jugs, in the same area they had served before the war. The dairy was given the name, the Hollywood Dairy, and it was a fixture in the Gorge until Joseph Bucher could not longer continue his route work because of problems with his legs. During the years the Buchers operated their dairy business in the Gorge, many local youngsters (friends of the Bucher children) worked for them. The comments of these former workers and others reflect the high regard and esteem felt for the Buchers by these workers and by the family's former customers. When Joseph gave up the route because of his health problems, he started raising sheep.

Joseph and Elma Bucher

Photos courtesy of Carol Royse.

Each of the Bucher children attended Bonneville Grade School. Carol started high school at Stevenson, but finished at Cascade Locks, graduating in 1948. She married Ray Hogenson and had two girls, Sharon and Carray. The latter died in her first year. In 1962 Carol married Hershel A. Royse of Stevenson, Washington, and they had a birth daughter, Nickie Jo. Hershel Royse served as a towboat Captain on the Columbia for 43 years. Sharon Hogenson, b. September 28, 1949, married Joe Nolin of Cascade Locks, and has two daughters, Rachel and Erica. Nickie Jo Royse, b. September 19, 1967, is married to Jerry McConnell.

Lillian (Bucher) Herschback graduated from Cascade Locks High School. She had seven children, 3 boys and 4 girls and worked as a fish counter at local dams. JoAnne (Bucher) Mohr graduated from Cascade Locks, raised three boys and a girl and also worked at local dams as a fish counter. Conida 'Connie' (Bucher) Cyrus lives on a ranch near Sisters, Oregon, where she and her husband raise hay, sheep, potatoes and some cattle. They have a family of five, 1 girl and 4 boys. She also graduated from Cascade Locks High School. Joseph 'Joby' Bucher became a schoolteacher and retired from Damascus as a school administrator. He has three boys. Susan (Bucher) Nolan graduated from Cascade Locks and now lives in Salem. She works for Farmers' Insurance Company and raised two boys. *Carol (Bucher) Royse*

The Bucher's Hollywood Dairy at Dodson.

61

Henry W. Canzler
Kathryn L. (Kern) Canzler

Henry William Canzler was born in Pennsylvania November 4, 1859 and Kathryn Lydia Kern was born in Indiana January 16, 1860. The couple lived near Lincoln, Nebraska where their five children were born: Clara A. Colby, b. November 8, 1884; George A., b. December 12, 1886; Laura M. Lucas, b. May 8, 1888, Lillian A., b. April 15, 1889 and Arthur L., born in 1891. Henry and Kathryn brought their family to Springdale the spring of 1905 and purchased property from the Jubitz family, bounded on the west by what is now Lucas Road and on the south by what is now the Columbia River Highway. Mr. Canzler also purchased 25 acres from the Crowstons and 17.5+ acres from Grant Bell. On April 6, 1905, Henry purchased six hens from Sutliff Bates for $2.50. April 23, 1905, he sold 35 cents worth of salt, 80 cents worth of butter and 40 cents worth of honey (no quantities given).

Henry and Kathryn built a home just west of where the Springdale Grade School now (1998) stands. The family was among a group of families affiliated with the Church of the Plymouth Brethren that settled in Springdale shortly after the turn of the century. The Canzlers farmed and established a dairy herd. Kathryn Canzler, a graduate of Northwestern University, had the responsibility of testing grade school students in East Multnomah County to determine if standards were being met. She continued this work until ill health forced her retirement. She passed away February 27, 1928. Henry died two years later, July 16, 1930.

A granddaughter, Dorothy Canzler, wrote of her memories of the Canzler Place:

"Grandpa and Grandma Canzler's place in Springdale holds an honored niche in my memory. It was just across the highway from our house, which made it a perfect place to which to escape, which as the oldest of nine children I often had the need to do. I can still feel the rush of air as I would dash across the busy paved road, pound up the wooden steps and across the garden on the path to the wooden veranda, which in summer was screened by a glory of purple clematis.

The Canzlers

Kathryn and Henry Canzler.

Canzler Home

L to R: Clara (Canzler) Colby, Lillian Canzler and Laura (Canzler) Lucas.

Photos courtesy of Sandy Cartisser.

Before I was old enough to cross the highway by myself I can remember approaching this veranda and seeing two grandmas in full skirts to the floor, gray, with long white aprons, rocking, rocking, in wooden chairs. One was Grandma Canzler, who appeared quite old even then, and the other was her mother, Grandmother Kern, who died when I was four. Aunt Lillian, doing the chores, seldom had time to rock, except in the evenings when she would take me on her lap and sing songs which I can remember to this day: "Twenty Froggies" was a favorite and also "Jackie Frost: and "Little Red Bird."

Grandpa Canzler was always busy doing something; he was a great gardener. I may have inherited my love of gardening to a great extent from him. As a grandchild came near he always greeted him or her with a cheery "Heigh-Ho," (high tone on the first word and a low tone on the last). He often sang gospel choruses in a firm voice. I especially remember "Romans Ten and Nine" floating in the air as he did his gardening. Besides wonderful vegetables there was a wealth of flowers in that big garden in front of the house. For several years Grandpa specialized in gladioli. He had many varieties and planted them in rows, keeping the varieties separate. In the fall the corms were stored in boxes in the back rooms.

All the old-fashioned flowers could be found in this yard. A favorite of mine was bleeding heart, with its graceful curved sprays loaded with 'hearts.' But probably the most memorable was a huge clump of simply gorgeous gold-banded lilies. Aunt Lillian helped with the flowers, and this was an especial pride of hers. We children could always count on her help to get a beautiful bouquet to present to Mamma on Mother's Day or other special times.

Inside the house, the kitchen-dining-living room had a scrubbed smell, redolent of various kinds of foods. There were always sugar cookies in a jar in the pantry. Fried potatoes were a stable supper dish, so that smell clung dimly at all times. The large oblong table had a spotless white cloth and thick padding, with oilcloth mats at each place. A smaller white cloth covered the appointments in the center between mealtimes. The spoon holder was there, the syrup tumbler, sugar (bowl), salt and pepper (shaker),

Canzler Home

Canzler Home showing some of the flowers of which Dorothy reminisces.
Photo courtesy of Sandy Cartisser.

etc. One was always encouraged to take some Karo syrup to spread on the white homemade bread. Sorghum had been a delicacy to the Canzlers back in Nebraska. Now they delighted in good old Karo. 'Sauce' was the dessert along with sugar cookies at every meal. Part of the table setting ritual was accompanying Aunt Lillian down steep stairs outside to the dank little cellar where canned goods were kept, and choosing the kind of 'sauce' for that day. One never chose 'pears' or 'peaches,' but 'pear sauce,' 'peach sauce,' etc.

'Mush was a regular breakfast item. Toast was made on a rack in the wood stove oven. Hot water to wash the dishes came from the reservoir on the side of the stove. Nearby on the worktable was a small crock of salt, among other condiments. A small desk was an important item of furniture in this room. It had a green, gathered curtain. Catalogs, record books, the Bible, etc. were kept on this small desk, which was Grandpas place to keep records. After breakfast he always took the Bible out and read a chapter. Then we all knelt at our wooden chairs while he prayed. Bare floors, hard chairs and Grandpa's gentle voice combined for a far-reaching influence...

65

On the back porch was the marvelous wooden washing machine. On wash days it was so exciting to see the steamy clothes being put through the hand-turned wringer. Later they had a more modern model, but that old wooden one was enchanting…

Upstairs were three old-fashioned bedrooms, complete with chamber pots. The beds were high, and mounded with beautiful quilts. Aunt Lillian's room was largest, with two beds. I would occasionally spend a night with her and she would let me choose which bed we would sleep in. Either bed was a thrilling choice, with a soft downy mattress and starchy pillowcases and the articles on the dressers were so fascinating to inspect.

In Uncle Arthur's room his harmonica was in a prominent place. His habit was to play a few songs in bed before retiring. How beautiful it did sound! In the morning I would help Aunt Lillian make his and her beds. The cover had to be thrown back and aired for an hour or so first. The third room was called the 'spare room.' Also upstairs was a large open storeroom. Uncle Arthur kept his very valuable cabbage seed there. He had worked up a profitable industry in growing cabbage seed. To see the big, bulging sacks was a treat.

Grandpa had raised pigs in Nebraska. He carried on here, and had built the most beautiful pigpen. It had separate rooms and cement walkways all around with lovely gates partitioning off the sections. It was raised above the yard and was always very clean. I was most intrigued with this perfectly appointed building and believe it was the cause of my unreasoning fondness for pigs as a barnyard animal.

However, I was terrified when visiting the hen house with Aunt Lillian. I would accompany her on this chore, but never became comfortable around chickens. Getting the feed out of the bin on the back porch was a novel procedure for me. I could do that, and throw the seed to the hens, and gather eggs from the nest boxes, but never could raise a hen up to see if there were eggs under her.

Grandpa and Uncle Arthur raised Holstein cows and milked quite a few. The barn was a beautiful, mysterious place with three levels. There was a separate milk house – a cold cement and stone place with a deep, cold water tank to hold the milk cans…(missing narrative)…(behind the) pens was a shady wood with a sparkling small stream running through it. Alfred and I spent many an hour playing there. Grandpa was clearing it up to look like a park. He named the two sections on the east and west sides of the path 'Dew-Drop-Inn' and I loved all the different plants and bushes and especially remember with rapture the red huckleberry. And oh, the moss and springy, soft duff!

Grandpa had a beautiful car long before my father was able to have one. It was called 'the rig,' black, with side curtains, and it seemed huge and luxurious to me. I do not know its make, but it was not a Ford. I can remember going places with Grandma and Grandpa and Uncle Arthur and Aunt Lillian, but do not remember my brother Alfred or sister Mildred being with us. I always was alone it seems, on visits to the Canzlers. I hope they got their share of visits too, for those visits are some of the most wonderful memories a person could ever have."

George Canzler married Martha Bourgeois June 24, 1914. Martha was born October 19, 1893. The couple purchased a place across the highway from the home place and adjacent to (west) the Church of the Plymouth Brethren where they raised their family. Their children are: Dorothy, b. April 3, 1915; Alfred, b. August 27, 1916; Mildred, b. March 14, 1918; Katie, b. April 16, 1923; Florence, b. August 31, 1925; David, b. February 21, 1928; and Richard, b. January 17, 1930. The youngsters all grew up in Springdale and attended Springdale Grade School. Because they had a choice, some of the Canzler children attended CHS while others chose to attend other schools. Those who attended CHS include Dorothy ('32), Alfred ('34), Mildred ('35), and Florence ('43). Katie graduated from Gresham High School; David from Benson Tech and Richard earned his diploma through the equivalency program (G.E.D.). The youngsters have memories of swimming in the Sandy River, earning money picking berries and peas, the County Bookmobile, which provided reading material for all interests, and music. Family members played musical instruments and all loved to sing. They would gather around "Dottie's piano" and sing together. The four sisters sang four-part harmony with either Dorothy or Florence on the piano. When the winter hit, with the east wind howling through the Gorge, sleds and skates were brought out for sledding and ice-skating.

George Canzler became a noted building contractor in the area. Among other buildings, he worked on the View Point Inn, which is lo-

Maxwell House

Among other structures, George Canzler helped build the Maxwell House.
Photo courtesy of Steve Lehl.

cated on Larch Mountain Road about one-quarter mile from its intersection with the Columbia River Highway. He also worked on the construction of the "Maxwell House," which was built for Ann Hebler and Nettie Arnold on the Columbia River Highway west of Bridal Veil.

He built many other buildings including the Springfield (Egypt) School. Of course, he built the family home in Springdale. He also built several barns in the community. His older sister, Clara, attended business school. Laura married Verne Lucas (see "Verne S. Lucas"), while Lillian and Arthur 'Art' did not marry. Art and Lillian lived on the home place until it burned. They then moved to a place south of Ernie Groce's store on the highway. Art farmed the Canzler place for years. The hill behind the Canzler home was usually planted to cabbage and it was quite an impressive sight from Lucas Road or the highway.

After graduating from CHS, Dorothy attended and graduated from Oregon Normal School in Monmouth. She taught in Douglas County and on the coast above Reedsport for many years. She married Richard 'Dick' Weatherly. Mildred also attended Oregon Normal School and taught in Sams Valley and Gold Hill near Medford for 25 years. She married Gilbert Mack, a rancher and school administrator, who was a principal in Gold Hill many years. They had two sons, David, who recently retired from the U.S. diplomatic service, and Dr. Herschel Mack, a professor at Humboldt State University in Northern California. Mildred, widowed since 1975, lives in Gold Hill.

Alfred enlisted in the U.S. Navy and was assigned to an oil tanker at Pearl Harbor when that base was attacked. He saw action in the Pacific Theater during World War II, participating in such engagements as the 'Marianas Turkey Shoot.' Among his assignments after the war, he served on an icebreaker in the Bering Sea. He retired from the Navy as a Chief Petty Officer after more than 22 years service. He married Elizabeth Cartisser, who had three boys, Roland, Joseph and Richard, by a previous marriage. Roland graduated from CHS in 1958 and Joseph graduated in 1960. The couple had six birth children, Mary, Arthur, Rodger, Gordon, Leona and Linda, who graduated from CHS in 1963, 1965, 1966, 1969, 1970 and 1972, respectively.

Florence Canzler married James 'Jim' Scudder and the couple had three children, James, Candice and William 'Bill,' two of whom graduated from CHS: Candice (1972) and Bill (1976). Divorced in 1975, Florence married Bob Groce in September 1985, knowing she was very ill with cancer. She died two months later. David graduated from Linfield, married Chantal Lamenoise and the couple had four children. After completing a hitch in the military he served two years with the American Field Service after which he returned to earn his MA and Ph.D. from the University of Oregon. He taught for many years at Central Washington in Ellensburg and now lives in Marysville, Washington. Richard is married to JoAnne (surname unknown), lives in Tacoma, Washington, and has eight children. Though retired, he, two of his sons and a son-in-law own and operate Tree Service, Incorporated, in Tacoma.

Mildred (Canzler) Mack

Dewey Carpenter
Rena (Harmon) Carpenter

The Carpenter family lived on Mershon Road less than one-half mile from its eastern terminus at the Columbia River Highway. Dewey Carpenter was born in Woodstock, Illinois, February 3, 1898. Rena (Harmon) Carpenter was born in Wauseon, Ohio, May 16, 1904. While Rena was an infant, her mother died and an aunt, Lucinda Harmon, adopted Rena and raised her. Rena married Dewey Carpenter August 25, 1921 in Benton Harbor, Michigan. The family moved to Oregon from Wabash, Indiana (where their first two children were born) in 1923, settling first in Springdale. According to family lore, they were headed for Washington, but when they came to the Columbia River Gorge, they decided "this is it." They loved the beautiful scenery and the fertile soil for growing crops. When five acres of land with an orchard became available on Mershon Road, Dewey and Rena purchased it, and moved their family there in 1924. They had eight children, Bethel, b. June 8, 1922 in Wabash, Indiana; Leo, b. December 5, 1923, also in Wabash; Willa, b. August 5, 1926 in Gresham, Gertrude, b, July 8, 1928 at Corbett; Carol, b. November 13, 1930 at Corbett; Margaret, b. May 24, 1934 at Corbett; Nolia, b. April 24, 1936 at Corbett; and Rita, b. December 5, 1939 at Corbett.

Dewey was a carpenter by trade as well as by name. He built several homes in Gresham and Portland. During World War II he worked at the Swan Island shipyard. After the war he worked for the Dock Commission on Swan Island. Rena Carpenter was a wonderful homemaker, raising eight children and caring for her invalid mother, who had accompanied the Carpenters to Oregon. Rena Carpenter loved to cook and made scrumptious home made bread, biscuits and donuts. In 1946 she took the Greyhound bus to Portland and applied for a job with Meier and Frank Company. She got the job and worked in the Company tearoom for many years, which she thoroughly enjoyed. Both Dewey and Rena loved to hunt and fish. Dewey would often go hunting with Claude Woodle, who owned Corbett Hardware.

Memories of the children during their "growing up" years included picking strawberries for Louie Berney, Cary Kirkham and Art Duncklee. They earned from two cents per pound (before the war) to four and five cents per pound later. One time Gertrude was planting cabbage for Louie

A New Home

Rena Carpenter and her oldest daughter, Bethel, enjoy apples from the orchard at their new home.   Photo courtesy of Carol (Carpenter) Daiber.

Berney when she caught her hand in the pack wheels and had to have stitches at the doctor's office. Both Gertrude and Carol hoed cabbage for Louie Berney for seventy-five cents per hour. According to Carol, the Carpenter kids were all great tree climbers. They had two large walnut trees to climb in the front yard as well as trees in an orchard and in the woods behind the house. The wooded area behind the house seemed gigantic and the youngsters would roam through the area, picking wild flowers and imagining great adventures. The fruit trees bloomed in the spring and provided all kinds of fresh fruit in the fall. A large garden provided fresh vegetables for the family. Dewey plowed the ground with 'George,' a white workhorse. The loess soil was rich and held moisture so well the garden did not require watering, even in the hottest of summers. The Carpenters had a cow for milk, raised chickens for eggs and fryers, and raised one or two pigs each year for meat.

Walking to Groce's store in Springdale or Arneson's store in Corbett for candy created lasting memories for the kids. During the summer the youngsters would walk to the Sandy River to swim at 'Big Rock,' then stop at Edna Parson's ice cream parlor for one of her double or triple dip five-cent ice cream cones on the way home. When winter came, the east wind would pile snow into huge drifts that blocked traffic on many of the

71

Carpenter Sisters

Gertrude and Carol. '46 Cohimore photo (excerpt) courtesy of David Rees.

L to R, Nolia, Rita and Margaret. Photo courtesy of Carol (Carpenter) Daiber.

roads. Also silver thaws would often coat the countryside with several inches of ice. This provided a great past time for the kids, who would take to their sleds and slide down the long hill on Mershon Road. If the weather was too bad, one could listen to such radio programs as "I Love a Mystery," "Jack Armstrong, the All-American Boy," "Jack Benny," "Burns and Allen," Fibber McGee and Molly," "Ma Perkins," "Bob Hope" or "Amos 'n' Andy." If storms caused a loss of power, one had books from the County bookmobile to read by candle light or kerosene lantern.

The Carpenter children attended Corbett Grade and CHS, riding the school bus to school. Harley Bates drove the bus, which picked up students on the loop that included Corbett Grade, Chamberlain Road and Mershon Road. While still in grade school, Bethel started taking Gertrude and Carol to the old Imperial Skating rink in Portland to roller skate. As the girls grew older, they would take the Greyhound bus to Portland and catch a streetcar to the Oaks Rink to skate. Both Gertrude and Carol met their future husbands at the skating rink.

After graduating from CHS in 1940, Bethel married Jack Baker. She and her husband purchased the house adjacent to her parents' property on the east. (The October 6, 1951 *Cardinal* mentioned the sale of Bethel's home to the Dhone family.) Bethel had two children, Ben and Terry, before divorcing Jack. Later she married William 'Bill' Paul, with whom she had four children, three boys and one girl. After this marriage, she and her family moved to Iowa, where Bill Paul attended Bible College. Thereafter they moved several times as his work as a minister took him to different locales. Currently, Bethel and her husband live in Seattle, Washington.

Leo enlisted in the U.S. Navy before he completed high school. He served in both the Pacific and Atlantic theaters, and was assigned as part of a naval cadre to merchant ships crossing the Atlantic Ocean, which was hazardous duty with German U-boats plying the shipping lanes. Upon his discharge, he married Minnie Syverson, who lived in Corbett with her family at the time. Leo and Minnie had seven children. They lived on Gordon Creek Road for several years before moving to Lyons, Oregon, where Leo worked in a mill.

Before she completed high school, Willa Carpenter married Eldon Gilson, who was in the Navy at the time. She and Eldon had five children, four boys and one girl, including twins. They moved to St. Johns for a time, then later moved to Lyons, Oregon, where Eldon worked in the same mill as Leo Carpenter. Later still they moved to Salem, where they became caretakers for an outdoor gun club. Currently, Willa and her husband live in Stayton, Oregon.

Gertrude Carpenter, who would have graduated from Columbian High in 1947, married Marvin Cross, U.S. Army, before she completed her senior year. The couple moved to Fort Lewis where Marvin was stationed. After his discharge, they moved to Milwaukie, Oregon. About two years after the birth of her fifth child, Gertrude died of Hodgkin's disease February 3, 1957, age 29.

Carol Carpenter married Don Daiber before she completed high school (CHS Class of 1949). She earned her high school diploma through David Douglas High and attended Business College. Carol worked for the Carnation Company, for Hudson House and sold Avon when her primary job as a homemaker permitted. She is an accomplished artist, working in oils, and sells her paintings and craft work at various venues. Don worked as a machinist during his working years, and was a supervisor for Hyster when he retired. Carol and Don had four children, Steven, Mark, Sue and Troy, all of whom attended school in the Centennial District. Steven graduated from Oregon State University and now works for Safeco Insurance Company. He is married to Vicki Kutcher, lives in West Linn and has two children. Mark has followed his father's example and works as a machinist for Precision Castparts. He married Linda Doney, lives in Sandy and has one child. Sue works for the David Douglas School District, lives in Portland and has three children. Troy, a graduate of Oregon State University with a degree in Engineering Physics, works as an engineer for Boeing in Seattle. He married Maureen Gannon, lives in Kent, Washington and has three children.

Margaret Carpenter contracted rheumatic fever during her grade school years, which damaged her heart. She married Lyle Schavin in 1953. The couple lived in Portland and had a daughter before Margaret died of a heart attack the evening of her mother's funeral, November 10, 1965, age 31.

Nolia Carpenter graduated from Columbian High in 1954. She attended Portland State College and the Northwest School of the Bible. She married Byron Pickering in 1961. They lived in Portland for one year, moved to Scotts Mills and Stayton where Byron served as pastor at the Church of Christ in each location. Later they moved to Lincoln City, Oregon, where they lived for 27 years. In Lincoln City, Pickering was in the ministry for 15 years, built eight houses and a large fine arts gallery. He became noted for his oil seascapes. Nolia worked in the gallery for 13 years, displaying and selling the work of her husband and other artists. Nolia and Byron have raised many foster children, and they continue to take children into their home. Currently the couple lives in Otis, Oregon. Byron teaches classes in painting and sells his work to collectors and others.

Rita Carpenter graduated from Corbett High School in 1957. She married Curtis Smith, also a graduate of CHS ('55) and son of Raymond and Wilma (Lucas) Smith. Rita and Curtis both attended Portland State College from which Curtis graduated in 1959. Rita completed an associate's degree in physical therapy at Mt. Hood Community College and works as a physical therapist for a spinal specialist. She enjoys music and plays a digital keyboard for her personal enjoyment, at church functions and an occasional wedding. She is not seriously considering retirement as she "enjoys work too much." Curtis worked as a produce wholesaler in Portland, and continues to work in that field. Curtis and Rita have two boys, Dana and Brian, and live on Curtis Road between the Columbia River Highway and Smith Road.

Rena (Harmon) Carpenter died November 6, 1965. Her husband, Dewey Carpenter, died May 13, 1970.   *Carol (Carpenter) Daiber*

Albert F. Chamberlain
Margaret (Shelley) Chamberlain

Albert 'Bert' Chamberlain and his family lived on the 'home' place of the Chamberlains, which comprised more than 115 acres at one time. The property was located on Chamberlain Road, about 1/2 mile north of its intersection with Mershon Road (George Perry Jr. lived there for several years). Bert married Margaret 'Maggie' Shelley, and they had 6 children: H. Bennett, b. November 8, 1902; Arthur L., b. December 1, 1904; H. Burton 'Si', b. March 31, 1906; Earl L., b. July 27, 1908, Eugene B. 'Gene', b. November 18, 1911; and Ervin 'Irvy', b. March 28, 1919. All the children were born on the 'hill.' Bert farmed, fished commercially and brined cucumbers for Libby, McNeil and Libby (and also made dill pickles of local renown). He was born in Iowa October 1, 1876; Margaret Shelley was born in Canada December 11, 1881.

George and Bert Chamberlain are brothers. Their father was Elijah D. Chamberlain, who came to the area in 1881 by boat from San Francisco, and by steamboat to Latourell (see "Elijah D. Chamberlain," *Pioneer History*). The family first settled in Springdale, then moved to what later became the Alvin Kinney Place, (which is on the west side of the Corbett Grade just uphill from its junction with Reed Road). Eventually the family moved to the property located on what is now Chamberlain Road (and which locale gave the road its name). This place is where Bert Chamberlain and his family later lived. In addition to Albert and George, there were two other children, Nettie and Arthur 'Logan' (one daughter, Florence, born in Kansas in 1878, lived only 11 months). Logan drowned in an accident while working the seine at Rooster Rock June 4, 1903. Nettie married Archie Kincaid December 30, 1897 (see "Archie Kincaid").

Of Bert's children, Bennett died in Portland in 1920 at age 17. Arthur Logan married Emily Jonas October 8, 1926. They had four children, George A., b. January 25, 1929; Donald A., b. March 1929 (died at 4-months of age); Donna L., b. November 13, 1931; and Paul R., b. March 20, 1935. Arthur, who worked as an electrician, died November 16, 1937. Burton 'Si' married Margaret Jonas June 1, 1926. The family lived on the scenic highway just above its intersection with Smith Road during the years their two boys, John and Wayne, were in school.

Earl Chamberlain

Earl Chamberlain, CHS graduate, 1926 Cohimore photo.

John, b. December 16, 1927, in Gresham, graduated from CHS in 1946. He married Nina Britton June 26, 1948 and the couple lived in East County for many years. They had three children, Lynn, Muriel and Jonny. Nina Chamberlain passed away February 23, 1993. John currently lives in Wenatchee, Washington. Wayne, b. July 20, 1933, graduated from CHS in 1951. He married Flora Davis (see "Irenus F. Davis") July 22, 1953. They had three children, Chris, Kathy and Michael. Wayne worked for Reynolds Metals in Troutdale. Flora worked for the Corbett School District for several years. She died July 30, 1990, and Wayne died September 18, 1997. Both are interred in the Mountain View Cemetery, Corbett.

Earl Chamberlain must have attended Pleasant View Grade School on what is now Wand Road. He graduated from CHS in 1926. After high school he attended Oregon Normal School (Western Oregon State College), from which he graduated in 1931. He taught at Bull Run, Three Links and Sandy in Clackamas County and at Powellhurst Grade in Multnomah County. He became a school principal after several years teaching. Earl married Velma Owen November 2, 1930. She had a daughter, Ellen R. Dyer, from a previous marriage. Earl and Velma had two birth children, Owen and Hazel. Owen now lives on the Jasper Mershon place on Wand Road. Earl Chamberlain died September 10, 1987, in Portland.

Gene Chamberlain graduated from CHS in 1929. He attended Northwest Christian College and became a minister. He married Verna Grider of Condon May 19, 1935 and they had a daughter, Vera. Later he took a pastorate in Visalia, California. He married a second time to Jean, who worked with him in his ministry. Gene Chamberlain passed away in May 1999. Ervin 'Irvie' Chamberlain married Virginia Williams December 4, 1943 in Seattle, Washington. He served in the U.S. Navy a number of years. Irvy and Virginia had two children, Lee C., b. March 4, 1945 and Patricia J., b. January 1, 1947. Virginia died in Houston, Texas June 30, 1949 (see "Chamberlain Clan History," *Pioneer History*, Volume II). Irvy married Margaret E. Pierce December 17, 1949. After retiring from the Navy, he worked in the law enforcement field in California.

The Chamberlain Family

George H. Chamberlain
Virginia (Owen) Chamberlain

George Chamberlain was born in East Multnomah County December 13, 1882, shortly after his family arrived in Oregon. His father, Elijah, lived for a time in Latourell, then located in Springdale and later near Lower Corbett before buying a place on what is now Chamberlain Road. His son, George, met his future bride, Virginia Pearl 'Virgie' Owen, in Corvallis where he was attending college. The couple married in Corvallis October 10, 1907. She was born in Wren, Oregon, May 6, 1884 of the pioneer 'Oregon Trail' Owens family. Her parents were part of the "Lost Wagon Train," which came to Oregon from Missouri in 1853. Virgie attended school in Monmouth and had moved to Corvallis, where she met her future husband. After the marriage, they moved to Corbett and purchased a place located on Evans Road just south of its intersection with Pounder Grade. They operated a small store there.

George Chamberlain served as a medic during World War I, even though he was 35 years of age with four young children at home. Assigned to medical duties as a volunteer because of his religious beliefs (conscientious objector), he wrote a letter from France to his wife, Virgie:

> "...I don't suppose you will believe it but I have changed my mind about our soldiers' smoking. (A wounded soldier asked for a cigarette when George was attending to his needs.) ...That night I bummed every cigarette I could get hold of from the fellows along my corridor. (I) was proud to put the cig(arette) in a soldier's mouth and light it for him so he might get his mind off his pain. ...You can bet that the next time I go to the hospital I will have a pocket full of cigarettes. I have one fellow in the ward that had both arms hit by shrapnel and has them both strapped into slings. Don't you think I would be glad to light a cigarette for him?"

After the Columbia River Highway was built, George and his family moved from Evans Road to a place along the Columbia River Highway, where they built another store (which was later sold to Perry Settlemier). They also owned a campground with some cabins and camping spaces adjacent to the store. George and Virgie had 6 children: Harold, b. December 3, 1908; Elsie 'Pearl,' b. February 25, 1911; Mabel, b. October

Chamberlain Family at Crown Point

Rear: Arlie Kincaid, Ellen Chamberlain, Virgie Chamberlain, Elijah Chamberlain, Mabel Chamberlain and Lucille Kincaid. Front: Pearl Chamberlain, Harold Chamberlain and Ernest Chamberlain.
Photo courtesy of Mickey Chamberlain.

19, 1912; Ernest, b. August 1, 1915; Catherine, b. December 30, 1919; and Margaret 'Marmie,' b. August 8, 1921. All completed elementary school at Corbett Grade School and attended CHS, from which Harold graduated in 1925, Pearl in 1928, Mabel in 1931, Ernest in 1933, Catherine in 1937 and Marmie in 1939.

Mr. Chamberlain was active in the Troutdale Fruit and Vegatable Growers Association. Members shipped produce, principally cauliflower, cabbage and lettuce, to markets across the country. To illustrate the scope of the Association's business, 160 carloads of cauliflower were shipped out of Troutdale in 1925. Some farmers, including George Chamberlain, also grew 'pole' peas for processing. His daughter, Pearl, remembers picking peas for her father. The Association faded during the depression of the 1930's. The Chamberlains also grew gladiolas, asters and iris. Virgie Chamberlain sold flowers, principally gladiolas, for many years from a stand in front of their home. The trade was brisk during the era when the Columbia River Highway carried all east and westbound traffic to and from Portland.

Chamberlain Youngsters

Laura Wilson with from L, Mabel, Pearl and Harold Chamberlain at the place on Evans Road.   Photo, the author.

George Chamberlain Family

Rear: Mabel, Harold, George, Virgie, Ernest and Pearl. Front: Marmie and Catherine.
Photo courtesy of Mickey Chamberlain.

79

George and Virgie Chamberlain with Granddaughters

L to R: Janice Chamberlain, Virgie, George and Barbara Chamberlain. Photo courtesy of Mickey Chamberlain

Anyone who attended Corbett Christian Church during George's life will remember his booming baritone voice singing the 'old-time' gospel hymns. Later in his life, George Chamberlain worked for Claude Woodle at Corbett Hardware. He maintained that the job was necessary in order for him to qualify for Social Security, as farmers were not covered in those days. George's daughter, Catherine, had the job of mail messenger for the Corbett Post Office. This required her to pick up and deliver mail to Corbett Station. One bitter-cold, icy winter day with the east wind howling, George insisted that he deliver the mail to Lower Corbett rather than Catherine. His car slid off the road and he was forced to walk home. When he walked into the house, he clutched his head and fell to the floor, dead of an apparent heart attack. He died February 23, 1957.

After George Chamberlain's death, Virgie moved to a small cottage in Milwaukie. She lived independently for the remainder of her life, except in her final years. She lived with her daughter, Pearl, in SE Portland for a time and lived in a care center for a couple of years. She loved poetry and wrote verse, which a grandson published. Virgie (Owen) Chamberlain died June 27, 1985, age 101 (see "Chamberlain Clan History," *Pioneer History*).

Harold Chamberlain received an appointment to the U.S. Naval Academy and spent more than two years at that institution. After leaving the Academy, he had a daughter, Patricia, with Margaret Robards. Later Harold met Martha 'Mickey' Linderholm on a blind date. The couple married October 15, 1931. Harold and Mickey had eight children: Claire, b. September 24, 1932; Barbara, b. December 1, 1934; Janice, b. September 16, 1936; Sylvia, b. December 12, 1937; Michael, b. July 29, 1942; Patrick, b. January 11, 1947; Dennis, b. November 2, 1949; and Robert, b. July 19, 1951. Harold decided to attend Northwest Christian College in Eugene, but attended just one year. He then worked in sales and on the farm for his father. When the family returned to Corbett, they lived in a cottage close to Corbett Hardware owned by Clara Salzman. Mrs. Salzman lived in an adjacent home. She wrote this poem about her neighbors, the Chamberlains:

My Neighbor
by Clara Salzman
(c 1939-40)

I have a little neighbor, whose yard's adjoining mine;
Her house is filled with laughter, there's washing on the line.
Her windows smudged with fingerprints, her porch is strewn with toys;
And always there's confusion, and quite a lot of noise.

Sometimes the children straying, forget the boundary line;
And play awhile in my yard, and I pretend they're mine.
Sometimes they break my tulips, or my daffodils so gay;
To better reach a sailboat, as beside my pool they play.

My house has long been empty; (My children all are grown);
Forsaken like the robin's nest, where all the birds have flown.
So I don't mind the broken flowers, I like the merry din;
I still have children 'round the house, though there are none within.

As World War II approached, ships and men were needed to transport supplies to Europe and the Pacific. Harold joined the US Merchant

Harold Chamberlain Family

L to R: Claire, Janice, Mickey, Michael, Sylvia and Barbara.

Visitors at the Chamberlain Home

L to R on horse, Sharon Dooley, Rose Dooley, Majorie Stephens, Carol Stephens, Sylvia Chamberlain, Janice Chamberlain, Violet Dooley and Michael Chamberlain. Harold Chamberlain in background.   Photos courtesy of Mickey Chamberlain.

82

Cousins

Claire Chamberlain and George Stephens.
Photo courtesy of Mickey Chamberlain.

Marine. George Chamberlain remodeled one of the cabins on the home place for Mickey and the children. Harold continued his service in the Merchant Marine after the war. His wife and family lived on the home place until 1952, when Mickey had an opportunity to buy a home in Happy Valley. The children attended Corbett schools until the family moved. Claire was the only child to complete her elementary and secondary years in Corbett, graduating from CHS in 1950. Barbara completed three years at CHS, but graduated from Milwaukie High School, as did the other youngsters.

Claire worked at Good Samaritan Hospital and also worked in various office jobs. She married Paul McAllister and had two children, Brian and Bruce. She passed away March 22, 1973, age 40. Barbara worked as a police officer and for Kaiser Permanente. She married Paul Clanton and had three sons, Michael, Eric and Jon. She now lives in Milwaukie with her mother (Mickey). Janice married Bruce Holson and they have three children, Leslie, Lynne and Edward. She and her husband live in Louisiana where he works for Shell Oil Company. Sylvia married Paul

Chamberlain Sisters

From L:, Mabel, Pearl, Marmie and Catherine Chamberlain.
Photo courtesy of Marge (Stephens) Soesbe.

Bader and they have four children, Kevin, Jeffrey, Kristin and Gregory. Paul owns a steel business and he and Sylvia raise emus and ostriches as a sideline. Michael married Janice Otterson and they have three children, Kimberly, Pamela and Stephen. He owns Rem Steel and also lives in Milwaukie. Patrick has not married, lives in Milwaukie and works as a caretaker. Dennis is married to Patricia Munson and has four children: Brittany, Aiden, and two birth children, Gabriel and Grace. He is a licensed marriage and family counselor and lives in Portland. Robert had three children, Sarah, Amy and Leah, from his first marriage. He is now married to Debra Anderson and they have two children, Daniel and Emily. He works for a steel company, has an (online) antique business and lives in SE Portland.

After graduating from CHS, Pearl attended the Oregon Normal School in Monmouth to earn a teaching certificate. She taught in the Porter District (near Estacada) her first year. She married James 'Jim' Stephens and the couple had three children, George, b. April 1, 1933; Marge, b. March 20, 1936; and Carol, b. October 19, 1937. Jim and Pearl purchased a place on Chamberlain Road adjacent to the former Chamberlain place. She did not teach during her children's early years. Before she could resume teaching in the 40's, she was required to complete another year at Monmouth in order to regain her teaching certificate. She resumed teaching at Lakeview, then taught at Selma, near Kerby, Oregon. In 1946 she married Ray Wilson (see "Raymond Wilson"). They purchased a farm in Beavercreek, where they raised their combined family of six children. Later Ray and Pearl moved to SE Portland, then to Milwaukie.

Pearl taught for many years, completing her teaching career in the Milwaukie School District, from which she retired in 1972. After both Ray and Pearl retired, they purchased a home in a church-sponsored community in Morton, Washington. They lived there for a number of years before returning to live in Gladstone. Ray Wilson passed away March 24, 1995. Pearl has lived independently at her home in Gladstone until recently, when she had knee replacement surgery.

George Stephens married Roberta Fortune. They had two children, Pamela and Rick. Later he married Judith Buss and they had two children, David and Deborah. George and Judith now live in Boring, Oregon. Pearl's oldest daughter, Marge, married Jim Soesbe, and the couple now lives in Aims. Their two children, Wallace and Laurie, graduated from CHS in 1979 and 1982, respectively. Marge had a son, Norman, from a previous marriage, who lives in Milwaukie. Carol Stephens married Stanley Stockwell and the couple had four children, Randy, Roger, Cheryl and Susan. Carol and her husband live in Utah.

Mabel attended Northwest Christian College in Eugene where she met her future husband, Charles P. 'Paul' Moore, of Los Angeles, California, who was studying for the ministry. Mabel's cousin, Eugene 'Gene' Chamberlain introduced Mabel to Paul. Paul's first full-time pastorate was at the Christian Church in Athena, Oregon. Mabel and Paul had seven children, Paul Jr., Dale, John, Thomas, Daniel, Matthew and James. After serving 23 years in Athena, Paul was sent to Rupert, Idaho, where he served as pastor of the First Christian Church. His next assignment was the Christian Church in Sweethome. After retiring, he accepted a pastorate at Holly, near Sweethome. He also became a municipal court judge in Sweethome. Mabel's musical abilities, her voice, piano and organ playing skills, contributed much to the Paul's ministry wherever he served. Paul Moore passed away July 30, 1996. Mabel (Chamberlain) Moore lives in a retirement home in Turner, OR.

Ernest also attended Northwest Bible College in Eugene and became a minister. In 1936 he married Zella Webb and the couple had a daughter, Gloria, and adopted another child, Martha. Ernest earned a Master's Degree from Butler University and ministered throughout the Northwest during his career. He taught at Boise Bible College for many years. He and his wife retired to Turner, Oregon.

Catherine married John Roley, of Savannah, Georgia, September 27, 1941. John came to Oregon with a contingent of the CCC's, which is how he and Catherine met. John was born June 20, 1920 and attended school in Washington, D.C. and Savannah, where he graduated from a military high school. He worked at the Bridal Veil mill and the Troutdale aluminum plant until he passed the exam requisite for employment in the Portland Police Department. He and Catherine had seven children, John E., b. May 19, 1942; Mary 'Ginger,' b. September 11, 1945; Stephen, b. October 1, 1947; Janette, b. November 15, 1948; Nancy, b. November 2, 1950; Anita, b. April 9, 1953; and Margaret 'Marmie,' b. August 8, 1957. All attended Corbett schools, with John graduating from CHS in 1960, Ginger, in 1963, Stephen in 1965, Janette in 1966, Nancy, ex-'68, Anita in 1971 and Marmie in 1975.

Catherine remained at home to care for her family for the most part. She did work as a mail messenger at Corbett for 13 years and worked in the Corbett Post Office on a part-time basis as needed. In 1961 she started work at Tektronix in Beaverton and worked there for more than 10 years. She loved to sing and performed in school productions, the church choir and at various other places. She sang with the Portland Symphonic Choir and among other performances, sang in a presentation of Handel's Messiah during the Christmas season of 1960. She also played the piano and organ. She and John lived in the family home in Corbett. After renting it for some time, they eventually purchased the historic dwelling and property.

John Roley retired from the Portland Police Department as a Lieutenant in 1979, after completing more than 30 years service. Prior to his retirement, John and Catherine sold the Chamberlain home to a daughter and moved to an apartment in Rockwood. In 1978 they purchased a home in Gearhart, Oregon where they now live.

Marmie Chamberlain married Rex Snook in Oakland, California June 11, 1941. Rex served in the US Navy from which he retired after completing 20-years service. He and Marmie had four children, Susan, Becky, Gregory and Richard. After Rex was discharged, the couple returned to Northwest and made their home in Portland. Rex Snook passed away in February 1991. Marmie continues to live at her home in Portland.

The Chamberlain Family

Leora (Philippi) Cheney

Mrs. Leora Cheney started teaching at CHS the fall of 1936. She was born January 26, 1896, in Eastern Oregon, where her family owned the famed Philippi Ranch. The ranch stretched from the John Day River east to Philippi Canyon, and started with a full section that Mr. Philippi had homesteaded about 1890. By the late 30's, the family had added surrounding acreage as it became available until it encompassed approximately 55,000 acres. Leora Philippi attended a one-room schoolhouse at the edge of the ranch her grade school years, and boarded in The Dalles to attend high school, from which she graduated at age 16. She then attended Oregon Agricultural College (now Oregon State University) for three years, obtained a teaching certificate in mathematics, and started teaching.

Leora Philippi's first teaching position was at Umapine High School, where, since she was only 19, she found some of the students older than she was. She completed work for a degree at O.A.C., and moved to Portland to teach at Benson. In 1927, while teaching in Portland, she met and married Willard C. Cheney. The couple had a son, David, b. August 3, 1928. Mrs. Cheney separated from her husband, and returned to Eastern Oregon to resume her teaching career at Arlington.

In 1932, Mrs. Cheney moved to Condon High School, and she taught there the next four years. Her son, David, started grade school in Condon, and completed his first two school years there. The next move was to Corbett, where she was to spend eleven years teaching high school students in this community. Though her specialty was mathematics, because of the high school's numbers, she taught Home Economics, Physical Education, Biology, and other science courses as well. David Cheney started at Corbett Grade School in the 3rd grade, and completed his remaining elementary and secondary school years here. Mrs. Cheney purchased a home on Crestview Lane in 1943. It was totally run down, and there was no money to hire work done. In keeping with her indomitable spirit, she set about making the place habitable. She pounded nails, installed electricity and plumbing, painted and wallpapered. When finished, she had a very nice place with lovely gardens. She became an active member of the Columbian Garden Club, and could always be counted on to have a beautiful display at any Garden Club show.

Leora Cheney

Classmates and Friends

Leora Cheney at CHS.. '47 Cohimore photo courtesy of David Rees.

George Perry (left) and David Cheney at Menucha. Photo courtesy of George Perry Jr.

In 1947, Mrs. Cheney obtained a teaching position at Gresham High School, and taught mathematics there until she retired in 1964. Starting in 1915 and ending in 1964, her teaching career spanned a total of 49 years, of which 41 years were actually spent in the classroom. Mrs. Cheney attended the First Presbyterian Church in Fairview. Appointed as the first female elder in the church, Mrs. Cheney commented to a critic who believed a woman was not qualified for such a position, that "men and women are no different from the shoulders up."

After graduating from CHS in 1946, David Cheney joined the U.S. Navy destined for its flight training program. The Navy sent him to the University of California at Berkley spring term, 1946, to Oregon State College (now OSU) from 1947-49, then to flight training. He served as a pilot in the Navy until 1951 after which he returned to Oregon State to complete another year of college. He enrolled at the University of Washington in 1952 and had completed one quarter when he was hired by American Airlines in its pilot training program. He served as a pilot with American for 35 years, retiring in 1988. During that span, he completed work for a college degree at San Jose State in California, graduating in 1958.

88

Wilma Dearixon

Wilma Dearixon, CHS freshman 1946-47. '47 Cohimore photo courtesy of David Rees.

On January 28, 1951, David married Wilma R. Dearixon of Corbett. Wilma is the daughter of Clarence and Irene (Dorzab) Dearixon, who moved to this area from Hood River the summer of 1942, when Dearixon got a job in the shipyards. In 1961, David and Wilma purchased a 900-acre ranch in Eastern Oregon, close to Ione. They added acreage, as adjacent land became available, until the ranch reached 4,600 acres in size. David's job with American Airlines permitted him to work the ranch, as he was able to "commute by air" to his duty station at San Francisco. David and Wilma have seven children, four birth sons and three adopted daughters of Asian-American extraction. David and Wilma sold the ranch in 1994, and now (1999) live in Walla Walla.

Mrs. Leora Cheney continued to live at her home in Corbett until her death August 22, 1985. The community lost a person respected and esteemed by everyone who knew her (most particularly by her former students, of whom the author is one). The children of David and Wilma are grown. Daniel R., b. July 4, 1952, married Susan Glasgow. They have two sons, and live in Fairfax, VA. He works as a computer consultant. David M. 'Mark,' b. September 6, 1953, married Denise Winger June 28, 1977. They have two daughters, and live in Prescott, AZ. He is a Captain for Southwest Airlines. Douglas A., b. February 17, 1957, married Rebecca Perry in 1982. He is now married to Lynda Dally. They live in Boise, ID, and have two adopted children from Bulgaria. He works as a Program Manager for Hewlett-Packard. Dennis T. 'Tim,' b. November 6, 1958, married Tami Harrison. They have three children, live in Boise, ID, and have a farm. Carol I. and Christine L. are twins (b. in Seoul, Korea October 24, 1962), and were adopted from Korea when they were a year old. Carol works at Planned Parenthood and lives in Portland. Christine also lives in Portland and works for Gardenburger Inc. Cathy M., b. September 17, 1962, was adopted in 1968. She lives in Houston, TX, and works at a printing firm. *David Cheney*

Oris A. Childers
Clara M. (Moul) Childers

Oris A. and Clara 'Kay' Childers purchased 40-acres located on Gordon Creek Road between Buck and Gordon Creeks in the early 40's. They lived in SE Portland at the time. Oris Childers was born in Missouri March 6, 1909, while Clara (Moul) Childers was born in McMinnville, Oregon March 29, 1912. Oris had two children from a previous marriage, Richard, b. December 11, 1931 and Sandra b. April 29, 1939. Kay Childers also had two children from a prior marriage, Colleen Innes, b. April 26, 1931 and Carroll Innes, b. March 15, 1935. The family moved into a small home located on the property on Gordon Creek Road in the summer of 1947. Colleen, who had been attending Franklin High School in Portland, entered CHS that fall as a junior. Richard enrolled as a sophomore at CHS while Carroll and Sandra enrolled at Corbett Grade School in grade 7 and grade 3, respectively. Both Colleen and Richard graduated from CHS, in 1949 and 1950, respectively. Oris and Kay Childers had one birth daughter, Mardee, b. December 3, 1948, while living on Gordon Creek Road. In 1952, because of Oris' health problems (asthma), the Childers moved to Bend.

April 28, 1950, Colleen Innes married Clarence Mershon (see "George W. Mershon"). After his discharge from the Air Force, Clarence and Colleen moved into the Gordon Creek home and lived there approximately five years. After Richard Childers graduated from CHS, he enlisted in the US Navy. During the Korean War he served on the carrier, USS Princeton, in the Sea of Japan. He decided to make the armed forces a career and served in both the Navy and the Air Force until he retired with a disability in the early 60's. Thereafter, he lived and worked in Portland. Richard Childers passed away January 11, 1994, of cancer.

When the Childers moved, Shirley Pounder, a classmate of Carroll Innes, wrote an editorial in the *Cardinal* about her friend:

"There is a vacancy left in the halls and hearts of Columbian High as one of our most charming schoolmates leaves us for Bend, Oregon. It is always a pleasure to know a lady and how well Carroll Innes deserves the title! Carroll joined the present junior class in the seventh grade at Corbett. She was the class secretary for three years in succession and was always willing to help in

Clara and Oris Childers

Clara and Oris Childers at their home on the Sandy River between the mouth of Gordon Creek and the mouth of Buck Creek.

Childers at Gordon Creek Home

L to R: Colleen Innes, Clara Childers, Mardee Childers [in front of] Oris Childers, Sandra Childers and Carroll Innes.

any project. Her excellent grades helped raise the junior class average to a high mark and her quiet manner and charming personality were the admiration of teachers and students alike. As Corbett realizes its loss, may Bend realize its gain!"

Carroll graduated from Bend High School in 1953, then attended Linfield College. She married John Stenkamp of Bend. The Stenkamps had two children, Kilby and Heidn. John recently retired from a position with the Internal Revenue Service.

Sandra Childers graduated from Bend High School in 1957. She then returned to East County to live with the Mershons. She started a career in medicine, working in Portland for Dr. Ernest Rudey. August 29, 1958, she married Ron Evans, of Corbett, who was in the Navy at the time. In 1964, the couple moved to Corbett, purchasing the former Walker home on Mershon Road. In 1960, Sandra went to work for Dr. Marshall Brown in Gresham. She has worked in the same office since, though Dr. Brown sold his practice a few years ago. Ron and Sandra have one birth son, Brian, b. May 3, 1959. In addition, they raised Linda Peterson's two children, Michael and Martha, after Linda (Ron's sister) was killed in an automobile accident on Hurlburt Road in 1970.

Carroll Innes

Carroll Innes holds her sister, Mardee, at her Gordon Creek home.

Richard and Sandra Childers

Richard and Sandra Childers at their Gordon Creek home. Photos courtesy of Colleen (Innes) Mershon.

After his discharge from the Navy, Ron worked for Coast Crane until he went into the crane repair business on his own in 1986. In the early '80's, Ron and Sandra purchased 20 acres from Murray and Stella Evans on Mannthey Road. They moved to the place in 1984, living in the shop building until they completed construction of a home on the property in 1985. They planted part of the acreage to Christmas trees and also took some of the Evans' daffodil stock when Murray and Stella retired. Ron has retired from his repair business and Sandra is looking forward to retirement soon. Currently they are building a retirement "hideaway" near Mitchell, Oregon.

Brian married Sue Walters, who had two children, Heather and Ashley, from a prior marriage. Brian and Sue have a son, Brandon, b. June 23, 1993. Brian and Sue now live in Gresham.

Mardee Childers also returned to East County and lived with the Mershons. She married Jack Rover, of Canby, and had a son, Tyler. Mardee (Childers) Tucker now lives in Texas.

James W. Cowling
Lula M. (Drew) Cowling

James W. Cowling was born July 28, 1904, in Sweet Home, Oregon, son of Thomas 'Tom' and Maude (Calkins) Cowling. Tom Cowling, along with his father and four brothers, came to the United States from Cornwall, England in the 1870's and 1880's. They had been tin miners. Some of the family continued to mine after arriving in America, while others turned to farming for their livelihood.

After homesteading near Sweet Home, Tom met Maude J. Calkins. The couple married March 27, 1892. Tom and Maude spent the first years of their married life in that area. They had seven children, Maude A., b. February 12, 1893; Thomas B., b. October 21, 1894; Alice F., b. June 15, 1897; Kate B., b. October 17, 1900; Alfred H., b. May 20, 1902; James W., b. July 28, 1904; and Esther, b. August 27, 1911. In 1900, Tom became involved in evangelical work, and the family moved temporarily to Troutdale. For the next two years, Tom served East Multnomah County as an itinerant preacher with the United Evangelical Church (later to merge with the Methodist Church). The first year in Troutdale, their fourth child, Kate, was born. During the second year, the family rented a farm on Christensen Road, near Gage (later Springdale). Their fifth child, Alfred, was born on the farm.

Using his horse, Dolly, and a buggy for transportation, Tom Cowling preached in two or three different churches each Sunday. An August, 1901 diary entry shows a typical two-Sunday, rotating schedule for preaching:

"Sunday, May 5, 1901:   Morning, Latourelle
                Afternoon, Springdale
                Evening, Troutdale

Sunday, May 12, 1901:   Morning, Bullrun
                Afternoon, Aims."

Church services were held in schools, campgrounds and homes. Tom and Dolly had a good workout on weekends.

In the fall of 1902, the Cowlings returned to the farm near Sweet Home. Besides farming, Tom worked as a miner and in the Boothe-Kelly

Thomas Cowling Family c1902

From L, Maude (holding Alfred Henry), Maude
Adelia, Alice Francis (seated), Thomas Berdic and
Thomas (holding Kate Beatrice). Photo courtesy
of Tom Cowling.

lumber mills of the Mohawk Valley. On October 26, 1923, Tom wrote in
his diary: "I was received as a patient at the Oregon State Tuberculosis
Hospital. Silicosis is Miner's consumption, an occupational disease." In
April 1930 he died in the hospital, leaving a wife, seven children and
four brothers as survivors.

In 1938, James W., Tom and Maude's youngest son, applied for work
at Bridal Veil Lumber and Box Company as an assistant saw filer. He
had worked as a saw filer in the lumber industry starting as a young man.
On July 5, 1935, James married Lula M. Drew in Vancouver, Washington. He went to work for the Bridal Veil Lumber and Box Company as a
saw filer and worked there until the mill closed. James and Lula had
three children, Thomas J. 'Tom,' b. July 25, 1938, Robert L. 'Bob,' b.
September 24, 1940 and Patricia L. 'Pat,' b. January 25, 1945. The family lived at Bridal Veil and all three children attended schools at Corbett.
Tom and Bob graduated from CHS in 1956 and 1958, respectively. After

the mill closed, the family moved to Parkrose, where Pat graduated from high school.

Tom Cowling graduated from the University of Oregon. On July 7, 1962, he married Janice H. Hinton. Tom and Janice have two children, Donna and Peggy. Tom Cowling owns his own business and practices as a financial planner. Bob Cowling also attended and graduated from the University of Oregon. He is a principal in a legal firm in Medford. He has two children, Timothy and Peggy, from his first marriage to Margi Pittam. In 1993, he married Jean Bolton and they live in Medford. Pat Cowling graduated from the University of Oregon and is the school nurse at the Oregon Episcopal School. She is married to Philip J. Smith, a teacher at Franklin High School, and has three children, Tiffany, Chad and Amanda 'Mandy.'

After the move to Parkrose, James Cowling opened his own business, Cowling Saw Service, which he operated until he retired. Lula Cowling passed away November 29, 1990; James Cowling died May 1, 1993.

Bourgeois Home. Springdale c1915.   Photo courtesy of Sandy Cartisser.

Sam K. Cox
Ollie (Richardson) Cox

The Cox family came to Oregon from Nebraska in 1939, settling first in Dallas. The family moved to Springdale in 1943. Sam K. Cox was born in Nebraska; Ollie 27Richardson was born in Axtel, Kansas. The couple married November 9, 1909 in Burchard, Nebraska. They had four children: 27Ada M., b. June 12, 1910; 27Leslie L., b. July 3, 1912; 27James R. 'Jim,' b. July 3, 1922; and 27Sam K. Jr., b. November 9, 1924. All were born in Burchard, Nebraska except Leslie, who was born in the nearby town of Axtel, Kansas. The two eldest children completed their education in Nebraska before the family moved to Oregon. Jim and Sam Jr. completed high school in Oregon at Perrydale High. Sam Jr. later continued his education at Portland State College, where he completed two years.

Sam and Ollie Cox lived in their home on Hurt Road until Mr. Cox was stricken by a stroke and passed away in August 1962. He had been caring for his wife, who had health problems for several years. Mrs. Cox sold the home and lived with her youngest son, Sam Jr., and his family. Sam's older sister, Ada, also lived with them for several years. Ollie Cox succumbed about two and one-half years after the death of her husband, passing away in January 1965.

Jim Cox enlisted in the U.S. Marines, was assigned to the 2nd Marine Division and participated in the invasions of Tarawa, Saipan, Okinawa and Tinian islands. Dwain Whitney, another "East County" marine, joined the 2nd Division for the invasion of Saipan, though in a different company. Dwain recounted seeing Jim Cox after Jim's company took out a Japanese machine-gun. Jim raised his shirt to show Dwain where a bullet from the gun had made about a 12" slash/burn wound across his chest. When Jim returned to the states, Dwain helped him get a job at the Bridal Veil Mill. Unfortunately, Jim survived the war only to be killed in a car crash on Bell Grade above Springdale in 1946.

Sam 28Cox Jr. was drafted into the Army in 1943. He was sent to Fort Lewis for training, and was bound for the Air Corps. However, a need arose for a cadre of specialists to help process former prisoners-of-war. The requirements were an ability to type; qualification in a variety of small arms; and the ability to drive a half-track. Sam said, "I had to take lessons to learn how to drive a half-track." The cadre was dispatched by troopship to the Philippines to process American troops who had been captured by the Japanese and held there. The former prisoners particularly desired cigarettes, so Sam, who didn't smoke, started collecting as many as possible. For the next assignment,the cadre flew to Japan, passing over the U.S. fleet, including the U.S.S. Missouri, anchored in Tokyo Bay. They landed at a base in Japan before the formal surrender had been signed. Sam, dragging a duffel bag full of cigarettes, approached the gates of the compound where American prisoners anxiously awaited their liberators. As he neared the gate, a C-54 flew over and dropped "thousands of cartons of cigarettes," according to Sam, totally deflating the exuberant welcome he expected. In fact, said Sam, "The prisoners preferred the brand dropped to what I brought, and I couldn't give mine away."

Sam and the others in the small cadre who had landed supervised the surrender of several thousand Japanese troops, The Japanese marched by, several abreast, and stacked their arms as they had been directed to do by the Emperor. Sam was surprised somewhat by their small stature. He said Americans literally towered above the Japanese. A couple of GIs three blocks away stood out from the multitude because of their size. After completing his military obligation, Sam returned to the states to resume his life as a civilian. He worked at the Bridal Veil Lumber and Box Company for a time before getting a job at the Troutdale Aluminum plant. He married Nettie Seyler May 27, 1950, daughter of a neighbor family who lived close to his parents on Hurt Road. At the time they married, she was working for Pacific Northwest Bell Telephone Company. The couple lived with Nettie's parents while they built a home on a 2.5-acre lot on Ogden Road, adjacent to the Mershon place.

When they moved into the home, Nettie said they had a hard time keeping warm. They expected to heat the dwelling with an oil stove, but when the East wind howled, they found the stove was inadequate. After that winter, they installed a furnace, but said Nettie; "We still had trouble keeping warm." Sam and Nettie Cox lived in this home for 12 years. They then bought a home on a 7+ acre place at the West End of Woodard Road where it intersects with the Columbia River Highway. Nettie remarked, "We found a place out of the East wind!" Sam and Nettie adopted four children: Jon L., b. October 20, 1954; Lisa L., b. June 15, 1955; Tori L., b. January 17, 1963; and Jarin K., b. January 4, 1970.

Cox Brothers

Sam (L) and Leslie Cox.

Nettie and Sam Cox

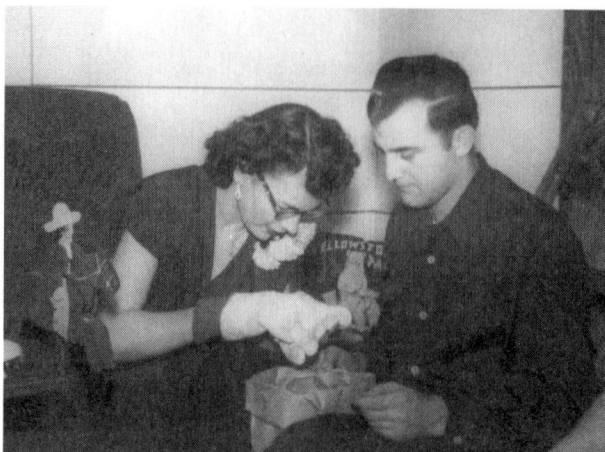

Nettie and Sam Cox celebrate New Year (1951) at the Mort residence, Springdale.

Cox Residence

Sam stands in front of their newly built home on Ogden Road.   Photos courtesy of Nettie Cox.

Cox Family

From L: Jarin Cox (held by) Lisa Shaer, Sam, Nettie, Ada (Sam's sister) behind Tori Cox.

Sam Cox served on the Troutdale City Council for 10 years, from 1972 to 1982. He became Mayor in 1982, and served in that capacity for another ten years. He continued to work at Reynolds Aluminum, retiring in 1983 after 36 years with the Company. The Cox's eldest son, Jon, died at age 15. Lisa lives in Gresham and operates a dance studio in the Rockwood area. Tori is married to Tim Muck, and lives in Troutdale. She and Tim have a son, Brandon. Jarin is not married and lives with his parents in Troutdale. Sam Cox Jr. died from injuries suffered in a fall September 16, 1998.

Sam Cox Jr.

Abraham L. Davies
Ellen (Lucas) Davies

The Davies family lived on a farm located just east of the Springdale School, and north of Bell Grade Road. The place was bordered on the east and north by the Eugene Berney place, and by the Canzler place on the west (north of Springdale School). Mr. Davies was married to Ellen 'Nell' Lucas, sister of Verne, Hazel and Eva Lucas. Before moving to Springdale, the Davies lived in the Trout Creek area (Aims), but Mrs. Davies felt too isolated there, which concern prompted the move. The Davies had three children: Gaylord, b. 1906; a second son who died in infancy; and Thelma, b. 1910. Gaylord was in the third grade when the family moved. It was about this time that the Columbia River Highway had been completed through the Gorge. Raleigh True, who owned the store across from where Bell Grade intersects the highway, got into a dispute with the State Highway Department. Because Bell Grade was too steep (grade greater than 6%), engineers directed that the highway be diverted south and east, which caused a sharp bend in the highway at that point. Raleigh decided to build an addition to the store, taking it to the edge of his property. The Highway Commission objected and shortly workers appeared to take down the addition. There was just one problem, Mr. True's addition was legal at the time, and he got on the phone to the Highway Commission to complain about the trespass. The official talked to the workers, and they left. Somehow the problem was worked out, perhaps because Mr. True sold the store soon thereafter.

Fred Salzman and Harley Bates built a garage in Springdale in 1915 (see *Pioneer History*, Volume II). Fred bought out Harley and brought his brother, Bill Salzman, into the business. They purchased additional land west of the garage (to Northway Road) from Bill Northway, and a meat market, small hotel and a camping area became part of a thriving business. An ad in the 1926 *Cohimore* reads: "Columbia High Service Station, Salzman Bros., Proprietors. Automotive Electrical Service, Complete Stock Auto Equipment, ...Auto Camp – 35 cents per night. Authorized Ford, Chevrolet and Buick Service." According to Gaylord, his mother used to prepare meals for Fred and Bill Salzman. Some of the proceeds helped Gaylord's father purchase his first car from the Salzmans. Showing uncanny and fortuitous timing, the Salzman Brothers sold the business in 1929.

The Davies family farmed, growing cabbage, cauliflower, lettuce and cucumbers. They also sold milk, chickens, eggs and firewood. Mr. Davies contracted with the school to provide firewood, for which the price varied, but Gaylord remembers the price being around $5 a cord. In addition to the farm work, Gaylord worked for his uncle, George Atkinson, at his store. The Atkinson grocery store was located west of Parson's garage and east of Lucas Road on the south side of the Columbia River Highway. Mr. Atkinson also had a warehouse built just east of and adjacent to the store and Parson's garage, which survives as an apartment building (1999). Gaylord kept the warehouse in order, stocked store shelves and generally made himself useful. On weekends he often drove his Uncle's milk truck, picking up 10-gallon milk and 5 gallon cream cans from local dairy farmers. George's milk route took him up Lucas Road, along Chamberlain Road and points west, while Earle Atkinson's route was to the east and south to Hurlburt, Loudon Road, Littlepage Road and other points.

Gaylord and Thelma both attended Springdale Grade School, from which Gaylord graduated in 1921, Thelma in 1925. Gaylord started high school at CHS, which at that time was located on the north side of the Columbia River Highway where the (abandoned) grade school now (1997) stands. He completed his freshman year in the high school at this location. The following summer (1922), his father noticed a large pall of black smoke to the east, and told Gaylord, "There's a fire - it looks like someone's house might be burning." It turned out to be CHS, which was gutted by the fire. Consequently, Gaylord spent his sophomore year going to school at the Grange Hall. Large curtains divided the main hall of this building into two "classrooms." Another "classroom" utilized the balcony room, where Gaylord said, "Miss Joy Crockett (later Mrs. Perry) taught us Spanish." The basement was used only sparingly as the Grange held its meetings there.

Gaylord's junior and senior years were spent in the new CHS, which was built during 1922-23, and opened for use in the fall of 1923. CHS now had a gymnasium, which gave its students a home floor for basketball for the first time. Gaylord remembers playing basketball with Ted Berney, Ray Wilson, Lloyd 'Red' Bramhall, Earl Chamberlain, Leonard Carter and Roy Pulliam. Gaylord graduated from CHS in 1925. His sister, Thelma, also attended CHS, graduating in 1929.

Gaylord Davies at CHS

'25 Cohimore photo (excerpt) courtesy of Ann (Reeves) Steers.

After graduating from high school, Gaylord attended the Oregon Normal School in Monmouth for two years. He taught school in Maupin, Grass Valley and The Dalles his initial years in the classroom. He then resumed his studies at Oregon State College, earning a Bachelor's Degree in 1931. Meanwhile, he continued to work for his Uncle George Atkinson and for ranchers in Eastern Oregon while he was attending college and even after he started teaching, having summers free to do so. In 1931, Gaylord married Margaret Dowley. He and Margaret had three children: Diane M. Plumridge, b. 1934, who now lives in Portland; and twins, John and Julie Ann. b. 1938. John now lives in Longview, Washington, and Julie A. Searcy lives in Corvallis, Oregon. Gaylord continued his educational pursuits, eventually earning a Master's Degree from the University of Washington. He concluded a 43-year teaching career with the final 25 years being spent at Longview, Washington, teaching business courses at Lower Columbia College. Gaylord Davies died May 1, 1998, age 91.

Thelma F. Davies also attended the Oregon Normal School in Monmouth, and taught school in Aloha, Oregon and other Washington County schools in the 30's and early 40's. In 1940, she married Carl Etling, son of Frederick Etling (see "Frederick Etling," *Pioneer History*). The Etlings lived on the Columbia River Highway almost directly across the road from the Portland Woman's' Forum Overlook. Carl Etling attended Corbett Schools, graduating from CHS in 1929. He served as a District Judge in Multnomah County for many years. He and Thelma had two children, Carl D. Jr., and Marilee K.

Irenus E. Davis
Flora (Jemes) Davis

Irenus 'Toye' Davis was born in Greenville, Tennessee July 17, 1891. His wife, Flora Jemes, was born in Conway, Missouri January 16, 1892. The family moved to Oregon from Nebraska in 1937. After their arrival they lived on MB McKay's farm, and worked for him. In 1939 they purchased the 10-acre Harding Place on Woodard Road. There were 10 children: Gladyce, b. February 4, 1916; Ralph, b. October 6, 1917; Wauneta, b. April 27, 1920; I.E. 'Shorty,' b. December 13, 1921; Rankin, b. April 30, 1923; Wanda, b. February 27, 1925; Wesley, b. November 10, 1926; Dean, b. October 26, 1928; Duane, b. August 7, 1930; and Flora, b. September 19, 1933. Toye farmed and sold his crops through the Troutdale Fruit and Vegetable Growers Association.

Gladyce, Ralph, Wauneta, Shorty, Rankin and Wanda completed their elementary and secondary education in Nebraska. Wesley, Dean, Duane and Flora all attended Corbett Grade School and all graduated from CHS, Wesley in 1944, Dean in 1947, Duane in 1948 and Flora in 1951. The younger Davis children worked for various farmers in the area, picking berries and working in the other crops, such as potatoes, cabbage, bulbs, corn and other grains. Duane worked for Howard Winters and Tood Larson during his high school years, which was typical of local employment for each of the Davis youngsters.

Ralph Davis enlisted in the U.S. Navy and served in that branch for twenty years. During World War II his ship operated out of Pearl Harbor in the Pacific Theater. Wuaneta married George Wand January 20, 1945. Rankin Davis was also in the U.S. Navy during the war. He served on the USS Carteret, a troopship. He was stationed at Kodiak Island, Alaska a considerable period of time and was discharged in Bremerton, Washington early in 1946. He married Sue Seyler September 13, 1952, and has four children, Penny, Cathy, Elaine and Ted. Wesley entered the U.S. Army shortly after graduating from high school. He was sent to the Philippine Islands about the time the war ended. He also was stationed in Seoul, Korea. November 24, 1956 Wesley married Donna Peterson, who grew up across Woodard Road from the Davis family. Wes and Donna had two children, Scott and Cheryl. Both Dean and Duane Davis were in

Wesley Davis

Wes, US Army 1945. Photo courtesy of Wes Davis.

Dean Davis

Dean, Student Body President CHS, '47. Photo courtesy of David Rees.

Flora Davis

Flora, Corbett Grade School. Photo courtesy of Joan (Ellis) Benner.

the service during the Korean War. Dean was in the Air Force stationed in Japan and Duane was in the Army stationed in Okinawa.

Duane went into a partnership with Tood Larson in 1949 as 'Larson and Davis.' The partners purchased the Canby-Aurora Truck Service in 1953 and added the Leighty Truck Line in Woodburn in the early 60's. The business operated under the latter name until the partnership was dissolved and the business sold in 1972. Flora married Wayne Chamberlain, son of Burton 'Si' Chamberlain, July 22, 1953. After graduating from high school, Flora worked for KASO plastics for a time, then worked for the Corbett School District. In 1982, she purchased M&M Video in Hood River. She and Wayne had three children, Chris, Kathy and Michael. Flora died of a heart attack July 30, 1990, at Wallowa Memorial Hospital in Enterprise.   *Wesley Davis*

Plowing with the Cletrac

Duane Davis plows a straight furrow on the Larson place.   Photo courtesy of Dorothy Larson.

Sherwood M. Davis
Anna I. (Shultz) Davis

Sherwood M. Davis had a 58-acre farm on Gordon Creek Road by Big Creek, which was originally part of the Hurlburt Place. It extended south toward the bluff above the Sandy River across from the Perkins' place. Sherwood married Anna I. Shultz and the couple had two children at the time they moved to the Hurlburt area in 1902. Eventually they had nine children, two of whom were born in Kansas, Delbert F., b. November 15, 1900, and Fernie I., b. November 12, 1901. Mary M., b. June 26, 1904, Ruth M., b. March 19, 1906, Albert M., b. July, 1908, John E., b. July 19, 1910, Estella L., b. October 12, 1913, James S., b. July 12, 1917 and Norah M., b. July 29, 1923, were born in Multnomah County. The family raised grain, hay and stock (see "The Family of Sherwood Melville Davis and Anna Isabelle (Shultz) Davis," *Pioneer History*).

Delbert F. 'Fay' Davis married Bertha Barr; Fernie married Walter H. Quier; Mary married Bill Udey. Ruth married Alex T. Nordin and the couple had five children, Everett, Gary, Galen, Sandra and Darrell. Albert married Frieda Heitzman and had two children, Frederick and Richard. John married Betty Meyers and the couple had two children, Jack and Sunny June. Estella married Murray Evans (see "Murray W. Evans").

James Davis married Ruth Bush of Oklahoma and the couple settled on the home (Davis) place. Later they purchased part of the original Hurlburt place, which lies to the north of the Davis place. James and Ruth had six children, Sherwood, Lloyd, Pamela, Daniel, Raymond and David. Raymond died in an automobile accident September 15, 1975. Presently, Sherwood lives on the home place. The youngest of Sherwood (senior's) children, Norah, married Johnnie Vasey. After World War II, Vasey served in the allied occupation force in Germany. Norah accompanied her husband on a transatlantic voyage via a U.S. Army troop transport. According to a letter Norah wrote to her sister, Mary Udey, the voyage took twelve days. After disembarking in Bremerhaven, the couple traveled to Germany where John reported to his new duty station. During his tour, Norah reported, "The Germans prefered to receive all tips in the form of candy bars, chocolate, cigarettes or other scarce articles. Most of the materials of value in Germany are sold on the black market." John and Norah had three children, Karen, Janis and Joel.

Sherwood Davis Family

Rear, L to R: Clara Lasley, Gladys Lasley, Weltha Lasley, Gladys Truesdell, Archie Truesdell, Ella Laughlin, Ruth Davis (held by) Amber Shultz, Nelly Truesdell, Leila Lasley, Isabel Davis, Sam Laughlin and Fred Lasley. Front, Forest Shultz, Sherwood Davis (holding) Albert Davis, Fernie Davis, Milly Truesdell, Fay Davis, Esther Laughlin, Leula Lasley, Esther Davis, Estelle Truesdell, Mary Davis, "Grandma" Shultz and Ray Lasley. Photo courtesy of Herbert Salzman.

Hurlburt Classmates c1921

L to R, Hazel Johnson, Estella Davis, Hazel Deverell and Mildred Ellis. Photo courtesy of Sandra Evans.

Hurlburt Schoolmates

From L, Mary (Davis) Udey, Doris (Emily) Bramhall, Selma Soderstrom and Frances (Evans) Henkle reminisce about the 'early days.' Photo courtesy of Pat (Bramhall) Paget.

Herbert Dooley
Hannah (Jett) Dooley

Herbert Dooley's parents, Thomas and Samantha Dooley, came to Oregon in 1935. They moved to Corbett in 1937 first living in the Chamberlain campground until a home was built for them on their son's place across the Columbia River Highway (where the RV park is now located). The Thomas Dooleys had ten children, many of whom picked berries for Elmer Larson after the family came to East County. Two sons, Herbert and Walter, purchased 47 acres across from the Bell Garage and divided the place between them.

Herbert Dooley, born August 26, 1910, was one of ten children, five boys (Luther, Gilbert, Walter, Herbert and Clifford) and five girls (May, Alma, Rose, Maude and Edna). Herbert married Hannah Jett of Gaston, Oregon, June 1, 1934. Hannah's father, William Jett, had worked on the construction of the Vista House, which may explain how the family became interested in moving to Corbett. During the construction, he lived on the Island across from Latourell, rowing a boat across the slough in order to get to work. When Herbert and Hannah moved to Corbett, they lived in one of the cabins located in the Chamberlain campground behind Bell's garage and service station. The couple had eight children: Violet, b. August 1, 1935; Rose, b. April 21, 1937; Sharon, b. April 18, 1940; Jim, b. February 26, 1942; Mary, b. August 18, 1944; Shirley, b. July 20, 1946; Linda, b. December 8, 1948; and Steve, b. October 25, 1954.

During World War II, Herbert worked at Swan Island shipyard. After World War II, Herbert and Hannah built a home on the property they had purchased across the highway from the Chamberlain place. Herbert continued in the boat-building trade, working for a company that manufactured barges and yachts. He also raised several varieties of berries that his children could pick. The children's playmates continued to be Harold Chamberlain's children since the new home was just across the street from the Chamberlain place.

Violet recalls visiting her Uncle Gilbert and Aunt Frances who rented a place on Northway Road in Springdale. She described an apple tree on the place that had huge apples growing upon it. She also recalled crawling under the fence at Weatherly Farms to gather pheasant eggs from some of the pens.

106

Chamberlain Campground

Thomas and Samantha Dooley living in the Chamberlain Campground.

Dooley Sons

From L., Luther, Gilbert 'Doc,' Clifford, Herbert and Walter Dooley

Picking Raspberries

Hannah and Frances Dooley picking raspberries for John Larson.
Photos courtesy of Violet Dooley.

Dooley Place

From L, Rear: Sharon, Rose and Violet (holding Shirley). Front: Mary and Jim Dooley. Background left, Settlemier's store; Bell garage and house build by Harley Bates behind tractor.

Violet Dooley

Violet Dooley stands in front of the Bell Garage.

Photos courtesy of Violet Dooley.

All of the Dooley youngsters attended Corbett schools, with Rose graduating from CHS in 1955, Sharon in 1958, Jim in 1960, Mary in 1962, Shirley in 1964, Linda in 1967 and Steve in 1973.

Violet married Renault McLaughlin and had four children, 2 boys and 2 girls. She now lives in Gresham. Rose married Wayne Burke and had 3 boys. She is now married to Jim Tracy and lives in Silverton. Sharon married Bill Rickert and had 3 boys. Sharon passed away April 20, 1985. Jim married and had four children, 2 boys and 2 girls. He now lives in Enterprise. Mary did not marry and lives in Gresham. Shirley married Terry Cornielson and had 2 boys. She is now married to Larry Carpenter and lives in Jerome, Idaho. Linda married Jim Farless, had 2 daughters and lives in Lostine, Oregon. Steve is not married and lives in Gresham.

108

Walter C. Dooley
Ruth (Grinstead) Dooley

The Dooley family came to East Multnomah County from Iowa in 1941. They rented the Bourgeois place on Northway Road in Springdale for a time before purchasing 47 acres at Corbett across from the Chamberlain place and adjacent to the Leader place. Walter Dooley and his brother, Herb Dooley, purchased the property together and each took 23.5 acres. Walter Dooley was born in Iowa in 1905, Ruth Grinstead in 1909. The couple married in Bloomfield, Iowa in 1929. The Dooleys had seven children, Donald, b. 1930; Paul, b. 1932; Delores, b. 1933; Ivan, b. 1935; Betty, b. 1938; John, b. 1945; and Robert, b. 1950. The five oldest were born in Iowa while John and Robert were born after the family came to Oregon.

Walter Dooley worked for John Larson after his arrival. He then obtained work at the wool pullery and aluminum plant in Troutdale before going to work at the Vancouver shipyards. In 1945, the family moved to the property in Corbett, where Dooley built a home. Upon the closure of the shipyard, he went to work for McGill Nursery in Gresham, and worked there until he retired. Walter Dooley passed away in 1968.

The youngsters attended school in Springdale until the family moved to Corbett in 1945 at which time they enrolled in Corbett schools. Donald left school before graduating. He was drafted into the Army and served in Germany. He married Janet Deutsch and they had two children. He worked on the docks at Swan Island until his death in 1979. Paul also did not complete high school, going to work for McGill Nursery in Gresham. Paul enlisted and completed two years in the Army, including service in a mortar unit in Korea. He was wounded in action July 12, 1953 for which he was awarded the Purple Heart. After his discharge he met and married Janes Potter. The couple had two children, Mike and Kathy. Paul went to work at Bridal Veil and worked there until the mill closed in 1960. He purchased part of the former Salzman property in Springdale on the corner of Northway Road where it intersects with the Columbia River Highway. After the mill closed, he worked for Overhead Door in Portland for a short period of time. He then obtained a job at a mill in Aberdeen, Washington, and moved there in 1962. After 20 years spent at

Gilbert Dooley Family

From L, Doc, Frances, Dorothy, David and Tom Dooley (in front) beside the Bell Garage. Photo courtesy of Violet Dooley.

the Aberdeen mill, he returned to the Portland area to work for McGill Nursery. Paul now lives in NE Portland.

Delores left Corbett before graduating and returned to Iowa. She married David Boley and had two children, Vickie and Daniel. Ivan enlisted in the Army at age seventeen. He served three years including 18 months in Korea, where he served in the signal corps. Ivan married Norma Fox and they had three children, Ivan, Becky and Mary. Ivan worked at Boeing's Portland plant for many years. He is now married to Jane Sweeney and lives in Rhododendron. Betty also left CHS before graduating. She married Robert Cunningham and had five children, Susan, Robert, Joseph, Jerry and Ricky. Betty passed away in 1978.

John continued to live in Corbett for several years in a trailer located on the family place. He married Linda Payne and they have five children, Nicholas, Natalie, Duane, Charlotte and Christopher. John started working for Sunbeam-Oster in small appliance repair and continued with the same firm when the association with Sunbeam was discontinued. The family moved to Gresham where his youngsters completed school. He is now married to Sharon and continues to live in Gresham. Robert completed school at Gresham High School. Ruth Dooley passed away January 3, 1983. Robert now lives in the family home at Corbett. Since completing high school, he has worked for the McGill Nursery.

110

Francis M. Driver
Jean E. (McKillop) Driver

Francis 'Frank' and Jean Driver purchased their place in Springdale from Vernon and Gertrude Jameson in 1947. According to Jean, "We fell in love with the creek, wooded acre and gentle hillside." Frank's mother, Edna Driver, was acquainted with the Jamesons. Frank was born in Portland, Oregon January 21, 1921. He attended school in Milwaukie, graduating from Milwaukie High School in 1939. In August 1939 he enlisted in the U.S. Navy. After completing basic training at San Diego, the Navy assigned him to the battleship *USS Idaho*, on which he served 19 months. During the summer of 1941 a transfer took him to the *USS Otis*, a subtender bound for Cavite Naval Base, Manila Bay, Philippine Islands.

When Japanese carrier planes attacked Pearl Harbor December 7, 1941, US military installations in the Philippines also came under attack. Because of the virtual destruction of the capital ships of the US fleet and because strategic outposts in the Pacific were also under attack, US forces in the Philippine Islands found themselves cut off from supplies and reinforcements, destined for a bitter battle for survival. The Navy kept one large subtender, the *USS Canopus*, at Cavite to tend the submarines that provided the only tangible link to US forces elsewhere. With little storage capacity, the incoming subs brought only critically needed items to the beleaguered forces. The outbound subs did not evacuate personnel; the cargo did include such items as the Philippine Government's gold cache.

As the Japanese invaders advanced from Lingayen Gulf in the North and from Lamon Bay on the Philippine Sea southeast of Manila, the defenders fell back to Bataan and the Island of Corregidor. Fort Drum, a concrete fort nearly impervious to attack, mounted 14-inch guns. Unfortunately, the Japanese attackers advanced from the north and the east rather than from the sea, and the huge guns could not be brought to bear. When Bataan fell, only Corregidor held out. Frank Driver and other navy personnel from Cavite dug in with the remnants of other American units on the Island. Subjected to almost constant bombardment, lacking ammunition and supplies and with Japanese tanks advancing on the Island, the Americans capitulated May 6, 1942. The defenders became prisoners of war (POW's).

The Japanese took the prisoners captured on Corregidor to a prison in Manila from which they were taken by train (and foot) to Camp Cubantuan, about 90 miles north of Manila. Asked about conditions at the POW camp, Frank said the prisoners actually organized the camp and the Japanese dealt only with the leader (or spokesman) for the group. He said, "The prisoners had little contact with the Japanese, but that changed later." After about six months the prisoners embarked upon a prison ship bound for Manchuria. The ship stopped in Formosa (Taiwan) to refuel before proceeding to Pusan, Korea. Traversing Korea by train, the prisoners crossed the Yalu River into China enroute to Manchuria. The Japanese had occupied Manchuria in 1932, building a number of factories to take advantage of the natural resources found there.

Frank Driver was assigned to work in a machine tool factory. Only enlisted personnel worked in the factories – officers remained at the prison. The living quarters for prisoners were quite primitive, heated only by a tiny stove. According to Frank, supplies seemed to be issued "only by direct order of the Emperor," so clothing, bedding, food and other supplies were always inadequate. He 'enjoyed' corn meal gruel served "boiling hot in a metal container" for lunch every day he spent in captivity. After a typical American protest (the gruel was left uneaten), spoons were issued rather than chopsticks, which made it possible to get the 'meal' down in the 30-minute time period allotted.

One threat the prisoners heard the Japanese reiterate as Japan faced an invasion of the home Islands was this, "All prisoners-of-war will be executed when American forces land." Prisoners took the threat seriously and believed that the bombing of Hiroshima and Nagasaki, which caused the Japanese to surrender before an invasion occurred, likely saved their lives. When the war ended, five Office of Strategic Services (OSS) personnel landed by parachute at the camp. Russian troops liberated the prisoners and told them, "You're free." Asked about his physical condition at that time, Frank said, "I thought it was fairly good, but I had lost a lot of weight." This assessment was certainly too optimistic as health problems related to the depravations experienced in captivity showed up later.

Taken by train to Port Arthur, the former POW's were placed aboard a ship bound for Guam. Unfortunately, the former prisoners' ordeal was not over, as a typhoon overtook the ship and made life miserable for them for three storm-tossed days. Next the ship hit a mine, causing casualties among the crew, but the craft finally reached Saipan. When Frank arrived in Guam a few days later, his cousin, Les Woodcock, found him and they had a happy reunion. After two weeks in the hospital there, Frank returned to the States. Granted "leave" by the Navy, he spent the next three months in the hospital at Camp Adair, where he recuperated from his ordeal and received his pay for the three years, three months and ten days he spent as a prisoner of the Japanese. Three days after his discharge, Frank got a job at the Kaiser Oregon shipyard as an operating engineer, anxious to resume a 'normal' life.

Jean McKillop was born in Seattle, Washington November 15, 1925. She completed her elementary and secondary school years in Seattle. Jean came to Oregon in 1943 to enroll in the School of Nursing at Good Samaritan Hospital in Portland, from which she graduated as a registered nurse in 1946. Frank Driver and Jean McKellop were married May 10, 1947, in Seattle, Washington. The Drivers made payments of $100.00 per month to pay the Jamesons for the Springdale property. Jean's starting pay, as a nurse at Good Samaritan was $130.00 per month. By this time Frank was also working at 'Good Sam' as an operating engineer. With $800.00 paid to Frank for his former interest in a logging business, he and Jean built a house based upon the *Good Housekeeping* 'Starter Home' plan. They did much of the work themselves, including the wiring, the plumbing and the finish work. Completed just in time for the severe winters of 48-49 and 49-50, the Drivers found the electric heaters inadequate for a severe winter. Frank joked that the first two winters reminded him of winters in Manchuria.

Frank and Jean Driver had three children, Frank S. 'Stuart,' b. June 5, 1948, Mary C. 'Catherine,' b. June 5, 1950 and Laurie J., b. August 3, 1955. All were born at 'Good Sam' in Portland. The Drivers added to their 'starter' home when more room was needed as the children were born. While raising her children, Jean Driver worked part-time as a nurse at Good Samaritan Hospital. When the children were grown, she took a full-time position with the NW Urological Clinic, working there for nearly 14 years until she retired in 1987. However, she continued to work at the clinic on an 'on-call' basis until 1994. After completing 13 years at 'Good Sam,' Frank took a position with the American Sterilizer Company, covering the State of Alaska as a sales and service representative. He retired from the Company in 1993 after 26 years service.

The Frank and Jean Driver Family

From L, Roger Anderson, Sally Driver (in front), Catherine Driver, Stuart Driver (kneeling), Budd Ledbetter, Laurie (Driver) Ledbetter, Mary Stovall (Jean Driver's sister), Jean Driver and Frank Driver.   Photo courtesy of Jean Driver.

Frank and Jean Driver have both been active in community affairs. Frank became a volunteer fireman when the Corbett Fire District was formed, and served as Chairman of the Board for ten years. He also took an active part in the Veterans of Foreign Wars, Corbett Post. The children attended Springdale Grade School until the consolidation with Corbett. Jean took an active role in school affairs while her children were in school. Stuart attended Springdale Grade School, then transferred to Corbett his 7th year. He completed his grade school years at Corbett, then attended Jesuit High School, from which he graduated in 1966. Catherine also started at Springdale, transferred to Corbett her 5th year and completed grade and high school at Corbett, graduating in 1968. Laurie also completed grade school at Corbett. She attended Barlow and Tigard High Schools, but gained her diploma from Portland Community College in 1973.

114

Stuart is currently living with his wife on a 45-foot boat that he built himself. According to Jean, he is "living a dream," and at the present time (1999) is anchored in Mexico. Stuart has a daughter, Stacy Jean, from a prior marriage. He and his wife, Sally, live on the boat. Catherine and her husband, Roger Anderson, own Vista Balloon, flying out of Newberg, Oregon. They also reside in Newberg, and have no children. Laurie lives with her husband, Budd Ledbetter, in Maui, Hawaii. She has three children, Travis, Tara and Shane.

In 1950, Frank and Jean gave Frank's mother an acre of land for Christmas. Frank started to build her a home at that time, which was completed in 1951. When she passed away November 28, 1961, this home was sold. The Drivers retained approximately 3.5 acres after the sale. In 1983, the Drivers received some daffodil stock from Murray Evans, and have since been involved in the business of growing daffodils. They are active in the Oregon and American Daffodil Societies, and now grow standard, intermediate and miniature varieties. They conduct a mail order business selling daffodil bulbs.

Murray Evans' daffodil field.   Photo courtesy of Stella Evans.

James D. Dunken
Nellie (Wilde) Dunken

James D. 'Delbert' Dunken brought his family to Oregon in 1937. The depression and the tribulations experienced on a Nebraska farm during the "dust bowl" caused the Dunkens to consider moving west. Delbert was born February 2, 1905; Nellie March 22, 1907. The couple married March 2, 1926, setting up housekeeping in Nelson, Nebraska. The dust storms of the 30's devastated the countryside, destroying crops, covering pasture and impoverishing the population. Nellie remarked, "We lived on eggs until the chickens stopped laying, then we lived on chicken." Swirling dust created dirty drifts along fences and behind obstacles. It came through cracks around doors and windows into the house to such an extent that it created a reddish halo around a lighted bulb in a room. People gathered under a dampened sheet draped over furniture in order to get a breath of filtered air. An opportunity came that the Dunkens pondered, and because of the circumstances, decided to take.

Delbert's sister and her husband, Walter Gibson, newlyweds, determined that they would head west in their 1926 Model-T sedan. They offered Delbert and his family a ride. The Dunkens sold all of their possessions except for a few personal items and Nellie's sewing machine at auction, netting $8.00. With the sewing machine strapped to the back of the automobile and a mattress and other belongings tied on the top, the journey began. Walter Gibson drove while his wife, the four Dunkens and a bulldog, Midge, rode as passengers.

Delbert and Nellie had two boys, Robert 'Bob,' b. May 31, 1928 and William 'Bill,' b. November 21, 1930. When the two families left Nebraska in August 1937, they had hopes of earning some money en route by picking apples. Unfortunately, it was not harvest time when they reached Idaho, so they pressed on to Oregon with the hope of finding Nellie's sister, Mildred Evans, in Portland. In Eastern Oregon a tire on the Model-T gave out, and the families sat on the roadside contemplating their plight: no money, a worn-out tire, no food and little hope. Fortunately a 'samaritan' came along driving a Model-T who happened to be carrying an extra tire. With the tire supplied by the stranger and with renewed hope because of the kindness and generosity of the man, they resumed their journey to Portland. After seven days on the road the family reached their destination. However, Mildred Evans no longer lived where the Dunkens expected to find her. Delbert made inquiries and discovered that the Evans family had moved to a place called Corbett.

Upon reaching Corbett, Delbert sought help at Rickert's garage and café, but no one knew "E. Boyd Evans." Finally, someone figured out that "E. Boyd" was Everett, and directed the Dunkens to Murray Evans' place on Evans Road. Stella happened to be walking along Evans Road when the Dunkens pulled up, and she stood on the running board to direct them to Everett's place on Gordon Creek Road. Abel Blanc had a small shack at his dairy, which provided a place for the family to stay. For a place to live and for all the milk the family could use, Delbert was to clean the barn morning and night. Both Delbert and Nellie marveled at the fruit and vegetables available for the asking. Nellie made carrot salad and fried carrots with milk gravy for a meal. After Delbert found a job, he moved his family to the Perkins place located at the junction of Rickert Road with Gordon Creek Road. The rental cost $5.00 per month.

Murray Evans worked at the Bridal Veil mill. Nearly every day Delbert rode to Bridal Veil with Murray to ask if help was needed. When the answer was "No", he walked home. Toot Evans hired him to cut firewood for $1.00 per day plus $1.00 per cord, cut and stacked. Delbert continued to be turned down at the mill until Johnny Hobnick said one morning, "You really want to work, don't you," and gave him a job. Delbert worked at Bridal Veil from August 1938 until the mill closed in 1960. With employment, Delbert was able to purchase three acres from Everett Evans on Pounder Grade, and built a house on the parcel. Later, he purchased two acres from Abel Blanc, which is the parcel where a future granddaughter, Susan Dunken, now lives with her husband, Paul Mershon.

Bob and Bill started school at Corbett Grade School in 1937, Bob in grade five and Bill in grade two. They rode the same bus that brought youngsters from Aims to Corbett via Gordon Creek Road. Bob worked for several farmers, including Vic, Jim and Bob Ellis, Ward Evans and Toot Evans. One job he had was cleaning Ward Evans' cannery. During his high school years, he worked for Toot most of the time. He also worked at the Corbett store for Mr. Benoist. Bob graduated from CHS in 1945, serving as Student Body President in 1944-45. Because he was younger than most of his classmates, he did not enter the service during the war. With the departure of many of his classmates, only seven seniors (compared to the 24 enrollees of 1941) attended the graduation ceremony at

Bob Dunken

Bob Dunken, CHS Student Body President, 1944-45. '45 Cohimore photo courtesy of David Rees.

year-end. During the war years, activities and sports were curtailed, which meant students did not have many school related functions to attend. There were no dances as MB McKay, school board member, was adamantly opposed to them. Cars sat in the drive because of gasoline rationing, though some enterprising high school students found an alternate supply. Bob says, "I best not talk about that!"

Bob Dunken started working at the Bridal Veil mill in 1946. He earned $1.00 per hour and asked to be placed on the swing shift to gain an extra 4 cents per hour ($1.04). Bob married Bette Jean Muck June 28, 1947. In 1952, Bob Kerslake approached him to see if he would like to go to work for the County Road Department. After some delay and thought, he decided to take the job. Bob worked for the County thirteen years. During the time he worked for the County, Bob decided his family needed extra income, so he took a part-time welding job at Carver where a mill was under construction. This second job led to an unexpected opportunity for Bob later.

After the mill was completed, the owner asked Bob if he would consider taking the job of millwright. Bob's first response was negative. He told Bette that he would prefer continuing with the County if he could work on heavy equipment, but Pat Kerslake offered no encouragement along those lines. Bob said he told Betty, "I don't want to wake up at age 60 thinking about why I hadn't tried something different," so he decided to take the sawmill job. Suddenly he was earning $300.00 *per week* compared to $400.00 *per month* for the County. Bob worked at the Carver mill for about seven years until it closed. He had many job offers and decided to take a job with the forest products division of Portland Machinery because of his positive experiences working with that Company during his tenure at Carver.

Bob started as Shop Superintendent at $1000 per month plus a car. One day the President approached Bob and asked, "Where's John?" Bob responded, "I don't know." As it turned out, the President was looking for John, the Manager, to give him his walking papers. He then appointed Bob Dunken as General Manager. Seven years later, Bob and his partner, Kirk Cooper, bought that branch of the company and moved it to 140th and NE Sandy Boulevard. They changed the name to the Portland Saw-

Reconditioned Mill Machinery

Mill machinery purchased from Publisher's Mill, reconditioned, and sold to a mill in British Columbia.　　Photo courtesy of Bob Dunken.

mill Machinery Company, with Bob Dunken President and General Manager. In addition to manufacturing sawmill machinery, the company purchased used machinery, reconditioned it and sold it all over the world. Oftentimes the company bought an entire mill that had closed, removed and rebuilt its machinery for resale and demolished its buildings.

One time, Bob related, the company bought a large mill in Potlatch, Idaho for a million dollars less two hundred thousand dollars for clean up costs, and the deal was sealed with a handshake. Bob had worked with this Company previously and the principals felt no written contract was needed. Removing machinery, salvaging building materials, leveling and cleaning the site took about a year and one-half. After Gene O'Neil retired, he and Frieda often drove the Company's truck on long hauls. One time Bob called from California and asked them to go to the shop, pick up the truck and drive to a farm in Sebastopol, California, as he had purchased a tractor there. Meanwhile Bob flew home. He worried about the purchase, and flew back to San Francisco to make certain the deal went through – he wanted that antique tractor! He arrived at the

Holt Caterpillar Restored

The Holt Tractor Bob Dunken bought in California and wanted 'out of town' before the previous owner changed his mind. Hauled to Portland by Gene and Frieda O'Neil.
Photo courtesy of Bob Dunken.

farm about the same time as Gene and Frieda, and told them to "get the tractor out of town." Gene and Frieda hauled it to Portland, where Bob and his crew restored it.

Gene and Frieda picked up and delivered machinery quite often for Bob in the period '79-'81. They made trips to such diverse places as DuBois, Wyoming, stopping at Yellowstone on the return trip; to Crescent City, California, where they felt right at home as a fire alarm rang during the night; to Potlatch, Idaho, where they had an opportunity to visit Walt Knieriem; and to Medford, Oregon, a trip they made several times. Bob's brother-in-law, Bill Muck, also drove the Company truck to pick up or deliver machinery. On one haul Bill delivered machinery to Mississippi and picked up a load in Louisiana for the return trip.

Bob and Bette developed a personal hobby similar to his sawmill machinery business. Rather then mill machinery, they restored historic automobiles. Bette delighted in finding clothes appropriate to the vintage of the automobile to be restored. Both participated in numerous parades and other appearances that permitted them to demonstrate the automobiles and 'fashions' of an earlier era. They joined the Horseless Carriage Club and Bob served as President of the National Club in 1974.

Somewhere in Utah

Gene and Frieda O'Neil run into a slight problem in Utah while delivering machinery for Portland Sawmill Machine. Photo courtesy of Frieda O'Neil.

He and Bette restored seven antique (pre-1916 era) automobiles and displayed them often.

Bob and Bette had three children, Christine, b. January 5, 1948; Jerry, b. March 2, 1949; and Susan, b. October 19, 1953. All three attended Corbett schools. Christine graduated from CHS in 1966. She edited the *Cohimore* and delivered the valedictory. Jerry graduated in 1967 and Susan followed in 1971. Bette Jean Dunken passed away two days before Christmas in 1986. Her passing was a great loss to Bob and his family, but they express gratitude for having been blessed with such a wonderful wife and mother for 39 years.

In 1990, it appeared to the partners that the sawmill machinery business was in a decline so they decided to sell. The machinery and inventory was sold at auction, which ended Bob's long association with sawmills and the sawmill machinery business. Shortly thereafter he and the same partner built a 360-unit mini-storage facility on NE Simpson, which Bob manages. They are now in the midst of an expansion, which will give them more than 500 units. Bob has been successful in his business ventures, and the storage facility is "full with customers on a waiting list." The business is located close to the airport between Airport Way and the Owens-Illinois glass plant.

Bill Dunken's school experiences were quite similar to Bob's though sports and other school activities were nearly back to "normal" after the war years. Bill's working career began in the berry fields during his grade school years. He also worked for Ward Evans, who grew corn, potatoes and bulbs. Later he worked for Dick Ellis, who grew vegetables and bulbs. One summer Bill worked under Frank Fagan at the Corbett Water District. Bill graduated from CHS in 1948. After graduation, he went to work at the Bridal Veil mill and had completed two years when the Korean War caused him to enlist in the US Navy for a four-year hitch. Bill's principal duty station was Japan, where he worked in the aviation logistics office. After completing his tour with the Navy, Bill resumed his job at Bridal Veil. He worked there until 1958, when he had an opportunity to go to work for Tektronix in Beaverton.

Bill married Barbara Bowling and the couple had one son, James, b. January 12, 1957. Bill and Barbara lived on Hurlburt Road for many years until Bill went to work for Tektronix. They then moved to Forest Grove. He spent thirteen years with that firm. When he reached age forty, Bill said he got "itchy feet," and wanted to try something on his own. In 1971, he "sold himself" to Honda Motor Company in order to obtain the franchise for Honda motorcycles when that Company first entered the US market. He owned the franchise for five years, which became quite lucrative as Honda's reputation for quality grew among American consumers. Bill says, "I got in at the right time." His brother, Bob says, "He also provided excellent service. One time when I was at his home, a customer called from the coast with a breakdown. Bill apologized and left immediately to take care of the problem. He worked hard."

After selling the motorcycle business Bill opened a men's wear store in Newberg. He then sold automobiles for six years. In 1980 he purchased a mobile home park in Redmond, which he sold in 1992. Meanwhile he opened a Papa Aldo's franchise outlet in Salem, Oregon in 1986. He kept this store until he retired in 1990. Bill is now married to Karen, has "totally" retired and lives in Bend, Oregon.

Robert J. Ellis
Evelyn (Hewitt) Ellis

Robert J. 'Bob' Ellis was born May 18, 1911 at Corbett. His parents, William J. and Dorothy (Heise) Ellis, had purchased a farm off Evans Road from Victor Ellis, William's brother (the Ellis family had earlier homesteaded a place on Brower [later Larch Mountain] Road). Bob attended Hurlburt Grade School and CHS, from which he graduated in 1930. He then attended Oregon State College for a year, after which he obtained a job with the US Forest Service, stationed at Cascade Locks. While on the job, he was driving across a bridge in an outlying area when the planks separated, causing the automobile to drop and throwing him forward. The rearview mirror caught his eye, causing a severe injury and costing him his right eye.

Subsequently, Bob Ellis returned to the farm to help his father, whose health was deteriorating. Bob married Evelyn Hewitt of Troutdale. Evelyn's parents, Mr. and Mrs. Raymond Hewitt, moved to Troutdale in 1925 when Mr. Hewitt became Principal at Troutdale Grade School. Later he became postmaster at the Troutdale Post Office from which position he retired in 1959. Bob and Evelyn had three children, Robert, b. January 15, 1943, Larry, b. October 15, 1944 and Victor, b. December 27, 1949.

Bob and his brother, Dick, worked the farm as partners until the mid-40's, when Bob and Evelyn purchased the Charles Bates farm in Springdale, off Hurlburt Road. Bob and Dick continued to work together in growing daffodils, but each grew other crops separately. Bob took a leadership role in agriculture, working in soil conservation and serving on the board of the East Multnomah Agricultural District. In addition to the principal crop, daffodils, he raised berries and cattle. Evelyn Ellis worked at the First National Bank as a teller for many years. When farming became unprofitable in the late 60's, Bob obtained a job with the Multnomah County Parks Department (starting in 1970). In 1976 he retired and he and Evelyn moved to Stayton, Oregon. Bob passed away in March 1986. Evelyn continued to live in Stayton until her death August 28, 1988.

Of their children, Robert graduated from Oregon State University, earning both a bachelor's and master's degree in ichthyology. Formerly

123

Ellis Brothers

Bob (L) and Dick Ellis display a bobcat caught in a trap. Photo courtesy of Joan (Ellis) Benner.

Mildred Ellis

Mildred Ellis, CHS graduate 1932. Photo courtesy of Donna Monoske.

married to Janet Larson, with whom he had two children, Kristin and Robin. Robert is now married to Nancy. He and Nancy have one birth child, Shannon. Robert completed a Ph.D. program at Penn State University, is a self-employed ichthyologist and now lives in Estacada.

Larry Ellis graduated from Oregon State University after which he joined the Navy. He served in the submarine service for about two and one-half years. After his discharge he obtained a job with Wagner Mining Equipment. He is now married to Shelly Wells, has one son, Robert 'Bobby,' and lives in Portland. Victor graduated from the University of Oregon, obtained a commission in the Air Force after completing the ROTC program there and served as a Navigator on transport aircraft for many years. He now works as a self-employed property appraiser.

Bob and Dick's sister, Mildred Ellis, graduated from CHS in 1932. She married Ted Wright, owner of Gresham Transfer. She and Ted had one child, Barbara, and lived in Gresham. After Ted sold Gresham Transfer, the couple moved to various locations in Eastern Oregon. They lived in Redmond, John Day, The Dalles and Rufus, which is where they were living when Ted passed away. Mildred then returned to Redmond to live. She died in June of 1999.   *Ruth (Ellis) Smith*

Victor E. Ellis
Myrtle M. (Evans) Ellis

Victor 'Vic' Ellis came west with his family from Pennsylvania in 1883 when he was seven years of age. He was born April 24, 1876 in Titusville, Pennsylvania. He worked in the woods during his early years and went to work in the shipyards in World War I. He married Myrtle Evans, daughter of another pioneer family, Tom and Hannah Evans, July 2, 1903. They had two sons, Kenneth, b. October 6, 1908 and Clifford, b. August 8, 1916. Vic farmed 20-acres that he had obtained from Myrtle's parents. He grew potatoes and daffodils, among other crops (see "Victor Emmanuel Ellis, *Pioneer History*). When Charlie Bramhall was killed accidentally while fighting fire, Vic Ellis replaced him as custodian at CHS. He worked at the high school until he retired in 1945 after fifteen years service. The 1945 *Cohimore* is dedicated to Mr. Ellis in these words: "…We will miss him but there will always be a remembrance of him, who has given so much of his energy to make us comfortable and happy," Vic Ellis died December 28, 1956. Myrtle Ellis passed away December 21, 1976, age 94.

Kenneth Ellis married Frances E. Bradley (born March 16, 1909 in Hillsboro, North Dakota) June 28, 1930. They had a daughter, Joan, b. April 10, 1933. The family lived on Evans Road next to Clifford Ellis, in the home once owned by Tom Evans, and purchased from the Evans family. Kenneth was once a plasterer, but later farmed, growing bulbs, and worked as a machinist. He also drove school bus for the Corbett School District. Frances Ellis passed away May 12, 1959. Kenneth married the widow, Gayle (Amidon) Goddard, of a former Corbett Grade School principal, Paul Goddard, after the death of Frances. Gayle died April 16, 1988. Kenneth Ellis passed away June 9, 1990.

Joan Ellis attended Corbett Grade School and CHS. She graduated from the latter in 1951. She married Don Carnathan had a son, Dana Mark. She later married Edward Benner and they had a birth son, Scott. Edward Benner was born October 18, 1932, in Pittsburgh, Kansas. Both Dana and Scott attended school in Corbett, Dana Benner graduating from CHS in 1973 and Scott in 1980. Joan went to work for Reynolds Metals in Troutdale in 1956 and was promoted to buyer in 1972. She has been active in the Purchasing Management Association of Oregon, serving as

Ellis, Victor

Victor Ellis, custodian, CHS. '45 Cohimore Photo courtesy of David Rees

Frances and Kenneth Ellis

Frances and Kenneth Ellis on a winter trip in the Cascades. Photo courtesy of Joan (Ellis) Benner.

Joan Ellis

Joan Ellis, CHS '51 and Editor 'extraordinaire.'

its first female President in 1983. She served on the Board of Directors for the National Purchasing Managers Association, a 28,000-member organization. She continues in the position of Purchasing Manager at Reynolds Metals and lives with her husband, Ed, on the home place on Evans Road.

Clifford Ellis married Helen Kandell, born March 6, 1918 in Portland, Oregon. After graduating from CHS in 1934, he apprenticed in the plastering trade and continued in that vocation throughout his working life. He also grew daffodil bulbs as a side line business. He and Helen had one daughter, Arlene, b. September 13, 1939. She attended Corbett schools, graduating from CHS in 1957. She attended Oregon State College where she

Vic and Myrtle Ellis Family

Joan, Frances, Kenneth, Victor, Myrtle, Clifford, Helen and Arlene Ellis celebrate Vic and Myrtle's 50th wedding anniversary.

Photo courtesy of Joan (Ellis) Benner

Ellis Home

The Vic and Myrtle Ellis home on Evans Road.

majored in education. She married Pat Allen and had two children, Barbara and Patrick. She is now married to John L. Williams. She taught in elementary schools, and is currently teaching second grade in Yerington Elementary School, Yerington, Nevada. She expects to retire from the teaching profession in a couple of years. She and her husband raise llamas and have a large alfalfa ranch.

127

William R. Ellis
Ruth (Butler) Ellis

William Richard 'Dick' Ellis, son of son of William J. and Dorothy (Heise) Ellis, was born April 1, 1913 on the farm acquired from Vic Ellis (a brother to William J.) off Evans Road. His parents had been farming the family homestead on Brower (later Larch Mountain) Road, but had moved from there before their two sons were born. Dick grew up on the farm, working for his father. He attended Hurlburt Grade School and CHS, from which he graduated in 1931. He then attended the Oregon Technical Institute in Klamath Falls for a couple of years before returning home to help his father on the farm. Dick's brother, Bob, returned to help on the farm also, due to their father's poor health. The brothers farmed as partners from the mid-30's until about 1945.

Dick Ellis married Ruth Butler of Bridal Veil May 21, 1938. Ruth, b. May 20, 1919, had graduated from CHS the previous spring. The couple lived with Dick's parents for about seven years before building a little home next door to Dick's parents. The Ellis brothers raised cucumbers (sold to Libby McNeil and Libby), cabbage (sold to Pacific Fruit), carrots (sold to Pete Binn), strawberries and raspberries (sold to Gresham Berry Growers) and daffodils. The blooms of the latter crop were sold to Chase Gardens and the bulbs were sold to Fred C. Gloeckmer in New York. Mr. Gloeckmer became a regular account, buying daffodil bulbs from the Ellis brothers for many years.

Asked for the names of youngsters who had worked for them, Ruth quickly named many: the Lofstedts (Sophia, Gussie and Frieda), the Arrington children (Adele, Janet and Audrey), Wayne Chamberlain, the May youngsters (Joretta, Zorada, Donford and Wymard), Richard Childers, Colleen Innes, the Dhone kids (Rosemarie, Joan, Claude, Jack, Jim, Rod and Bob) and several of the Howells, including Mitzie. Dick and Ruth farmed until 1970. From about 1945 to 1970, the Ellis brothers worked together in the bulb business, but farmed separately with regard to other crops. Bob had purchased the former Charles Bates place off Hurlburt Road, which he farmed. In 1970, Dick had an opportunity to work for the Multnomah County Parks Department. Assigned to the park at Blue Lake, he worked there until his death December 8, 1974.

128

Dick and Ruth Ellis had two children, James R., b. April 1, 1943 and Marjorie R., b. June 20, 1952. Both attended Corbett Grade School and CHS, James graduating from the latter in 1961, Marjorie in 1970. Both youngsters worked for their parents on the farm. After high school, James 'Jim' attended Oregon State University, graduating in 1965 with a degree in chemical engineering. He married Patricia Coleman June 20, 1964. The couple had two children, Kari, b. December 13, 1966 and Angie, b. March 22, 1970. Kari teaches school in the Evergreen School District, Vancouver, Washington. Angie is a medical assistant in a Vancouver medical clinic. Jim and his family returned to East Multnomah County in 1979. Currently, he is President of the Wacker chip plant in North Portland.

Marjorie also attended Oregon State University earning a degree in marketing in 1974. She was married to Peter S. Turner, with whom she had two children, Peter, b. February 13, 1971 and Bradley, b. June 18, 1973. Currently Majorie lives in Woodinville, Washington and serves as Vice-President of the Bon Marché Store in Seattle, Washington. Ruth Ellis married Raymond Smith July 27, 1987. He too, had lost his spouse of many years. Presently, Ruth and Raymond live in a home on Loudon Hill.   *Ruth (Ellis) Smith*

Corbett Christian Church after an ice storm, December 1963.   Photo, the author.

129

Roy E. Emily
Jessie K. (Morgan) Emily

Roy E. Emily, born December 10, 1881, of pioneer parents Frederick and Mary J. (Esson) Emily, was the first of their children to be born at Hurlburt. He grew up on the farm where his father had intended to build a sawmill. However, a terrible windstorm swept through the area, uprooting the timber on the 40-acre place, which ended the sawmill plan. Frederick added 40 more cleared acres to the farm, but had to clear the original 40 of the downed logs and debris left by the storm. Frederick Emily completed the construction of a home on the property in 1881. The house stood until removed by Walter and Marie Vockert when they built a new home on the place in 1961.

Jessie K. Morgan, b. July 13, 1884, and Roy E. Emily married March 3, 1906. Art Johnson and Lee Evans served as witnesses. Roy went to Wardner, Idaho in order to work in a silver mine. Jessie gave birth to the couple's first child, Doris, December 14, 1906, at Wardner. Two months earlier, October 6, 1906, Roy's father died of a self-inflicted gunshot wound. He had been suffering excruciating pain from (it was thought) some sort of cancer. The family decided that Roy Emily should return to Hurlburt to manage the farm (see "Descendants of Frederick and Mary Jane Emily," *Pioneer History*).

In addition to the house Frederick had built on the place, other farm buildings included a combination storage and woodshed, a prune dryer, a smokehouse, an equipment shed, a barn, a chicken house and, of course, an outhouse. The Emily barn, one of the largest in the area at the time, had stalls for horses on the main level, (East End). Stanchions for cows were found below the main floor on the West End, where cows were fed and milked. Large double doors on both the south and north side allowed for large loads to be brought into the structure. Above the main floor a haymow permitted the storage of a quantity of hay. There was also a grain storage area on the main floor. A trap door on the main floor permitted feed to be dropped to the cows. Later, two silos were added at the west end of the barn. Adjacent to the barn on the north side, basement level, stood a cooling shed for milk. Frederick Emily built the barn himself, with help from Mr. Gandy, a neighbor. Year's later Walter Vockert

Emily Home c 1881

The Emily House built by Frederick Emily in 1881. Used by the Vockerts until 1961.
Photo courtesy of Pat (Bramhall) Paget

Emily Barn

This barn, built before the turn of the century by Frederick Emily and 'Mr. Gandy,' is still used by Karl Vockert. Photo courtesy of Pat (Bramhall) Paget}

told Doris Emily that he knew "A German had built it because it was so solidly done (and held together) with square wooden pegs." The prune dryer, about 900 cubic feet in size, had a capacity of about three tons. After the demise of the prune orchards, it was used to store grain or produce.

Roy and Jessie Emily had three other children who survived infancy, Owen, b. June 23, 1912, Gerald, b. November 15, 1913 and Shirley, b. September 8, 1918. All the youngsters attended Hurlburt School, which

Hurlburt School c 1914

Geneva Wright stands in front of the Hurlburt School

Hurlburt Students, 1913

Rear, L. to R: Johnny Thompson, Earl Pounder, Lloyd Ough, Cecil Pounder (in front of Lloyd), Victor Rickert, Fay Davis, Beth Pounder (in front of Fay Davis), Selma Soderstrom, Fernie Davis, unidentified, unidentified, Mary Davis. Front: Albert Pounder, Albert Davis, Albert Soderstrom, Ray Lasley, Irene Evans, Ruth Davis, Doris Emily. Photos courtesy of Pat (Bramhall) Paget.

was located on Hurlburt Road about one-half mile west of the farm. Among the children's teachers were Miss Dewey, Miss Lyda Bramhall, Miss Hazel Johnson, Miss Geneva Wright and Miss Minerva Powell. Doris had Hazel Johnson as teacher in the third grade. Miss Johnson took Doris to her Portland home that year to meet her two sisters, who made her welcome for a weekend. Doris was much impressed by the home's lovely furnishings, a winding staircase and the bathroom. Two members of Miss Johnson's family had died of TB. Later that same school year Miss Johnson became so ill she could not complete the year. That fall, Doris came down with TB and spent three months, October, November and December, in bed. Though she liked Miss Johnson, Doris wrote, "I think it strange she didn't realize she was endangering my life."

At Hurlburt, children acted as 'janitors,' which consisted of cleaning the blackboards and sweeping the classroom, cloakroom and porch after school. The two students selected for the job were paid $9.00 each at year end. Doris graduated from Hurlburt, while Owen, Gerald and Shirley completed grade school at Corbett because the family moved to Corbett in 1924. All four youngsters graduated from CHS, Doris in 1925, Owen and Gerald in 1931, and Shirley in 1936.

Living on a farm had its advantages. The first good early apples came from "yellow transparent" trees, followed soon by Gravensteins. Winter apples included Northern Spy, Greenlings, Kings, Red Snow and a hardy red apple. Nearly everyone had Royal Anne and Bing cherry trees. Though the prune orchards did not survive the ice storm of November 1921, many farms had an Italian prune tree, a pear tree or two and perhaps, a peach-plum tree. Persimmon and apricot trees were found in a few fruit orchards and walnut trees often bordered the road. A concord (and similar white variety) grape arbor provided many families with grapes for eating, juicing and jelly. Newcomers were usually astounded of the 'bounty' while 'old timers' used what they wanted and left the remainder on the ground.

Roy Emily milked from 12 to 16 cows. A plank walkway led to the manure pile, which received its replenishment twice a day. A hired man used the manure shovel to clean the gutters and wheeled the waste to the manure pile with a wheelbarrow. The cows were milked by hand twice a day. Three-legged milk stools held the milker, who directed streams of milk into a shiny, three-gallon milk pail. The milker strained the milk into 10-gallon cans, which were placed in a trough of cold water in the

Spring Plowing

Roy Emily stops plowing for a moment to visit with a neighbor, Art Johnson.   Photo courtesy of Arlene (Johnson) Marble.

cooling room. There some of the milk might be put through the separator, which separated the cream from the milk. In early days the cream went to the creamery in Gage (Springdale). Later whole milk in ten-gallon cans was shipped by truck to the processing plant in Portland. Doris recalled that George Shelley drove the milk truck that came to the farm each day to pick up the milk. Emily raised pigs, which received the 'skimmed' milk from the separator to help them put on weight. Of course they were fed grain and other feed as well. Emily usually butchered in the fall and marketed the 'sides' in Portland.

The Emily's closest neighbors were the Loyal Rickert family. The Thompson family lived beyond (east of) the Rickerts. William Thompson carried the mail, though sometimes Jane Thompson or his son, Johnny, substituted for him. According to Doris Emily, Jane Thompson had "gorgeous red hair." She died in the flu epidemic of 1918-19. A daughter, Alma, graduated from CHS in 1917. She attended Oregon Normal School and Oregon State College. She taught school in Oregon for more than 34 years. Married to Dewey Quier, she settled in Eastern Oregon. Emily Thompson also graduated from CHS in 1917. She and John Gorsline married in 1918 and had a son, Robert. She, too, became a teacher. Johnny served in the Navy Seabees during WW II. After the war he settled near Astoria in Jewell (see "William James Thompson," *Pioneer History*).

134

Elihu 'El' Rickert's widow, Anna, lived south of the Thompsons (see "Elihu G. Rickert," *Pioneer History*).

The principal crops grown by Roy Emily included hay and grain, including corn, which went for livestock feed. He also grew some vegetable crops, such as potatoes. After the hay crop was cut and dried, a team of horses hauled it to the barn by wagon. A contraption called a hayfork carried the hay into the barn. Upon reaching the barn, Emily unhitched the team from the wagon, re-hitched the doubletree to a pulley to which a hayfork was attached, rammed the hayfork into the load and marched the horses forward. This lifted part of the load to an arm extending outward from the top of the barn. When the hay reached the arm, a catch was tripped and the load was carried inside. Pulling a second rope caused the hayfork to release the load in the haymow. The process continued until the wagon emptied, then the team took the wagon back to the field for the next load. Sometimes huge stacks of hay were formed in a convenient place, accessible to the baling crew when they came.

The thrashing machine came annually after the grain ripened. The engine, fired by wood, operated the machinery by steam power. The thrasher separated grain from the stalk, blowing the waste straw by means of a large tube-like appendage to a pile behind the machine. The grain poured from an outlet on one side of the thrashing machine into a sack held by sharp hooks. As a sack filled, the 'sacker' pushed a lever to divert the grain into another sack attached in the same manner. The filled sack was sewn shut with twine so that two ear-like handles were formed. This helped the workers stack the grain into a neat pile. Thrashing continued until the bundles of grain, which had been stockpiled in a convenient location, were gone. The baler followed the thresher to bale the straw and other hay. Corn was fed to the cows directly from the field. By the time it grew too old for feed, most of it had been harvested. Later, of course, it was chopped for ensilage and stored in silos.

Women worked extra hard during the harvest season. Sometimes neighbor girls were hired to help with the household chores or to care for the children when meals were prepared for the harvest hands. Doris mentioned two hired from 'Loudon Hill,' Laura Wilson and Louretta Udey. After Union High School District #1 formed in 1914, Gladys Barr came to live with the Emilys to attend CHS at Corbett. She had completed grade nine and wanted to complete high school. She earned her keep by helping with the household chores and came to be considered one of the

Gladys Barr

Gladys Barr, training to become a nurse. Photos courtesy of Pat (Bramhall) Paget.

Hurlburt School c1920

From L: Doris Emily, Ray Lasley, Selma Soderstrom, Albert Pounder and Irene Evans. Seated, Miss Margaret Patterson.

family. She rode the Emily's horse, Babe, to school. Gladys Barr graduated from CHS in 1917. She trained to become a nurse, but suffered an acute appendicitis attack and died.

Typical household chores at the time included some long since forgotten. Coal oil lanterns furnished light. To keep them efficient, the lamp chimneys required frequent cleaning, the wicks needed to be trimmed and the oil chamber filled. The lamps did come in handy for heating metal curling irons for curling one's hair. Bathing involved heating water on the kitchen stove or dipping it from the stove's water reservoir, pouring it into a wash tub, adding cold water to obtain the desired temperature and shooing others out of the kitchen while one bathed. In Doris' experience, being the oldest, she bathed first, followed by Owen and Gerald, who used the same water. Another chore required the replacement of the ticking in straw mattresses. This necessitated a trip to the barn to remove the 'old' straw and to obtain fresh straw from the straw mow. The ticking was changed every ten weeks or so.

A family member mentioned frequently in Doris Emily's reminiscences is her Aunt Connie (Emily) Smith. The Emilys visited Uncle Charlie and Aunt Connie quite often. The Smiths lived on a houseboat, which was anchored at various locations on the Columbia River. Charlie Smith fished commercially and had obtained the job of lighting the channel markers on the banks of the river east of Lower Corbett each evening. Charlie and Connie had one son, Esson (Hartwell), who followed his father's model by working on a river tugboat. Charlie bought a ferryboat for the run between Cascade Locks, Oregon and Stevenson, Washington shortly after the Columbia River Highway was completed through the Gorge. It soon became a lucrative business, and two more ferryboats were added for the run. The three ferries kept busy, particularly on Sunday, carrying automobiles and passengers between the two towns. After Charlie and Connie divorced, he started a ferry run at Hood River and later, one at The Dalles (see "John T. and Roxanna Smith," *Pioneer History*).

When five area grade school districts (Hurlburt, Mountain, Pleasant View, Springfield and Taylor) petitioned the Boundary Board to form a union high school district, an election followed at which the petition received a favorable vote in all five districts. Thus Union High School District #1, Multnomah County, came into existence. Its first classes were held starting in September 1914, in classrooms rented from Corbett Christian Church for $10 per month. The new four-room high school building opened to students December 7, 1915 (Dorothy Klock, *Crown Point Country Schools*, pp. 12-13). Prior to the establishment of CHS at Corbett, local students who wished to continue their education had to make arrangements to attend high school in Portland or Gresham, if indeed, they wished to continue. Each of the five districts elected a board member for the new Union High School District. Hurlburt District elected Roy Emily to the post.

Doris Emily started at CHS in 1920. Usually, Irene and Jennie Evans would join her for the two-mile hike to school. Irene and Doris became fast friends at Hurlburt and the friendship continued during their high school years. In 1921, Doris developed "rheumatism" in all her joints, which caused her to miss the rest of the school year. It also cost her credits, so that fall she returned as a freshman. Thereafter she was in the same class as her cousin, Dolores Morgan. Doris Emily often dated Harold Barr while in high school. Sometimes a foursome of Fay Davis, Bertha Barr, Harold Barr and Doris joined the dancers at the Palmer Mill hall. They also frequented the dance hall behind Knight's Grocery in Corbett.

On July 3, 1922, after school was out, a fire spread from Knight's to Columbia High School. The grocery, the dance hall and the high school burned to the ground. Consequently, Doris completed her sophomore year in the Columbia Grange building. A member of the *Cohimore* staff,

High Jinks at the Hulits

From L, Doris Emily, Lloyd Bramhall, Francis Henkle (partially obscured), Mabel Harding, Horace Evans (partially obscured) and Maude Henkle enjoy watermelon at the Hulit Home on Woodard Road.

Emily Family

L to R: Shirley, Jessie, Roy, Owen (in wheelchair), Gerald, Doris. Photos courtesy of Pat (Bramhall) Paget.

she helped complete the 60 annuals published by the staff of 1922-23. A new teacher, Joy Crockett, served as advisor. After Knight's dance hall burned, dances were held at the grange hall. In February 1923, Doris dated Lloyd Bramhall for the first time.

In the summer of 1923, Doris Emily worked six days a week for Mrs. Henderson at the Crown Point Chalet. According to Doris, the waitresses cleaned the dance floor, dining room, outdoor eating areas and wiped the dishes before the evening working hours. The day started at 10:00 a.m. and ended at midnight. Waitresses received $1.00 per day plus tips. The girls stayed in dormitory rooms and had one day off each week, which started the evening of the preceding day and ended at 10:00 a.m. the subsequent day. Doris worked at the Chalet two summers.

After graduating from CHS in 1925, Doris worked the summer for Mr. Johnson at Johnson's Café at Crown Point. He generally hired only one waitress and her day ended at 8:00 p.m. Sometimes Lloyd picked her up and they watched the eastbound 10:30 train pass through the tunnel near Reed's Landing from Crown Point. That summer she sometimes worked a banquet or special event for Mrs. Henderson, but not often.

In 1920, Roy Emily had purchased approximately 21 acres of the Corbett Estate, which was being subdivided and sold off at the time. Roy

138

Emily had a small shack built on the north side of the highway for a wood cutter who helped him clear the 18 acres parcel south of the highway. In 1924, Roy Emily moved his family to Corbett. Earlier he had hired Cecil Pounder to build another small home north of the highway. This home became the first Emily residence at Corbett. The following fall, Gerald and Owen decided to go fishing at Big Creek, close to the farm. Both boys caught a cold, but Owen's "stayed with him," according to Doris. Dr. H. H. Hughes came and called the County Health Officer. The latter determined that the illness was infantile paralysis or poliomyelitis. He placed Jessie Emily and Owen in quarantine for six weeks, during which time the terrible disease damaged Owen's nervous system so severely that he lost the use of his legs. The disease affected his upper body as well and Owen struggled for years to regain partial use of his arms and hands.

Neighbors provided support and encouragement for Owen and the family during the ordeal and afterward. Of course, Owen faced many obstacles and through sheer will power and effort, developed what physical strength he could muster and became an avid reader in order to develop his mind. His school friends gratified the family by being so thoughtful. They included Owen in their activities, even tying a rope to his wheel chair in order to take him to Lower Corbett with them. The rope held Owen back on the trip down Corbett Grade and was used to help pull him up on the return trip. Because he missed so much school, Owen and Gerald became classmates and graduated from CHS together in 1931. Owen Emily gave the valedictory at the graduation ceremony that year.

In 1924, Roy Emily became the janitor at Corbett Grade School, which was erected upon the foundation of CHS, which had burned. The new high school was built west of its former site on the south side of the highway. Summers, Roy worked for the US Forest Service on the lookout on Pepper Mountain. Later, both he and Jessie worked for J. Ward Evans in his cannery during the corn season. The trees and stumps had been cleared from the 18 acres adjacent to the new high school by 1926. That year Art Johnson helped Emily harvest 18 acres of hay. Thereafter the 18 acres continued to be farmed. After Owen and Gerald graduated in 1931, the Emilys went into the flower and bulb business. A stand, built close to the highway, became a stop for both weekend sightseers from Portland and visitors passing through.

Doris Emily married Lloyd Bramhall September 5, 1926. As mentioned, Doris first dated Lloyd during her sophomore year. Lloyd built

First Crop, 1928

Art Johnson helps Roy Emily harvest the first crop of hay at Corbett.

Owen Emily's First Flower Stand

'Aunt Kate,' Mrs. Olinger, Owen Emily, Alma Bramhall and Gerald Emily at Owen's flower and bulb stand.

Photos courtesy of Pat (Bramhall) Paget.

them a home on property the Emilys gave the couple, part of the 18-acre piece south of the highway. Lloyd Bramhall went into the trucking business with Albert Pounder (see "Charles Bramhall" and "Albert C. Pounder"). When Jessie Emily's health began to fail, Doris returned to the Corbett home to live with her for a time. During that interval, her daughter, Beverly Bramhall, attended and graduated from CHS (1948).

Emily Place from the Air

The Emily Place, showing Owen's new stand, the home and garage built by Lloyd Bramhall, the cottage and bulb shed. Lower left is the Van Speybrock residence. The new Corbett Grade School sits on this site.   Photo courtesy of Pat (Bramhall) Paget.

Later Jessie Emily moved to Beaverton to be close to the Bramhalls, which is where she lived at her death on June 10, 1964.

After Owen graduated from high school, he managed the flower stand at which many varieties of flowers and bulbs were sold, but gladiolas became the mainstay. The Emilys built a bulb shed and the balance of the eighteen acres soon came to be devoted nearly totally to gladiolas and daffodils. After Roy Emily died August 26, 1940, Owen managed the farm, hiring all work done for the next several years. He opened a flower stand on Sandy Boulevard, which he operated until two days before his death from a heart condition August 30, 1951. In addition to the farm, Owen kept books for a logging company, worked at the telephone office, wrote short stories, wrote a narrative history regarding Fred Shoulz for the Pioneer Association and helped younger students, who knew of his scholarly reputation, with school papers and assignments. Doris wrote: "Owen's family remember all of the many nice things that were done for him by friends-also the many projects they sponsored to raise money for doctor bills and other needs during his illness and through his life. We thank all who knew and did for him."

After high school, Gerald Emily joined the US Navy. He helped on the bulb farm until it was discontinued, then worked for the Multnomah County Road Department. Later he became school custodian at a Rockwood Grade School. He married Dorothy Littlepage May 15, 1945. They lived in Troutdale for several years, during which time Dorothy worked for the Multnomah County Educational Service District under Superintendent Thomas Sommerville. Gerald and Dorothy had two children, Pamela (Mocobee) and Penny (Garner). Gerald Emily passed away July 12, 1975.

After Shirley graduated from CHS in 1936, she married William Mishey in October of that year. They moved to Gresham where two children were born, William O. and Kay Sharon. In 1939, the Misheys purchased the Springdale store from the Bramhalls, and managed it for several years. Later George Atkinson bought the merchandise, moved it to his Pleasant Home store and the store in 'West' Springdale closed. The Misheys moved to Madras to farm, raising potatoes and seed clover principally. Both youngsters graduated from Madras High School. Shirley clerked at the Rainbow Market on the Deschutes River near Warm Springs for several years. She married William Porter after separating from William Mishey. *Doris Emily*

County Garage-Corbett c1928

The garage sat across from the high school behind the houses on the highway.   Photo courtesy of Pat (Bramhall) Paget.

Erick Enquist
Anna (Enquist) Enquist

Erick Enquist, born in Finland in 1884, immigrated to the United States in 1902, landing in New York, then proceeding to Portland to join his sister, Louisa, arriving June 5, 1902. During his youth in Finland, Erick worked at farming, fishing, logging and saw milling. When Erick reached age seventeen, a family council determined that one of two brothers had to leave – the farm could not support both. Erick, who had been thinking about America, volunteered to leave. Hence, in 1902, he found himself in Portland (see "Erick Enquist," *Pioneer History*).

On August 5, 1905, Erick Enquist married Anna Enquist (same surname, not related), also a native of Finland. She had been working at the Brown Palace Hotel in Denver before moving to Salt Lake City. From Salt Lake City the couple returned to Portland where Erick worked for the Southern Pacific railroad in the car repair facility. He also fished commercially when the salmon runs hit the Columbia River.

The Enquist's first child, a daughter, Aino E., was born March 10, 1906. Shortly after her birth the family moved to Bradford Island to work a fishwheel. Later they moved to Warrendale, where Erick worked for Frank M. Warren, President of Warren Packing Company, who operated a cannery at Warrendale as well as several fishwheels on the Columbia. According to reports, Erick seemed to have a knack for locating fishwheels and building the leads so that more salmon were caught. Warren offered to finance a start for Erick Enquist in the fishwheel business, but he lost his life when the SS Titanic sank in 1912. Thus Enquist's venture was delayed until he obtained another backer, J.H. Gallagher of the Diamond Lumber Company. Eventually Enquist owned eight fishwheels on the Columbia River and operated them until that method of catching salmon was banned, first by the State of Oregon in 1926 followed by the State of Washington in 1934.

In 1934 Enquist went into the construction business. He built 'Enquist's Addition' at Warrendale, which provided cottages for Bonneville Dam construction workers. He also was involved in the real estate business. By 1920, he had purchased 40 acres in Springdale fronting on the highway and Lucas Road. Erick and Anna had three more children, Alfred 'O,' Erick R. 'Rolf' and Robert S. 'Bob.' Anna passed away in January 1953. Erick Enquist died February 15, 1976.

Erick Enquist Fishwheel

From L, Anna, Rolf (in carriage), Aino and Erick Enquist at his fishwheel located on Bradford Island.   Photo courtesy of Aino (Enquist) Ferrington.

Aino Enquist attended high school in Corbett, starting in 1920, but did not graduate from CHS. She married Glen H. Ferrington, who worked for the Corps of Engineers during the construction of Bonneville Dam. The couple lived in Dodson during this period. Later they purchased property in Springdale from her parents and located there. Glen and Aino had two sons, Dale, b. May 29, 1931 and Gary, b. May 11, 1941. After moving to Springdale, the couple started a dairy herd, but the cows contracted Bang's disease, which put them out of the dairy business. When the aluminum plant opened, both Glen and Aino worked there, he as a carpenter and she, in the personnel office. Glen took an active part in the formation of the Corbett Volunteer Fire Department, serving as its Chief for several years. He died at a Gresham fire August 28, 1958. In his memory, Aino Ferrington donated two acres of land to the Springdale Community Bible Church on Lucas Road. Fire District 14 also memorializes Glen Ferrington at the fire station in Corbett. Aino Ferrington married Clarence Bossio after Glen's death, but he too, passed away. Aino (Enquist) Bossio passed away August 31, 1999.

Enquist Family, Five Generations

From L, Clarence Bossio, Joretta (May) Ferrington, Bob Ferrington (behind), Aino (Enquist) Bossio, Dale Ferrington, Erick Enquist (seated), Louise (Ferrington) Jones, Neely Jones(baby), Glenda Ferrington and Richard Jones.

Photo courtesy of Joretta Ferrington.

Both Dale and Gary Ferrington attended Springdale Grade School and CHS from which Dale graduated in 1950, Gary in 1959. Dale served as a volunteer firefighter for District 14 before becoming a paid firefighter for District 9, Multnomah County. He worked as a firefighter for 30 years, his final years with the City of Portland Fire Department. Dale married Joretta May of Corbett February 7, 1952. The couple had three children: Louise, b. 1954, married Charles Jones and had two children. Bob, b. 1955, married Victoria Dow and they have two children. Glenda, b. 1964, married Robert Ekblad and has two children. Dale and Joretta have retired and live in Gresham.

After graduating from CHS, Gary attended Portland State College, from which he earned his BA Degree. He completed a masters program in Instructional Technology at the University of Southern California after which he taught at the University of Oregon. He recently retired after spending 31 years at the U of O, completing his career in the position of Director of Instructional Technology. Gary Ferrington continues to make Eugene his home.

J. Ward Evans
Rae S. (Perkins) Evans

J. Ward Evans was born in Corbett November 4, 1883, son of Tom and Hannah 'Jane' Evans, who purchased land on what is now Evans Road in 1882. Tom Evans (Ward's father) operated a large prune dryer, which could handle 8 tons of this crop during a drying cycle. A heavy ice storm in November 1921, destroyed the prune orchards, and with it, this business (see "Thomas L. and Hannah J. Evans," *Pioneer History*). Ward Evans married Rae Sarah Perkins March 17, 1907.

In 1912, Ward and his wife decided to try canning corn since they had a surplus of corn that they could not sell. The initial year they hand packed the corn in cans, soldered them shut, and processed the product on the kitchen stove. With encouragement from a manufacturer of canning equipment in Portland, Evans bought some processing machinery, built a cannery in 1916, and produced 200 cases (4800 cans) that year. One of the first stores to market Evans "Golden" brand was the Sealy-Dresser Company in Portland. Meier and Frank Company also marketed the 67Evans' "Original Golden Sugar Corn, grown and packed by J. Ward Evans, Corbett, Oregon."

The business continued to expand until the Evans planted more than 100 acres of an improved Golden Bantam corn for processing. The Golden Bantam corn grown by Evans came from a strain propagated by Fred N. Lasley. The cannery did a thriving business because of the high quality of the product. Even during the depression year of 1930, more than 6000 cases (144,000 cans) were produced. The corn, planted around May 10, took approximately 120 days to mature. In September, processing began. Coming from the field, the corn passed through the 'husker' at the rate of 150 ears per minute. Workers placed the ears in 'slots' that carried them into the machine. The husked corn then ran through a water bath onto another belt where workers removed any imperfect ears and remaining silk. Next the corn traveled along a belt of Mr. Evans' design to the cutting machine where the corn was removed from the cob.

Buckets of corn kernels were carried to a large table where workers filled cans with corn. "Salt, sugar and water enough to cover" were added to each of the cans, which were then placed in a machine to be preheated. The next step took the cans to the sealing machine, where the

146

Tom and Hannah Evans Family

Rear, Victor and Myrtle Ellis, Ward and Toot Evans. Front, Hannah and Tom Evans.
Photo courtesy of Joan (Ellis) Benner.

Evans CornField

Golden Bantam corn matures – note Evans home in background.
Photo courtesy of Belle Evans.

Evans Cannery Labels

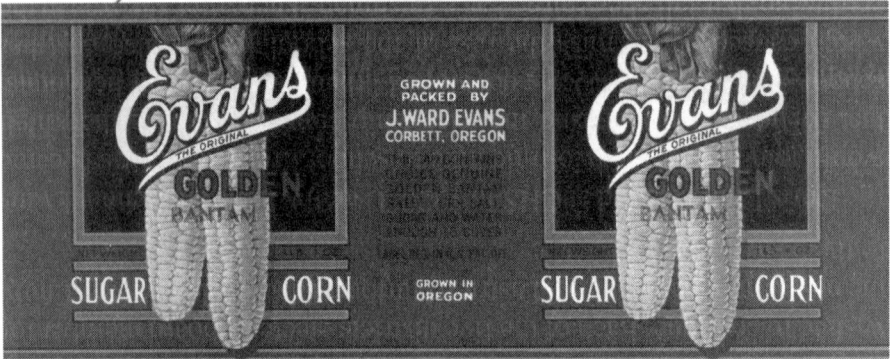

Evans Golden Bantam Sugar Corn Label

Evans Golden Red Raspberries Label

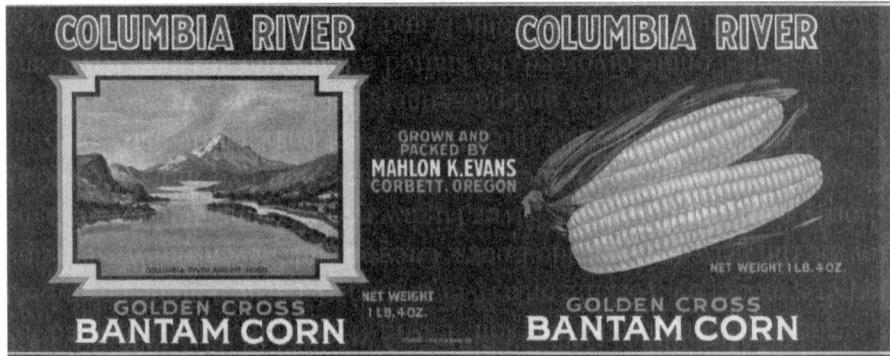

Columbia River Golden Cross Bantam Corn.   Labels courtesy of Keith Evans.

tops were put on. The cans (648 or 27 cases) were then placed in a huge crate, which was lowered into the retort to cook for 70 minutes at 250 degrees. After the cans cooled, they were ready for labeling, packing and shipping. The husks and some other portions of the waste were fed to cattle. Much of the other waste was used for fertilizer. The cannery operated for about 20 days in order to process the crop, which was grown

Evans Bulb Digger

Horace (left) and Ward Evans operating the mechanized bulb digger.
Photo courtesy of Belle Evans.

only on the Evans' farm. The cannery required about 30 employees during the season.

In addition to corn, Mr. Evans tried packing berries. He used the same brand, "Golden," on this crop. Apparently canned berries did not sell as well as the corn, as the product was soon dropped. An interesting sidelight to this story is the fact that corn was processed and sold under another label, "Columbia River Golden Cross Bantam Corn, grown and packed by Mahlon K. Evans, Corbett, Oregon." The cannery shut down during WWII because of the shortage of tin and sugar, and because Mr. Evans did not take well to the dictates of the government bureaucrats who allocated these resources.

Ward Evans loved flowers and grew bulbs as a hobby. This hobby developed into an important part of his farm operation. Benefiting from the introductory efforts of County Agent S.B. Hall, Evans started growing King Alfred daffodil bulbs, which had been imported from Holland by Hall. By 1930 Evans had more than 10 acres in daffodils. Another important Evans' crop was potatoes. Ward Evans was a progressive farmer and businessman, and a leader in developing the agricultural potential of East Multnomah County. Ward and Rae had five children, Horace (b. January 3, 1908), Adeline (Adams) b. April 17, 1910, Mahlon b. March 1, 1912, Lois M. (Dunkin) b. January 29, 1915, and Rosemary (Nichols) b. March 13, 1923.

The February 27, 1946 *Cardinal* reported: "Mrs. Rae Evans was called to her farm at Alsea about a week ago by the caretaker of her bulb farm,

Haying Time

From left, Horace, Rae and Mahlon Evans, 'Fred' standing on load. (Evans' home on left.)   Photo courtesy of Belle Evans.

who said the daffodils were ready to be picked for market. Mr. Kenneth Ellis and Mr. Marshall Dunkin have gone to the beach to help Mrs. Evans in harvesting her flower crop." Ward Evans passed away January 25, 1944. Rae Evans died May 17, 1976. Both are interred at Forest Lawn Cemetery in Gresham.

Horace Evans attended and graduated from Oregon State College after graduating from CHS. He worked for his father on the farm for about four years, then worked at Bonneville Dam as a shift foreman for two years. Next he worked for a contractor in The Dalles after which he rejoined the Army Corps of Engineers in 1940 to serve in a supervisory capacity during the construction of the Fort Richardson project in Alaska. His duties in Alaska took him on inspection trips to projects in the Aleutian Islands about the time the Japanese launched an attack on Dutch Harbor. Later during the war his duties included working on several airfield projects in the Northwest. For about a year, he worked as a contract expediter with Boeing Aircraft Company in Seattle. From the Northwest he went to New Mexico as a supervisor in the construction of the White Sands rocket testing grounds.

Horace Evans returned to the Northwest in 1946 to resume a career as a bulb grower on property his father had purchased near Waldport. He married for a second time on January 10, 1944. In the May 1948 primary, Evans won the Republican nomination to represent Lincoln County

150

Mahlon and Belle Evans Family

Belle Evans, Ward (standing), Larry (held by Belle), Mahlon Evans (Keith in front).
Photos courtesy of Belle Evans.

in the legislature. August 22, 1948, he died in a plane crash at Lake of the Woods with four other Oregon Republican leaders. His widow, Marie (Jordan) Evans, and a daughter by a previous marriage, Judith Carol b. September 1935, survived him.

Adeline Evans attended Oregon State College and became a teacher. She married Robert L. Adams June 6, 1934. He worked for Pacific Power and Light Company. She taught in the Roseburg area most of her teaching career. She and her husband had three children, Roberta (Freytag), Sara Rae (Tiffany), and John.

Mahlon Evans married Juanita Endicott, and they had one daughter, Sandra (Shardlow), b. July 1, 1936. On December 8, 1942, Mahlon married Belle Campbell. Mahlon and Belle had three sons, 46James W. 'Ward,' b. September 16, 1943, Mahlon Keith b. September 10, 1944 and Lawrence 'Larry,' b. September 2, 1946. Mahlon started a trucking business, Northwest (or Northwestern) Motor Freight, with Bill and Louis Mishey after graduating from high school. The business hired several local individuals, including Bill Gebhardt, Dan Holgate, Bob Shelley, George Shelley, Jimmy Wilson and Howard Winters. A terrible accident involving one of the firm's trucks, which occurred east of The Dalles, ended the trucking business for Mahlon.

Mahlon then helped his father with the farm and took over its operation when his father died in 1944. By then the daffodil business was thriving. In April 1946, Mahlon sold three tons of daffodil blooms (144,000 blossoms) to the City of San Francisco for its "Spring Comes to Maiden Lane" festival. The shipment was sent via United Airlines. In later years when farming in the Corbett area was on the wane, he drove truck and sold automobiles for the Hessel dealership in Gresham. Mahlon died January 21, 1979. Two of his sons have also passed away, Larry, September 2, 1987, and Ward, May 8, 1998. Larry married Vickie Hollingsworth and the couple had three children, Larry Jr., Letecia M. and Caroline R. Ward worked for Multnomah County and lived on a 10-acre parcel of the home place. Keith has worked at a number of jobs, including the U.S. Postal Service, Zimmerman's and Fred Meyer. He has one child and currently lives on a 24-acre parcel of the original Evans property. Belle Evans lives on 10 acres that belonged to her son, Ward. She also owns 20 acres of the 50 acres she and Mahlon purchased earlier, which is adjacent to the original Evans property.

Lois Evans married Marshall 'Marsh' F. 47Dunkin of Santa Ana, California October 12, 1938. The couple met at Oregon State College. Marsh qualified for the 1932 Olympics in the high hurdles. He served in the U.S. Army during and after World War II. During the war Marsh served on General Douglas MacArthur's staff. An article in the April 7, 1964, *Oregonian* reported Marsh Dunkin's association with General MacArthur as one of his staff officers during World War II. Mr. Dunkin commented in the article, "It was a great privilege for me to be about as close to him as anyone except his chief staff officers. Nobody really got to know the General intimately. He had a reserve and an aloofness about him."

Marsh added, "Those who worked under the General felt themselves fortunate and none could serve with him and fail to come away a better individual." An article in the November 9, 1962 *Cardinal* reported that Captain Ben Goodling, Vice-Principal, CHS, was retiring from the guard, and that Colonel Dunkin was his commanding officer. Later Marsh commanded a unit of the U.S. Army Reserve. He served a total of 30 years in

152

the Army and retired a Colonel. He and Lois had two sons, David b. March 26, 1939, and Marshall, b. January 24, 1944. Both Lois and Marsh were very active in community affairs. Lois took an active role in the East Multnomah County Pioneer Association for many years and served as its President. Marsh served as a director of the Corbett Water District for 8 years.

In the mid-40's, Lois established a business in her home on Gordon Creek Road selling home baked goods including pies (the pies, featuring Evans' blueberries, were among the best the author ever tasted). She had a thriving retail and wholesale business for several years. After they "retired," Lois and Marsh made furniture in their own shop for several years. Marsh passed away March 25, 1987 and Lois died October 25, 1995.

Rosemary Evans attended Oregon State College and became a teacher. She married Bob Nichol September 5, 1947. Bob served in the U.S. Navy during World War II. The couple had seven children, 68Roberta, Gregory, Jason, Scott, Lucinda, Stewart and Garwood. After Rosemary retired from raising her family and teaching, and Bob retired from the real estate business, they opened an antique store located at Tidewater, Oregon, on the Alsea Highway to the coast.

Menucha Greenhouse c1944

From L: Lois Dunkin, Frances Ellis and George Perry Sr. examine orchids grown at the Menucha greenhouse during the war.   Photo courtesy of George Perry Jr.

Murray W. Evans
Estella L. (Davis) Evans

Murray Evans, son of Wilbur and Alice (Neely) Evans, and grandson of Tom and Hannah Evans (see *Pioneer History*), was born Christmas Day, 1912, in Corbett. He attended school at Hurlburt Grade School. His parents lived on Pounder grade about a quarter-mile below Evans Road. Later the family moved to Lower Corbett to a house on the hill behind what is now the Chinook Inn. On September 29, 1934, Murray married Estella 'Stella' L. Davis, daughter of Sherwood M. and Anna I. Davis. Stella grew up in the Hurlburt District, where she attended Hurlburt Grade School. She completed her education at CHS, graduating in 1933 (class Valedictorian).

The couple married during the hard times of the 30's, and they worked whenever and wherever an opportunity arose. Murray's uncles were daffodil growers, and both he and Stella put in many hours on their uncles' farms during the season. His uncle Toot permitted the couple to dig rogues (volunteers) from his field, and sometimes they took their pay in bulbs. During these years, they lived in Tom Evans' (Murray's grandfather) old house on the home place. When World War II started, Murray and Stella had accumulated enough daffodil stock to plant about three acres. They rented land on Henkle Road in which to plant their bulbs. According to Stella, one could make about $1000.00 per acre from daffodils in 1940, selling cut flowers and bulbs.

Murray was drafted into the U.S. Army in 1942. While he was in the service, Stella worked at the Bridal Veil Lumber and Box Company. Murray spent time at various places, including Pendleton, Oregon, Oklahoma and Illinois, where the Army sent him to school to learn the machinist trade. One year he took his leave during "bulb" season, as they had to get their bulbs dug. This year they replanted on ground rented from the Gebhardts on Loudon Road. Stella worked six days a week at the mill, and took care of the bulbs as best she could. When it came time to dig the bulbs, the rows had to be plowed out as the weeds were thick, and some bulbs were lost.

When Murray was discharged in 1946, he became aware of the fact that veterans could get a loan through the Farm Security Administration at 3% interest. The Evans bought the Miller Place of 180 acres at the end

Estella Davis c1933

Estella Davis, CHS Valedictorian, Class of
1933.   Photo courtesy of Sandra Evans.

of Mannthey Road from the Ihrkes for three thousand dollars. The house
on the property was in disrepair, so they had to work to make it more
livable. Furthermore, there was neither electricity nor running water to
the house. A ram water pump supplied water to a tank in the yard, but it
frequently stopped because of leaks. In order to get water, the leak had to
be found, repaired and the ram restarted. Finally, Murray improved a
spring located on Mannthey Road, and they hauled water from it for
several years. This, too, was a burden, as they had to ration water use.
Water problems continued for thirteen years before the couple got enough
money together to have Frank Fagan install a water system to replace the
ram. The Evans finally had water piped into the house.

Murray and Stella continued building their daffodil stock, but the
market was not as good as before the war. The embargo of agricultural
products from Europe was lifted, and Dutch producers flooded the U.S.
with daffodil bulbs. In order to improve their financial situation, Murray
purchased a combine and a "Cat," the former to do custom work for
other farmers and the latter to do some logging on the 120 acres not in
cultivation. When they harvested grain for others, Stella drove the tractor and Murray rode the combine. He used the Cat to drag logs to the

landing for sale. This helped pay the bills during the lean years. Stella had to keep the daffodils weeded while Murray worked elsewhere. She also worked for Toot Evans and Jim Udey in their bulbs. Then an opportunity came that changed the direction of their lives, and became Murray's passion.

Because of the GI Bill, Murray was able to attend nursery school at night, and was paid $93.00 per month while enrolled. Mr. Nuffer of Mountain View Nursery taught the course, which took four years to complete. During Murray's schooling, the class took field trips to the Grant Mitsch Bulb Farm in Canby. It was there that Murray learned daffodil hybridizing and developed an interest that was to become the central theme of his working life thereafter. Murray developed a friendship with Grant Mitsch, and helped him by locating a bulb digger, as he had been plowing the bulbs out previously. Murray and Stella also worked for him, taking their pay in some of the newer bulbs and hybridized seedlings. Murray was soon hybridizing daffodils from some of his own stock as well as from that obtained from Mr. Mitsch. Initially, Murray hybridized because of his fascination with the process, and it was more of a hobby than a vocational pursuit. However, that changed when other growers discovered what he had accomplished by his interest, skill and meticulous attention to detail.

In 1949, with help from family and friends, the Evans salvaged enough lumber from the Miller home and another house being razzed to build a new home. Progress was slow as they adopted a "pay as you go" policy rather than borrowing money. They bought a big wood furnace, which came from the Springdale Hotel and built a fireplace for supplemental heat. They used large windows in the living area so that they could enjoy watching the abundant wildlife, which included deer, bear, grouse, quail and wild turkeys. The winter of 1949-50 was exceptionally severe, with driving snow and cold weather. Many roads were closed by drifted snow. Fortunately, Murray had parked their pickup on Loudon Road, which permitted them to get out. They were unable to get a vehicle to their house for six weeks. Stella says, "We worked out," which means they worked at other jobs in order to keep farming. She took a job at Grahn's Market in Springdale to help pay the bills while Murray worked with the daffodils. At one point, Murray took a job as a machinist for a short time in order to earn some money to keep the bills paid.

Murray started hybridizing with some of his own varieties and with some of Grant Mitsch's seedlings. What started as a hobby soon devel-

Growing Daffodils

Prize-Winning Blossoms

Murray Evans tends his daffodil crop.

Murray and Stella Evans' hybrids.
Photos courtesy of Sandra Evans.

oped into an entirely different approach to the bulb business. Murray and Stella joined the American Daffodil Society and met two people there who would impact their lives greatly. One was Bill Pannill, of Pannill Knitting Mills in Martinsville, Virginia and the second was Bill's friend, Harry Tuggle. According to Stella, they "knew more about daffodils here and abroad than we could ever dream." Both sent their seed to Murray to grow, as the Northwest climate is much more favorable for daffodils than that in Virginia. They also sent other bulbs for use in hybridizing. Both visited the Evans farm the following spring and urged Murray and Stella to publish a price list and sell retail. Thus they embarked on a "new" phase in growing daffodils. At this point they decided to sell their own hybridized cultivars (varieties). While this required close attention to detail and much record keeping, it seemed to have the potential for providing a better income. Most importantly, the hybridizing process absolutely fascinated Murray. In 1954, Murray and Stella closed out much of their commercial stock.

To understand the scope of Murray's work, an outline of the process of hybridizing daffodils follows. The "parent" blooms are chosen. Murray would scrape pollen from the stamen of the male "parent." He would then (or later) apply it to the pistil of the female "parent" by brush or fingertip. Usually he had several blooms of the same parentage so that he would obtain thousands of seeds after the seed pods matured. He collected the seeds, careful not to mix seeds from different "parents," and the seeds from the various cultivars would be planted that fall in rows. The next spring, when the seeds germinated, tiny shoots would appear in the seedbed. Nothing was done to them that first year except for weeding

157

and applying a thin mulch. The second year was much the same. A small shoot would appear, and again, the seedbed would be weeded and mulched. The third year, a tiny plant would appear, and this year the "seedling" was dug after the plant died back. When the seedlings were replanted that fall, they were placed a little deeper in the soil. The fourth year the plants were larger, but rarely bloomed. The seedlings were again dug and replanted in the fall. The fifth year the plant would normally flower and the bulb would have grown to be about the size of one's thumb. At this stage the bulb is called a "round." This round is replanted in the fall, and the blooms the sixth year are evaluated for commercial potential. Even though the seedlings' parentage is the same, each offspring differs. Murray examined each bloom for its attributes: coloration, strength of stem, texture of its bloom, and other characteristics. Most of the seedlings would be rejected at this point, and only the selected rounds replanted in subsequent years. Each subsequent year also served to give one an opportunity to reject any stock deemed not worthy of commercial development.

Murray kept meticulous records, as required if one wished to register a cultivar with the Royal Horticultural Society in England. Murray's notes reflect his absorption with his work, and the intensity he brought to it:

"(April 12, 1957) "A 2B seedling given to us by Grant and mentioned in my notes of 1955, from Dick Wellband and Mary Longstreet (varieties), shows promise as a market and garden flower. The "Twink" type Dutch double, Insulinde, deserves a place in more gardens for, regardless of weather conditions; it consistently displays its brilliant red color, and is absolutely sunproof. Flamenco has proven its worth as a garden and market flower – free blooming, bright color and virtually weather proof. I would cast my vote for Duke of Windsor in the 2B division for the number 1 spot for garden decoration. In warmer climes it may open with a yellow cup, but an impressive flower even without the bright orange color it usually opens with here."

When a "seedling" was selected from among the rest because of its potential, much work remained. The rounds were planted to become "mother" bulbs, which usually took another three years. At that time, "slabs" could be removed and planted to become mother bulbs in turn. Repeating this process for another 12 to 15 years produced enough of the desirable cultivar to consider selling a few of the bulbs. Their first successful variety was "Celilo." Their first major prizewinner was "Descano." The most Murray and Stella ever received for a bulb was $100.00. Murray had five bulbs of "Cataract" listed at $100.00 each and all five sold quickly. Stella was pleased with "Little Bell," as that "open" variety came from seeds Stella discovered on a daffodil plant in the field.

The Evans' customers grew flowers to enter in various flower shows. As mentioned, one of his early cultivars, "Descano," twice won "Best of Show" honors. His "Foxfire" was pictured in the Royal Horticultural Society's Daffodil Yearbook one year. At the 1967 National Daffodil Convention in Philadelphia, one of Murray's cultivars was voted the outstanding one shown, and he duplicated the feat the subsequent year (the convention happened to be held in Portland). In all, Murray and Stella developed and registered more than three hundred different daffodil cultivars. As his reputation grew, and honor upon honor received, the Evans hosted visitors from around the world. As Stella remarked, "Visitors have come to our fields from England, Ireland, Holland, Australia, Tasmania, Canada and all over the USA, and I thought no one would ever visit us!"

Growing daffodils is a challenge in itself. Murray and other growers waged a constant battle with bulb flies. These pests lay eggs on the plant, the larva from which invades the bulb and essentially ruins it for sale. One can remove the larva, but the bulb must be replanted with hope that it can be saved. Murray went after the flies with a 410-gauge shotgun, and kept a tally of his "kills." Bulbs were sometimes treated for diseases, such as botrytis, or pests, such as nematodes and greater or lesser flies, by "cooking" them in a water-formaldehyde solution. The bulbs were placed in slatted containers and immersed in the solution. The solution was brought to a constant temperature between 110-111.5 degrees Fahrenheit, and held for three to four hours, depending upon the size of the bulbs.

Bulbs are planted in the fall. The plant appears quite early in the spring, and farmers hoped for an Easter bloom. This gave an impetus to the start of the flower season. Holidays such as Mother's Day also bolstered sales. Blooms could be held in cold storage for a short period, if that would help sales. If not picked for the floral trade, the daffodils were "headed," that is, the bloom snapped off to channel energy for growth of the bulb. When the plants died back in the summer, the bulbs would be dug with a bulb digger. The bulbs were picked up, sacked and hauled to the bulb shed. There they were placed in boxes for drying. Of course, each cultivar was kept separate from others. After drying, "slabs" were removed for replanting, the bulbs were graded for sale and those not sold were replanted in the fall, when the cycle started anew.

Murray and Stella Evans had no children. They have bestowed their daffodils upon a nephew, Ron Evans and his wife, Sandra 'Sandy,' and a niece, Diane Tribe, and her husband, Bill. Frank and Jeannie Driver have entered the daffodil business, and are growing some varieties obtained from the Evans' stock. Murray's journal again provides a clue to his feelings about what became his life work.

(1959) "While I never really relished growing older, the prospect of viewing our new seedlings, plus a number of normal varieties to date almost makes one feel he is being reborn rather than growing a year older. How wonderful it would be, if everyone had as much to look forward to with each passing year."

Murray and Stella "officially" retired in 1975. They sold 140 acres of their land to Publisher's Paper Company, and later sold 20 acres to their nephew, Ron Evans. In 1983, cancer struck Murray and in 1986, Stella underwent breast cancer surgery. Shortly thereafter, it was discovered that Murray's cancer had spread to the bones and kidney area. He passed away November 8, 1988. Stella recovered from her bout with cancer, and still lives in the house where she and Murray made their home. Recently she sold another 5 acres of the place to her nephew, Ron Evans.   *Stella Evans*

Trickey Home, Palmer c1906. Photo courtesy of Janet Lucas.

160

Wilbur Evans
Alice (Neely) Evans

Wilbur was a son of Thomas and Hannah Evans who settled in Corbett in 1882. Wilbur married Alice Neely and the couple settled where Weltha Wilson later lived (on Pounder Grade). The family moved from there to Lower Corbett, living on the hill above what is now Corbett Station. Wilbur had 4 children by this marriage, Frances J. (Henkle), b. April 1, 1909, Everett B., b. January 12, 1911, Murray W., b. December 25, 1912 and Melvin L., b. May 17, 1915. When Wilbur and Alice divorced, Melvin went with his mother. Wilbur then married Grace Swalberg, and had two more children with her, Forrest H., who went to Alaska, and Catherine (Riz) who also moved from the area. Wilbur Evans, born in Corbett June 7, 1889, died November 19, 1944, age 55. He lived in SE Portland at the time. Wilbur was a nature lover and was well known for his hobby of studying birds and flowers.

After graduating from CHS, Frances Evans attended the Oregon Normal School and gained certification to teach. She taught in Springdale one year. On June 2, 1929, she married Francis Henkle, born in Aliceville, Kansas on March 12, 1902 (see "William F. Henkle"). The couple made their home in Gresham. She operated a greenhouse and flower shop at Linneman Junction and Powell Boulevard for many years. Frances Henkle took an active role in the affairs of the East Multnomah County Pioneer Association and provided many of the flowers for decorations for the event. She and Francis had two children, Thomas, b. March 26, 1930, and Eleanor, b. March 23, 1932, both in Gresham (see "Thomas L. and Hannah J. Evans," *Pioneer History*).

Everett Evans married Mildred I. Wilde, born in Kansas August 8, 1912. Everett grew up in Corbett, attended local schools and worked for Fred Shearer and Sons in Portland for many years. He and Mildred raised three children, John, b. March 2, 1931 in Louisiana, Ronald, b. June 12, 1937, and Linda, b. February 17, 1942. Ronald and Linda were born in Portland. The family lived on Pounder Grade north of its intersection with Littlepage Road. Everett sold three acres of land to the Dunken family, who lived immediately south on Pounder Grade. John, Ron and Linda attended Corbett schools. Mildred Evans died October 26, 1992. Linda (Evans) Peterson died in an automobile accident June 13, 1970.

Mildred and Everett Evans

Mildred and Everett enjoy a day at the beach. Kenneth Ellis and daughter, Joan, in the background. Photo courtesy of Joan (Ellis) Benner.

Everett now lives with his son and daughter-in-law, Ron and Sandra Evans, on Mannthey Road.

Ron Evans served in the U.S. Navy four years. He married Sandra Childers, who moved to Corbett in 1947. They have a son, Brian, b. May 3, 1959. Ron worked as a diesel mechanic for several years, then went into business for himself, repairing heavy equipment, principally cranes. He is now retired. Sandra worked for Dr. Marshall Brown in Gresham for many years until he retired. She now works for the Adventist Health Group, which took over Dr. Brown's practice. Ron and Sandra purchased 20 acres on Mannthey Road from Ron's Uncle Murray Evans and built a home on the acreage. When Murray and his wife, Stella, retired from the daffodil business, Ron and Sandra took part of their stock. Sandra learned how to hybridize to create new varieties and hopes to develop some that might be prize winners (see "Murray Evans").   *Everett Evans*

Frank J. Fehrenbacher
Josephine (Lampert) Fehrenbacher

Frank Fehrenbacher's father, Joseph, and Joseph's wife, Rosalia (Scheller), were born in Indiana. They moved westward to South Dakota in 1887. Frank, the youngest of eleven children, was born in South Dakota May 6, 1890. When Frank was three years of age, the family moved to Portland, Oregon. They settled in Montavilla where Joseph and the older boys in the family earned a living cutting firewood. In the late 1890's, Joseph moved the family to a section of land between Biggs Junction and Arlington near Early, Oregon, about 7 miles eastward from the mouth of the John Day River. The ranch was adjacent to the Philippi Ranch, and one of Frank's older schoolmates at the one-room school he attended in Early was Leora Philippi (see "Leora Cheney"). The Fehrenbachers stayed on the ranch for about ten years, moving back to Portland when Rosalia had enough of the isolation of the ranch. Frank had quit school after completing grade 5, but resumed his education in Portland, attending the Christian Brothers Business College.

Joseph purchased 20 acres on "cabbage hill" around 1912. The place was located off Wand Road across from the C.W. Post place. Frank moved there to farm the property in 1912. He met and married Josephine Lampert, daughter of Alexander and Julia Lampert, November 18, 1916 (see "Alexander Lampert," *Pioneer History*). Frank worked for the Multnomah County Road Department during the construction of the Columbia River Highway, and was riding on the back of the dump truck loaded with gravel that broke through the Sandy River Bridge at Viking Park. Frank found a splinter buried under his skin near his temple when he arrived home. Charlie Bramhall's arm was broken in the accident, and Jum Mershon was apparently not injured. Two other workers were on the truck when it fell to the river.

Frank and Josephine had two children, Jerome F., b. September 9, 1917, and Evelyn, b. October 30, 1918, before moving to Central Oregon in 1920 to look into buying a ranch near Millican. While living there, Josephine gave birth to a third child, Joseph. Unfortunately, she died October 1, 1922, in childbirth. Joseph lived only 16 months before dying from complications related to measles. Frank moved his family back to the Troutdale farm that winter after the ranch deal fell through.

Jerome started grade school at Pleasant View, completing grades 1 and 2 during the school year 1923-24, the year Pleasant View closed. His father, now a widower, sent Jerome and Evelyn to stay with relatives in Portland, where both attended Catholic schools. After completing grade 5, Jerome returned home, and completed grade school at Corbett. Evelyn remained with relatives, and completed grade school in Portland before returning to the farm. Both attended CHS, Jerome graduating in 1934, and Evelyn in 1937.

After graduating, Jerome worked at various jobs, including a summer in the wheat harvest in Eastern Oregon. He also worked one summer on the horse seine at Rooster Rock for the Kruckmans. Jerome drove the team that his father provided while his father tended net on the skiff. The net had to be stowed in a particular way so that it "played out" properly, and Frank was assigned this task by Harry Kruckman (see "Harry Kruckman"). The seine crew worked for shares, with Mr. Kruckman taking 50%, and the crew receiving 50%. Kruckman furnished the boats, the net, supplies and food; the crew furnished teams of horses and labor. The crew's share was divided equally, each man getting one share, and each team of horses getting one share. Any member of the crew not involved in another job, such as holding up the cork line and keeping the lead line down to keep the salmon from escaping, was expected to wade into the boiling melee of trapped fish to help throw them into the waiting scow.

When Jerome first started, he eagerly jumped into the churning mass to grab a salmon. The experienced hands held back "to watch the fun," Jerome remarked. He took a huge Chinook by the tail, reached below it to give it a heave into the scow when it gave a flip and smacked him a good one on the head. Jerome said, "Do you know a salmon's head is all bone and gristle? That salmon nearly knocked me senseless!" He soon learned from the veterans that the proper method was to turn the fish on its back before giving it a heave into the scow. Fishing that particular summer (pre-dam days) was excellent, and each share earned an average of about $4.00 per day. For the Fehrenbachers, that amounted to $12.00 each day of the fishing season.

Jerome also worked at the planer mill at Bridal Veil until a fire destroyed much of the mill in November 1936. Thereafter, he worked for various farmers, including Johnny Van Speybrock, who grew dahlias, John Seidl, potatoes and cabbage, and Kendall and Parsons, gladiolas.

Later in 1937 he got a job at the Stimpson Lumber Co. in Gaston, Oregon. He and Rod Bates drove to Gaston to start the week, stayed in the crew bunkhouse during the week, ate in the cookhouse and drove home for the weekend. While Jerome was home one weekend, A.D. Kendall, who was the Union Pacific Station Agent in Troutdale, and for whom he had worked earlier, asked him if he was interested in learning the telegraph trade. Because Jerome thought that might provide a better future than the mill's green chain, he accepted the offer. He worked for the Union Pacific Railroad for forty years, progressing from telegraph operator to train dispatcher, safety officer and trainmaster. He worked at various stations, including Troutdale, LaGrande, Pendleton and others, returning to the Portland Station dispatcher's office in 1962. He worked there until his retirement in 1978.

On February 8, 1942, while at the Pendleton Station, Jerome married Kathleen Higgins. Kathleen was born in Hermiston July 24, 1917. The couple had five children: Jerry Ann, b. January 23, 1943; Michael J., b. July 23, 1945; Mary Jo, b. August 30, 1950; Kathleen, b. January 23, 1952; and Daniel M., b. May 17, 1956. Jerry Ann Heaney lives in Sun Valley, Idaho, and has two boys. Michael lives in Haley, Idaho, near Sun Valley, owns a retail paint store and has two boys and a girl. Mary Jo Hunsaker lives in Boring, is married, but has no children. Kathleen Roth lives in Ketchum, Idaho, where she and her husband operate a business selling wood stoves, pellets, hot tubs and related wares. They have two boys. Daniel lives in Edmonds, Washington, has two boys and works for PepsiCo. Jerome's first wife, Kathleen, died February 9. 1991. On May 2, 1992, he married Lenore Durning, a long time acquaintance and widow of a close friend. The couple now lives in SE Portland.

After graduating from CHS, Evelyn went to San Francisco to stay with an aunt. During World War II, she joined the Coast Guard Auxiliary. In 1946, she married a fellow Coast Guardsman, Bruce McCaleb. Mr. McCaleb passed away in 1982. The couple had five children. Evelyn McCaleb continues to live in Phoenix, where she and her family located in 1950.   *Jerome Fehrenbacher*

Henry A. Fehrenbacher
Caroline E. (Stopper) Fehrenbacher

Henry's father, Joseph, and Joseph's wife, Rosalia (Scheller) Fehrenbacher, were born in Indiana. Henry, the 8th child in the family, was also born in Indiana February 13, 1886. When he was about one year of age the family moved to South Dakota. A few years later, when he was seven, they moved to Portland, Oregon. Later, when Henry was in his early teens, the family moved to a ranch near Biggs Junction (see "Frank Fehrenbacher"). When this ranch was sold, he accompanied his parents' back to Portland. After the return to Portland, Henry married Caroline Stopper January 5, 1910, in Portland. Caroline was born in Toledo, Washington May 12, 1890. The couple had returned to Eastern Oregon where their first child, Henry R., was born October 8, 1910, at Condon. Henry (Sr.) had joined his brother, William, on the ranch.

The couple had four more children: Rosalie, b. October 16, 1911; Willamina M., b. January 24, 1914; Robert W., b. July 5, 1919; and Dolores R., b. November 6, 1928. Rosalie and Willamina 'Billie' were born in Portland, Robert 'Bob," in Walla Walla, and Dolores, in Milton-Freewater. Henry, Rosalie, Billie and Bob all started school in a rural school near the ranch. When the family moved to a ranch near Milton-Freewater, the older siblings were of high school age and attended McLaughlin High School in that town. In the early 30's the family moved to a farm on the "hill" located adjacent to Frank Fehrenbacher's place off Wand Road. Henry and Caroline Fehrenbacher purchased some land from Caroline's parents. At the time the two oldest children, Henry and Rosalie, were no longer living at home. Henry was working and attending college and Rosalie had married

The family lived in a small house located on Grandfather Joseph's place while Henry built a new home on the property. Henry farmed the approximate 20-acre place, raising two principal crops, cabbage and certified seed potatoes. The family also had chickens, pigs, a milk cow and a large garden. The youngsters still living at home helped with the chores and the farm work. To supplement the family's income, Henry worked for the Kruckmans during the fishing (seine) season and at the main Portland Post Office over the Christmas holidays. Bob went on to complete grade school at Corbett, then attended CHS, graduating in 1938.

166

Dolores Fehrenbacher

Dolores Fehrenbacher, CHS. Photo, '47 Cohimore courtesy of David Rees.

Dolores attended Corbett Grade School all eight years and completed high school at CHS, graduating in 1947.

Mr. and Mrs. Henry Fehrenbacher left the "hill" in 1951, staying in Philomath for a short time before moving to Portland and then back to the farm. In 1957, due to Mrs. Fehrenbacher's health, they returned to Philomath to stay with Dolores and her family. Caroline Fehrenbacher passed away December 6, 1957. After her death, Henry returned to the farm and sold it about a year later. He then returned to Philomath to live with Dolores and her family until his death, November 27, 1976. Both Henry and his wife, Caroline, are buried at the Forest Lawn Cemetery in Gresham, Oregon.

During World War II, Henry (Jr.) joined the Merchant Marine. Sent to the South Pacific, he was able to visit his younger brother, Bob who was at a base hospital in New Guinea after being wounded in battle. After the war Henry married Helen Jacobs and they had three daughters, Sigrid, Frieda and Gretchen. (Sigrid married Bud Clark, who became the Mayor of Portland, Oregon.) Henry Jr. died in November 1977. Rosalie married Alfred Lewis and they had three children, Alfred, Callie and Diane. After her first husband died, she married George Durrie and they had a birth son, George. Rosalie passed away in July 1990. Billie had completed high school before the family moved to the East County area. She married Terry Gray, with whom she had four sons, Terry, Dan, Bob and Mike. After her first husband's death, Billie married Allan Lewis and they had a daughter, Judy.

After graduating from CHS, Bob worked for his father for a time before enlisting in the Army. He had completed training just before Pearl Harbor and was supposed to have a leave at home. Instead he found himself on a troop transport bound for Australia. He was dispatched to

167

New Guinea, where he was wounded. After being stabilized at a base hospital there, he returned to the States to recuperate further. He was awarded the Purple Heart because of his wounds. After his return, he married Florence Powers and they had one son, Phillip. Bob and his family lived in SE Portland. Bob Fehrenbacher died in September 1992.

As mentioned, Dolores really "grew up" on the "hill." She walked to Wand Road to catch the school bus, which was driven by Alvin Kinney. She remembered the year (1937) when the snow and ice was so bad her father had to pound nails into an old pair of shoes so he could get to the barn to take care of the animals. The snow was so deep that year that the path to the outhouse was "like a tunnel," according to Dolores. Before electricity came in, small candles lighted the family's Christmas tree. Of course family members were very careful and attentive when the candles were lit.

Dolores certainly enjoyed her high school years at CHS. She took an active part in extra-curricular activities such as plays. She performed in two senior class plays (*Miss Smarty* and *Lady, Be Good*) and four student body plays (*Don't Take My Penny, Pigtails, June Mad* and *A Date With Judy*). Since Dolores' father was a farmer, he could obtain gasoline during World War II. He provided gasoline for students who needed it to get to play practice. Mrs. Fehrenbacher enjoyed having teen-agers around, so Dolores had many parties for her high school friends. She remembers a time when two fellow students stole some gasoline from a car, siphoning it from the car's gas tank. They went before a judge and were given a choice – jail or the Army. Both opted for the Army.

Of course living on a farm also involved work. Dolores worked in the fields during the summer months, planting cabbage and potatoes, hoeing and other farm work. She also worked for neighboring farmers, including Ed Klinski and Ferd Lampert. Dolores graduated from CHS in 1947. After graduating she visited her brother, Henry, in Corvallis and met a young man, Henry 'Hank' Gerding. About a year later, July 5, 1948, the couple married. She has lived on a ranch near Philomath, Oregon since. She and her husband have six children: Henry E. III, b. October 13, 1949; Gregory S., b. May 30, 1951; Peggy A., b. June 20, 1953; Timothy A., b. January 11, 1955; Terrence J., b. January 1, 1959; and Thomas P., b. March 28, 1961. Dolores and Hank Gerding celebrated their 50th wedding anniversary July 5, 1998.

Dolores (Fehrenbacher) Gerding

William H. Fehrenbacher
Sarah C. (Fox) Fehrenbacher

William H. 'Will' Fehrenbacher was born in Evansville, Indiana, and moved to Oregon in the 1890's. He met Sarah C. Fox, and the couple married. They homesteaded a place near Gwendolin, Oregon, which is between Arlington and Condon. They had five children: Cecelia M. (Kirsch), b. November 2, 1906; Mary (Bergeron), b. February 13, 1908; Leo, b. May 27, 1910; George, b. November 1, 1914; and Rita (Rodgers), b. November 27, 1920. The oldest three children were born in Gwendolin and the younger two, in Lowden, Washington. From Gwendolin the family first moved to Milton Freewater, then to Lowden where they located on a 1500-acre wheat ranch. All of the children spent some (or all) of their grade school years at Lowden Grade School. William, together with Frank and two other of his brothers, went to Bend, Oregon in 1920 to look into buying the Smith Brothers' Ranch. However, the deal fell through when they found it heavily mortgaged, and Will returned to the ranch in Lowden.

Two of the girls, Cecelia and Mary, graduated from St. Mary's Academy in Walla Walla. Both then attended the Oregon College of Education in Monmouth and became teachers. After Cecelia graduated in 1928, she taught three years at rural schools, including one near McMinnville. She applied then at Springdale Grade School, and taught there for a period of 8 years (1933-41). June (Bates) Law said, "She was the best teacher I ever had. The kids just worshiped her." She taught at Troutdale, and then at Powellhurst Grade School. She met John J. Kirsch of McMinnville, and they married in 1943. She invited her "Springdale kids" to the wedding. She had two sons, John, b. February 14, 1945, and Richard, b. April 18, 1947. When her boys had enrolled in school, Cecelia found herself back in the classroom at St. James parochial school, where she taught another eight years. At a Springdale School reunion, held at the Corbett Fire Hall in the late 80's, Mrs. Kirsch (Miss Fehrenbacher) came, and, according to June, "looked 30 years younger than her years."

Will Fehrenbacher sold the wheat ranch in the early 30's, and moved to Springdale. First, he leased Herman Blazer's dairy farm on Seidl Road. After a few years, he purchased a 20-acre place located on Seidl Road at its intersection with Haines (now Ogden) Road. He built a house, and his family lived there several years. While she taught in Springdale, his daugh-

169

Cecilia Fehrenbacher

Cecilia Fehrenbacher at Springdale
Grade School, where she taught from
1933-1941. Photo courtesy of Grace
(Kerslake) Stolin.

ter, Cecelia, lived there also. Will's son, George Fehrenbacher, completed
grade school at Corbett, and graduated from CHS in 1933. Leo also joined
the family at the Troutdale address. George and Leo took over the lease
of the Blazer Farm for a time, but both decided to try farming. Leo purchased a place on Seidl Road (which Howard Winters later purchased),
and George purchased a place on Seidl Road (later purchased by John
Seidl). When Leo sold to Howard, he purchased a ranch in Central Oregon near Terrebonne. Leo Fehrenbacher married Lillian Keyes, and they
have six children, three boys and three girls. George later sold his place
and moved to Central Oregon, also. He married Lucille Berney, daughter of Charlie Berney, and they have two children, a son, Douglas, and a
daughter, Kay. When George retired, he and Lucille purchased a home in
Prineville, where Lucille makes her home. George died in 1992.

Cecelia (Fehrenbacher) Kirsch

William J. Fehrenbacher
Helen L. (Strahm) Fehrenbacher

William J. "Bill" Fehrenbacher was born on a wheat ranch near Early, Oregon, August 16, 1900 (see Frank Fehrenbacher). He was the third of eleven children. When his grandfather, Joseph Fehrenbacher, sold the ranch, his father, Joseph Jr., moved his family to Lowden, Washington, to continue wheat ranching there. Bill had started school in Early, and completed his grade and high school years at Lowden. After completing school, Bill's work frequently took him out of town. During one of his trips, his young sister, Helen, wrote to him about her teacher, Miss Strahm, who was "really nice." Bill decided he wanted to meet her, and they met on a wintry day at an ice pond to go skating. Bill and Miss Strahm started dating, but didn't marry then, as times were tough.

Helen L. Strahm was born in Dayton, Washington October 14, 1906. She attended a one-room school in Dayton her grade school years, and completed high school in Walla Walla. After graduating, she attended Eastern Washington State College in Cheney for two years, obtaining a teaching certificate. Her first job was in Lowden, where she taught for two years, 1925-27. She not only met her future husband there, she also taught his younger siblings, Joe, Margaret and Helen, and met Rosalie, Leo and Henry, who attended Lowden High School. Helen moved to Rosalind and then Centralia, Washington, where she taught for the next six years (1927-33). On June 6, 1933, she married Bill Fehrenbacher.

Bill had a garage business in Troutdale, Oregon, located approximately where the Troutdale City Hall now stands. Helen did not teach for a couple of years, but started at Troutdale Grade in 1935 when asked to do so by the Principal. The couple rented a beautiful home located on the south side of the Sandy River (across from what is now Tad's Restaurant) for $12.00 per month. In 1939, they could have purchased the home from Mrs. Ball, the owner, for $2,950.00, but Helen said, "We were worried that we couldn't make the payments." Instead they purchased a large lot (2.5 acres) on Mershon Road. The prior owner had started to build a house on the property, but it was not finished. With help from Mr. Leslie Emerson, Bill put a basement under it. During the next year, Bill and Helen worked weekends and evenings to make the place habitable and moved there in 1940. The property had a good stand of timber, which, when sold, helped pay for the improvements.

Corbett Staff Members

From L, Ruth Sommerville, Helen Fehrenbacher, Paul Goddard. Photo (excerpt) courtesy of Joan Benner.

The Fehrenbachers loved to travel. A neighbor had found gold in a mine in Mexico, and received a permit to do further exploratory work. He invited the Fehrenbachers to accompany he and his wife on this adventure, which they were pleased to be able to do. The two couples traveled into the mountains near Chihuahua, Mexico, reaching the end of the road and traveling by packhorses to reach the mine. Unfortunately, Bill became ill, which ended this escapade, but Helen indicated this was just one of the adventures experienced by them. They traveled Mexico extensively by trailer or motorhome, where she said, they did much fishing, and where "I got my marlin!"

Over the years they motored throughout the United States, Canada and Alaska, and took several trips abroad.

When World War II erupted, Bill went to work for Hammond Construction Company, which had a contract on the aluminum plant under construction in Troutdale. Promoted, he eventually became the Company's supervisor of concrete jobs, and worked for them 28 years. At the invitation of Mr. George Lusby, Principal of Corbett Grade, Mrs. Fehrenbacher moved to that school to teach in 1943. She finished her teaching career at Corbett, retiring in 1965 when her husband retired from his position. The couple had purchased a cabin in Willapa, Washington, and spent much time there the 17 years they owned it. Bill Fehrenbacher passed away September 24, 1993, age 93. Helen sold the home on Mershon Road, and now lives in Gresham Manor. She will be remembered by all of her former students who were in her capable hands during the twenty plus years she taught in this community. When asked what they recalled about Mrs. Fehrenbacher, several mentioned that she taught shop. Sandra (Childers) Evans said, "She taught us how to use a hammer, a saw and other tools. She gave us confidence that we could take the tools in hand, and get the job done!"

Helen Fehrenbacher

Arthur Groce
Edith (Lidgate) Groce

Arthur 'Art' and Ray Groce purchased the Springdale store across from the grade school from Raleigh True in 1923 (using, in Art's case, savings his wife had accumulated). Art was born in Raymond, Washington, October 31, 1890, son of Earnest and Carrie Groce. Earnest was working as a sawyer for a mill in Raymond at the time. Later the family moved to Portland, where Earnest worked as a sawyer for the large Eastern-Western Mill. Art's youngest brother, Clyde, was born after the family moved to Portland. Art married Edith Lidgate, of Basin, Montana, born February 12, 1896. Art's parents moved to a farm on Christensen Road at about the same time that Art and Ray purchased the grocery store. Clyde Groce built a service station around the corner from the grocery soon after Art purchased the property. Art Groce bought out his brother Ray's interest approximately a year after the original purchase.

Art Groce had an extensive credit business in the store. Each credit customer had an account book in which sales were recorded together with the balance due. The author's parents would often send him to Groce's store with a list of items to buy. Then one said, "charge it," and was on his way, groceries in hand. Given the family's circumstances, we were fortunate to have this arrangement. On one occasion Louis Baker got a contract to supply cordwood to a buyer from Portland, who was to pay $3.00 per cord (f.o.b.). Louis hired a crew to cut the wood for $2.00 per cord. After the first week, the buyer picked up the first loads and paid cash. The second week the buyer didn't show up. Louis kept his crew cutting wood. Finally, Louis realized that his buyer had reneged on the contract. He told the story to Art Groce, who told Louis, "Have your workers come in. I'll give them groceries for the amount you owe them, and you can pay me when you get the money." Needless to say, the Bakers continued as loyal customers for years thereafter.

Another customer, Bill Wright, was building a new home in Springdale. He asked Art to extend the time period for payment of his bill as he was building on a pay-as-you-go basis. Art gladly did so as he knew Bill Wright would take care of the obligation. It's probably safe to say that Art Groce carried many families through some difficult times during the depression.

Art Groce's Springdale Store

Art Groce purchased this store from Raleigh True in 1923. George Shelley's feed store was located where the sliding door shows on the right.

Another view of Art Groce's store in the 20's.

Photos courtesy of Bob Groce.

Art and Edith Groce owned approximately 300 acres of land toward Aims, beyond the Baker place. He purchased 100 acres at a tax sale, and accumulated adjacent parcels over the years. Some were purchased and some were acquired when the owners turned over the property to settle debts for groceries. Art continued to operate the store into the early 40's. At that time he turned it over to LaVern Van Ausdel, who managed it for a time. Later H.P. Lewis leased the store after the Van Ausdels left and continued its operation until 1958. Mr. and Mrs. Doyle Staples then leased the building until it burned in 1962. When it burned, a room full of Raleigh True's belongings burned with it. He had paid $10.00 a month to Art Groce to store the items in an upstairs room after he sold the business to Art and Edith Groce in 1923. Unfortunately, the items, some of great value, were still in the room when the fire destroyed the building, according to Bob Groce.

The Groce's living quarters were located in the 2nd story of the building. Bob Groce attended school at Springdale Grade School, completing 8 years there in 1936. He then attended CHS from which he graduated in 1940. After graduation, Bob attended the Oregon Technical Institute, completing a course in automotive and diesel mechanics. He then went to work in a machine shop, Premier Gear. On March 25, 1944, he enlisted in the Army Air Corps and was accepted into the air cadet program. He was still in training when the war ended and was discharged in November 1945. He married Donna Davis of LaGrande, who was born September 14, 1927. The couple had two children, Linda, b. July 12, 1945 and Nancy, b. September 13, 1954. The two girls attended school in Parkrose where Bob and Donna Groce settled after the War. Donna Groce passed away February 24, 1984. Later, Bob married Betty (Baker) Groce, widow of his cousin, Tom Groce. The couple now lives in Gresham.

When Art leased the store, he moved to a house at 33rd and NW Vaughn, which his parents had built in 1905. Art paid off the mortgage on the property in 1942. He rented a building at 22nd and NW Thurman and established a 2nd hand store. He purchased bankrupt and fire stock for resale. Eventually he opened four such establishments. Art Groce died during the summer in 1955. His wife, Edith, passed away in the summer of 1987.   *Bob Groce*

Clyde Groce
Bertha (Zilm) Groce

Clyde Groce purchased the property upon which he built a service station from his brother, Arthur 'Art' Groce. The station was located in Springdale on the Columbia River Highway adjacent to Art's grocery store. Clyde, son of Earnest and Carrie Groce, was born in Portland May 1, 1898. He married Bertha Zilm, who was born in Portland March 28, 1899. The couple opened the station in the early 20's shortly after Art and Ray Groce purchased the grocery store and adjoining property from Raleigh True in 1923. When the station opened, Clyde was a dealer for 'Gilmore' gasoline. Later he became a Union Oil dealer.

Clyde and Bertha had two children: Thomas 'Tom,' b. June 15, 1925; and Mary Lou, b. May 20, 1929. Both attended and graduated from Springdale Grade School, which was nearly across the road from their parents' business establishment. Tom attended high school in Portland, graduating from Benson Tech in 1943. Mary Lou attended CHS from which she graduated in 1946.

Shortly after completing high school, Tom Groce was drafted into the United States Army. After undergoing the tests and evaluations given to inductees, he was assigned to the U.S. Army Air Corps for flight training. While he was in cadet training, priorities changed and he was reassigned to gunnery school. After completing training, he was sent to England where he was assigned to a B-17 bomber group as a tail gunner. His unit conducted bombing raids over Germany. When he had completed his requisite "missions," and after hostilities ended, he returned to the States, where he received his honorable discharge.

Shortly after his return, Tom had an opportunity to serve as a substitute mail carrier for Bill Wright out of the Troutdale Post Office. He soon obtained a full-time position as a postal clerk in the Troutdale station. He was promoted to Assistant Postmaster before taking a rural route. Later he became a rural mail carrier working out of the Corbett Post Office. Tom married Elizabeth 'Betty' Baker January 30, 1949. Betty was born September 29, 1931, lived in the East County area and attended Rockwood and Lusted Grade Schools. She graduated from Gresham High School in

Clyde Groce's Springdale Service Station

Clyde Groce's station sits to the right of Ernie Groce's stand and store.

Photo courtesy of Bob Groce.

1949. The couple had three children: Michelle, b. December 16, 1949; Gail, b. May 16, 1951; and Jacqueline 'Jackie,' b. June 15, 1960.

After Tom's father, Clyde Groce, died November 29, 1959, Tom and Betty purchased the family service station business from Tom's mother. When Tom's grandfather, Earnest, passed away, the 'Log Cabin Grocery' building was torn down and Tom and Betty purchased the property. They built a house located approximately where the grocery stood. Tom and Betty's children attended Corbett Schools, Michelle graduating from Corbett High School in 1968, Gail, in 1969, and Jackie, in 1978. Michelle is married to Tim LeDoux and lives in Portland. Gail married Mike O'Neil, had two children, a son who died, and a daughter, Megan. Gail and Mike live in Corbett. Jackie is married to Chris Grosek, has one girl, Annie, and lives in Troutdale.

Tom and Betty operated the service station (except for a short interval) until Tom was diagnosed with cancer in 1988. Thereafter the station was leased to Albert Kimbley until the government decreed that the station's gasoline storage tanks had to be replaced. Rather than undertake that task, Betty decided to close the station. Eventually the site was sold to Mark Kruckman, Rob Kruckman's son (See "Harry Kruckman"). Tom died of cancer August 5, 1988. Betty has since married Tom's cousin, Robert 'Bob' Groce and lives in Gresham.

After graduating from CHS, Mary Lou Groce obtained a job with Meier and Frank Company in Portland. She met Robert 106Hallwyler, who owned a small printing company, Hallwyler Printing, in Portland. A

177

Mary Lou Groce

Mary Lou Groce, CHS graduate. '46 Cohimore photo courtesy of David Rees.

Springdale Friends

Front, L to R: Michelle Groce, Gail Groce, Becky Law. Rear, Lynne Law. Photo courtesy of June Law.

former marine and Portland native, b. May 19, 1926, he had just returned from occupation duty in Japan. He was a member of the 5th Marine Division, which served as the 'spearhead' division for the invasion of Okinawa. The couple married April 24, 1948. Hallwyler Printing eventually merged into the printing business, Graphics Arts Center, in which Robert was a partner. He sold his interest in the business in 1987, and retired. Mary Lou and Robert have three children: Fred, b. January 22, 1952; Wendy, b. June 10, 1954; and Rick, b. May 8, 1961. Mary Lou became a homemaker, caring for and raising her three children. The children attended Riverside Grade School and Putnam High School. Mary Lou and Robert continue to live in Milwaukie, Oregon, which has been their home for the past 48 years.

Betty (Baker) Groce and Mary Lou (Groce) Hallwyler

Earnest Groce
Carrie (Matteson) Groce

Ernie Groce in his Springdale Store during WWII.
Photo courtesy of Bob Groce

Earnest and Carrie Groce moved to Springdale to a farm that later became part of the Weatherly holdings. Formerly Earnest was employed as a sawyer in a Raymond, Washington sawmill and also worked as a sawyer at the large Eastern-Western mill in Portland. Mr. Groce wanted to stay in Portland, but Mrs. Groce insisted on a place in the country. She prevailed, and Mr. Groce later agreed that hers was the better choice. They produced vegetables on the farm, and set up a stand in Springdale on property owned by their son, Arthur. The business prospered, and they gradually enlarged the operation. When prohibition ended, the Groces built an addition to their 'stand' to put in a tavern. The location was just far enough from the Springdale Grade School to be legal. However, Mrs. Groce was not too happy in that business, so it was later closed. The business evolved into a grocery store and candy shop. Mr. and Mrs. Groce built a structure for the business, which they named the 'Log Cabin Grocery.'

Earnest and Carrie Groce had four boys: Arthur, b. October 31, 1890, Ray, b. 18, Eustes, b. 18, and Clyde, b. May 1, 1898. Arthur 'Art' owned a grocery store in Springdale (see "Arthur Groce"). Clyde owned a service station in Springdale (see "Clyde Groce"). Ray was a partner in the Springdale store for about a year. After WWII, Eustes lived in Springdale in a place adjacent to the Log Cabin Grocery for a short period of time.

Earnest Groce passed away February 26, 1951, having been seriously ill for several months.   *Bob Groce*

179

William F. Henkle
Della (Rooney) Henkle

William F. and Della Henkle came to the Northwest in 1903. After their arrival, one of Henkle's first jobs involved working for a contractor who participated in the preparation of the site for the 1905 World's Fair (Lewis and Clark Centennial Exposition) in Portland. In November 1905, William Henkle signed a lease to rent the 142-acre Haynes place on Ogden Road, of which 27 acres was in cultivation. The terms for the first 11 months were: "$155.00 in gold, 10 sacks of spuds and 6 boxes of good sound winter apples." The lease period was from January 1, 1906 to November 30, 1906.

The Henkles had three children, Francis R., b. March 17, 1902 (in Kansas), Maude M., b. January 4, 1904 (in Portland) and Rosetta W., b. August 31, 1909 (in Troutdale). Mr. Henkle, who came from a farm family in Kansas, began raising such crops as potatoes, hay and grain, and livestock, including pigs, calves and cattle. The lease was renewed thereafter each December 1. While still leasing the Haynes place (June 5, 1909), Henkle purchased a 40-acre farm in Springdale. After the purchase, he continued to farm the rented place though he commenced construction of a home on the Springdale property. His 'calendar' entries include references to working at the "place" clearing brush (July 1, 1909: "Went to place to slash") to building (August 16: "Went to place to see Kerslake about hauling lumber"). From mid-August to early October 1909, Henkle worked on the house pouring a foundation, among other tasks. His entries mention, "Harding helped," referring to Mr. Harding, a neighbor who lived on Woodard Road.

During 1910 and 1911, as farm work on the 'hill' permitted, Henkle continued to work at the Springdale place. Apparently, Mr. Henkle also helped his neighbors in bringing phone service to the Pleasant View area during this period. A 'calendar' entree March 2, 1910 reads: "Went to telephone meeting" and another March 27, 1910 continued: "Built telephone wire.") The phone wires at this time were strung on whatever was handy, fence posts, trees, etc.

In December 1911, the family began to move ('calendar' entree December 27: "Loaded hogs and brought them to the place." December 28 and 29 entries: "Brought range and machine to the place in Curry's hack,"

180

Henkle Home under Construction

Della Henkle stands beside the New Henkle Home in Springdale. Photo courtesy of Rosetta (Henkle) Heitzman.

and "Brought load to place.") Once established at the Springdale farm, Henkle continued to raise crops similar to those grown on the Haynes place. He also cleared more land for cultivation and put in fences. Numerous 'calendar' entries in 1914 indicated that he worked on the construction of the Columbia River Highway. The usual notation was "On road." For this work he received $2.25 to $2.50 per day, or $5.00 per day when he worked with his team. An interesting notation to the author was the entry of February 9, 1914, which read: "Chased coyote with Mershon (on our way) to Troutdale."

In the spring of 1916, William Henkle's father asked him to return to Kansas and take over management of the home place as the elderly Henkle's health was failing. Therefore, on June 28, 1916, the Henkles auctioned off most of their belongings, leased the farm and returned to Kansas. (A sample of the items sold included a kitchen cabinet for $3.50, sold to J.C. Wilson (the author's grandfather); 3 leather and 1 cane chair for $3.00 to Ralph Rogers; a dresser for $5.25 to Charles Berney; two couches and a mattress for $2.25 to Evo Speybrock; a mattock and a round shovel for $.75 to Louis Mershon. More expensive items included a cream separator for $38.00, to S.R. Kitzmiller; a black and white cow for $50.00 to R.W. Larson; a 6-year old black gelding for $110.00 to Jim Pounder; a 9-year old black gelding for $80.00 to J.C. Wilson; a spotted cow for $39.00 to Art Johnson; and a bay gelding for $39.00 to Robert Kerslake. Two red pigs went for $3.70 each to Fred Etling while R.W. Larson obtained 3 white pigs for $3.00 each.) As Rosetta recounted the experience in Kansas, she said her father quickly found that "he and his father didn't see eye to eye." After a few short months, the Henkles left Kansas, headed west once again.

Grain Harvest c1914

Bill Henkle works an Ox team binding grain.
Photo courtesy of Rosetta (Henkle) Heitzman.

Raking Hay

Bill Henkle raking hay at his Springdale farm.
Photo courtesy of Rosetta (Henkle) Heitzman.

Since the Springdale farm was leased for three years, the family settled in Yakima, Washington when Henkle obtained work there. Della, Francis and Maude found work in the orchards picking fruit. In 1919, the Henkles returned to East Multnomah County, staying with the Charlie Bramhall family until the tenant vacated the Springdale farm. Once re-established on the farm, Mr. Henkle apparently decided to concentrate on raising chickens. He continued raising other crops, but his 'calendar' entries clearly reflect this new emphasis. June 19, 1922: "Took broilers and eggs to town (Portland). February 17, 1923: "Took seven cases of eggs to

Thrashing Machine

The thrashing crew visits the Henkle farm.

Steam Tractor for Thrashing

Power for the thrashing machine was supplied by this steam tractor. Francis and Maude Henkle stand by a front wheel.

Photos courtesy of Rosetta (Henkle) Heitzman.

Portland." February 22, 1923: "Went to Portland with eggs." During the 20's the Henkles built up an impressive poultry business. Several 'hen' houses were constructed as well as a place to kill and dress broilers.

Although the family worked hard, recreation had its place. In August 1923, relatives visited from Kansas. William Henkle hired a guide and he, Francis, Maude and some relatives "climbed to the top of old Mt. Hood." Occasionally, Henkle worked as a carpenter. For example, starting September 6, 1920, he worked for Hugh Reeves, who was building a

Henkle Place Planted to Gladiolas, c 1937

Kendall and Parson's raised gladiolas on the Henkle Place. Note the 'hen' houses in the background, reflecting the Henkle's principal farming activity in the 20's and early 30's.

Photo courtesy of Rosetta (Henkle) Heitzman.

Gladiolas for the Floral Trade

From L, Arnold Lampert, A.D. Kendall, Clarence Parsons, Jess Coons and Roy Malcolm cut and load gladiolas at the Henkle place. Note Bates' barn in the background.

Photo courtesy of Rosetta (Henkle) Heitzman.

The Henkle Home

The Henkle Home as it appeared after remodeling, c1939.

The Henkle Family

From L, Francis, Rosetta, William Henkle, Della Henkle and Maude.
Photos courtesy of Rosetta Heitzman.

new home on the Columbia River Highway (on the corner opposite from the point where Smith Road intersects the highway). He worked for Hugh Reeves for more than a month.

Of the Henkles three children, Francis attended Pleasant View and Maude started school there as well. After the move to the "place," the youngsters attended Springdale Grade School. When the family returned to Springdale in 1919, Francis had completed high school in Yakima. Maude enrolled at the Behnke-Walker Business College in Portland and Rosetta, who had been attending school in Yakima, completed grade school at Springdale. Rosetta then enrolled at CHS, from which she graduated in 1928.

The Henkle place was sold in 1947. The family had rented it to others for some years. In 1937, Kendall and Parsons rented the place as an ideal location for gladiolas. William Henkle, who was active in the Grange movement and the Masonic Order, died April 29, 1948. Della (Rooney) Henkle passed away August 25, 1964.

After Francis Henkle visited a relative in Coos Bay who was an electrician, he came home with an idea that he should learn that trade. He had an opportunity to work with Mr. Mendenhall at the Bridal Veil mill, which heightened his interest even more. He decided to complete a program to become an electrician and traveled to Chicago to attend a trade school. Upon his return, he took over a shop in Springdale. The 1931

185

Cohimore carried this advertisement: "Francis R. Henkle, Licensed Electrical Contractor. Radio, House Wiring, General Electrician, Radio and Electrical Supplies."

June 2, 1929, Francis Henkle married Frances Evans, daughter of Wilbur and Alice (Neely) Evans (see "Thomas L. and Hannah J. Evans," *Pioneer History*). The couple had two children, Thomas R., b. March 26, 1930 and Eleanor A., b. March 29, 1932. As a licensed electrician, Francis found employment in that trade during his lifetime. After the couple moved to Gresham, Frances operated a flower shop at the junction of Linnemann Road and Powell Boulevard for many years. Francis Henkle died July 20, 1977; Frances (Evans) Henkle passed away February 10, 1982. Maude Henkle married Fred Hicks, b. May 21, 1894, in Palmer. The couple had two children, Meridell, b. April 13, 1927 and Willis, b. April 11, 1928. Maude Henkle passed away April 26, 1998.

After graduating from CHS in 1928, Rosetta Henkle completed a general business course at the Northwestern School of Commerce. She paid her school expenses by becoming a 'mother's helper.' After completing the course, Neidermeyer and Martin Lumber Company employed her as a bookkeeper. Driving out Stark Street one evening, she lost control of her vehicle and had an accident. After missing a few days work because of her injuries, she found herself out of a job. One of the families for whom she worked came to her rescue and helped her get a job at Woolworth's. During the depression she lost this job because, as her boss explained, "You're single, can live at home and others need a job more than you."

In 1932, Rosetta obtained a position with the Western Oregon Lumber Company as a bookkeeper, a position she kept until her marriage to Murray Heitzman September 30, 1938. Murray's father worked at the Ridge Lumber Company and the family lived in mill housing there. Murray Heitzman owned a body shop in Gresham, which did much work for McRobert Ford. In addition to operating his own shop, he worked for Fanchers and McRoberts. During the war years, Rosetta worked at Portland General Electric as cashier and bookkeeper.

In 1946, with a start from an uncle and at the urging of Roy Malcolm, Rosetta and Murray went into the gladiola business, buying bulbs and raising flowers. They had a place in West Gresham on Powell and later, 5 acres at Linnemann Junction. From 1959 to 1962, Rosetta worked in the offices of Marckx Bakery in Gresham. Later Murray and Rosetta

The Heitzmans

Rosetta (Henkle) Heitzman, Murray Heitzman and their son, William.
Photo courtesy of Rosetta (Henkle) Heitzman.

purchased farmland in Boring, and continued raising gladiolas at that location. Rosetta and Murray had three children, William M., b. July 17, 1946, David A., b. November 26, 1949 and Elizabeth D., b. July 1, 1952. Murray Heitzman passed away February 2, 1992. Currently Rosetta (Henkle) Heitzman lives in an apartment at her son, William's home in Boring.   *Rosetta (Henkle) Heitzman*

Springdale Grade School c1938.
Photo courtesy of Rosetta Henkle.

Willis G. Hicks
Mary (Crowston) Hicks

Willis Hicks married Mary Crowston in 1893 (see *Pioneer History*, "Willis G. Hicks"). The Hicks family settled on a tract of land near Chanticleer Point, which had been purchased from Mary's parents in 1898. Their children included Fred, b. May 21, 1894, Charles, b. Mary 9, 1897, Arthur, b. March 28, 1899, Clarence, b. March 31, 1904 and Laura, b. June 1, 1914. All attended Mountain Grade except Fred, who started at Brower, and Laura, who attended both Mountain and Corbett Grade. Willis Hicks operated a donkey engine in Brower, Palmer and Bridal Veil, and worked on the construction of the Columbia River Highway. Willis Hicks died of pneumonia in 1916 when Laura was an infant and Mrs. Hicks carried on with raising her family with the help of the older youngsters. Fred operated the farm until he moved in the mid 20's. From that time until 1935 a hired man known as "Ashby" ran the farm.

Fred Hicks worked on the construction of the Larch Mountain Road. He married Maude Henkle and they had two children, Maridell and Willis. When his mother moved to Eugene in 1935, Fred returned to the farm and operated it until it was sold in 1941. Charles served in the Army during World War I and died of influenza in Tours, France in 1919. Arthur moved to Canada in his early 20's and settled there. Clarence Hicks operated a garage on the Columbia River Highway adjacent to the Ross store (near the intersection of Knieriem Road with the highway). He married Irene Knieriem and they moved to Modesto, California. They had one son, Donald.

Laura graduated from CHS in 1932. In 1931, she got a car, which gave her and her friends an opportunity to take many "outings." They became known as "The Holy Seven." After graduation she attended Northwest Christian College for two years. Mary Hicks moved to Eugene in 1935 to be with Laura and passed away about a year later (1936). Laura married Byron Boyles in Eugene March 9, 1937. The couple had four children, Laurance, b. July 27, 1938, Clifford, b. February 16, 1940, Marcia, b. March 15, 1947 and David, b. April 11, 1949. Both Laurance and Clifford attended Corbett High for a time, but graduated from Benson Tech in Portland. Laura married Chester A. Heman of Portland May 3, 1953. He passed away March 13, 1994. Laura lived with her daughter, Marcia Mathieu in Sequim, Washington until her death early this year (1999).

The Hicks Home c1898

From L, Willis Hicks, Frank Hicks, Mary (Crowston) Hicks, William Crowston – Children: Fred W. Hicks, Charles E. Hicks. This home sat across from Chanticleer Point.
Photo courtesy of Laura Hicks

The Hicks Family

Rear from L, Fred and Charles Hicks. Front, Arthur, Laura, Mary and Clarence Hicks.
Photo courtesy of Marcia Mathieu.

189

Hicks Home c1921

The Hicks Home after it was remodeled in 1921.

Photo courtesy of Laura Hicks.

Corbett c1932

From L, Eva Barker, Ruth Berney and Clarice Mishey stand beside Laura Hicks' automobile. Note Woodle's Corbett Hardware and Arneson's across the highway. Photo courtesy of Laura Hicks.

Laura Hicks

Photo courtesy of Mickey Chamberlain.

William Jackson
Emma (Peterson) Jackson

William 'Bill' Jackson was born in Butte, Montana. After he came to Oregon, he met and married Emma Peterson, b. September 1, 1893, daughter of Ernest F. Peterson (see "Descendants of Ernest F.C. Peterson and Emma Barbara Peterson," *Pioneer History*). They lived off Ogden Road at its intersection with Woodard Road (on what is now Springhill Road). The Jackson's raised vegetable crops, chiefly cabbage and cauliflower. They had two sons, Walter, b. October 19, 1914, and Frank, b. September 30, 1916. Both attended Pleasant View Grade School until it closed, then finished at Corbett Grade. Walter graduated from CHS in 1933; Frank, who served as Student Body President, in 1934. Both also attended Pacific University.

From L, Mr. Walter Jackson and Mrs. Joy Perry. '47 Cohimore Photo (excerpt) courtesy of David Rees.

Walter Jackson majored in science at college, and also completed course work to become a teacher. He married Helen Wehrley and they have three children, Donald, who is an electrical engineer, Harold, who is a physician, and Nancy, who is a schoolteacher. Mr. Jackson taught at Gold Beach before returning to Columbian High as a teacher in 1947. At CHS he taught science courses and became head basketball coach. He left Corbett in 1952 to take a position as principal in Falls City. Later he took an administrative position with a School District near Sacramento, California. He earned his doctorate in education at the University of Colorado in 1963. Currently, Mr. and Mrs. Jackson live in Rio Linda, California, near Sacramento.

Frank Jackson earned a doctorate in chemistry at the University of Pittsburgh. He worked as a research chemist for Proctor and Gamble Corporation, Cincinnati, Ohio. Frank Jackson, according to an item in the October 2, 1951 *Cardinal*, "is working in the field of radio isotopes-atomic energy, in the research laboratories of Proctor and Gamble at Ivorydale, Ohio."

Arthur F. Johnson
Geneva (Wright) Johnson

Arthur 'Art' Johnson, son of Anderson F. and Amanda M. Johnson, was born in Hurlburt November 10, 1882. His sisters included Iphi, Geneva, Exenia and Catherine; his brothers were Homer and Morris (see "Descendants of Anderson Foster Johnson and Amanda Melvin Johnson," *Pioneer History*). Arthur worked at various mills including a mill located in Clatskanie early in the century. He purchased 40 acres on Loudon Road adjacent to the Emily place after attaining his majority. Art married Mabel Evans July 2, 1907 and a son, Orval K., was born August 30, 1909. Mabel Johnson passed away in May of 1914 from tuberculosis.

Art Johnson added 60 acres to the original 40 he had purchased earlier, including the 40-acre Garbarino place on Loudon, 10 acres from the Phillips and 10 acres from the Emilys, which gave him 100 acres to farm. Art was always active in community affairs. Elected to the Board of Directors, Hurlburt School District, he was serving in 1914 when a new teacher, Geneva Wright, was hired for a three-month period that year. Miss Wright came to Hurlburt from Powell Valley, where she had started her teaching career. Art Johnson married Geneva Wright September 23, 1915. She was born May 30, 1895, a descendant of two pioneer families. On her maternal side, the Wilkes family came around Mt. Hood with the Barlow party in 1845. On her paternal side, the Wright family settled in Powell Valley in 1880. Art and Geneva had three children, Margaret, b. September 16, 1916, Arlene, b. August 17, 1919 and Ross, b. September 30, 1925.

During World War I, Art worked at the Cameron Hogg Mill in Aims and his family lived in mill housing during that period. He returned to farming in 1920. Later, Art worked at the Ridge Lumber Company on Gordon Creek Road as a "turn down" man, which involves guiding logs onto the carriage track on the ramp that takes logs from the millpond into the mill for processing. During this era, the Johnson dairy supplied milk to mill workers and to cooks at the company cookhouse. The Johnsons established and maintained a dairy herd until 1956. The Johnsons also raised other crops, such as cucumbers, which became a 'cash' crop during the depression.

Johnson Family c1916

Rear, L to R: Catherine, Xenia, Arthur, Iphi. Front: Morris and Homer.

Cameron-Hogg Mill Housing c1920

Margaret Johnson plays 'horse' behind Cameron-Hogg mill housing in Aims.
Photos courtesy of Arlene (Johnson) Marble

Ridge Lumber Company

'Turn-down' Art Johnson, L, and 'pond-man' Vern Pitts took the logs from the pond to the saws.   Photo courtesy of Ross Johnson

Both Margaret and Arlene started school at Hurlburt Grade School, transferring to Corbett Grade School when Hurlburt consolidated with Corbett in 1929. Margaret completed grade 8 at Corbett and Arlene started in grade 6. Shortly after the consolidation, Corbett School District hired Geneva Johnson as school clerk, a position she held until she retired in 1961, serving 32 years. Later she worked in the Corbett Grade School cafeteria for four years. Ross attended Corbett schools grades 1-12. Each of the three youngsters graduated from CHS, Margaret in 1934, Arlene in 1936 and Ross in 1943. Ross served as Student Body President his senior year, 1942-43. According to Arlene, even though she sometimes worked outside the home, Geneva Johnson always considered herself a homemaker. She enjoyed needlework. In her later years she worked at Camp Menucha. Arthur Johnson died July 24, 1955; Geneva (Wright) Johnson passed away May 11, 1995.

Orval Johnson lived with his Aunt Exenia 'Xene' (Johnson) Knighton many of his childhood years. Xene's first marriage was to William Maffett of Latourell, and they had one son, Harold. William Maffett owned a lumber mill in the Brower area. Later Xene married Sigardland 'Sig' Knighton, who was a barber. The family moved several times, which meant Orval attended many different schools. When the highway came

194

At the Farm

Rear, L to R: Anna Johnson, Art Johnson, Margaret (Johnson) Warren and Elsie Warren. Front, Jean Warren, Albert Warren and Ross Johnson. Photo courtesy of Ross Johnson.

through Corbett, Sig and Xene built a small store, barber shop and confectionery about a mile west of Corbett. The 1924 *Cohimore* carried this ad: "Knighton's Confectionery and Grocery, one mile west of CHS. Barber shop in connection. A good place to trade." (The store was located on the south side of the Columbia River Highway about where Mershon Road now intersects with the highway.) Later, Knightons moved to a location in Corbett across from Rickert's garage. In addition to groceries, the Knightons sold sandwiches and light drinks. In 1926 the Corbett store was sold to the Arnesons (who purchased Roy Anderson's store to the west shortly thereafter). Exenia Knighton died in 1929.

Orval Johnson married Olive Rich and the couple had four children: Leona C., b. September 29, 1931, Arnold A., b. December 13, 1932, Orval K. 'Keith,' b. June 1, 1944, and Robert S., b. December 16, 1946. The family lived on Loudon Road when Leona and Arnold were small. Leona remembers when electricity came to the Hurlburt area in the 30's, which meant "no more kerosene lamps (and) no more scrub boards." After living elsewhere for a period of time, the family returned to East County after WWII. Both Leona and Arnold attended CHS in the late 40's. At that time the family lived at the end of Rickert Road on the Thompson place. Leona had five children, Randy D., Sherri L., Terri L.,

Ross and Arlene

Ross, L, and Arlene Johnson pose at home.

Margaret Warren

Margaret (Johnson) Warren with her children, Albert and Jean.

Photos courtesy of Ross Johnson.

Lorri A. and Susan M. She now lives in Seaside. Arnold had seven children, Michael E., Mitchell R., Kathleen R., Debra M., James A., Noel D. and Perry L. He now lives in Prineville. Keith has two children, Danielle and Daniel, and lives in Milwaukie. Robert 'Bob' also has two children, Jennifer S. and Robert Z., and lives in Gresham.

September 17, 1934, Margaret Johnson married Milton Warren. The couple purchased 40 acres that had been foreclosed, which was located off Loudon on O'Regan Road. Milton worked as a logger his entire working life. Margaret worked as a clerk in a store for a brief period and as a teller at the Troutdale Bank. She also worked for Corbett Water District for a time. Milton and Margaret had two children, Jean, b. September 13, 1935 and Albert, b. August 3, 1937. Jean completed grades 1-12 in Corbett, graduating from CHS in 1953. Albert, however, attended high school in Northern California after the family moved to Honeydew (near Garberville), where Milton had taken a contract-logging job. During his senior year, Albert stayed with his Aunt Arlene at her home in Burlingame, California, graduating from high school there in 1955. On August 29, 1955, about 3 months later, Albert was killed in a logging accident in California. Albert Warren is interred in the Evans cemetery at Corbett. After spending about 8 years in California, Milton and Margaret returned to their home in Oregon.

Winter Wood

From L, Orval Johnson, Geneva Johnson, Ross Johnson, Vance Evans, Art Johnson and Arlene Johnson getting wood for the coming winter. Photo courtesy of Arlene (Johnson) Marble

Livestock Feed

Ross Johnson cuts oats for hay.
Photo courtesy of Ross Johnson.

After graduating from CHS, Jean attended Oregon State University (OSU), graduating in 1957 with degrees in home economics and education. She taught at the middle school level, completing 4 years in Colorado and 21 years in California. She took early retirement in 1990 and moved back to Oregon. Jean married Jack Carter in June 1957 and they now live on the former Deverell place. She and Jack have three children, Linda, James 'Jim' and John. Linda married Jeff Hargens, has two children, Jared and Kimberly, and lives with her husband in Corbett. Jared and Kimberly attend Corbett middle school. Jim Carter graduated from OSU with a degree in engineering. He married Sue Worley, has two children, twins James and Rachel, and lives in Pacifica, California. John Carter graduated from the nursing program at Oregon Health Sciences University, is married to Kelli Dudley, has three children, Steve, Heather and Kent, and works at OHSU as a surgical nurse.

During her high school years, Arlene Johnson worked for Ward Evans during the summer. In addition to working in the bulbs, she worked in the corn cannery. Among her jobs, she fed the husker with Jack Evans. The husker had slots that carried the corn into the machine, which removed the husks. Arlene also worked on the conveyor where individuals looked for bad spots on the corn as it passed on its way to the cutter. She and others removed the defects before the corn reached the cutter. After

Johnson Barn

Albert Warren harrows Grandfather Art Johnson's field. The Johnson barn, built by C.P. Woodle and Fay Davis, stands in the background.

Photos courtesy of Ross Johnson.

Johnson Field Corn

Arthur Johnson holds Bud Warren on his shoulders to demonstrate the heighth of his corn.

the cutting machine removed the kernels from the husks, liquid, including a sweetener, was added to the corn before it was cooked in a steam cooker. Arlene said the workers could prepare an ear of corn for lunch and cook it in steam. "It was delicious," she remarked. However, she said, one thing always bothered her. "We had to clean up *after* our lunch period started and *after* the work day was over."

Arlene graduated from CHS in 1936 after which she enrolled at Oregon State College. She completed two years there and was accepted into the nurses training program at Good Samaritan Hospital, which she completed in September 1942. While at OSC, she met Harold Marble, and the couple married September 26, 1942. They spent the next two years in Cleveland, Ohio, then moved to Hollywood, California. Harold worked as a mechanical engineer for the American Gas Association. His specialty involved gas combustion. Eventually he obtained a position in San Francisco, which is where they lived while raising their two children, Bill, b. January 8, 1945, and Kathleen, b. November 16, 1946.

Harold and Arlene Marble returned to Corbett in 1964. Arlene obtained a position as a nurse in the gynecology department at Good Samaritan Hospital, working there from 1967-1973. Harold Marble passed away September 15, 1995. Son Bill Marble has two children, Steve and Julie, who graduated from CHS in 1986 and 1990, respectively. He now

198

The Marbles

Arlene (Johnson) Marble, Harold Marble and son, Bill.

Photo courtesy of Ross Johnson.

lives on Loudon Road and is married to Cheryl (Meyer). Kathleen (Marble) Dixon is now single, lives on Hurlburt Road and owns a riding stable.

Ross Johnson started school at Corbett Grade rather than Hurlburt, as the latter closed after consolidating with Corbett in 1929. During his youth he worked for his father on the farm, which was primarily a dairy operation. He attended CHS, served as Student Body President in 1942-43 and graduated in 1943. Ross enlisted in the US Navy and soon found himself in the Admiralty Islands, Bismarck Archipelago, stationed at the huge naval supply base on Manus, Island (New Guinea). Though the natives were classified 'head-hunters,' the United States military personnel stationed there had no problems. The natives either fished or farmed. Their crops included pigs, yams and corn. Ross remarked, "In contrast to the primitive existence of the people at that time, today the natives communicate with the outside world over the Internet." Ross stayed on Manus until the war concluded in 1945 and arrived home in 1946 after his discharge.

Ross Johnson on Manus Island

Ross Johnson, stationed on the Navy supply base at Manus Island during World War II. Photo courtesy of Ross Johnson.

Ross worked with his father on the home place until his father passed away in 1955. On August 6, 1949, he married Thelma Lundbom of Gresham. When first married the couple moved into the house on the Johnson place located close to Loudon Road. After Arthur Johnson died, Ross moved his family to his parents' home and his mother, Geneva Johnson, moved into the home in which Ross and his family had been living. Ross mentioned, "I'm now living in the house I was born in." Ross and Thelma had two children, Curt, b. January 18, 1952 and Carl, b. September 30, 1953. Both youngsters attended school at Corbett, with Curt graduating from CHS in 1970 and Carl in 1971.

Ross worked at the Bridal Veil mill, at the aluminum plant and in construction for the Guy F. Atkinson Company before obtaining a more permanent job. September 29, 1958, he went to work for the Corps of Engineers at Bonneville Dam. He worked as a fireman/first aid man for about 21 years. In 1979, he was assigned to the navigation locks, which is where he was working when he retired in May 1986. Thelma was secretary to the Superintendent of Gresham Union High School District for many years. She worked at Corbett Grade School as secretary for some time, then returned to Gresham. Offered the position of School Clerk, she turned it down (with some regret in later years). Thelma Johnson passed away August 2, 1989. Ross continues to live in 'retirement' on the home place, and raises beef cattle.

Morris D. Johnson
Anna M. (Nordin) Johnson

Morris Johnson, the 5th child of Anderson and Amanda Johnson, was born in Portland July 18, 1875. He married Anna Nordin in 1908, and the couple lived on the original Johnson place for many years on what is now Gordon Creek Road. They had five children, Neill, b. February 1911, Louise, b. March 5, 1913, Gladys, b. December 1914, Norwood, b. June 8, 1916, and Verna, b. October 1918. The children attended Hurlburt Grade School until its closure with those youngsters still in grade school transferring to Corbett. Louise (1931), Gladys (1932), Norwood (1932) and Verna (1936) graduated from CHS.

Neill Johnson lived on Hurlburt Road (now part of Ellis Road) just east of the Klocks. He owned a drift right at Lower Corbett and fished commercially for years. In 1947 he, together with his brother, Norwood, and two brothers-in-law, Russell Akin and Howard Gilson, went into the lumber business, building a mill on Neill's property on Hurlburt Road. The partners operated the Big Creek Lumber Company for approximately four years. After the mill closed, Neill fished commercially, worked on a dredge for the US Corps of Engineers and worked for the Corbett Water District for a time.

Louise Johnson married Roland Erickson and moved to the Kelso area. They had one son, Wayne, b. 1941. Roland worked as head sawyer in various mills over the years, including the Big Creek Lumber Company that was owned by his brothers-in-law.

Gladys Johnson married Howard Gilson in the mid 30's, and they had one son, Dennis. Gladys and Howard purchased two acres (part of the original Johnson place) from the Errend family. Howard became a partner in the Big Creek Lumber Company (see above). Gladys and Verna Akin grew strawberries on the place in the late 40's. Colleen and Carroll Innes and Richard and Sandra Childers picked berries for Gladys and Verna. In 1951, Howard and Russell Akin moved the mill to Beaver, Oregon. When that mill closed Gladys and Howard moved to a ranch in Paisley, Oregon. Gladys Gilson now lives in Bend, Oregon.

Norwood Johnson joined the Army during World War II. Assigned to the Army Air Force, he served in the African campaign. After the war,

Neill Johnson

Neill Johnson, US Navy, WW II

Norwood Johnson

Norwood Johnson, Army Air Force, WW II. Photos courtesy of Ross Johnson.

July 14, 1945, he married Betty Akin. They had two children, Gail, b. May 2, 1947 and Stephen, b. November 9, 1948. As mentioned above, Norwood was a partner in the Big Creek Lumber Company until it closed. He worked with sawyer Roland Erickson as setter. When Big Creek shut down, Norwood purchased a working share in a plywood mill located in Linnton where he worked a short period of time. He traded this share to Ed Sworden for Ed's drift right at Lower Corbett, and then fished commercially until 1959, fishing both the upper and lower drift. During the off season, he often worked on a dredge for the US Corps of Engineers.

In 1959, Norwood started working at the Corbett Post Office, later transferring to the Troutdale Post Office. Betty spent a good deal of time on the boat with Norwood when he fished commercially. Both Gail and Stephen attended school at Corbett, Gail graduating from CHS in 1965 and Stephen in 1966. Gail attended Portland State University, graduating with a Bachelor's degree in Political Science. Stephen served in the U.S. Navy for four years after which he completed college, earning both a bachelor's and a master's degree in business.

Norwood Johnson passed away in February 1999. Betty Johnson continues to live in the family home on Gordon Creek Road, which overlooks Oxbow Park on the Sandy River. She keeps busy doing volunteer work at the Legacy Mt. Hood Medical Center in Gresham and has been active with the Gresham Historical Society.

Road Building

L to R: Neill Johnson, Frank Fagan and Gordon Osborn, building the road to the water source on Gordon Creek.

Photo courtesy of Julia Fagan.

In 1941, Verna Johnson married Russell Akin of Gresham. He too, became a partner in the Big Creek Lumber Company (see above). During the period when the mill operated, Russell and Verna rented a home behind the Johnson house. He and Howard Gilson moved the mill to Beaver, Oregon in 1951. When the mill at Beaver closed, Russell and Verna returned to the area in 1960, purchasing Troutdale Sand and Gravel. They operated this business until 1978, when it was sold except for the parcel upon which their home was located. Verna and Russell had one child, a daughter, Judy, b. in 1943. Judy Akin worked for the Walrad Insurance Agency for years, retiring from that firm in 1997. Verna Akin died May 20, 1989 and Russell Akin passed away in 1996.

Charles Jones
Antonia (Trevares) (Silva) Jones

In the late 20's and 30's Charles 'Charlie' Jones lived on Chamberlain Road in a summer home owned by Francis Blakely of *The Oregonian*. Charlie was a veteran of World War I. According to reports, he enlisted in the Canadian Army in order to get involved and served two years in France fighting for the allied cause. When the United States entered the war in 1917, U.S. citizens among the troops were given an option of transferring to the U.S. Army, which Charlie did, and thereafter he fought with the U.S. forces. He stayed in the army for several years after the war, and was discharged as a sergeant.

After his discharge, Charlie Jones returned to East Multnomah County. According to Jum Mershon, Charlie had cut cordwood before the war, which was hauled to Corbett Station and sold to the railroad. Sometime after the war he married Antonia (Trevares) Silva, who had five children by her previous marriage, Frank, George, Eddie, Marie and Tony Silva. In the 30's Charlie worked on the seine and for various farmers in the area. Two of his wife's children, Eddie and Marie Wall, often visited. While visiting, Eddie met a neighbor girl from across Chamberlain Road, Sybil Quier. The couple started going together and later they married. Marie had two children by her first marriage to Joseph Wall, David L., b. April 14, 1928, and Louise, b. January 6, 1931. David and Louis lived with Mr. and Mrs. Jones for two or three years in the early 30's. David used to walk with Quinten and Sybil Quier to Jum Mershon's place to catch the school bus. One time George Chamberlain, who was about David's age, was staying with Bert and Maggy Chamberlain. David told him, "Let's go stand by the road. Wait'll you see what happens when the rich people come by." They waited until a big, yellow LaSalle pulled up and stopped. David said it "took half an hour to pass from the hood ornament to the door handle." The "rich people" (the Tullys) handed each of the boys a candy bar and continued on their way. The Tullys lived on Chamberlain Road about a quarter-mile beyond the Blakely place.

While visiting her mother, stepfather and children, Marie Wall met Ray Wilson, a friend of Charlie Jones. Ray and Marie started going together and they married in April 1935. Marie and Ray Wilson had three

Ray and Marie Wilson

Front, L to R: Ray Wilson (holding Myra), Jean Warren, Milton Warrren, Louise Wall, Marie Wilson (holding Del) and David Wall (others unknown).
Photo courtesy of Ross Johnson.

birth children, Myra, b. September 15, 1937; Delos 'Del.' b. September 24, 1938; and Donna, b. February 21, 1941. The family lived on Wand Road in the old Pleasant View schoolhouse that Ray purchased at auction and remodeled. Of course, David continued school at Corbett, and Louise enrolled there in 1936.

Until World War II started, Ray worked as an electrician with Ig Wand and worked on construction projects in Gresham and Troutdale. After the war started both he and Marie worked at the Kaiser Swan Island shipyard. They decided to move to North Portland in order to be closer to their jobs. David Wall had graduated from Corbett Grade School in 1942 and was attending CHS at that time. After the move he attended Roosevelt High School until he joined the Merchant Marine in 1945. Louise Wall also attended Corbett Grade School until grade seven. After the move, she attended Portsmouth Grade in Portland. Ray and Marie divorced in 1945. After the divorce, Louise remained with her mother while Myra, Del and Donna stayed with their father (see "Ray Wilson").

Antonia Jones died in 1938 and Charlie lost his position as caretaker of the Blakely summer home. He purchased an acre of ground across Chamberlain Road and built a small shack in which to live. When the

Rooster Rock Seine Grounds

David Wall holds a spring Chinook salmon caught in the seine net. Photo, the author.

Japanese bombed Pearl Harbor, Charlie enlisted in the U.S. Army. Because of his experience, he was commissioned and eventually sent to the European Theater of operations. He served in France and Germany advancing to the rank of Captain. According to David Wall, he returned after Germany's surrender "with a trunk full of souvenirs, all covered with swastikas." While in the service, he sent an allotment to Marie Wilson.

After Charlie returned from Europe, he contacted Ray Wilson and gave him a hunting rifle that he had brought back from Germany. This was the last contact that former neighbors and relatives had with Charlie Jones. Reportedly, he stayed in the army, and was sent to Korea, but this information can not be verified. When he retired from the Army he apparently lived in California, where his second wife lived. According to reports, he died on a trip with his wife to Alaska in the 50's.

After David Wall left the Merchant Marine, he met and married Shirley Carden July 27, 1948. The couple has three children, Patricia M., b. September 29, 1949, David L. Jr., b. April 17, 1952, and Robert A., b. December 2, 1953. David and Shirley live in Milwaukie, Oregon. After she left home Louise moved to Los Angeles. She married Stanley Price and has two boys, Steven and Daniel. Later Louise married Hector Mascorro. They had one birth son, David, and currently live in Pittsburgh, PA.

Allan B. Kerslake
Jessie O. (Hart) Kerslake

Allan B. Kerslake was born in Woodstock, Canada July 26, 1877. After he came to East County, he worked as a woods boss for various lumber camps, and was working in the woods on Larch Mountain when he married Jessie O. Hart. Jessie was born in Washougal, Washington October 23, 1881. The couple's first child, Clara Jeannette, was born June 22, 1898 at the Deverell Camp, which was located at the foothills of Pepper Mountain in the Brower Area. According to Clara, the family lived in logging camps until she reached age seven (1905), at which time her parents purchased 20 acres near Springdale located between Henkle and Christensen Roads. The family lived in a rented house until a house was built on the property. Six more children were born to Allan and Jessie Kerslake: Allan R. 'Bob,' b. November 20, 1903; Harold F. 'Pat,' b. February 1, 1906; Dorthy E., b. August 4, 1912; Fred E., b. October 21, 1914; Grace L., b. February 28, 1919; and Daniel M. 'Dan,' b. July 2, 1923.

During the period of time while the children were small, Allan Kerslake was working at the Kelly and Wilon Mill in Aims, riding a horse to and from work. When Allan worked at the mill, railway ties were stockpiled for the annual "tie drive" to Troutdale. The ties were rafted down the Sandy River during high water (spring freshet) and were subsequently shipped by rail from Troutdale.

One time Allan encountered a cougar on his way home. The cougar started to stalk him from the hill above Gordon Creek, emitting a scream now and then. Togo, Allan's dog, became agitated and kept running under the horse's hooves. When Allan realized the cougar was after him, he picked up the dog and put his horse into a gallop. The cougar followed him down the hill to Gordon Creek and up the long grade to the top of Buck Creek Hill. The horse had lathered up considerably by the time level ground was reached, but Allan continued to press him toward home, uncertain at this point if the cougar was continuing the chase. By the time the trio reached home, the horse was frothing at the mouth, totally lathered and exhausted. Togo was also thoroughly shaken and, according to family lore, was visibly quaking in Allan's arms. All had survived a frightening experience.

Donahue Lumber Camp c1889

A.B. Kerslake (middle foreground [left] with sledge) worked for M.C. Donahue, who contracted to bring logs to the Bridal Veil Lumbering Company rail line, by which logs were transported to Palmer. Young Mike Donahue rides the horse.

Key and Douglas Mill

A.B. Kerslake also worked at this mill. He is standing in the yard near one of the oxen teams. Photos courtesy of the Kerslake family.

208

The Kerslake family kept dairy cows and took the milk to Springdale in a horse drawn two-wheeled cart to meet the milk truck. The milk was then hauled to Portland for processing. Later Allan Kerslake worked for the Multnomah County Road Department, eventually becoming road foreman. He supervised the building of several roads in East Multnomah County, including the road to Aims and the Larch Mountain Road, which was completed in the 30's.

Clara started school in Springdale at age seven, graduating in 1913. Since there was no high school in the area, she became in her words, "everyone's helper." She accompanied her Aunt Libby, who was terminally ill, to the coast after she had undergone surgery in a Portland hospital. Clara stayed with her Aunt for several months during which time she "learned to cook." After the sojourn to the coast, Clara returned to the farm and worked for her parents. The new Columbian High School building constructed in Corbett opened in 1915 and Clara enrolled. She walked from the farm to school, which is more than two miles. She intended to take nurses training and needed one year of high school in order to qualify.

At the end of the year Dr. H.H. Hughes advised her to wait another year, so she completed an additional year at the high school. During this interval, the qualifications changed, and one had to have a high school diploma to qualify for nurses training. Clara then decided to become a teacher, which required three years of high school. However, her mother became ill, which forced her to quit school and stay at home to help. She did complete a third year by an early version of a 'correspondence course.' Her teachers outlined work for her to complete, tested her knowledge of the material and gave her further work to complete. Many years later, in June 1988, Corbett High School awarded Clara an honorary diploma, which thrilled her.

Clara met her future husband, Louie Baker, when she was twelve. His parents had rented a neighboring farm and were moving from Eastern Oregon. Louie preceded the family to the farm and a storm hit about the time he arrived. His new neighbors, the Kerslakes, invited him to stay with them until the storm abated. Clara said that though she was too young to have an interest, "all the girls in the area were thrilled by that good looking young cowboy with his pretty horse, chaps and trimming." Subsequently, she and Louie became better acquainted as he went to work for her father and consequently "was around a lot." The Baker

The A.B. Kerslake Family

Rear, from L: A.B. Kerslake, Clara (holding Dorthy) and
Jessie. Front, Bob and Pat Kerslake.

Kerslake Home

From L, Bob, Pat, Dorthy (on Chappie), and Clara Kerslake.
Photos courtesy of the Kerslake family.

family did not long remain in the area, returning to live in Friend, Oregon (near Dufur). Louie and Clara corresponded, but saw each other rather infrequently.

World War I intervened and Louie Baker was drafted and soon sent overseas. Clara rolled bandages for the Red Cross, solicited for victory bonds and corresponded with soldiers who threw their addresses along the road as they passed through by truck. Clara and the other girls picked them up and wrote letters to them. Clara was picking apples with her friend, Esther Kincaid (Settlemier) when the war ended. Shortly, one Texas trooper with whom she had corresponded showed up for a visit, but a friendship did not materialize. When Louie returned from overseas, he contacted Clara. When his parents moved to Cottrell, he started courting Clara in earnest. Clara and Louie Baker married March 21, 1921 (see "Louie Baker" {this volume}, and "Louie and Clara (Kerslake) Baker," *Pioneer History*).

Bob also attended grade school at Springdale Grade, graduating in 1915. He attended CHS for a year before joining his father, who was working at the Cameron Hogg Mill in Aims. While working there, he met and married Alice McMannamy August 14, 1925 (see "Allan R. Kerslake/ Alice McMannamy) Kerslake").

Similarly to his siblings, Pat Kerslake attended and graduated from Springdale Grade School. According to family members, he was not much interested in high school, and could often be found at Roy Parsons' garage, where he had an opportunity to learn about machinery. He also enjoyed catching a ride into Portland with the milk truck. At age 14, Pat obtained a job with the County Road Department as a laborer. This job didn't suit him, so his boss put him to work driving truck. During this period of time he lived at home. Later, he transferred to the County shop in SE Portland. Pat married Iola Urbach August 1, 1931. The couple lived in Portland where they raised an adopted daughter, Marian J., b. September 3, 1938. Pat Kerslake became foreman for the road department in East Multnomah County in the 30's. He continued in that role until World War II started, when he joined the Seabees, US Navy, and went in as a Warrant Officer.

Pat served in the South Pacific on various Islands. His most exciting duty assignment was on Iwo Jima when the 8th battalion, to which he was assigned, went ashore to build an airstrip for US Marine pilots. He was there when the US flag was raised on Mt. Suribachi. During his

Aunt, Uncle and Nephews

From L, Aunt Grace Kerslake, Jim Baker, Uncle Dan Kerslake and Allan Baker.
Photo courtesy of the Kerslake family.

service, he was promoted to Chief Warrant Officer. When Pat returned home after the war, he was made an Assistant County Roadmaster with jurisdiction over all the Districts in Multnomah County. According to his sister, Grace, Pat "Got ahead because he got along well with people." Pat Kerslake lived at various homes in Portland while working for the County. He passed away December 6, 1964 at age 58.

Dorthy Kerslake grew up with her siblings on the home place off Christensen Road. She completed grade school at Springdale Grade, then chose to attend CHS in Corbett. The 20's were sometimes referred to as "the golden age of sports for women," as the high school fielded teams in several sports, including basketball, for girls as well as boys. (For some reason, this changed during the 30's.) Dorthy excelled in basketball, perhaps establishing the "Kerslake" tradition. In keeping with the times of the "Roaring 20's," Corbett girls were fashion conscious, wearing the latest in bloomers with elastic at the knees, and learned the Charleston, the Fox Trot and the Waltz. The dance hall in Springdale attracted dancers, but, unfortunately, a few drunks as well. Of course, liquor was not legal at the time. The girls complained that few boys "marked" their cards.

Violet Parsons was going with a soldier stationed at Fort Vancouver, and introduced Dorthy to her boy friend's buddy, Jimmy Pomante. Dorthy started dating Jimmy and the couple married February 28, 1930, about 3 months before her graduation from CHS. She continued in school, graduating with her class in 1930, the first of Allan and Jessie Kerslake's children to graduate from high school (see "James Pomante/Dorthy (Kerslake) Pomante").

Fred Kerslake completed grade school at Springdale and started high school at Corbett in 1928. He had attended CHS for about one and one-half years when a mumps epidemic hit the area. The family was subjected to a 6-week quarantine when one of his siblings came down with the mumps, which was renewed when another family member caught the disease. Though Fred never did get the mumps, he missed a lot of school, and decided to quit and farm. Because of her experience living in several lumber camps, Jessie Kerslake always encouraged her children to stay put once they settled on the farm. She always hoped that one of her youngsters would develop a love for the farm that she had. Fred fulfilled Jessie's hopes. He lived at home and farmed, raising hay and grain, principally. He also increased the size of the dairy herd. Fred purchased the Stevens' place in the 30's, which added more acreage to the original 20. Henry Campbell and Ada Morden held the mortgage. According to Grace, "Fred finally achieved his dream. He had his farm."

During World War II, Fred obtained a draft deferral and continued to work the farm those years. When Dan returned from the Navy, he and Fred became partners. They increased the dairy herd to the point where they were milking approximately 140 head. According to Grace, after she lost her husband and returned to live at home, Fred helped care for her daughter, Claudia. Grace is grateful as "Fred gave Claudia the attention a father would have provided." Grace describes Fred as a gentle, soft-spoken individual who was good to everyone in the family.

Fred did not marry until his mother, Jessie, died February 19, 1959. Her husband, Allan had passed away almost exactly seven years earlier (February 21, 1952). Fred married Lyda McCreary December 27, 1962. Fred and Lyda had no children. In 1984, Fred was diagnosed with cancer of the colon. The cancerous growth was removed, and he was transferred to the new Gresham hospital as its first patient. Nurses were walking him in preparation for his going home, when he collapsed from a massive heart attack and passed away November 4, 1984. His widow,

Fred Kerslake

Planting Grain

Fred drills grain while Virginia Pomante, Richard Kerslake (in front) and Harold Kerslake play in the foreground.

Photos courtesy of Grace (Kerslake) Stolin.

Fred Kerslake with his pony, Babe.

Lyda, continues to live on a parcel of the property that Fred purchased in the 30's.

Grace Kerslake graduated from Springdale Grade School in 1933. She then enrolled at CHS, from which she graduated in 1937. After graduation she continued to live at home. Grace, Dorthy and Fred raised a few acres of strawberries and cucumbers to earn a bit of extra money. Grace married Claude Urbach February 9, 1941. They had one daughter, Claudia, b. June 17, 1945. Unfortunately, Claude became ill shortly after Claudia's birth and died July 11, 1945.

Grace remained in Fred's house for a few months, then moved home to help when her mother's illness became progressively worse and more debilitating. As Grace explained, "She needed help and we needed a home." When Claudia grew old enough to get around, she loved to follow her Uncle Fred around everywhere possible. Grace continues to express her love and admiration for Fred who did so much for her and Claudia.

214

Kerslake River Cabin

Fred Kerslake stands on the porch of his cabin on the Sandy River. Photo courtesy of Grace (Kerslake) Stolin.

Grace started working as a cook at Springdale Grade School in the late 40's after Mrs. Shaw retired. While she worked, Dorthy would come to the house to take care of Jessie, Al and Claudia. Some family member was always ready to help out when needed. Until Springdale consolidated with Corbett School District in 1960, Grace was paid on a 12-month basis. During the summer months, lady volunteers and she would gather vegetables and fruit from local gardens and take it to a commercial cannery to be processed. The canned goods would be placed in the school's pantry for use the following year. After the consolidation, cooks were paid for the nine months school was in session. Consequently, she took a summer job at the County "poor farm" in Wood Village. Grace said, "I fed mouths in the winter and wiped 'ends' in the summer." Grace continued to work at the Springdale Primary School until after her marriage to Walter Stolin. Her replacement at Springdale was Barbara Case.

In 1962, she and Claudia moved to their home on Christensen Road. Her father had given her an acre of land after Claudia's birth and her brothers helped build a 'starter' home on the property. Grace married Walter Stolin August 10, 1963. She completed that school year (1963-64), but did not work outside the home after 1964. After the marriage,

Tamara Becker

Tamara Becker, CHS Homecoming Queen, 1985.

Tricia Becker

Tricia Becker, CHS State champions, 1987. Photos courtesy of Claudia Becker.

Walter remodeled and enlarged the home. Walter Stolin passed away December 2, 1993. Grace continues to live in the house situated on an acre of the home place that her father gave her years before.

Claudia married Robert Becker and now lives on Stevens Road, close to the home place. She has four daughters, Tammy, b. October 25, 1967, Tricia, b. September 22, 1969, Tina, b. January 29, 1975 and Trudi, b. March 22, 1977. Each attended school at CHS and graduated in 1985, 1987, 1993, and 1997, respectively. In addition to her exploits in athletics, Tamara served as Homecoming Queen her senior year. Tricia also established an enviable record in sports, earning a spot on the All-State volleyball team her senior year after helping CHS take the State Championship in that sport. She also played on the State championship team her sophomore year and on the State runner-up team her junior year. Tricia played on the girls' basketball team that earned a State tourney berth her sophomore year. Tricia was named to the State 'all-star' team. She played on the State runner-up team her junior year, and on the CHS girls' team that took the State Championship in 1987. Tina and Trudi continued the family's sports accomplishments during their high school years. Both were named to the District softball all-star team in 1993.

Dan Kerslake had quite a career at CHS, playing on two CHS basketball teams of local renown. As a junior, he played on the 'Big-Nine'

216

Dan Kerslake, US Navy

Dan Kerslake served in the South Pacific during WW II.
Photo courtesy of Ross Johnson.

championship team of 1939-40. The following year, he played on the team that was the State runner-up, CHS' first tourney team. After World War II started, Dan lived at home helping on the farm. However, he said, "All my friends were going into the service, so I decided to join, also." He enlisted in the U.S. Navy and spent eighteen months in the South Pacific. On one occasion, he was summoned to appear by an officer. Thinking he was in trouble, Dan was much surprised to find the summons came because his brother, Pat, was at the same base.

January 22, 1946, while home on a 30-day furlough, Dan and Doris Gravett were married. After his discharge, he and Fred became partners in the farming operation, and continued to increase the dairy herd. Dan and Doris had three children, Carol A., b. September 9, 1946, Steven R., b. December 30, 1948 and Nicholas A., b. January 21, 1962. All attended Springdale Grade School until the District, because of action at the State legislature, consolidated with Corbett in 1960. The youngsters completed their remaining elementary years at Corbett, and graduated from CHS in 1964, 1967 and 1980, respectively. After Fred's death in 1984, Dan thought the time opportune to sell the dairy herd, which was accomplished in 1985. Dan now farms the Kerslake place with his youngest son, Nicholas.

Columbian High School c1941.   Photo courtesy of Norma (Bratley) Taylor.

217

Allan R. Kerslake
Alice (McMannamy) Kerslake

Allan Robert 'Bob' Kerslake, son of Allen and Jessie (Hart) Kerslake, grew up in East Multnomah County. Alice McMannamay, born in Weiser, Idaho May 29 1906, came to Oregon with her family in the early 20's. Alice's brother-in-law worked at the Cameron and Hogg sawmill in Aims. Alice traveled to Aims to visit and obtained a job at the mill cookhouse. She met Bob Kerslake, who worked for Cameron and Hogg as a high climber and train brakeman. The couple married August 14, 1925. Bob built a house in Springdale, located on Christensen Road, to which they moved in 1928. In 1927, Bob Kerslake started working part time for the Multnomah County Road Department driving snowplow. During the depression years, truck drivers drove three days per week; thus twice as many men had work. This permitted Bob to take part-time work for various employers such as Ridge Lumber Company as a high climber. He also worked some as a carpenter for Claude Woodle, who permitted him to select lumber from his scrap pile to use for building purposes. Bob drove truck for the County until 1941, when he became District (East County) Foreman. Building and maintaining County roads in East Multnomah County became his managerial responsibility. He remained in that position until he retired in 1969 (see "Descendants of Allan B. and Jessie Kerslake," *Pioneer History*).

Bob and Alice Kerslake had five children: Allan R. b. December 9, 1926 (who died shortly after birth); Harold A., b. September 22, 1928; Richard E., b. September 5, 1931; Jean L., b. July 18, 1933; and John A., b. June 18, 1937. Each attended Springdale Grade School from which Harold graduated in 1942, Richard in 1945, Jean in 1947 and John in 1951. The entire family was intensely loyal to and supportive of the Springdale school, its teachers and programs, and opposed the consolidation vote with Corbett schools that occurred in 1954 (failed) and 1960 (passed). According to Bob Kerslake, "newcomers" were responsible, but the legislature made consolidation almost mandatory when it specified that every school district must have a grade 1 to 12 program.

The Kerslake youngsters all attended CHS, Harold graduating in 1946, Richard in 1949, Jean in 1951 and John in 1955. The squabble concerning consolidation did not carry over with regard to the high school, which

Cameron Hogg Woods Crew

The Cameron Hogg logging crew pose at the mill cookhouse. Bob Kerslake sits on the step, right.

Bob Kerslake Driving Snowplow

Bob Kerslake, shown with his father, took a job driving a snowplow for the County in 1927.   Photos courtesy of the Kerslake Family.

Bob and Alice Kerslake's Children

From L, Richard, Jean, Harold and John Kerslake.
Photo courtesy of the Kerslake family.

the family always supported and which provided Bob and Alice's children an opportunity to gain a fine education.

Upon Bob Kerslake's retirement in 1969, an anonymous community member penned:

To Bob Kerslake, March 19, 1969, presented by his community on the occasion of his retirement:

In a quarter of a century, Bob Kerslake grows on a man. At first he seems blunt, uncompromising, even stubborn. Gradually, what seemed to have been stubbornness, turns out to (be) deep convictions about important things. What seemed to have been brutal bluntness turns out often to have been the unvarnished truth. Opinions he held that seemed so manifestly wrong, turned out, reluctant as we are to admit it, far too often have been just about dead right.

Bob typifies a fast shrinking band of self-reliant, second-generation pioneers who built our community and gave it character. The code they lived by was based on old-fashioned virtues. They are considered too tough and outmoded by today's loose standards; but whoever aspires to do better will have to produce a substitute for dedication to duty, fearless impartiality, civic responsibility, and personal resourcefulness.

Mr. and Mrs. Kerslake were active in community affairs, maintaining memberships in the Troutdale Historical Society and the East Multnomah County Pioneer Association, among others. Alice Kerslake was active in the Springdale Grade School PTA and a group of women known as the 'Friendly Neighbor Club.' Bob and Alice Kerslake celebrated their 50th wedding anniversary in 1975. Bob Kerslake died July 24, 1985 and Alice Kerslake died October 23, 1994.

Harold Kerslake graduated from Oregon State College with an engineering degree. He worked for Peter Kiewit Construction and transferred to Alaska in 1968. He married Virginia McCreary in 1951, and the couple had five children, Robert, Scott, Jack, William and Lisa. Shortly after moving to Alaska, he formed his own construction company and also had a water treatment company. When the Alaska oil pipeline was under construction, Harold received an offer he "couldn't resist," and went to work for another construction company. When this project ended he worked for a construction company whose principal endeavor was building roads. He spent the balance of his working career in Alaska. He married for a second time to Charlotte Howard and had another daughter, Christine. He purchased the home place and divides his time between his place in Anchorage, Alaska and his place in Springdale.

Richard 'Rich' Kerslake married Dorothy Van Orsow. He worked for Multnomah County at different jobs, but eventually transferred to the wastewater treatment plant as Assistant Chief Operator. When the plant closed he transferred to a City of Portland plant from which he retired after more than 30 years with the County and City. Dorothy worked for J.C. Penney Company in Gresham until the store closed. She then transferred to the District Office in Clackamas and eventually to the Vancouver Mall. Richard and Dorothy had three children, Charles 'Chuck,' b. June 8, 1953, James, b. August 22, 1955 and Kathy, b. June 13, 1959. Chuck graduated from CHS in 1972, James, in 1973 and Kathy, in 1978. In 1997, Rich and Dorothy received the "Chief Heini Ziegler" Community Service Award from Fire District 14. Richard and Dorothy Kerslake live on Northway Road in Springdale.

Jean Kerslake married James 'Jim' Rhodes and they have three children, Michael, May 16, 1953, John, September 7, 1956 and Susan, b. March 31, 1961. Jim, who had enlisted in the Oregon Air Guard, was activated during the Korean War and served in the U.S. Air Force. After his discharge, he worked for Braley and Graham for several years, then joined the Multnomah County Road Department. In 1969, Jim became District Foreman (East County). Eventually he became Road Maintenance Supervisor for the entire County. Jean worked for Corbett School District for seventeen years, retiring January 1, 1992. Jim and Jean live on Knieriem Road, Corbett.

John Kerslake enlisted in the Navy after graduating from CHS. He married Mitzie Howell of Corbett August 31, 1958. After his discharge from the service he joined the Multnomah County Sheriffs' Department and served as a deputy until his retirement in 1987. He and Mitzie have two children, Timothy, b. November 24, 1959 and Jacqueline, b. February 27, 1961. John and Mitzie live on Northway Road in Springdale.

Latourell Landing c1890.   Photo courtesy of the Kerslake Family.

Albert R. Kimbley
Irene L. (Evans) Kimbley

Albert 'Bud' Kimbley married Irene L. Evans December 24, 1924, in Portland. Irene, b. December 20, 1906, daughter of Sylvester E. and Marcella A. (Moore) Evans, grew up on the place homesteaded by her father in Howard Canyon. Sylvester Evans taught school before establishing a store near the head of Howard Canyon. Irene Evans attended Hurlburt Grade School, completing her final year there in 1920. She then enrolled at CHS, from which she graduated in 1924. Irene wrote several literary selections for the 1924 *Cohimore*. She continued to write during her lifetime for her own, and others, enjoyment. Bud Kimbley was born July 2, 1893, in Damascus. After the couple married, they lived in a home on the Evans' homestead. Albert R. Kimbley served on the Board of Directors of Hurlburt Grade School, elected to the post in 1926.

The Kimbleys had three children, Irma, b. July 15, 1927, Joy, b. April 12, 1929 and Albert Jr., b. September 12, 1931. The three Kimbley youngsters all attended grade and high school at Corbett. Irma graduated from CHS in 1945, Joy in 1947 and Albert in 1949. Bud Kimbley worked at various places, including the Troutdale Vegetable and Fruit Growers Association in Troutdale, the Wood Pullery in Troutdale and the Bridal Veil Lumber and Box Company.

As mentioned, during the late 20's and early 30's the Kimbleys lived in a house located up Howard Canyon, part of the original Evans' homestead. Later they moved to a house located behind the Hurlburt School, which subsequently became the home for the Kuzmesky family. Eventually the Kimbleys bought a place on Hurlburt Road, where Albert Jr. now lives. When Hurlburt Road was straightened, a portion of the former Hurlburt Road became Kimbley Road.

A 45-46 issue of the *Cardinal* reported the marriage of Irma Kimbley to Pvt. Wilbur D. Biornstad, U.S. Army at the Corbett Christian Church, March 23, 1945. According to the article, Biornstad was to report to Fort Ord for overseas duty in the South Pacific. After Biornstad completed his military obligation the couple settled in Gresham. Joy Kimbley married Don Lampert and the couple made their home in Washington. They had three girls, but, tragically, two died in their childhood years. Joy now lives in Sumner, Washington.

Irene Evans at Hurlburt School

From L, Doris Emily, Ray Lasley, Selma Soderstrom, Albert Pounder and Irene Evans. Seated, Miss Margaret Patterson.

Photo courtesy of Pat (Bramhall) Paget

Irene Evans

Irene Evans, CHS graduate, 1924. Lloyd Bramhall, rear. '24 Cohimore photo (excerpt).

Irma Kimbley

Irma Kimbley, CHS graduate, 1945.

Joy Kimbley

Joy Kimbley, CHS graduate, 1947. Photos, '45 and '47 Cohimore, respectively, courtesy of David Rees.

Albert Kimbley

Recent photo of Albert Kimbley, CHS graduate 1949. Photo courtesy of Edith Pinto.

Albert Kimbley spent two years in the U.S. Army after which he lived on the Kimbley place off Hurlburt Road. He is now married to Karen. He helped raise nine children, of whom five were birth children and four were stepchildren. He operated the former Clyde Groce station in Springdale for a time and worked in the export trade. Seven of his children graduated from CHS, Dan Jenkins ('65), Bonnie Jenkins ('69), Robert Jenkins ('72), Timothy ('81), John ('82), Marcella ('83) and Derrick Wolfe ('98). John attended MHCC for two years, then went into the Air Force for four years. After his discharge, he planned a career in law enforcement. John was crushed while working on an automobile at home and died from his injuries in February 1989.

Irene (Evans) Kimbley passed away February 18, 1951. Albert 'Bud' Kimbley died March 16, 1968. Both are interred at Douglas Cemetery in Troutdale.

Church Easter Egg Hunt c1939

L to R: Jimmy Van Orsow, Don Lampert, Steve Kuzmesky, Juanita Berney, Bob Van Speybrock, John Evans, __?__, Joretta May and Glenna Trussell.
Photo courtesy of Joretta (May) Ferrington..

225

Chester K. Kincaid
Verlena (Owen) Kincaid

Chester 'Kenneth' Kincaid was born in Corbett, Oregon January 3, 1901, on the 15-acre family farm located on the West side of Mershon Road near its eastern terminus at the highway. Kenneth worked on the family farm, logged and fished commercially for the Reeds before enlisting in the U.S. Navy in 1916. Apparently, he attended Taylor Grade School and CHS, but his age when he enlisted must have cut short his high school years (See "Esther Kincaid Settlemier," second volume, *Pioneer History*). Kincaid served in the Navy through the war years (WW I), completing his five year 'hitch' in 1921 after which he re-enlisted in the Navy for four years. While he was in the service his parents sold the farm on Mershon Road to Harley Bates.

On September 21, 1925, before his discharge from the Navy, Kincaid married Verlena Owen, who was born in Eugene, Oregon, November 26, 1907. The couple had two children, Alvin A., b. November 3, 1927 and Clyde E., b. August 12, 1930. Kincaid fished commercially and farmed the Chamberlain place on Chamberlain Road until 1932. He then moved with his family to Lovell Berney's place on Salzman Road, off what is now Larch Mountain Road. Kincaid operated a dairy farm at this location. Both Alvin and Clyde started grade school at Corbett Grade.

In 1939, Kincaid purchased five acres of land on Lusted Road near Pleasant Home. He worked for the State Highway Department until World War II commenced, then attempted to enlist in the Navy. When this failed, he went to work at the Oregon Shipyard as a crane operator. He left that job when he was accepted into the Merchant Marine as a fireman/watertender. During his Merchant Marine service, he rose to the position of chief electrician. Meanwhile Alvin and Clyde completed their grade school years at Orient and Lusted Grade Schools. Both then attended Gresham High School.

After the war, Kenneth Kincaid sold the place on Lusted Road and purchased a home with two lots in Crescent City, California. During the move, Verlena Kincaid was working on a ladder cleaning the ceiling in the newly purchased home when she fell. She died from her injuries August 30, 1945. Both Alvin and Clyde were in Oregon to pick up a load of furniture. After the accident, Kincaid went back to sea, Clyde went to

Alvin Kincaid and Friend

Alvin Kincaid (left) and George Perry at Menucha, c1937.
Photo courtesy of George Perry Jr.

Picnic at the Crump Place

Front, from L, Mr. Crump, Mrs. Crump, Isabelle Mershon, Clyde Kincaid, Alvin Kincaid, George Mershon, Clarence Mershon, Antonia Jones. Rear, Charlie Jones, George Mershon Sr., Verlena Kincaid, Kenneth Kincaid and Laura Mershon.   Photo, the author.

stay with his Aunt Esther Settlemier in Corbett and Alvin returned to Gresham. Kenneth Kincaid remained in the Merchant Marine for six more years. He married Agnes Kalana of Hawaii, and returned to East Multnomah County. He purchased two acres on Clara Smith Road, fished commercially and worked as a logger during this interval. In 1956, he and Agnes divorced. In 1957 he married Mary Milliken, and the couple lived on the place thereafter. Mary died in 1985. Kincaid continued to live on the place until 1991, when he moved in with a stepson, Keith Milliken. He remained with Keith for about six months, then fell and broke a hip. He spent the final two years of his life in a rest home in Oregon City, where he died April 3, 1993.

Alvin joined the Merchant Marine in April 1944 and served in the South Pacific until February 1945. He married Alys Korsund in Vancouver, Washington in July 13, 1945. The couple had two daughters, Julie A., b. June 27, 1946, and Linda J., b. May 15, 1948. Alvin enlisted in the U.S. Air Force in 1945 and served for three years. After his discharge he worked at Southern California Edison for 20 years. Alvin married a second time to Arleta Crawford on August 13, 1957. Arleta was born in Salem, Oregon January 11, 1938. They had two birth children, Michael A., b. September 27, 1969, and Megan A., b. February 8, 1976. After completing the twenty years at Southern California Edison, the family moved to Bremerton, Washington, where Alvin worked at the Puget Sound Naval Shipyard. He retired December 3, 1989, as a Utilities Operation Foreman. He and his wife, Arleta, now live in Milwaukie, Oregon.

During World War II, Clyde Kincaid served in the US Navy (air service). He married Grace E. Riddle October 1, 1954. After Clyde left the service he worked in the auto parts business. Currently he and his wife live in Prescott, Arizona.

William C. Kirkham
Mary E. (Raybourn) Kirkham

William C. 'Cary' Kirkham and Mary E. Kirkham moved to East County in 1923, renting the former Sumpter place near the junction of Chamberlain Road with Corbett Grade (NW corner). At the time, the couple had three children, Dortha, b. September 27, 1914, Susie, b. February 20, 1918 and Marion, b. March 6, 1922 (all born in Portland). A fourth child, Virgil, was born November 7, 1924 at this place, where the family lived until the spring of 1925. Next the family moved to the former Farquhar place off Christensen Road in Springdale. Dortha had started school in Portland before the family moved to East County; Susie started at Corbett, transferring to Springdale in 1925; Marion started school at Springdale when he was five years of age. In the fall of 1927 the Kirkhams moved to the Delano place on Smith Road, which they contracted to purchase. Marion completed the school year at Springdale, though the family now lived in the Corbett 'area.'

After the move, the youngsters attended school at Corbett. Dortha graduated from CHS in 1932 and almost immediately went to work for Libby, McNeil and Libby at its pickle plant off Powell Boulevard in SE Portland. Susie finished grade school at Corbett, and graduated from CHS in 1936. She attended Oregon State College for a year. Marion restarted grade one at Corbett Grade School and completed grade school there. He graduated from CHS in 1940, a member of the championship basketball team of 1939-40 featuring Carl and Clarence Lofstedt that took the Big Nine Championship with a 9-1 record in league play. At that time, there was no state tourney. Virgil completed both grade and high school at Corbett, graduating from CHS in 1942. He attended Oregon State College one term.

During the depression years, Cary Kirkham worked at a number of jobs. He drove school bus for Corbett School District, which paid a steady $30.00 per month. Another job involved working for the PWA at the headwaters on Gordon Creek when Corbett Water District built a system to utilize water from that source. In order to reach the job site, workers walked in from Larch Mountain Road on the Bridal Veil Lumbering Company railroad line that extended toward Walker Prairie. The men worked a five-hour shift, but it took them two hours to reach the job site

Kirkham Family

Rear, Mary and Cary Kirkham, Front, Susie, Marion, Virgil
and Dortha.   Photo courtesy of Dortha Kirkham.

and two hours to return. Of course they were paid only for the time they actually worked on the job. The work involved digging the ditch in which the pipeline was to be placed. Another place of employment for both Cary and Mary Kirkham was Ward Evans' corn cannery, where both worked during the canning season. One year, the Kirkhams took King Alfred daffodil bulbs for the pay they had coming, and planted them at their place. By 1940, the initial stock had increased considerably. During these years, Mary Kirkham, Susie, Marion and Virgil sometimes worked picking berries for John Larson.

Though primarily a homemaker, Mary Raybourn had proved her mettle before she married. When she reached age 21, land was still available for homesteading in some areas of the country. She homesteaded a half section (320 acres) in NE New Mexico. A desolate location, then and now, she lived on the place the requisite time to 'prove' her claim, and the land belongs to the family to this day. Several years ago hopes were raised among family members when an oil company leased the land. Exploratory wells were sunk, but as far as the family knows, no commercial amounts of oil or gas were found.

During the 30's, the PWA extended Smith Road through to Evans Road, which had previously ended at Kirkham's driveway. Workers excavated the 'cuts' by shovel and moved dirt to level the grade with wheelbarrows. Workers shoveled dirt into dump trucks, which dumped the contents into the one large fill on the extension. This and similar projects provided local farmers an opportunity to earn a few dollars to pay bills.

As Marion remarked, "The men worked doing something. It wasn't just a handout."

At age 12, Marion got a job working for Orland Zeek on his horse-powered hay baler. His job involved keeping the horses going in a circle, which powered the compactor that formed the bales. As the horses circled the dust grew deeper and deeper under their hooves, soon becoming ankle deep in the ruts. Of course the dust flew, and everyone on the job had to breathe it.

In the fall of 1941, Marion had an opportunity to go to Sitka, Alaska to work on a construction job. He was in Sitka when Japan bombed Pearl Harbor. The job paid well, which turned out to be fortuitous as when he arrived home the family faced eviction from the place they had called home for 14 years. During the depression years, the Kirkhams had not made payments required by the contract they had signed to purchase the Delano property. Mr. Delano had died, and the estate wanted to be paid, or the property would be sold. Fortunately, opportunities to obtain work had brightened with the war underway in Europe, so the Kirkhams scraped together the funds necessary to pay what they owed. The payment was made and the Kirkhams finally owned the property clear.

During World War II, Cary Kirkham worked in the shipyards. He established a route calling on various stores that stocked daffodil bouquets that he supplied. He stopped at each store twice a week during the 'bloom.' If necessary, he took time off from his job at the shipyard to take care of the route. During the period when the Kirkhams worked to increase their bulb stock, the flowers were 'headed,' which caused the energy to be displaced from the flower to the bulb, hopefully increasing the size of the bulb.

Dortha, who had worked for Libby through the depression years, joined the Women's Army Corp (WAC's) during the war. After completing basic training she was sent to the South Pacific, eventually to Guam. She spent three years in the Army, attaining the rank of Tech 3 (T-3). After completing her tour, she returned to Libby, McNeil and Libby. When the Portland plant closed, she transferred to Salem. She said, "I went from pickles to canned fruits and vegetables." Dortha retired after completing 50 years with the Company. She built a house on 5 acres she owns that is adjacent to other family holdings on Mershon Road. Currently, because of health problems, she lives with Charles and Barbara Kirkham at their home on Smith Road.

Dortha Kirkham (on right) in New Guinea with 'GI Joe.'

Susie Kirkham, c 1944.

Photos courtesy of Dortha Kirkham.

After leaving Oregon State College, Susie Kirkham worked at the Bridal Veil Lumber and Box Company. Later she obtained a job at Consolidated Freightways, which is where she was working when she married Richard Stief in 1951. The couple lived in Portland and had three children, Richard (who is deceased), David and Mary. David purchased 10 acres on Mershon Road (that belonged to the author at one time) and works for American Airlines. He married Diane Woo and has two girls, Jamie and Kelly, both of whom attend CHS. Later Mary joined her mother at the Kirkham residence on Mershon Road. After the original house burned, a replacement was built on the property and Mary lived with her mother there. Susie Kirkham died May 22, 1995 of Leukemia. Mary married Dominic DeHoyos and has a son, Alvaro.

Marion, who had returned from Alaska, expected to be drafted. He had heard about a program that ostensibly trained individuals to become flight instructors for the Army. He registered at Lewiston State Normal School in Idaho and registered for the program. No pay was involved, but he did receive room and board. Later those involved in the training were paid a small stipend. He took flight training at the Lewiston-Clarkston Airport. After completing primary and secondary training, he was sent home, and the US Army called. Joining the Army in August 1943, Marion took boot camp at Kerns, Utah where the recruits lived in tents heated by coal-burning stoves. Because of his background, the Air Corps accepted Marion into the Air Cadet program and sent him to Kansas State Teachers College for preliminary schooling. He completed this phase satisfactorily, was transferred first to Albuquerque, New Mexico and then to Amarillo, Texas, where (it seemed to him), he was in 'limbo' for a time. Finally, orders sent Marion to Santa Anna, California for fur-

232

Made It

Air Cadet Marion Kirkham in an AT-6.
Photo courtesy of Dortha Kirkham.

ther pre-flight training. He completed primary training at Lancaster, California and secondary training at Merced, California. Finally, he earned his wings and his commission at Luke Field near Phoenix, Arizona in August 1945.

Mary Kirkham passed away August 2, 1945. The Army Air Corps gave Marion an emergency leave home to attend her funeral. By the time he returned to Luke Field, the war had ended. He received his honorable discharge in October of 1945. He returned home and started farming in 1946. He grew certified seed potatoes, strawberries and daffodils. Marion married Ethel Cowings June 5, 1948. They had met during the war, corresponded regularly and saw each other on occasion. They moved into the home place on Smith Road. Meanwhile, Cary Kirkham had purchased 10 acres on Mershon Road from John Flanagan. He added a five-acre parcel at the north end of that piece. Dortha purchased an adjacent five-acre parcel, as did Susie. Thus the Kirkhams had sufficient farmland to keep both Marion and his father busy. In 1962 after 17 years experiencing the 'ups and downs' of farming, Marion decided he wanted to try something else. There were just too many 'down' years.

Bill Soderstrom's nephew, Keith Soderstrom, had become interested in plastics while working for Boeing. Keith, who lived in Federal Way, Washington, had invented an air-injection-molding machine for shaping plastics that he thought had potential. When Bill talked to Marion regarding the possibility of manufacturing parts using the machine, both decided to provide capital to proceed. Marion also had a building (the former bulb shed) and Keith, the machinery and the expertise needed to start production. Thus KASO (Keith A. Soderstrom (0) Plastics was born. The business provided custom molded plastic parts to such customers as John Fluke Corporation and Tektronix. After the business had proved profitable, Marion and Bill bought out Keith, who had other business plans. Later Bob Kiesel purchased Keith's share. The plant operated 24 hours a day and hired more than 10 people at various times. When asked about past employees, Marion quickly named Thelma Beeman, Barbara Case, Flora Chamberlain, Gloria Collins, Mitzie Kerslake, Jean Rhodes, Louise Rhodes, Linda Roley, Linda Stiles, Linda Tarpley and Gladys Wilson. He said, "I know I've missed some."

Foresight saved the business when what could have been a disastrous event occurred, the death of Bill Soderstrom in an accident. The partners had a 'buy-sell' agreement backed by life insurance package that paid off Bill's heirs, and the business continued with Marion and Bob. When Bob Kiesel wanted to sell, Marion purchased his share. Later, Marion sold out to Duane Cartier, who moved the business to Washington. Though Cartier later sold it, the business continues to operate. Because of a 'no compete' agreement, Marion and his family could not go into the plastics molding business for five years. After that period passed, Marion and Chuck's wife, Barbara, decided to reopen the business, purchased machinery and established Kirkham Custom Molding, Inc., which Barbara 'Bobbie,' now manages.

Marion and Ethel had three children, Marilyn, b. November 19, 1949, Chuck, b. December 14, 1951 and Irene, b. July 19, 1955. Marilyn attended Corbett schools, but completed her secondary years at Marshall High School. During the time she attended Marshall she lived with her Aunt Dortha. Both Chuck and Irene completed school at Corbett. Chuck graduated from CHS in 1970 and Irene graduated in 1973. Irene gave the Valedictory address at the '73 commencement. Marilyn married Doug Van Patton, lives in Homer, Alaska and teaches school.

Chuck trained with Norv Shuster, who operated a tool and die business in Corbett. When Norv moved the business to Clackamas, Chuck decided to open his own tool and die business, Comp Tool. He now operates Comp Tool in the same location as Kirkham Custom Molding. Chuck married Barbara 'Bobbie' Willis and lives in a home built on the home place located on Smith Road. He and Bobbie have two sons, Charles

234

Virgil Kirkham

Virgil Kirkham, CHS Class of 1942.
Photo courtesy of the Kirkham Family.

'C.W.' and Timothy 'Tim.' Irene married Loran Leighton, lives in Springfield, Oregon and has three children, Andrea, Leanne and Lindsey.

After Virgil graduated from CHS, he attended Oregon State College for a term. In January 1943 he visited Marion, who was going through pilot training at Lewiston. Virgil decided to join the Army, hoping to gain acceptance into the pilot training program. He moved through the training phases without pause and was commissioned a 2nd Lieutenant at Luke Field, Arizona in the summer of 1944. The Air Corps sent Virgil overseas, assigned to the 377th Fighter Squadron based in France. Formed to provide ground support for the advancing Allied armies, the 377th flew P-47's, a rugged fighter plane designed for air to ground combat.

Virgil flew 83 missions in 1944 and 1945. He and his fellow pilots took 'R and R' in such places as Paris and the French Riviera. These diversions, however, did not keep them from their principal task: to harass, interdict and destroy enemy formations and traffic, including convoys, trains, barges, airfields and aircraft, armor or other military targets. On April 30, 1945, the 377th flew its final mission of the war. Though he had completed his required number of missions, Kirkham and another pilot from the 377th volunteered for this mission. The two went after a German convoy in Czechoslovakia. Virgil was to strafe the target while his comrade carried a bomb to use against any target of 'opportunity' in the area.

As Kirkham made his run, his fighter was hit by ground fire, struck a tree, cartwheeled to a stop and burst into flames. Later his family learned that a bullet had pierced the cockpit, and he was likely dead before his aircraft struck the tree. The townspeople in a nearby village put out the flames and later placed a monument to honor and commemorate the courage and sacrifice displayed by an American pilot in helping to rid Czechoslovakia of the Nazi invader. The war ended just eight days later.

Lieutenant Virgil Kirkham

Lt. Virgil Kirkham stands beside his P-47 fighter plane in France, 1945.
Photo courtesy of the Kirkham Family.

Marion Kirkham and other members of the Kirkham family have visited the site in Czechoslovakia where Virgil's plane went down. They visited the memorial erected by the people of a nearby village to express their gratitude to an American who gave his life to help liberate their country. As Marion remarked, "These villagers know what it means to live under a dictatorship, know the suffering that war brings and have done many things to remind their descendants of the past. They remember the sacrifice of an American pilot, and continue to honor him and the country from which he came."

Because of contacts between the Kirkham family and people in Czechoslovakia regarding her Uncle Virgil's death during World War II, Marion and Ethel's daughter, Marilyn, arranged for a plaque to be presented to the villagers in the Chodso Region of the Czech Republic. The Mayor of Homer, Jack Cushing, signed the plaque, which reads in part:

> …"WHEREAS, the kind people of the (Chodsko) area gave courageous assistance and made personal contact with family members in Corbett, Oregon; and
>
> WHEREAS, the people of the Czech Republic have continued to honor Lt. Virgil Kirkham as well as all people and soldiers working toward peace, equality and justice, and...

236

Memorial Erected by Villagers in Czechoslovakia for Virgil Kirkham

From L, Marilyn Kirkham, Ethel Kirkham, Marion Kirkham, Irene (Kirkham) Leighton and Andrea Leighton visit Virgil's Memorial in Czechoslovakia.

Photo courtesy of Marion Kirkham.

WHEREAS, continuing efforts of friendship and understanding of citizens over great distances are a vital means to promote peace in the world and a better future for our children.

NOW, THEREFORE, I, Jack P. Cushing, Mayor of the City of Homer, do hereby proclaim a special relationship between our citizens, and offer a very sincere thanks to the people of the Czech Republic for recognition of Lt. Kirkham and for the deeds of all the people involved, then and now, in building goodwill and friendship between our citizens."

Edward W. Klinski
Ida E. (Berney) Klinski

Edward 'Ed' Klinski was born in Three Lakes, Wisconsin October 19, 1899. He came with his family to the Northwest shortly after the turn of the century, when they settled in Vancouver, Washington. Ed attended Benson Tech, where he learned the pattern-making trade. He worked at this trade even as he farmed through World War II. Ed and his brother started a dairy farm near Pleasant Home in the early 20's. Ed married Ida Elise Berney, daughter of Charlie Berney (see "Charles A. Berney") October 24, 1925. Ed and his bride then moved to this area, renting a farm close to the Grange Hall (later owned by Frank Windust). In 1930, Ed Klinski purchased 40 acres on Mershon Road at its junction with Wand Road. Later he added 23 acres to the west, 15 acres on Ogden Road, and also purchased the former Chamberlain place. Much of the property was sub-divided early in the century as Banner Acres, which is the name the family selected for the farm. Ed brought his dairy herd of approximately fifteen milking cows to the new place. He continued with his job as a pattern maker at Willamette Pattern Works during this time.

Ed and Ida had three children, Barbara, b. March 1, 1927; Thomas 'Tom,' b. March 27, 1930; and Marilyn, b. July 2, 1936. The children attended Corbett Grade School, riding the bus driven by Alvin Kinney. All graduated from CHS, Barbara in 1944, Tom in 1948 and Marilyn in 1955. Both Barbara and Tom served as Student Body President, Barbara in 1943-44 and Tom in 1947-48. In addition to the dairy herd, the Klinskis grew potatoes, cabbage, cauliflower, bulbs, strawberries and cucumbers. The principal crop, however, was potatoes, which were planted on from 50 to 60 acres each year. Because they were needed on the home farm, the youngsters did not generally work for other farmers in the area.

Ed joined with other farmers to form the Troutdale Potato Growers, organized by M.B. McKay. The growers grew seed potatoes that were shipped to California for early planting. During World War II farmers could market all their crops at good prices, and Ed Klinski took advantage of the opportunity. Because of the labor shortage, a camp was established for Mexican nationals at Viking Park. Farmers could order the number of workers wanted for the day and pick them up at the camp. After the war, Ed cut down on row crops and increased the size of the

Ed and Ida Klinski

Edward Klinski and Ida (Berney) Klinski at home. Photo courtesy of Barbara (Klinski) Wells.

Klinski Children

Barbara (holding Marilyn) and Tom Klinski in their yard. First Klinski home in the background. Photo courtesy of Delta Klinski.

dairy herd. However, the Korean War caused a pick-up in demand for vegetables, and the Klinskis grew more cabbage during this period, marketing the crop through the vegetable shed at Troutdale, managed by Pete Binn. Neighbors who worked for Ed Klinski included Alma Bramhall (daffodils), Hattie Keisel (daffodils), Gladys Lampert and her children, Lorraine, Barbara, Carroll, Colleen and Donna (strawberries), Jeff Overby (dairy), Andy Winters (general farm work) and Howard Winters. When Ed grew flowers, he had about ten acres of daffodils, 3 acres of tulips and a couple of acres of Dutch Iris.

In 1934 Ed Klinski received the Carnegie Medal for saving the life of a former neighbor, Mr. Lansdowne, who became unconscious while working in the depths of a well. Ed volunteered to be lowered into the well to bring him up. He was able to get a rope around Mr. Lansdowne and both were pulled to safety. In addition to the medal, Ed received a $1000 cash award, which was used to help pay for the property on Mershon Road.

Barbara Klinski started college at Linfield with a scholarship, but admits she became so homesick that she asked her parents to come and get her. Her goal was to become a teacher, and she regrets to this day her inability to deal with leaving home. She then obtained a secretarial job at the County Extension Office. After she left this job, she worked for Walrad Insurance Agency in Gresham for six years. She married James R. 'Dick' Wells June 6, 1953. The couple lived on the family farm until 1956,

Barbara Klinski

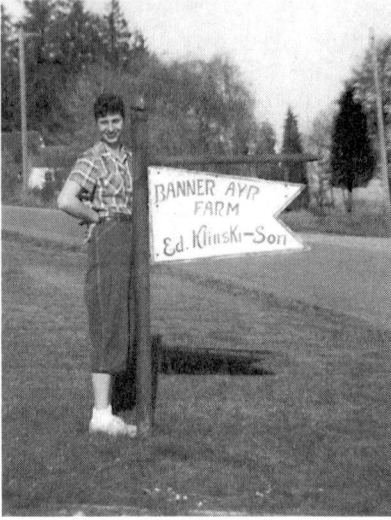

Barbara Klinski stands at the corner of Wand and Mershon Roads.

Tom Klinski

Tom Klinski on 'R & R' in Japan before returning to Korea during the Korean War.

Klinski Farm

Aerial view of the Klinski farm, Banner Acres. Note the Larson farm to the west.

Photos courtesy of Delta Klinski.

240

The Wells

Barbara and Dick Wells with their son, Jay. Photo courtesy of Delta Klinski.

Dick and Barbara Wells Family

From L, Dick Wells, Barbara Wells (holding granddaughter Kristin), Jay Wells (with Kyle) and Ida Klinski. Photo courtesy of Barbara (Klinski) Wells.

when they moved to Wood Village. Barbara's parents gave the couple a lot on the Chamberlain place (off Chamberlain Road). Barbara and Dick built a home on this place and have lived there since 1968. A son, Jay, was born October 5, 1956. He attended Corbett Schools after the move and graduated from Corbett High School in 1974. Dick worked for Reynolds Metals in Troutdale for 36 years. After working for Walrad, Barbara obtained a position with Western Skyways in Troutdale, where she worked for 29 years in the accounting department. Barbara recently underwent a heart operation and has recovered well from the ordeal.

Tom Klinski always preferred dairying to some of the other farm operations. After he graduated from high school Tom encouraged his father to increase the dairy herd. He much preferred milking cows, baling hay and doing the other tasks associated with dairying to growing row crops. He remembers cutting cabbage with ice clinging to the leaves and said he would rather be in the barn milking cows. The Korean War interrupted Tom's farming years when he was called to serve in the U.S. Army in 1952. He spent two years in the service, which included a tour in Korea. Tom married Delta Stahl, whom he met in church, February 17, 1956. Delta was born in Langham, Saskatchewan December 9, 1934. They have three children, Todd E., b. November 5, 1958, Dawn M., b. August 24, 1961 and Melissa R., b. November 4, 1964. Tom worked with his father until Ed passed away August 15, 1977. Tom and Delta

Ida Klinski with Tom and Family

L to R: Rose Stahl, Dawn (Klinski) Hudson, Kevin Hudson, Todd Klinski, Ida Klinski, Tom Klinski, Delta Klinski, Paul Schweitzer and Melissa (Klinski) Schweitzer.

Photo courtesy of Delta Klinski.

continued to farm the home place. They operated the dairy until 1986, when they took advantage of the government sponsored 'buy-out.' The cows were sold for beef and the government paid Tom and Delta a set price for their milk production. When Tom and Delta sold the dairy herd, the "dairy era" ended in East Multnomah County, as the Klinski herd was the only dairy in operation in the area at the time. Since 1986 they have raised beef cattle.

Delta Klinski started working as a secretary at Corbett Grade School in 1970 and continued in that position for 26 years, retiring in 1996. The youngsters attended school in Corbett, with Todd graduating from Corbett High in 1976, Dawn in 1979 and Melissa in 1982. After selling the dairy herd, Tom started driving school bus for Corbett schools.

Marilyn Klinski married Allan G. Holms June 7, 1958. The couple moved to Missoula, Montana, where Allan was in the automobile business. The couple had three children, Allison, Tyler and Trent. Marilyn was interested in and practiced interior decorating. Her last job involved decorating a private railroad car for Mr. Denny Washington, who used it for his journeys across the country. Marilyn passed away July 31, 1990, in Missoula and Mr. Washington invited the Klinski family to join he and his wife in the special car after the funeral to reminisce.

242

Marilyn (Klinski) Holms with Her Mother

Marilyn (Klinski) Holms stands with her mother, Ida Klinski.
Photo courtesy of Barbara (Klinski) Wells.

Smelt fishing, Sandy River c1917.
Photo courtesy of Don Lampert.

Orval A. Klock
Dorothy M. (Wheeler) Klock

Orval and Dorothy Klock lived on the north side of Hurlburt Road near its junction with Ellis Road. The place was about three acres in size, with a large garden area. Orval, son of Harper and Oma (Kimbley) Klock, was born in Gresham, Oregon May 7, 1911. Dorothy was born in Gresham, August 4, 1915. Orval's parents had another son, Bruce, b. June 30, 1913. Both Orval and Bruce attended Hurlburt Grade School. At the time, the family lived on Gordon Creek Road south of the Davis place. After completing elementary school, Orval attended CHS, graduating in 1930. Bruce had gone to work to help support the family and to help Orval with his high school expenses. After Orval graduated, he was to return the favor, but Bruce turned down the offer as he had a job, difficult to come by during the depression era.

Orval and Dorothy M. Wheeler were married August 31, 1935. Orval worked at the Bridal Veil mill during the 30's. The Klocks also worked their three acres intensively. In addition to the garden, they raised berries, chickens and sheep. They sold eggs and dressed fryers to Strohecker's store in West Portland, among other outlets. Stroheckers also bought vegetables fresh from the garden. Dorothy Klock became very active as a volunteer with the Oregon State Extension Service, teaching craft classes and working with youth groups in the 4-H program for more than 60 years. She was an accomplished seamstress and worked in that field on a contract basis.

When World War II created a demand for ships, Orval, together with many others, went to work in the Kaiser Oregon Shipyard. He joined a car pool from East County with Jum Mershon and several others in order to conserve gasoline. When the war ended in 1945, Orval took a job at CHS in Corbett as a custodian and school bus driver. He also coached the freshman basketball and drove the activity bus to 'away' games. Those who played on the teams he coached will remember him for his calm and supportive attitude. He loved sports, and relished working with young people. In 1959, Orval accepted a similar position with David Douglas School District.

Orval and Dorothy Klock had two children, Glen, b. August 26, 1937 and Mary S., b. September 9, 1939. Both attended Corbett schools, with

The Klock Family

From (L), Dorothy, Glen, Orval and Mary Klock.

Photo courtesy of Clair Klock.

Glen graduating from CHS in 1955, Mary in 1957. While growing up, both Glen and Mary were active in 4-H projects directed by their mother. She taught sewing, cooking, livestock raising and chicken husbandry, among others. After graduation, both attended Oregon State College from which Glen graduated in 1959 with a degree in agriculture and Mary in 1961 with a degree in home economics.

As mentioned, Dorothy Klock taught courses through the extension service. Among the classes she taught was basketry. Dorothy became renowned for her work in making pine needle baskets, selling her work through local outlets and teaching others the craft. She was also interested in local history. She wrote a book, *Crown Point Country Schools, 1874-1974*. Now out of print, the East Multnomah County Pioneer Association has obtained the family's permission to publish a 2nd edition.

Glen Klock, after completing the ROTC program at OSC, went into the Air Force as a commissioned officer. He then completed a masters program at Iowa State University in Ames, Iowa and a doctorate at Oregon State University. He married Kathryn Wirostek September 13, 1958, and the couple had four children, Linda, David, Steven and Kevin. Glen now works as a Natural Resources Consultant and lives in Wenatchee, Washington. Glen participates in athletic events, and placed 3rd in the legendary 'Iron Man Division' of the April 1998 'Ridge to River' race,

Mary & Glen Klock

Mary and Glen Klock in their yard.
Photos courtesy of Clair Klock.

The Klocks c1963

Recent OSU graduate Mary at home with Dorothy and Orval Klock.

in which participants cross-country ski, downhill ski, run, bike and white-water kayak to cover the course. He also travels extensively. Places he has visited recently include: a two-week tour of Moscow, Tver and St. Petersburg, Russia; a backpack and Eurorail trip from Berlin, Germany to the Greek Island of Santorini; a trek in Nepal including a stay at the base camp for Mt. Everest climbers; a trip sailing the Turquoise Coast of Southwest Turkey in a gullet (Turkish wood sailboat) studying the ruins of Rhodes and enjoying the cultural amenities of Istanbul; and a self-guided tour of Costa Rica in 1998. In addition, he, together with a group of scientist from the United States, toured the length of Siberia, including Lake Bakal to study environmental degradation and related problems in Russia.

Mary Klock married John Rauch and has three children, James, John and Brian. John, who has a doctorate in physics, worked as a research physicist for Bell Labs, Lockheed Aircraft and other firms. The family has lived in Poway, California for 30 or more years. While she was raising her family, Mary did freelance writing. She now works as a legal assistant.

Bruce Klock worked at Bridal Veil Lumbering Company and other jobs in the logging industry until World War II. He was drafted and served with the 10th Mountain Division in North Africa and Italy. After the war he went to clock and watchmaking school and spent the remainder of his life as a watchmaker. On March 25, 1936, he married Amy St. Clair. She

246

Bruce Klock and Family

Grandfather Harper Klock (L), Bruce Klock with his children, Carol (L) and Clair.
Photos courtesy of Clair Klock.

worked in the shipyards as a welder and riveter. After the war, she returned to her job as homemaker. Bruce and Amy Klock had two children, Clair, b. March 29, 1951 and Carol, b. April 7, 1952. Amy passed away July 30, 1959 at age 42. In December 1963, Orval and Dorothy Klock took in Bruce's children because he had become ill with a brain tumor. Bruce died May 24, 1964 at age 50. At that time Clair was age 13, Carol, age 12. According to Clair, "The only silver lining in a time that was a dark cloud was the fact that Orval and Dorothy were willing to take us into their home. This was quite an adjustment for a couple in their early 50's who had children with families of their own."

Both Clair and Carol completed their elementary and secondary years at Corbett. Clair graduated from CHS in 1969 and Carol, in 1970. Clair then attended Oregon State University, graduating in 1974 with a degree in biology. On February 21, 1976, he married Beverly Bristow. Clair has worked in conservation and environmental education and as a full-time farmer. He is presently a Conservation Specialist/Habitat Biologist for the soil conservation districts in Multnomah County and a part-time farmer. He has about 4 acres of his 27-acre place on Salzman Road in cultivation. Carol moved to eastern Washington and worked in the fruit industry as a salesperson and broker. She is married to Max Williams, and now works as a real estate agent.

Frank Knieriem
Edith (Butler) Knieriem

Frank is the oldest son of George Knieriem Sr., who located on an 80-acre farm on what is now Knieriem Road in 1896 (See Pioneer History, pp. 107-108). Frank purchased a 40-acre farm adjacent to the family place. Frank's sister, Bessie, married Roy Muck, and lived just up Knieriem Road from Frank. His bachelor brothers, Fred and Robert 'Bob,' also lived up the road on the home place. Another brother, William E. Knieriem married Jessie J. Miller. They had two children, Herbert E., b. February 7, 1906 and Irene, b. October 11, 1907. William was killed in an auto accident April 26, 1931 that also took the life of George, his father. Shortly after (January 1937), William's son, Herbert was killed in an airplane crash (see "George Knieriem," *Pioneer History*). Frank married Edith Butler, and they had twelve children, only six of whom lived to adulthood. The family raised dairy cattle and grew feed for their livestock. In addition to farming, Frank Knieriem sometimes worked off the farm to supplement the family's income. Another brother, William E. married Jessie J. Miller.

On one such job Frank worked for the State Highway Department. He was hired to paint a white line to mark the center of the Columbia River Highway. (This original white stripe was later changed to yellow because it was thought that yellow could be seen better in foggy conditions.) Since there was no machine to accomplish this task, the painting was done by hand. Mr. Knieriem spent many days and hours on his hands and knees with a four-inch paint brush in hand painting this stripe. The centerline was marked by binder twine stretched along the middle of the roadway for the painter to follow. There were no 'flaggers,' as used today, so one took his chances with traffic on the road. In fact, on one occasion Frank was hit from behind by a car, but suffered no injury. However, a can of Prince Albert tobacco he was carrying in his hip pocket was smashed.

While the Knieriem kids were growing up, they worked for various neighbors on surrounding farms. They picked strawberries for the Uyetakes and planted cabbage for their Uncle George. The cabbage was always planted by hand. An older boy, girl or an adult with shovel in hand followed a marked row. He or she would scrape the top layer of dirt

Knieriem Family

In this picture of the Knieriem family, several appear to be wearing civil war era medals. Emily Knieriem is left of the post and George Knieriem is to the right.

Photos courtesy of Bob Dunken.

George and Emily Knieriem

George and Emily Knieriem with their daughter, Bessie.

William Knieriem Family

Rear, Jessie (Miller) and William E. Knieriem. Front, Irene and Herbert.

George Knieriem   **Bob Knieriem**

George Knieriem, World War I veteran.   Bob Knieriem, WW I veteran.

Photos courtesy of Bob Dunken

to show moisture, plunge the shovel into the ground and pull back so that a hole for the plant was made. The second member of the "team," usually a younger boy or girl carrying a handful of cabbage plants would insert a plant in the hole described above. The person operating the shovel would pull the shovel from the hole and simultaneously compact the soil around the plant with his/her foot. Acres of cabbage were planted in this manner. The 'old timers' say, partially in jest, "This was back breaking work that only the young could take."

Thrashing time was an annual event to which many looked forward with anticipation. Thrashing grain was done much differently in pre-combine days. Fred Knieriem had a binder, which was pulled by a team of horses. The binder cut the grain and tied it into bundles. These bundles were stacked heads up in the field for further curing and drying. When ready for thrashing, the bundles were hauled to a central location handy for the thrasher to reach, and stacked. These stacks were approximately 20-30 feet high, and about the same across. Each type of grain (wheat, barley, or oats) was stacked and thrashed separately. Alec Trickey oper-

250

Frank Knieriem Home

The Knieriem home off Knieriem Road.
Photo courtesy of Robert Knieriem.

ated one thrashing machine, which was reportedly owned by Gib Bates. His schedule was coordinated with each farmer so they would know when to expect his arrival. Of course rain would delay the sequence, and the schedule adjusted accordingly. The timing was crucial as neighboring farmers always helped with the thrashing and the wives and daughters would prepare the traditional huge meal for the participants. The thrasher was pulled and operated by a huge Case steam engine tractor. It was set up between the rows of stacked grain bundles. The tractor was turned about to face the thrasher and positioned so that the power pulley was aligned with the thrasher pulley. After the long 8" wide leather belt connected the two machines, the tractor backed up to take up the slack in the belt, and the machinery started to hum. Sometimes the tractor placement had to be adjusted so the belt would stay on the pulleys. The belt had a half (moebus) turn, which ensured even wear on each surface of the belt and caused the thrasher pulley to turn in the proper direction.

Alec kept the fire going to make steam and generally supervised the whole operation. Farm hands worked on the stacks pitching bundles onto the conveyor, which fed the thrasher. Straw flew from a movable stack at the back end of the thrasher, and was directed some distance away to make a straw 'haystack.' Grain poured from tubes on the side where sacks were attached, filled and removed. As the sacks of grain filled, they were sewn shut with sack-needle and binder twine. The grain was stacked nearby. When mealtime came, the rig was shut down and all hands washed up to eat. Everyone retired to the house for the feast. Many of the participants in these thrashing bees remark about the excellent meals. Either the meals were especially good, or the workers were especially hungry. After the meal, the work would resume until completed in a day or two. Alec Trickey would then move on to the next farm, the process repeated daily throughout the harvest season. The machine owner was paid so much per hundredweight, or he took payment by receiving a part of the grain if money was short (which it often was!).

Hay baling kept farmers busy during the summer, also. When he was about 14 years old, Robert Knieriem worked for Orland Zeek on the hay baler, a job that lasted about 2 or 3 weeks. Orland drove to the work site in a Model A Ford sedan, taking his helpers with him. Orland had a team of Belgian draft horses, which were left overnight where the baler had also been left to be used the next day. The team was soon harnessed and baling commenced. The baling machine itself was similar to the one operated in earlier years by J.C. 'Haywire' Wilson (see "Clarence Henry Wilson") in that it was powered by horses walking in a circle driving the reach, which powered the baler. Robert's job was to keep his eye on the bales and to holler when a new board had to be inserted between bales. If Orland didn't hear Robert holler, a very large bale would come forth. The operation ground to a stop and the bale had to be shortened while the horses took a break. This didn't improve Mr. Zeek's humor. Robert 'tied' the bales as they emerged. The 'boards' had slots on each side to permit baling wire to be pushed through and 'tied.' Each bale was weighed as it came out of the machine, and its weight posted on a small cedar chip which was inserted under the middle wire of the bale. The weight was also tallied on a record sheet, as Mr. Zeek was paid by weight. These tasks were all Robert's to perform. In addition, he had to 'buck' each bale upon the stack of finished bales.

Robert earned $2.00 per day for helping bale hay. The 'day' was about ten hours long by the time the team was unharnessed, curried down and fed, and the return trip to Orland's house was completed. Robert then had to jump on his bike, ride home, bring in the cows, milk them and then eat supper. Robert says he liked the job very much despite the hard work and the trouble he had in getting his own chores done at the end of the day. The mid-day meal was always a treat at the farmer's place where the baling was being done. There were exceptions, of course. One time Orland was baling hay for Charlie Sutton, who lived in Howard Canyon. The baler was set up near an orchard. Charlie was not overly concerned about cleanliness. This day Charlie left the field about 11:30 a.m. to prepare lunch. Mr. Zeek shut the baler down at noon, the team was fed and watered, and the crew filed into Charlie's kitchen to eat. Charlie had killed an old rooster, and boiled it for lunch, fried some potatoes and made some biscuits. According to Robert, the "chicken was tough and raw, the spuds half cooked and the biscuits showed evidence of the dirt on Charlie's hands from his handling them after baking." The crew soon withdrew to the orchard for a lunch of apples and pears.

The Knieriem girls had plenty to do. In addition to working for other farmers, and performing their chores at home, they had to take care of the home, with all the work that entailed. With the death of their mother, in 1927, the girls, Goldie and Eva, were faced with the task of preserving food for the winter months. As the fruit and vegetable crops came on, processing commenced. The girls canned cherries, applesauce, prunes, peaches, pears and berries as well as vegetables such as corn, peas, green beans, carrots and various kinds of pickles. In addition jams and jellies were made from the many fruits available, including wild varieties. A large copper boiler which held about 32 quarts was used for canning, The jars were stacked two high, separated by a wood layer made of lathe. Of course the wood stove was going full blast to cook the ingredients and to seal the jars during the hottest summer days. It was hard, hot work, but work at which the girls excelled. At times the boys, Walt and Robert were involved, such as with canning peas.

The task of shelling peas fell to the boys. Three or four gunnysacks of pole peas were bought from Paul Bosshardt, who was farming the Jim Ross' place at the time. That is a lot of peas to shell! After spending many hours at this task, Walt thought he had a great idea - use the clothes wringer. Thereafter, the boys filled a large galvanized tub with warm water in which to soak the peas and soften the shells. An old-fashioned hand clothes wringer was attached to the tub, and the shelling began. One boy pulled peas by the handful from the tub, and fed them into the wringer. The 'operator' turned the wringer and the peas popped from their shells. The idea worked famously, and the job, which had formerly taken hours, was accomplished in about 30 minutes. Sometimes a hard or monotonous task caused a creative mind to come up with a great, labor and timesaving idea.

As mentioned earlier, the Knieriems had dairy cattle. Sometimes the stock, particularly the younger animals, would eat larkspur (or "staggerweed" as it was called), which caused the animal to bloat, stagger about and go down. If not found quickly, the animal would die. To treat this condition, tallow or rendered fat was forced down the animal's throat. In a few minutes this usually caused the release of the trapped gas, and the animal would soon regain its feet. Another method used to treat the condition was to use a short knife inserted between the third and fourth ribs, which allowed the gas to escape. This was only used in an emergency as an infection could develop at the puncture site.

However, some of the tasks the Knieriem boys performed might not be considered 'normal' farm work. Everyone knows how the east wind howls through the Gorge. Tourists attracted to the area by the waterfalls or recreational opportunities would often stop at the Vista House. Because they lived nearby, Walt and Robert became entrepreneurs, relying upon the wind to help with their 'business.' When tourists unsuspectingly stepped from a car, the wind would often catch a hat and send it over the cliff. Walt and Robert knew this, so occasionally they would go to the Vista House, then carefully work their way down the bluff to retrieve the many hats thus lost. Back on top, they would offer their merchandise for sale, sometimes receiving 15 or 20 cents per hat. They thought they had a gold mine!

Another example of an 'unusual' practice involved getting wood for the winter. Walt and Robert were allowed to use dynamite and black powder for this task (Robert said he was 12 years old). Black powder was used in the splitting gun, a 1.5" round hollow steel tube open at one end and solid steel on the other so it could be driven into the end of a log. The hollow end was filled about three quarters full of black powder, then driven into the end of the log with a sledgehammer. The more the tool was driven into the wood, the more compressed the powder became. When the splitter reached the desired depth, a short 12" or so fuse was inserted into the hole provided for it, and lit. Something was propped against the 'gun' to keep it from becoming a projectile. The boys would scurry behind a stump or tree as it only took a few seconds for the fuse to ignite the powder. When it exploded, the log split apart. If the splitter became a projectile flying through the air, the boys kept their eyes on it in order to retrieve it for the next log.

To blow stumps, Walt and Robert bored holes beneath the larger roots and packed dynamite in the bottom of the hole. The middle stick in the pack would have a blasting cap inserted carefully into it with a trailing fuse long enough to give the 'lighter' time to get away before the blast. Another method used to get large trees down was by fire. One time Walt and Robert decided to bring down a large Douglas fir snag which had lost its top. It was only about 75' high, but was about 15' through at the butt. This particular tree had been 'tapped' in earlier days for pitch.

The original settlers sold pitch, which was used for many purposes, including as a sealant for ship planking and as the source material for making turpentine. A selected tree was bored to tap the pitch stream. After being bored, a vine maple plug was formed and inserted to close the hole to prevent the pitch from flowing. About twice a year, this plug was removed and the accumulated pitch was drained into buckets. It was then poured into barrels on a sled or wagon pulled by horses or mules, and taken to market. Before felling this particular tree, Walt and Robert removed the wood plug and obtained about 30 gallons of pitch, which was later used to start fires in their stoves.

To start the job of felling the snag, a two-inch hole was bored into the tree at a slight incline from the outside to the heart of the monster. Then a 2nd hole was bored to meet the first, but starting from a higher point. It took some time to bore these holes, as they had to be lined up properly. When the two holes were satisfactorily completed, a small ledge was axed in front of the bottom hole to make a shelf where a small fire could be built with pitch-laden chips. The holes created a powerful draft for the fire, and it would burn into the tree while smoke and sometimes flame poured from the upper bore. This slow, controlled process took about a week to complete. The fire was tended daily. When the tree finally fell, the boys threw dirt on the fire to put it out. Their next problem was finding a crosscut saw long enough to cut rounds for firewood. Fred Knieriem (the boys' uncle) had a power crosscut saw, but its blade was too short to do the job. Charlie Meistrell had a welding machine in his garage at Bridal Veil. He was able to braze two wood saw blades together to make a blade long enough to cut the rounds. There was not a single knot in the tree, and the rounds were quite easily split. The tree provided enough wood for two seasons (about 40 cords).

Of course, work didn't take all the Knieriem kids time. Roy Emily, who worked at the school, enjoyed taking students on fishing trips to favorite local spots, such as Herman Creek or Gordon Creek during the summer. Mr. Emily had a Model A Ford sedan, and could pile 5 or 6

Pepper Mtn. Lookout

Roy Emily mans the Pepper Mountain Lookout. This structure was replaced by an enclosed lookout in 1933. Photo courtesy of Pat (Bramhall) Paget.

youngsters in it for the trip. Everyone took a bedroll, food, cooking utensils and fishing gear. It was about a ten-mile hike into Herman Creek where the camp was set up. After unpacking, the kids headed for the creek. While the boys flailed around, hollering, jumping about and making noise, Mr. Emily would quietly fish upstream, away from the hubbub. The boys would catch a few fish, but Mr. Emily always caught enough to feed all. Another time, he took a group of boys to stay at a forest service cabin at the base of Pepper Mountain, where Robert's uncle, George Knieriem, was based and where Roy Emily sometimes manned the lookout. George's wife, Ruth, always welcomed the visitors. They stayed a few days, fishing in Gordon Creek, which was about a mile away. There were lots of wild blackberries growing everywhere, which, in the hands of a good pie maker, becomes an exceptional dessert. The only problem for Robert in going on these excursions was to find someone willing to do his chores for him. Usually he was able to prevail upon Walt to take care of them.

Another bit of fun Robert was involved with was an "experimental" car he and the O'Connell boys put together. Al Woodward had quite a collection of old worn out and discarded cars, which hadn't yet made it to the dump. The boys selected the best engine, which was in a Star frame, a Chevy transmission (which was installed backwards in order to get it to mesh), and a Model T Ford rear end and axle. According to Robert, it was a challenge to drive this "freak" because of all the possible speeds and getting the gears to mesh. He said it garnered "lots of attention and curiosity!"

When Robert was a high school junior, he got a job driving a "flag" truck for C.L. Deitrich, who had a logging operation. Robert's job was to intercept Mr. Deitrich's log trucks as they reached the Columbia River Highway off of Larch Mountain Road, and escort them to where they left the Highway at the Corbett Grade Road. The pickup was decked out with red flags and a sign, "Dangerous truck load of logs ahead." When the log truck driver turned onto Corbett Grade, Robert would turn around and speed back to Larch Mountain Road to meet the next truck. Later he worked for Mr. Deitrich as a grease monkey. After school he reported to the garage, greased the trucks and trailers in the shop, and changed any tires that needed changing. Changing a 900 x 20-truck tire with the tools available then was a difficult and dirty job, and it was all done by hand. Pry bars and sledgehammers came in handy for this chore. Since the rigs traveled over muddy, dirt logging roads, axles and undercarriages would be covered and caked with mud. One had to know where the zerk fittings were located in order to chip away the mud and get them greased. Robert was paid $.50 per hour, and was issued his social security card on July 23, 1938, while working this job.

The Knieriem children walked to the Columbia River Highway to catch the school bus. When the wind was blowing hard this was an adventure in itself, particularly the final 400-500 feet. If the east wind was blowing, the kids were pelted with dirt and sand particles as they traversed this stretch, struggling to take shelter at Jim and May Ross' stand on the north side of the highway. Frank Knieriem had built this sturdy structure for Mr. and Mrs. Ross, and part of it extended out over the bluff. When a strong gust hit the building, it would shudder, creak and rattle. That it stood while roofs blew off other buildings nearby indicates it was solidly built. As people said, "Frank used so many nails nothing could knock it down!"

The Knieriem children attended Corbett Grade and CHS. The grade school was heated by steam radiators, which were supplied with steam from a steam boiler heated by a wood furnace. It took a lot of wood to keep the building warm during the winter, perhaps 100 cords a year. Louie Baker of Aims generally furnished the wood. When brought to the school, the wood was stacked outside to dry. Roy Emily, the janitor, needed to get the wood inside, and he enlisted many of the grade school boys to get the job done. The boys would line up to help, and would lug the slabs in from outside, stacking them in the wood storage area. It took three or four weeks to get all the wood inside. When the job was completed, Mr. Emily would stop at Arneson's store, buy a box of Baby Ruth candy bars and distribute one to each of his helpers. The boys were happy to help, happy to get the candy and pleased to help Mr. Emily, who was well liked by all the kids.

Mignon Knieriem

Walt and Mignon Knieriem's Sons

From L, Jimmy, Alvin and Frances Knieriem.
Photos courtesy of Carlos Anderson.

Mignon Knieriem visits in San Francisco. Standing with her is her stepfather, Ellis Johnson.

When Robert enrolled as a freshman, there were 42 students in his class (1935). After four years of hard work, 28 graduated. Blanche Settlemier was Valedictorian and Maurice McKay, Salutatorian. Of the six children of Frank Knieriem to reach adulthood, all married and eventually moved from Corbett area, though Walt lived in the community for many years. The six are Aletha, b. 1904, who first married Charlie Meistrell and had two children. Later she married Mr. Jackson. Aletha is deceased. Frances M., B. 1907, first married Leonard Washburn (no living children). Later she married James 'Jim' Rose (no children). She and Jim live in Newberg, OR. 139Goldie, b. 1915, first married a Mr. Judson (one child). She later married Sherman Joy, (four children). Goldie is deceased.

Walter 'Walt' E. Knieriem married Mignon Anderson, daughter of Ollie (Wilson) Anderson. Walt and Mignon had three children, Alvin, Francis and James 'Jim.' Walt was born in Corbett January 10, 1918, where he was raised and educated. He was among the organizers of the Corbett Volunteer Fire Department, and served as fire chief in 1958. He worked a number of years for Pounder Truck Service as a truck driver. He also worked in the logging industry. Walt and his family lived on Hurlburt Road for many years before moving to the family place on

Frank Knieriem

Frank visiting the
Dave Butler family.
Photo, the author.

Robert and 'Buck' Beeman

World War II vets Robert Knieriem
(right) and Buck Beeman, Eva's
husband. Photo courtesy of Robert
Knieriem.

Knieriem Road. In 1963 he moved to Lewiston, Idaho with his family. His wife, Mignon, died on Thanksgiving Day in 1974. Walter died December 19, 1992. He is interred in Douglas Cemetery in Troutdale.

Robert E. Knieriem had a son, Robert Jr., by his first wife. Robert Jr. retired a Lt. Colonel from the Army National Guard. In 1949 Robert Sr. married Suzanne Eisenegger and they had a daughter, Cindy (Brown). Cindy had three children, Kevin, Emily and Jeff. Robert and his wife now live in Woodburn, OR. Eva married Buck Beeman. Buck had a band, "Buck Beeman and His Western Pals," which performed locally. For a time the group played for radio station KWJJ in Portland. The couple had two children, Loretta and Kenneth. Eva now lives in Portland, OR.

Robert Knieriem

Harry Kruckman
Clara (McQuillan) Kruckman

Harry Kruckman came to the East County area around 1920, sent by the McGowans (fishing interests) to supervise their seine at Rooster Rock. He had worked for the McGowans at their Ellsworth cannery just west of Fisher's Landing in Clark County, Washington for a number of years. Harry met his future wife, Clara McQuillan, while working at the cannery, and they were married at Toledo, Oregon in 1925. Clara had a child, Wayne, from a previous marriage. Harry was born December 6, 1887, and Clara was born July 13, 1888. At about the time fishwheels were banned on the Columbia River by the State of Oregon, the McGowans gave up the seine at Rooster Rock, and Harry Kruckman took over its operation. He moved to Rooster Rock, living in the foreman's quarters, which was located near the Union Pacific Railroad's section hand quarters. Harry built a bunkhouse on the Island, the land area stretching east of Rooster Rock, which no longer exists as an island. The bunkhouse housed workers while the seine operated. There was also a horse barn and corral located there.

This seine was a 'horse seine,' which means the nets were pulled ashore by teams of horses. There were four active teams, two for the 'tail,' and two for the 'head.' Often local farmers with teams were hired to work the seine. A 250 fathom net (maximum) was laid out by boat traveling across the Columbia starting at the upper end of the Island (toward Sand Island). The tail (beach) end was hooked to a team, as the net was set. As the net drifted downstream, the driver of the tail team kept abreast of the net, and kept it taut. The length of time it was allowed to drift depended upon the current, but it was usually about 30 minutes. When it was time to begin the pick-up, the 'head' boat turned shoreward and reefed the head of the net into the beach at Rooster Rock.

As the head (outer) end was brought ashore, one team hooked up, and started pulling the net ashore. As the net was pulled in, a large loop formed with both the head and tail being pulled ashore. When the first team ran out of room, the second team took a 'bite,' and continued the work. The first team then returned to the water edge ready to take a second 'bite' in turn. With each successive bite, the loop in the river became smaller and smaller. As this 'loop' approached shallow water,

Seine Ground at Rooster Rock

Seine fishermen hold the cork line up to prevent salmon from escaping. J.C. 'Curly' Wilson is the second fisherman from the L.   Photo, the author.

Team Working the Seine

The 'tail team' kept the net even with the 'head-end' in the boat as the net drifted downriver.   Photo, the author.

men surrounded it, held the cork line up and the lead line down to keep salmon from escaping. When the 'loop' came into water shallow enough to work in, the hands waded into the melee, grabbing salmon by the tail, and throwing them into the 'pot' scow. When the numbers had been reduced sufficiently, the cork line was draped over stakes in the gunwale of the scow, and the balance of the catch flipped in with the net.

The entire process, from laying out the net to harvesting the salmon, continued hour after hour and day after day during the open season. Clara Kruckman cooked for the fisherman who stayed in the bunkhouse. She sometimes would bring a big pan of donuts to the beach while the work was in progress. She told how kids who were sometimes on hand "gobbled them up."

The fish were picked up by the fish tender, usually operated by Alvin Kinney, and sent on to the cannery for processing. The McGowans purchased the salmon for years. Later Alvin delivered the catch to Faloma, where it was trucked to the Portland Fish Company. Faloma was located on the Oregon shore above Jantzen Beach. The Kruckman seine operated into the 1950's, continuing for a time under an injunction issued by a court after being outlawed by the State Legislature. However, the State prevailed, and fishing by seine was finished. Over the years, the seining season was shortened until in its final days, it was allowed to operate from May 1 to August 25, with weekend closures. Since the spring run was nearly over by May 1, not many of the premium spring fish (Royal Chinooks) were caught. The fall season opened September 10, and fishing ended when the run ended.

Bringing In the Seine Net

A team brings in the tail end of the net. George 'Jum' Mershon strides through the water in the foreground.   Photo, the author.

Completing the Harvest

The crew finish throwing the salmon into the scow. Jum Mershon is the sixth from left, Walt Preston is fifth from the right (with brimmed hat).   Photo, the author.

Many local people worked for the Kruckmans, including Frank Fehrenbacher, with his "outstanding" team (according to Wayne Kruckman), Jerome Fehrenbacher, George 'Jum' Mershon, Walt Preston, J.C. 'Curly' Wilson, Jasper Mershon, Lewis Deaver and many others. Sometimes men came in before the season opened who knew how to mend and rack the nets. Jum Mershon was sometimes called upon to do

Catch of the Day　　　　　**Seine Grounds at Rooster Rock**

Laura Mershon selects a couple of prime Chinook salmon to take home for canning.
Photo, the author.

The Rooster Rock seining ground with the McGowan cannery (bottom left) nestled beneath Rooster Rock. Note the causeway by which salmon were taken from the seine directly to the cannery.
Photo courtesy of Arlene (Johnson) Marble.

this. Wayne also mentioned the importance of stacking the net for layout. It had to be done in a particular way so that it came off the scow easily, didn't hang up, and didn't entangle anyone. Frank Fehrenbacher often performed this task.

The Kruckmans moved to Latourell from the 'Island,' and lived there until purchasing the George Joseph place just west of Latourell in 1941. They had two birth children, Betty, b. December 6, 1926, and 140Harry 'Buster,' b. April 27, 1929. The children attended school at Latourell Grade School, though Mrs. Kruckman moved Betty to Corbett in the sixth grade, and Buster moved to Corbett when Latourell Grade closed. All of the Kruckman children attended CHS in Corbett, Wayne graduating in 1938, Betty in 1944, and Buster in 1947. Harry and Clara continued to live on the farm and built up a dairy herd of about 25 head. Wayne Kruckman, after graduating from high school, worked on the dairy farm. After getting his draft notice in 1941, he enlisted in the Army Air Force and entered the service in July of that year. He was sent to Texas for basic and advanced training, and was ordered to a bombardier-training outfit. While stationed at Big Springs Army Air Force base, he attended an USO event one evening and met Virginia Howell, of Sweetwater, Texas, his future bride. They were married August 28, 1943, in the Airbase chapel. Virginia said hers "was not a farm or ranch background," despite her Texas roots. In 1944, Wayne, after undergoing overseas training in

Utah, found himself on a British troopship out of New Jersey on his way to the South Pacific. Though tons of beef carcasses had been taken onboard in New Jersey, the regular mess fare for the troops was mutton. In order to see the Panama Canal when the ship passed through, Wayne stayed up all night.

Wayne and his shipmates landed in New Guinea assigned to the 49th Fighter Group, Fifth Air Force. The pilots of the 49th flew P-38s, which the Japanese called the "fork-tailed devil." Major Bong was the leading ace in the 49th. Wayne served as an armorer, which involved taking care of the fighters' guns, loading ammunition and bombs, and similar duties. Four days after the invasion of the Philippines, Wayne's outfit landed at Leyte, and soon found themselves at a base near Lingayen Gulf, a former resort "with beautiful beaches." While based there, he traveled to Manila for R & R (rest and recreation). Wayne's next station was Okinawa, where he spent three to four months. He was stationed on Okinawa when the war ended, and was sent to Japan after the surrender to a base near Yokohama.

Wayne returned to the states in November 1945, and was discharged at Fort Lewis. He caught a train bound for Amarillo, where Virginia met him, and they were back in Latourell for Christmas. The couple rented a place there, and Wayne farmed and fished the seine with his parents. The flood of 1948 washed away the horse barn on the "Island," with water covering the bunkhouse floor to a depth of two feet. After the seine closed and the State Parks took over the "Island," the bunkhouse was torn down and rebuilt on the farm. While the couple lived in Latourell, they had three children: Robert, b. December 25, 1947; Brenda, b. March 24, 1950; and Jay, b. October 17, 1955. When Harry's mother, Clara, died in December 12, 1959, Wayne and his family moved to the dairy, which they had been working with his parents, to be with his father. Harry Kruckman died October 12, 1978. By this time, the dairy herd had increased to the point the Kruckmans were milking nearly 50 head. During the bad winter of 1969, a blizzard isolated East Multnomah County for several days, and milk to be shipped was covered by a snowdrift at Bridal Veil. The Kruckmans dumped several days' production.

After this experience, Virginia thought perhaps the family should "try something else," so Wayne let it be known the herd was for sale. Soon thereafter, a prospective purchaser from Boardman approached him. He put up $2500 in earnest money for the herd. Exactly 30 days later, on the day when the agreement was due to expire, the buyer showed up

Buster Kruckman

Buster Kruckman, CHS graduate, 1947

Ila Dempsey

Ila Dempsey, CHS 1947. '47 Cohimore photos courtesy of David Rees.

with a cattle truck. According to Wayne, the only question he asked was, "Do you have the rest of the money?" An affirmative answer led to loading the cows aboard the truck, and he and Virginia accompanied it to Hermiston. Wayne admits having a "tear in his eye", as the herd was unloaded at its new home. The Kruckmans then ran beef cattle on the place until it was sold to the State of Oregon in 1972.

When the State of Oregon purchased the farm in 1972, the Kruckmans moved to Springdale, Oregon. Wayne had gone to work for the State Parks Division after selling the dairy herd, and Virginia worked for Fred Meyer, Inc., at a store service center. When Fred Meyer closed their in-store service centers in 1974, she went to work at Portland Bottling Company as an accounts receivable clerk, and worked there until retiring in 1983. Wayne retired from the State Parks Division December 31, 1980. Wayne and Virginia sold their home in Springdale in 1990, and since that time, have been "on the road" in their 5th wheel RV unit.

After graduating from CHS in 1944, Betty Kruckman worked in the shipyards until the war ended. She married Bud McCleary, and they lived east of Gresham on Troutdale Road. The McClearys had four children, a son, Kelly, and three daughters, Susan, Kathy and Laurie. Later the family moved to a home on Marmot Road past Sandy, Oregon. They also have a cabin on a lake in British Columbia.

Harry "Buster" Kruckman graduated from CHS in 1947. He worked at the Bridal Veil mill for a time, then worked for Portland General Electric for many years, until "I was vested," he mentions. Buster married Ila Mae Dempsey November 7, 1948. Ila was his high school sweetheart, and the couple has two children, Jeff and Jeanette. The family lived off Hurlburt Road on Henkle Road, near the Kerslake place, for several years. After leaving PGE, Buster and Ila moved to Lostine, Oregon, where, Wayne avers, "Buster and Ila have a beautiful place." *Wayne Kruckman*

McGowan's Cannery at Rooster Rock

The McGowan Cannery before the river silted in blocking the channel.
Photo courtesy of George Perry Jr.

266

Alexander Lampert
Juliana (Grohs) Lampert

Sometime in 1882, Alexander Lampert and Juliana Grohs (pronounced "Gross") Lampert immigrated to America. Both were born in Germany, came to America as sweethearts and married here. (A grandson, Donald Lampert, has the travel trunk they brought with them, which has notices written in German and the year "1882" stenciled on it.) Alexander's United States citizenship application, dated February 11, 1891, states that he was "a subject of the Emperor of Austria." They lived a short time at Freeport, Illinois where their oldest child, Theresa, was born June 30, 1883. When the baby was three months old, the family took a train to Portland. This was most likely after September 8 when the Northern Pacific Railroad began continuous service from St. Paul, Minnesota to Portland, Oregon.

Where they stayed the first winter is not known for sure. A brief family history, apparently written by Emma Lampert (second child), has them living with friends when they first arrived. These may have been Franz Joseph and Katherine Frommelt, who were friends of theirs from Germany. The Frommelts arrived at Portland in the fall of 1882 and settled at Bethany, west of Portland. This somewhat agrees with family lore, which mentions that the family may have settled in the Tualatin Valley, but the farm was lost due to some misfortune. In the spring of 1884, the Frommelts moved to a 40-acre homestead on Chamberlain Hill, 3 miles east of Troutdale. A brother-in-law to Franz Frommelt, Joseph Morak, homesteaded 40 acres adjacent to and south of them. The Lamperts moved to a 160-acre place east of the Frommelts in March 1885. The property had been abandoned as the original homesteader had not "proved up" on the claim. Alexander was a carpenter and cabinetmaker by trade; Franz Frommelt was a stonemason, so the men helped each other build their homes. The Lamperts built their home in the northwest portion of the homestead. The original homesteaders did leave a small house that was later either demolished or moved.

The Lampert homestead was completely wooded at that time. Alex and Juliana cleared and cultivated about 1/4 acre the first season. Eleven years later, (1896), they had 12 acres in cultivation. Two wells provided water. One was north (and downhill) from where the barn was later built, and the second was uphill from the orchard, south of the house. The remaining 8 Lampert children were born in Oregon: Emma, b. May 24, 1985; Bertha, b. September 9, 1886; Ferd, b. September 16, 1886; Josephine, b. October 12, 1889; Arnold, b. September 16, 1890; Julius, b. March 4, 1892; Alexander, b. May 19, 1893; and Bernard, born sometime before July 1896.

Franz obtained his patent (property deed) in 1892. Alexander's took much longer to be approved and required considerable time and effort. In all, 23 forms were filed in order to obtain the grant. Several trips to Oregon City were made to file applications, affidavits and other paperwork. For example, in July (1896), Joseph Marok and Julius Lampert (son of Caroline, a distant cousin) accompanied Alexander to the Land Office. Each man filled out and signed an affidavit that Alexander had lived on the property continuously since March 1885 and had improved the property for farming. The certificate was finally approved in October and the patent issued November 6, 1896. Unfortunately, Alexander died August 23, 1896, so he died not knowing that the land belonged to him and his family. The patent remained at the Land Office in Oregon City until Frank Wand obtained it on behalf of Juliana Lampert about 5 years later.

The trip to Oregon City was an adventure of itself. Of course the Columbia and Willamette Rivers were travel corridors for many years. One could walk to the mouth of the Sandy and catch a boat to Portland then on to Oregon City. A much more likely and popular mode of travel was by rail. It was common for folks who lived along the tracks to wait and flag down a train bound in their direction of travel. Julius, Alex's eldest son, always told his family that Alex used a trail that started just below and north of the house to reach the railroad to catch a train. Another means was by horse. But farmers didn't always use their animals for transportation for fear of injuring a workhorse that was needed to work the farm.

And one could always walk. People walked everywhere and thought little of it. The *Pioneer History*, Volume Two, mentions early settlers walking to Oregon City to conduct business. It was an all-day trip one-way. Travelers likely stayed at a boarding house overnight and returned home the next day. Alexander made frequent trips on foot. The descendants of the family still have the packboard that he made and used. He carried butter and eggs westward down the bluff to a store in Fairview, where he traded his goods for flour and other staples. The distance was 5 miles if a person used the old Seidl trail to the Sandy River, crossed the river via the railroad bridge and followed the trail westward into Fairview.

Alexander died of tuberculosis and was buried on the homestead where a daughter of the Frommelts had been buried earlier. Alex and Juliana's youngest son, Bernard, who died on Christmas Eve, either 1896 or 1897, at the age of 2 years, was also buried there. In approximately 1920, Frank Wand moved the remains to St. Joseph's Cemetery on Powell Blvd. Julius Lampert and his mother, Caroline, distant cousins to Alexander & Juliana, who owned 160 acres west of the Frommelt place, were also buried at St. Joseph's. When Alexander died he left 35 year old Juliana to support nine children, the oldest 13 years of age, on the homestead. The Multnomah County records show that on August 20, 1896 (three days before Alexander died) Alexander and Juliana sold the east 40 acres of their homestead to Julius Lampert (Caroline's son) for $600. Juliana probably made good use of this money to get through the next few years. Julius split the 40 acres that he purchased from Juliana. The west 20 acres went to his cousin, Alyouisious, whose house was later used to store farm implements. George Wand now owns these 20 acres. The 20 acres to the east was later owned by C.W. Post, and may have had other owners in the interim.

Theresa Lampert's first job off the farm was at Aaron Fox's store in Troutdale. Mr. Fox's children, Milt and Mannie, also worked there. Emma Lampert worked for the Foehlers in Portland and the acquaintanceship developed into friendship. In 1899, Frank Wand moved to Portland and learned from the Foehlers that Juliana needed help on the farm. Though Franz Frommelt helped as much as he could, Juliana needed additional help. Frank went to work for her, and was given 20 acres of land on the eastern end of her property in lieu of wages. Thus with the sale and the exchange, Juliana's holdings were reduced to 100 acres from the original 160.

Frank Wand married Juliana's oldest daughter, Theresa, in January 1903. They lived on the Lampert Farm the first 4 years. Theresa wrote to her Aunt Annie Wand in Elizabeth, Illinois on April 17, 1907 that she and Frank were putting in crops on their 20 acres and were planning to move into their home in 2 or 3 weeks (see "Frank Wand/Theresa [Lampert] Wand").

From letters that Theresa, Emma and Bertha wrote to their Aunt Annie in Elizabeth, Illinois we get a glimpse at how the family survived the following dozen years or so. The girls worked out doing housekeeping in Portland. In August 1, 1907 Emma & Bertha were living in Portland doing housekeeping and Alexander & Julius were visiting them on their vacation. The Lampert's barn was built in 1912. The four Lampert brothers and Frank Wand provided the labor. Two carpenters were hired; John Livingston, who lived on 20 acres just east of the Lampert Homestead, and Billy Powell, who lived below the Suhr Farm on Stark Street. The main large timbers were hand-hewn logs cut from the West End of the Livingston Place. The barn was believed to have been the largest barn built east of the Sandy River at that time.

Clearing the homestead was a long-range project; the brothers and Frank Wand were still working on the East End of the 100 acres in the teens and early twenties. Julius finished clearing the steep portion (southeast corner) after he had taken over the farm. During the early teens, the four Lampert brothers paired off and alternately worked the farm and worked out for other farms in the area. Alexander and Julius (or Jack as he was called) worked out while Ferd and Arnold worked the farm. The next year, Alex and Jack worked the farm while Ferd and Arnold worked out. Jack worked for and boarded with the Bramhalls, whose farm was on the Woodard road near the intersection with Seidl Rd. The brothers were doing so well that in 1915 they pooled their money and purchased a Ford Model-T for $600.00, the first in the area.

Josephine married Frank Fehrenbacher in 1916. The reception was at the Fehrenbacher home on Wand road (see "Frank J. Fehrenbacher/ Josephine (Lampert) Fehrenbacher"). In April 1918, Jack was drafted into the army and in June, Alex was drafted. While they were in the service, Ferd and Arnold worked the farm. Jack completed basic training at Fort Lewis in July. Then his outfit went to San Diego and across the States via Chicago by train. The 91st National Guard Division arrived in France on July 23, 1918. Jack's brother, Alex, completed boot camp on August 6, 1918, in the 4th Company at Fort MacArthur, California. He too was sent to France and worked on a supply train in Cheffes, France until the end of the war (see Alexander A. Lampert).

Jack was in the 111th Infantry Regiment of Company J which was at the Front for 23 days, 17 of which were in battle. His outfit suffered 1454 casualties and 4654 wounded, advanced 21 miles and captured 2412 prisoners. He served in the Argonne Forest, had his rifle stock shot in half and was hit with the mustard gas. When assigned to guard prisoners, he spoke good German so they asked him why he was fighting the Moth-

270

Alex and Jack Lampert

Alex and Jack Lampert served in the army during World War I. Photo courtesy of Don Lampert.

erland to which he responded, "I am an American."

Every so often the Doughboys in the trenches would choose who would go to the nearest town to get wine. The time that Jack was chosen, they were under heavy bombardment and he didn't want to go. He was in the trenches when the last shot was fired on November 11, 1918 at 11:00 AM. All the soldiers were very nervous about someone starting the war all over again. Both brothers were still in France on February 14, 1919. When they came home, Jack carried his helmet, which was in the family until just after his wife Evelyn died. Family members have often commented that he came home with a much more serious disposition than the young, fun loving boy who left for war (see "Julius 'Jack' Lampert").

Back home during the summer of 1919, the young folk from the Troutdale area knew how to have fun! A large group of them piled into several Model-T trucks for a camping trip in the Mt. Hood National Forest. Among them were Ferd, Alex, Arnold, Opal Monahan, Emma, Cab Seidl, Evelyn Kendall and her sister Marge. They roughed it in tents, cooking over the open fire and did a lot of hiking. Fishing trips became part of the family folklore, passed on to younger generations. Ferd, Arnold and Herman Blazer spent a week in the High Rock area with a sheepherder's pack train in the early 1930's. They met the train at the end of the Skyline Rd, at Clackamas Lake Campground. The sheepherders enjoyed the company so much that the trip became an annual event. Ferd was an avid fisherman, hunter and outdoorsman. Years later, others accompanied Ferd, including Cab Seidl, Doc Hurt and Ignatius Wand. It is from the sheepherders that the fishermen learned how to make sourdough pancakes.

In 1919, Emma met James Fox when he visited Frank Fehrenbacher. The Fehrenbachers had lived on the Philippi ranch about the turn of the century, across the John Day River from Jim. Later, around 1910, the Fehrenbachers moved to the Troutdale area and were neighbors to the Lamperts and Wands. Emma married Jim around 1920 and moved with him to Early, Oregon on the John Day River. As stated earlier, Emma spent most of her childhood on the farm with a large family and lots of relatives about. She spent many of her teenage years in Portland as a live-in housekeeper. Now she had to adjust to a remote rural lifestyle where the closest farm, besides the In-laws, was a 2-mile hike up the opposite side of the John Day River.

In the early 20's, Alex and Julius "batched it" in a cabin on the Hurt Road property where Ferd later purchased and constructed a home (see "Ferdinand Lampert"). Jack married Evelyn Kendall on August 10, 1922. The couple bought out the other heirs and farmed the Lampert place. The property at this point included a parcel off Henkle Road, south of Springdale, as well as 100 acres of the homestead. Jack used a team of large horses, over 1600 pounds each, with which he could plow 2 acres per day. His largest horse, 'Big Red' weighing in at around 1800 pounds, got loose one night and foundered after helping himself to too much grain. That ended his days as a work animal, and Jack sold him (see "Julius 'Jack' Lampert").

In the teens, both the Lamperts and Wands raised potatoes as a main crop. Later, during the 20's, they switched to cabbage and cauliflower with 5 to 10 acres in those crops. The largest acreage in the area was Bob Larson who planted about 20 acres of cabbage. Jack Lampert used a one-row cabbage planter pulled by his team of horses. Two people set plants and one person sat on a water tank and drove the team. Later, Jack and Ed Klinski combined their planters into a two-row planter, which was pulled by a tractor. The Lamperts raised cabbage into the 1930's. They also had 5 to 10 acres of grain. Oats and barley were raised for livestock feed. A threshing machine was brought to the farm during the harvest. All the brothers and Frank Wand helped along with the crew that traveled with and operated the equipment. Neighbors helped each other during the harvest season. The crew and operator stayed with the equipment, often sleeping on the straw pile. Farm wives cooked for the crew and all hands. Three large meals a day meant a lot of cooking for the women! In the earlier years, Frank brought his grain to the Lampert farm for threshing. In later years he had enough on his own farm for the threshing machine crew to include him on their route.

In the early 1920's, Arnold purchased his own Model-T from Fr. Brunagle, of St. Henry's church. It had been used by Father Brunagle to get to Sandy to say mass every two weeks. In 1926, Arnold purchased a new Ford Model-T and sold his 1920 model to Jim Fox. In the 1960's, this and other Model-T parts were salvaged before the John Day Dam flooded the Fox Farm. These parts are still in the family. Arnold never married. He lived out his adult life on a small farm at the intersection of Wand and Hurt Roads. He died in 1964. Juliana Lampert died in Pendleton, Oregon, March 1927. She is buried in St. Joseph's Cemetery.

Life on the Lampert farm in the 30's and 40's was one of hard work. Everything needed in the way of food came from the farm except sugar and some other staples. With no electricity, no refrigeration and no running water, food had to be canned, preserved and stored for later use. Animals were butchered on the farm for fresh meat. Hundreds of quarts of fruit, vegetables and meat were put up for the winter. A cellar was used to keep milk cool in the summer. Two or three wood stoves were used for heat and cooking. Both Fred Riehl and George Wand helped on the farm at various times. George helped with the dairy work and Jack Lampert's girls enjoyed playing ball with him in the evenings for fun.

Flowering bulbs were raised during World War II. This was a profitable cash crop because the importation of European stock was halted. All the Lampert brothers and some nephews were raising lilies, gladiolas and tulips. A very large local industry was developed with bulbs crated and shipped by the carload to markets in the east. A caustic pollutant destroyed the bulb industry in the late 40's. After the War, farmers in the area raised certified seed potatoes. The quality of seed potatoes declined as disease organisms infected the soil and flea beetle invaded the crop.   *David Wand*

Bucher Barn, Dodson c1930's.   Photo courtesy of Carol Royse.

Alexander A. Lampert
Opal J. (Monahan) Lampert

Alexander 'Alex' Lampert was born in Troutdale in 1893, son of Alexander and Julia Lampert, who homesteaded on "Staggerweed Mountain" before the turn of the century (See "Alexander Lampert," *Pioneer History*, pp. 108-109). He attended Pleasant View Grade School. Alex married Opal J. Monahan May 17, 1922. Opal was born in Troutdale in 1903 and grew up there. She was a friend of Evelyn Kendall, who married Julius 'Jack' Lampert, Alex's brother. When Alex's father died at age 38, Frank Wand worked on the farm to help his mother. He was given the East End of the homestead in lieu of wages, which reduced the home place acreage somewhat. When Alex and Opal married they rented a nine-acre place on Hurt Road, located between the Ferd Lampert and Hurt farms. Their three children were born while they lived on this place.

When Julius A. Lampert (1st generation, not Jack) died, Alex purchased a small plot of land located less than a quarter mile west of the original Lampert homestead from his heirs. (Julius and his mother, Caroline Lampert, were relatives of Alexander.) The seven-acre plot had a three-room house on it, which Alex remodeled to make four rooms. Alex worked at the Wool Pullery in Troutdale until World War II intervened. During the war he worked at the aluminum plant. After the war he returned to the wool pullery and worked there until he retired. The family also did some farming, raising tulip and lily bulbs. Mrs. Lampert was at home until the children were grown. She then worked at the Edgefield Center near Wood Village until she retired.

Alex and Opal had three children, Kathleen, b. June 10, 1923; Nadine, b. May 2, 1926; and Donald 'Don,' b. February 4, 1933. Each of the youngsters attended and graduated from Corbett Grade School. Kathleen and Nadine attended CHS, Kathleen graduating in 1941 and Nadine in 1944. Donald attended Central Catholic High School in Portland, but attended CHS his senior year. He traveled by bus in order to attend Central. Don said that he, Kathleen and Nadine did not work for other farmers much. However, he worked for Toye Davis cutting spinach and also thinned carrots and parsnips. Alex Lampert died in 1966. His wife, Opal (Monaghan) Lampert passed away in 1989.

274

Pleasant View Roster c1903

SOUVENIR

1903

SCHOOL DISTRICT
PLEASANT VIEW ♦ OREGON

October 13, 1902 — June 5, 1903

Presented By
Clara E. Toof
Teacher

SCHOOL BOARD

Chas. Ogden	Fred Chamberlain
Will Rogers	Geo. Chamberlain

Pupils

Logan Chamberlain	Susie Shelly
Louis Mershon	Emma Shelly
George Larson	George Mershon
Olowis Frommelt	Ferdinand Lampert
Lucy Mershon	Lavina Shelly
Ethel Rogers	Winona Ogden
Jervis Zilm	Henry Seidl
Harry Larson	George Shelly
May Zilm	Arnold Lampert
Ada Preston	Ralph Rogers
Josephine Lampert	Anna Mershon
Ernest Zilm	Mary Seidl
Alexander Lampert	Victoria Peterson
Maud Ogden	Margie Mershon
Julius Lampert	Jesse Rogers
Coral Zilm	Grover Preston
Frankie Seidl	Rudolph Frommelt
Walter Preston	Alvia Ogden
Jesse Robins	Lizzie Seidl
Lora Preston	Emma Peterson
Louis Ogden	Joseph Frommelt
Burnice Woodard	Archie Graham
Grant Preston	Edger Ogden

Kathleen married Ted Reihl, who worked as an automobile mechanic in Montavilla. They lived in Portland and had nine children. Kathleen passed away April 18, 1986. Nadine married Donald G. Lane. The couple purchased a farm near Boring, where they raised berries and nursery stock. They had eight children. Nadine worked at the First National Bank in Gresham for many years. Nadine died January 24, 1990. Donald married Barbara Zimmerman of Portland and they had two birth children, twins Joy and Judy, born May 17, 1961. Barbara had three children from a previous marriage, so they had a family of five children. Don worked as a routeman for the American Industrial Service Company. His route took him to industrial customers in the Gresham and Estacada areas for many years. He is now in the wholesale nursery business (Columbia Plant Source), and lives in Sandy, Oregon. *Don Lampert*

Ferdinand Lampert
Gladys (Imlah-Hurt) Lampert

Ferdinand 'Ferd' Lampert, was born on the home place September 16, 1888, a son of the pioneer Lampert family (See "Alexander Lampert," *Pioneer History*, pp. 108-109). Ferd attended Pleasant View Grade School located on what is now Wand Road. In the early 20's, Ferd purchased a 22-acre place adjacent to the Lampert homestead on the south, which was reached from Hurt Road. When he bought the place, there were several older buildings on it. Close neighbors to the west were Mr. and Mrs. Frank Hurt, for whom Hurt Road is named. Their daughter-in-law, Gladys (Imlah) Hurt, was living with them. Her husband, Hugh Hurt, had been killed in a logging accident, leaving Gladys a widow with two small children, June, b. February 13, 1919 and H. William 'Bill,' b. August 12, 1923. She and Ferd were married at St. Henry's Church is Gresham, Oregon, September 22, 1924. They lived in a small house on the place while they built a new home on the property. The new home was completed in 1925.

Ferd and Gladys had five birth children: G. Lorraine, b. August 1, 1925; Barbara A., b. March 16, 1927; Carroll M., b. November 10, 1928; Colleen M., b. January 8, 1931; and Donna J., b. November 30, 1932. Upon reaching school age, all the Lampert children attended Corbett Grade School. Ferd had cleared some of the land to farm. Later he cleared the balance and built a large barn. Among the crops he raised were certified seed potatoes, cabbage, lettuce and, occasionally, cucumbers. Howard Winters said Ferd Lampert grew "absolutely the best lettuce in the country." Apparently Ferd marketed much of his produce to Kienow's stores. He belonged to the growers' cooperative in Troutdale, and probably experienced some of the same problems that other farmers did. The Lampert youngsters worked on the farm, but they also worked for other farmers in the area. Mrs. Lampert used to take the children to pick strawberries for Ed Klinski after they were old enough to work. Sometimes farmers exchanged labor. For example, Carroll Lampert and Dolores Fehrenbacher worked together on a potato planter at both the Lampert farm and the Fehrenbacher farm. The youngsters always had plenty to do during summer "vacations."

In the 20's and early 30's, there was no running water and no electricity to the farm. When the Corbett Water District was established, water was piped to farms on the "hill." It was a thrill for the families involved to have running water and electricity. The Lampert home was equipped to take advantage of the new "marvels" as the builders had wired the house when it was built. As Carroll said, "We didn't have to take a bath in the wash tub anymore." And one had only to flip a switch to have light!

The economic situation improved for farmers after World War II commenced in Europe. Ferd and his family continued to farm through the 30's, 40's and 50's. The prosperity that came with the war years meant new farm equipment could be purchased when it became available after the war. The Lamperts also purchased a new truck and a new car. Ferd continued farming until poor health forced him to retire in the late 50's. After her children were grown, Gladys worked as a dietician at the Edgefield Center in Troutdale for many years. Ferd Lampert died March 9, 1960. After his death, Mrs. Lampert sold the farm and moved to Gresham. She loved to travel and visited several states, particularly western states, Yellowstone National Park and Canada. She also enjoyed performing volunteer work at the Gresham Senior Center and at her church, St. Henry's. Gladys Lampert died October 29, 1981.

June Lampert attended St. Mary's of the Valley High School after completing grade school at Corbett Grade. She married James 'Jim' Allen, and they had four children: James, William 'Bill,' Bonnie and Mark. The family lived in Tillamook, then moved to California. Jim died in the late 50's and June later married Fred Riehl. June now lives in Prineville. Bill Lampert attended Columbian High, but dropped out to join the U.S. Army. He spent much of his service time in the Aleutian Islands operating heavy equipment. After his discharge, he married and had three children, William, Colleen and Patrick. Bill now lives with his wife, Connie, in Dallas, Oregon. Lorraine Lampert attended Madeleine High School in Portland after completing grade school at Corbett Grade. After graduating from Madeleine she attended Behnke-Walker Business College and worked as a stenographer until her marriage to Clint Pearson. They had three children: Dan (who was killed in a plane crash while he was in the Air Force), Anne and Stephen. The family lived in Arizona for several years. Clint Pearson died in 1980. Lorraine married Bud Walton in 1994, and they now live in Springfield, Oregon. Barbara Lampert, after completing grade school, worked as a kitchen helper at Corbett Grade School for

Donna Lampert

Donna Lampert, Corbett Grade School. Photo courtesy of Joan (Ellis) Benner.

several years. She then obtained a job working for the Sisters of the Holy Child in Portland. Poor health forced her retirement and she died in January 1993 of Lou Gehrig's disease.

Carroll Lampert attended Madeleine High School in Portland. After graduation she worked at the First National Bank, Gresham Branch, as a bookkeeper until her marriage in 1949 to Francis Gerding of Corvallis, Oregon. Carroll met her future husband when she served as Maid of Honor at Dolores Fehrenbacher's marriage to Henry Gerding, at which Francis served as Best Man. Carroll and her husband settled on a ranch in the Philomath area near Corvallis. The Gerding family owned a grocery and feed store business in Corvallis, which they operated until it was sold in 1979. Francis 'Fran' Gerding and Carroll raised turkeys, chickens, hogs, cattle and horses on the ranch. They have lived in the same house for 49 years, which is where they raised their family of six children: Robert, b. April 22, 1950; Bernard 'Ben,' b. May 20, 1952; Jerome 'Jerry,' b. May 26, 1953; Jeanne, b. February 1, 1955; and twins, Sharon and Sandra, b. March 2, 1960. Carroll and her husband have retired and enjoy traveling. They have been to Europe and have completed several cruises. They also have a travel trailer and enjoy outdoor activities such as hunting, fishing, crabbing, clamming and camping. They also are active in their church, St. Mary's, in Corvallis.

Colleen Lampert graduated from Corbett Grade School in 1945. She then attended St. Mary's High School in Portland. She married Albert Krebs in 1948. They have seven children: Michael (who died of cancer in 1996), Rick, Erick, Becky, Doug, Lori and Ben. She moved to California after her marriage, and now lives in Grass Valley. Donna also completed grade school at Corbett, graduating in 1947. She attended St. Mary's High School in Portland, graduating in 1951. After graduation, she started working for the Albertina Kerr Nursery, where she spent thirteen years. She married George Hart and they had four children, Mark, Carla, Debbie and Greg. She now works at the Mt. Hood Hospital in Gresham where she also lives.   *Carroll Gerding*

Julius Lampert
Evelyn (Kendall) Lampert

Julius 'Jack' Lampert was born on the family homestead of 160 acres March 4, 1889, son of Alexander and Julia (Gross) Lampert. The Lamperts located in this area together with the Frommelts in the early 1880's. When Jack was about six years of age, his father died from consumption, leaving his wife Julia with 8 children to rear (one child, Bernard, died in infancy). Jack helped his mother, taking care of the cows and chickens the family raised. Eggs, milk and butter were delivered to Troutdale to sell. The Lampert children, Theresa, Emma, Bertha, Ferdinand (Ferd), Josephine, Arnold, Alexander (Alex) and Julius (Jack), attended Pleasant View Grade School on the "hill." With the help of her children and neighbors, Mrs. Lampert was able to keep the family together.

Jack was drafted into the U.S. Army during World War I, sent to France, and saw action in the trenches. During his service there, he contracted "trench foot," a common ailment among the troops. After returning to the States, Jack resumed his acquaintanceship with Evelyn Kendall of Troutdale. Evelyn was born in Illinois February 8, 1901, daughter of Albert D. Kendall. The Kendalls came west when Mr. Kendall, a Station Agent for the Union Pacific Railroad, was transferred first to Biggs, Oregon, then a couple of years later, to Troutdale. Evelyn attended Troutdale Grade School and Gresham High School. Though she started to attend college in Seattle, something came up that caused her to return home. During her high school years she had worked at the Troutdale Station with her father, and when she returned home she decided to attend business school.

Her friendship with Jack Lampert developed into a courtship, and the couple married August 10, 1922. They first lived in a small house owned by Jack's brother, Ferd. Jack continued to farm the family place, and when his mother died in 1927, the couple moved to the farm. Jack purchased his brothers' and sisters' interest for $12,000.00. He expanded the herd of dairy cattle, raising feed for them and growing some vegetable crops. The Lamperts had seven children: Basil A., b. May 5, 1923; Lenore J., b. January 28, 1926; Delores E., b. August 24, 1928; Lucille A., b. July 21, 1931; Cecelia A., b. December 1, 1933; Evelyn M., b. November 2, 1936; and Eileen J., b. August 21, 1939. Jack Lampert

Working the Land

Harrowing with a three horse team on Jack Lampert's farm. Note the Lampert barn in the background.   Photo courtesy of Don Lampert.

continued to farm during the depression years, nearly always planting spinach, which provided an early spring "cash crop," cabbage, lettuce and a plot of carrots for the youngsters to tend. The children were expected to do their chores, which included getting the cows to the barn when they were pastured, milking them morning and night, piling the manure for later use on the fields and replacing the animals' bedding. Corn was cut, chopped, put into the silo, leveled and trampled down. Hay was cut, dried, stacked in shocks and hauled to the barn by wagon. There, a hayfork was used to lift the hay into the barn, where it was stored for use. A horse was used to lift the hayfork bearing the load into the barn loft. The work was hard, and times were tough, but, as Lenore remarked, "We always had plenty to eat, and were not short of money. If we did have some money, there was no place to spend it." The children all attended Corbett Grade School, but attended private Catholic schools their high school years.

The youngsters worked for various farmers on the "hill," including Alfred Moser, Frank Fehrenbacher, Bob Larson, John Seidl and Joe Frommelt. The jobs included planting cabbage and potatoes, picking berries, or cultivating and hoeing various crops. One time when Lenore was working for Bob Larson on a cabbage planter, she started to take her place when the team bolted. The row marker caught her leg, and she was dragged across the field. Fortunately, the shoe was in the ground, which slowed the horses somewhat, and the ground was well worked. She was

280

Thrashing Day

The team is ready to haul grain from the thrashing machine.   Photo courtesy of Don Lampert.

shaken and bruised, but had no serious injuries. When Mr. Larson came by that evening to see how she was, he found her in the yard cutting the lawn! When planting potatoes for certified seed, the seed potatoes were kept separate in boxes. Each box contained just one cut-up seed potato. That way, if a potato carried disease, the plants would be together in a row, which would make them easier to spot, and they could be rogued out.

During World War II, Mr. Lampert worked in the shipyards for a couple of years. It was at this time that he sold the dairy herd. The kids didn't mind! Lucille said, "Dad couldn't build a fence that would keep a cow in." The kids would have to find the cows, which were usually in a neighbor's crops, and they would "catch it." They thought Genevieve Frommelt was unfairly cross, realizing many years later that she had good reason.

After World War II, the Lamperts started raising gladiolas, selling bulbs and cut flowers. Evelyn's father, A.D. Kendall, was a well-known, established grower. Gladiolas are a rather labor intensive crop, requiring special handling. The bulbs are sorted by size before planting, as only the larger bulbs will flower. Smaller sizes and "bulblets" are planted separately until they reach a size sufficient to produce a flower. Bulblets took three or more years before reaching such size. When the bulbs are dug, each variety must be kept separate. The bulbs were placed in wooden sided containers with a wire mesh bottom. The Lamperts remodeled their barn to make a bulb "shed," which is where the bulbs were dried and kept at a set temperature. After the bulbs dried, "rooting" proceeded,

281

which involved separating the root wad from the bulb. The bulbs were sorted by size, the larger bulbs sold, and the smaller sized bulbs replanted the following spring.

Another requisite in growing gladiolas was to plant them where they had not been grown previously. Since not all the bulblets could possibly be found when the bulbs were dug, varieties would become mixed if that ground were replanted to glads. When emissions from the aluminum plant in Troutdale caused mottling and browning of the gladiola foliage, Mr. Lampert was forced to rent ground in the Orient area to plant the bulbs. Each year a different place had to be found. The November 1950 CHS paper, the *Cardinal*, reported that Reynolds Aluminum Company was installing "hoods" to remove fluorine from the plant emissions. According to the article, the modification "is expected to continue on through several years before the work will be completed." After Jack Lampert started raising gladiolas, the younger Lampert children usually worked for their father rather than other farmers.

When the Bonneville Power Administration placed a power line across the Lampert place despite the family's objections (later to be followed by a second line), Mr. Lampert said, "There's no future here." An early freeze in November, 1952, which caught the bulb crop still in the ground, did not help. (Note: The early freeze didn't help the author either, as he had ten acres of cabbage ruined, which ended his venture as a farmer.) As Jack and Evelyn Lampert advanced in age, the farm proved too much work. Sometime prior to 1960, they moved to the Kendall Home in Troutdale, near the present day Handy Brothers Garage.

In 1960, Robert and Delores Williams (a daughter to Jack and Evelyn) worked the farm. Sometime between 1960 and 1965, a strong windstorm blew the barn down. The farm was rented out for approximately 10 years and later sold. The farmhouse has given way to neglect and is no longer standing. Most of the orchard is gone. Fond memories of summer picnics, cold east windy, nights, hard farm work and a family bonded together with love remain.

Basil Lampert married Aloha Whitney in 1944. After he was discharged from the U.S. Navy, he worked for Columbia Telephone Company for approximately 20 years. In 1972, Basil and Aloha moved to Prineville, Oregon, where he worked in the woods as a timber faller. They had five children, Larry, Audrey, Beth, Shawn and Marjorie. Larry completed high school at Corbett before the move and was cited by his coach, Buck Monroe, as one of the finest basketball players he had coached. The other children completed their education in Crook County Schools. Basil Lampert died October 4, 1997.

Lenore attended Madeline Parish School High School, graduating in 1944. She married Herb Winters of Troutdale, who was in the U.S. Navy at the time. When Herb was discharged in 1947, the couple lived in various rentals in the Corbett area until they bought a "junior acre" in Gresham, where the family has since lived. Lenore and Herb have eleven children, Pamela, Cassandra, Herbert Jr., Randall, Colin, Beverly, Darlene, Sharon, John, Jay and Jeffrey.

Delores married Robert Williams, who was in the construction business. They located on Bluff Road, near Sandy, and had two children, Arnold and Charles (deceased). Lucille married William L. Tolbert from Orient, but lost her husband in 1971. She has no children, and lives in Fairview. Cecelia married Rudolf Misten, lives in Portland, and had five children, Eric, Marlene, Sonja, Joanne and Martha. Cecelia and two of her children, Eric and Marlene, are deceased.

Evelyn married Wayne Weien of Corbett, and had two boys, Carl and Perry, before she was widowed. She married Wayne Lewis, and had four more children, twins Greg and Garth, Casey and Stephanie. All of Evelyn's children attended school at Corbett. Their year of graduation from Corbett High School is, respectively: Carl Weien, 1974; Perry Weien, 1976; Greg and Garth Lewis, 1980; Casey Lewis, 1983; and Stephanie Lewis, 1985. Evelyn and Wayne are now divorced. Eileen married Edward Troxel, and has four children, Jeanette, Benjamin, Mark and Marsha. They lived in Troutdale, Gresham, Salt Lake City and Maupin before locating permanently in The Dalles, Oregon.   *Lenore Winters*

Robert W. Larson
Lucy J. (Mershon) Larson

The Larson farm (19.4 acres) was located on the west side of Ogden Road just north of its intersection with Mershon Road. Robert 'Bob' Larson was born in Wisconsin November 19, 1880, and came to Troutdale, Oregon, with his parents before the turn on the century. The family rented a "shack" located in the Hickland Bottom area east of Troutdale. Later, they located a house on the bluff above, which was first rented, and later purchased. Robert Larson's father commuted to Portland to work in a mill. On December 8, 1906, Robert Larson married Lucy J. 'Jane' Mershon, who was born March 16, 1889, in Cadiz, Kentucky, daughter of Alfred D. and Sarah Mershon. The Mershons had moved to the Pleasant View area in 1890. Bob and Jane moved onto the farm and Bob Larson farmed the place thereafter. Bob and Jane Larson had two sons, Robert Jr. "Tood", b. September 17, 1908, and Alfred Louis, b. February 14, 1911. Alfred died December 27, 1915, when an outbreak of diphtheria swept through the area.

Robert Jr. "Tood" Larson attended Pleasant View Grade School for 8 years, then started at CHS in Corbett in 1924, the second year in the new high school. During Tood's sophomore year, he was taking a science class from Mr. Willard, who asked, "What's the highest form of animal life?" Called upon to respond, Tood said, "A giraffe, I guess." Of course all the students laughed (The response does seem rather humorous), but someone was not amused, and the consequences caused Tood to walk out on the Principal, G.N. McKay. Tood did not return to high school. At age 16, he bought a truck and started hauling produce and hay for his father and other farmers. Later he obtained a Public Utility Commission permit (type #3) for the business, and was hauling throughout the Pacific Northwest. With this type permit, he was required to purchase the load, haul it to its destination and sell it there. Since this involved considerable risk, Tood developed many contacts throughout the region, which served him well later.

The Larsons had a new home built for them in 1918 by Quay Martin. Reportedly, Bob Larson won enough money in a lottery to build the home. Mr. Larson (Sr.), who was working at Crown Point while the Vista House was under construction, took home discarded pieces of the marble being

Larson Home

The Larson's new home, completed in 1918. Robert Larson salvaged discarded stone from the Vista House to build a fireplace. Left is Louis Larson. Jane Larson is in the center. The adult to the right is Bob Larson. Son, Tood Larson, to the far right.

Jane Larson and Robert Jr.

Jane (Mershon) Larson and her oldest son, Robert 'Tood.' Photos courtesy of Dorothy Larson.

A Load of Cabbage and Cauliflower

A semi-load of cauliflower and sacked cabbage bound for Lewiston, Idaho.   Photos courtesy of Dorothy Larson.

used in the building. Later, he used these discarded pieces for the fireplace when the new home was built. On the farm, the Larsons raised potatoes, cabbage, cauliflower and clover, but principally cabbage and clover, for hay. The Larsons used a two-person "New Idea" cabbage planter pulled by a team composed of a horse and a mule. Some of the local youngsters who worked for the Larsons on the cabbage planter included: June Bates, Rosemary Berney, Lenore Lampert and Herb Winters. June remarked that she learned to plant left handed because "hardly anyone could be found to plant from that side." She became proficient on the planter, and most of the time planted with Herb Winters, while Mr. Larson handled the team. Pacific Fruit bought much of the farm produce, which was shipped throughout the Northwest by the truckload during the harvest season.

During the spring of 1936, Howard Winters came to work for (and boarded with) the Larsons. Shortly thereafter, he bought a one-fourth interest in Tood's trucking business (Robert Larson's Truck Service), and later still, he increased his share to a one-half interest. Tood allowed Howard to pay for his interest from his wages. When Howard started, Tood paid him $5.00 per trip to Touchet, Washington, and back, and he loaded and unloaded at each end. Wishing to expand the trucking business, the partners purchased a second PUC permit (#1), from Si Chamberlain and Earle Atkinson, which allowed them to haul throughout the Pacific Northwest. They named the new business "Winters Truck Service" to avoid any confusion with Tood's other permit. A typical haul

286

Hay from Touchet, Washingon

Robert Larson Sr. (L) and Tood with a load of hay hauled from Touchet, Washington.   Photo courtesy of Dorothy Larson.

Howard Winters Plowing

Howard Winters plowing the Roberts' place. Custom work earned the partners $2.50 per hour.   Photo courtesy of Dorothy Larson.

found Tood hauling produce such as cabbage, cauliflower or potatoes to Walla Walla, and a load of hay on the return to Portland. On one trip to Walla Walla, Howard was to go on to Lewiston to pick up a load before returning to Portland. The Ford truck he was driving blew an exhaust gasket near Lewiston. The Ford garage in Lewiston sent a mechanic to replace the gasket, and charged Winters Truck Service seventy-five cents for the repair.

When Winters Truck Service hauled peas, customers were charged $1.50 per hour, $.50 of which went to the driver. The partners hauled peas from Puget Island (near Cathlamet), from Seaview, Washington (near Long Beach), and from Touchet, Washington (near Walla Walla). Peas were hauled to a plant where the peas were thrashed to be ready for processing. Winters Truck Service also served farmers in the East Multnomah County area, hauling crops such as cucumbers to Libby McNeil and Libby, in Portland. They hauled produce, such as cabbage, from this area to Seattle, Spokane, Klamath Falls, Medford and other locations (see Howard Winters). In addition to the trucking business, the partners purchased a small "Cat" (Caterpillar R2 and later a D2) which was used to clear land (especially around the Orient area) and to do other custom work, such as plowing and disking, for farmers. The going rate for such work in 1941 was $2.50 per hour.

In 1940, Robert Larson Jr. and Howard Winters formed another partnership, "Larson and Winters," to engage in farming, but retained the trucking and custom work business. During the next six years, the partnership raised potatoes, cabbage, strawberries, gladiolas, daffodils, grain and other crops. In 1940, the partners planted White Rose potatoes on the 10th of February. The potatoes were dug June 7th, and sold at the Farmers' early market at SE 9th and Belmont for $1.00 per orange box (70 lbs.). With war raging in Europe, potatoes brought a higher price that year than that of the previous (depression) year. After the United States became directly involved in the war after December 7, 1941, farm prices improved dramatically, and one could sell whatever was produced. In 1942, Larson and Winters sold potatoes at $3.50 per hundredweight (or an equivalent in today's dollars of about $35.00) to Pacific Fruit, and delivered 300 sacks per day over a three week period. Strawberries brought $3.00 per flat (or an equivalent $30.00) and cabbage sold for $1.40 to $2.00 per crate ($14.00 to $20.00).

When Japanese farmers were removed from the area in May 1942, Howard and Tood purchased some of their planted crops, and harvested them that year. During the partnership years, Howard purchased the McGill Place and the Bramhall Place in his name, and Tood purchased the Mershon Place and 18+ acres from Rudolf Frommelt on Woodard Road in his name. The partners rented ground from others, including the Davis Place (on Gordon Creek Road), the McGinley Place (on Lampert Road), and Wilson Place (on Pounder Grade). During this period, many local youngsters worked for Larson and Winters on their farm. This included work such as picking strawberries, cultivating, hoeing, dusting and harvesting the various crops. Among those who worked for them at this time were: Dorothy, Lucille and Alvin Hoecker; Bill, Gus and Johnny McCleary; Alfred 'Bud,' George, Clarence and Bill Mershon; Wes, Dean

Ford Semi Loaded with Potatoes

Each day during the potato harvest, two loads of potatoes went out, this semi-load (203 sacks) and the flat bed truck (100 sacks).

Photo courtesy of Dorothy Larson.

and Duane Davis; Herb and Merle Winters; David Rees; and Gerald "Jerry" Lambert (who had returned from the South Pacific after being wounded at Tarawa). As the older teenagers obtained higher paying jobs in the shipyards or elsewhere, younger workers came to the fore. Too illustrate farming techniques in use during this period, We will "follow" one crop, cabbage, from start to finish.

First the seed, which had been collected from selected plants saved for that purpose the preceding year, was planted by a hand-seeder in a bed. When the seed sprouted and emerged, the rows were "weeded" by workers on their hands and knees to remove emerging weeds. A push hoe was used to keep the area between the rows clear of weeds. Periodically the plants were "dusted" with sulfur, Black Flag (nicotine) and rotenone, a natural pesticide. The dusting was accomplished using a "Champion" duster, which was a pack-like device with a handle that pumped the dust by means of a bellows-like contraption through a tube to the plants. One pumped with one arm and directed the dust tube with the other, creating quite a cloud of dust in the process.

When the time came to transplant the cabbage plants, usually starting in mid-June, the plants were loosened with a fork, separated, sorted, and the roots dipped in water. The plants were placed in a cabbage crate, and kept moist until they were replanted. With a two-person planter, pulled by a team or by tractor, the plants were transplanted in the field that had been prepared for them. The "New Idea" planter had two seats close to the ground. Two boxes directly above each worker's legs held the plants, which were replenished after each round (trip) in the field. A water tank dispensed water, if desired, when the trip mechanism 'clunk' signaled one to insert a plant. The tank, which was seldom used to dispense water, sat behind the two workers doing the planting. It provided a place to locate the seat for the driver, if a team was pulling the planter. The "shoe," was lowered into the ground by levers at the start of each row. It formed a furrow into which the two 'planters' inserted a cabbage plant (alternately, from each side). Two packer wheels pushed soil around the plant's root stem and compressed it.

As the plants grew, they required regular cultivation, which was accomplished at this time by a horse pulling a single row cultivator handled by one person. Tood and Howard said a good man could "cultivate an acre an hour." Naturally, this became the author's goal when he cultivated with the horse, Pack. The field also required regular hoeing. If the person operating the cultivator did the job properly, many of the sprouting weeds were covered, which helped those doing the hoeing. In the fall, the cabbage was harvested, which involved cutting off the heads, and piling them on a bed of leaves for crating. Workers then packed the heads into wooden crates so that each crate was slightly heaped. Then a lid was nailed to the top, and the crates were loaded upon a sled, if the fields were wet, or on a truck, if conditions permitted. At this time seed heads were selected for planting the following spring for the crop to be harvested two years hence.

Much of the cabbage was marketed through Pacific Fruit where Emil Feltz was the manager. Both Tood Larson and Howard Winters mentioned that Pacific Fruit was an excellent firm to work with, and the partners hauled cabbage to the firm's branches throughout the Northwest. One's ability to market the crop became the final element in determining success or failure. If one developed a dependable market at a fair price, success was possible. If not, failure was certain.

On October 13, 1944, Robert Larson Jr. married Dorothy Hoecker, whose family lived across the Sandy River on Hoecker Road (off Kerslake Road). Dorothy was born at the family home December 12, 1926. Her parents are Frederick "Fritz" and Florence (Bramhall) Hoecker. After their marriage Tood and Dorothy added rooms to the original house located on the acreage purchased from Mr. Frommelt (which had been

290

Dorothy Hoecker

Tood Larson's bride, Dorothy Hoecker (center), her sister, Lucille (right) and Merle Winters at the farm.   Photo courtesy of Dorothy Larson.

rented to the Rees family), and made their home there. This home dated back to the turn of the century. In 1946, Tood and Howard Winters dissolved their farming partnership. They sold the P.U.C. permit for Winters Truck Service soon thereafter. At the split, Tood retained all the gladiola stock, and about one-half of the daffodil bulb stock which the partnership had accumulated, and he and Dorothy continued to farm his parents and his properties until 1956. In 1949, Tood formed a partnership with Duane Davis, "Larson and Davis." In 1953, the partners purchased the Canby-Aurora Truck Service, and Tood found himself back in the trucking business, which he loved. In the early 60's, the partners purchased the Leighty Truck Line of Woodburn, Oregon, and combined the two operations under that name. The partnership dissolved, and in 1972, the trucking business was sold.

As with other youngsters growing up in the area, Tood fished local streams, such as Pounder Creek, Big Creek, Eagle Creek and others. Later, he fished in Eastern Oregon and at the Coast. He also loved to travel by car. After his father died, Tood purchased a motorcycle, which he also enjoyed riding. Robert "Tood" and Dorothy Larson had three children: Janet, born in 1945; Fred, born in 1948; and Roberta "Bobbie" born in 1949. Fred now (1997) lives at the Larson home place on Ogden Road. Robert Larson (Sr.) died May 14, 1965; Lucy Jane died January 5, 1987; and Robert Jr. "Tood" died March 27, 1977. Dorothy continues to live in the home located on Woodard Road just west of its intersection with Ogden Road.   *Dorothy Larson*

291

Fred N. Lasley
Leula (Davis) Lasley

Fred Lasley came to Oregon the winter of 1988-89 by train. He saved money in order to bring his wife, Leula and their daughter, Leila, to Oregon the following spring (see "Fred N. and Leula A. Lasley," *Pioneer History*). Lasley moved his family to the East County area in the 1890's. In 1896 the Lasleys purchased 20 acres on Loudon Hill, which had to be cleared. Fred Lasley worked the first year to clear enough land for a garden and put up a barn. Whenever work was available through a neighbor or for the county, he was pleased for an opportunity to earn some cash. Roadwork paid 15 cents per hour and one worked a 10-hour day.

Clearing the land involved cutting up the best logs for wood, exposing the roots of stumps below plow level, piling debris to be burned in piles and keeping the fire going. Roots of the smaller brush such as vine maple and hazel were grubbed out with a mattock. By 1905 when Walter was born, the family had several acres cleared, an orchard planted, a team of horses and two or three milk cows. Mrs. Lasley sold butter and "never had to hunt for customers," according to Clara Lasley.

The Lasley children, Leila, Weltha, Gladys, Clara, Walter 'Ray' and Edwin, attended Hurlburt Grade School, which was about a mile distant. The older girls obtained jobs in Portland as live-in "mother's helpers" in order to attend high school. Leila went on to the University of California where she earned her BA and MA. Later she went to England where she studied at Oxford's Manchester College. In 1918 she married Charles Thompson, whom she met in college. He was killed in France during World War I. Leila Thompson taught at various high schools, including Columbian High. Later she became an ordained minister and had a church in Palo Alto. Leila died in Portland in 1971 and her remains are interred in Mountain View Cemetery.

Weltha graduated from Washington High School in 1912. She married Edward C. Wilson (see "Descendants of Charles and Nellie Wilson," *Pioneer History*). She and her husband built up a substantial acreage of daffodils and gladiolas. Gladys also attended Washington High for three years, but sickness kept her from completing one semester. Her

Salzman Homestead Near Donahue Camp

Wilhelmina 'Minnie' Salzman stands by the house (right). Her mother, Emelia Etling, with Fred and Albert Salzman, stands in the strawberry patch in front of the house. Note the high fence needed to keep deer and other wildlife out.

Photo courtesy of Herb Salzman.

senior year she attended the newly opened CHS, but was short credits and did not graduate. Years later she was awarded her diploma, graduating with the Class of 1981. Gladys married Claude Woodle in September 1915 (see "The Woodle Families," *Pioneer History*).

Clara attended Washington High for two years. By then the high school at Corbett had opened and she completed her final two years at CHS. She is the school's first graduate (1916). She married Albert G. Salzman in July 1916. Albert, one of the three surviving sons of Charles* and Wilhelmina Salzman, attended both Brower and Mountain grade schools. Charles 'proved' a homestead near the Donahue Camp, the rights to which he purchased from an earlier settler, Mr. Tompkins. Thus Albert's earliest years were spent in a rugged, almost wilderness setting on the slopes of Larch Mountain. When Salzman sold this place to the Bridal Veil Lumbering Company, he purchased 80 acres on what is now called Salzman Road. The other two surviving brothers were Fred and William.

*Charles given name Karl, was changed when he obtained his citizenship papers.

293

Lasley Home on Loudon

From L, Clara, Leula, Ray, Fred, Gladys, Weltha and Leila Lasley.

Lasley Family

Rear, Leula and Fred Lasley. Front, Clara, Gladys, Leila and Weltha. Of interest is the fact that four of this family lived to be 100+ years of age: Fred (father), Clara, Gladys and Weltha. Clara now (1999) lives in Aloha. Photos courtesy of Herb Salzman.

After the marriage, Albert and Clara moved to the 80-acre farm mentioned above. They farmed the place for several years. Later, because of health problems, the farm was sold. Albert worked at various jobs until World War II started, when both he and Clara went to work in the shipyards. Salzman worked as a layout man on the ways; Clara Salzman welded in the assembly area. According to Clara, her job "Was at the noisiest place in the yard and I am extremely deaf as a result." In the spring of 1945 Albert had an opportunity to take a job in Pearl Harbor. A few months after the end of the war Clara joined her husband in Hawaii. They returned to Oregon in 1947, moving to Aloha, where Clara celebrated her 100th birthday on March 9, 1997. Albert and Clara had two children, Marian ('36 CHS) and Herbert, who graduated from Benson Tech.

W. Ray Lasley graduated from CHS in 1923 and attended Oregon Agricultural College for a time, then worked in construction. He and Fay Davis owned a cement mixer and poured cement for many of the structures built by CP Woodle during the 20's and early 30's. He joined the Navy Seabee's (construction battalion) and served in the South Pacific during the war. He married Bernice Walters and they have a son, Harry. Ray worked as a lineman for the Bonneville Power Administration. He died in 1954 and is interred in Willamette National Cemetery, Portland.

In the mid-20's the Lasley farm on Loudon was sold. Lasleys bought land in what is now Lincoln City and built a few cottages to rent. Consequently Edwin graduated from Taft High School. He worked on tugboats on the Siletz River and later became a marine diesel engineer. He worked at Midway Island to help construct facilities for the Clipper Flying Boats that inaugurated flight to the Orient and a Navy oil storage depot. During WW II he joined the Navy and was stationed in Puget Sound, Washington and Dutch Harbor, Alaska. After the war he worked as a machinist and a crane operator. He married Dorothea Johnson and they have an adopted daughter. Edwin now lives at Manning, Oregon.

Clara has fond memories of her parents:

"Dad was always for progress. He served on school boards, county fair boards and was a 4H Club leader. He helped get a measure through the legislature allowing small districts to unite to form Union High School Districts. Our (Corbett) district was the first formed in Multnomah County and I was its first graduate. He was forward looking in farming too. When it was the practice to use small potatoes (culls) for seed (and sell) the larger, marketable ones as a cash crop, he was 'hill selecting." If he found an extra fine hill (with) several large, even-shaped tubers, he put it aside for seed. In a few years his yield was several times that of other farmers around. He raised the first "certified disease-free" potatoes in the County. He was a very outgoing person who, as they say, "Never knew a stranger." (Note: Fred Lasley also developed the strain of Golden Bantam corn seed used by J. Ward Evans for canning.)

Mother was a quiet person. She had a very strict Scottish Covenant Presbyterian childhood. She held her emotions in check, very self-effacing. She was very capable, could make a good meal out of almost nothing. She made all our clothes and never bought a pattern. We girls would look in the Montgomery Ward catalog and pick out a dress we liked. She would measure us here and there, lay out a piece of 'dry goods paper' on the table and cut her own pattern. Of course our underwear was made from flour sacks. She kept us clean and mended (with) no safety pins for missing buttons. She always said, "It's no sin to be poor, but you can always be clean." We went to school clean, starched and ironed, even though the clothes were washed on the old washboard and had to be ironed with the old irons heated on the wood cook stove. If we tended to slack she would say, "Have a little pride in yourself." So we held our heads high, even though our clothes were patched and our stockings darned, we were clean! And she sang! Old hymns (and) old Civil War songs, "Tramp, Tramp, Tramp," "The Vacant Chair" and ...silly songs (such as) "Frog a Courting He Would Go" (and) "Grandmother Slipper Slopper Jumped Out of Bed" and many, many others... Altogether, though our childhood was filled with hard work (we all had to pitch in and do our share), (it) was filled with many an incident that we look back on and remember with happiness, love and pride."

Leula A. Lasley died in 1950. Fred Newton Lasley died November 3, 1964, age 100 years, 5 months and 14 days. Both are interred in a cemetery at Hillsboro, Oregon. Weltha (Lasley) Wilson passed away September 11, 1999, age 106 years, 8 months and 10 days.

(Clara (Lasley) Salzman)

Charles A. Lofstedt
Clara M. (Mannthey) Lofstedt

Charles August Leonard Lofstedt was born May 23, 1887, in Malmo, Sweden. His father, Charles W. Lofstedt, worked as a fireman on steamers plying the Atlantic Ocean between Europe and the United States, where he sometimes worked while waiting for a return berth after being discharged from a ship. He and his wife, Christina, came to the United States in 1887, when young Charles was a few weeks old. The family traveled across the country, stopping for a time in Chicago, Illinois, but eventually located in Portland, Oregon. Charles' father obtained a position as a lithographer for L. Samuel, Publisher, and continued in that trade for the remainder of his working life. He also worked for the publisher of *West Shore* magazine. Another child was born to the Lofstedts in Portland, a daughter, Ellen E., b. December 11, 1889. Charles and Ellen's mother died in 1890 from pneumonia.

In 1891, Charles' father homesteaded a quarter section of land below Pepper Mountain near the community of Brower. The father continued to work in Portland while "proving" the homestead, staying in Portland the winter months and commuting to work from the homestead the rest of the year. Eventually the father brought the children's grandmother from Sweden to care for them. By the time the children were of school age, the family lived on the homestead year round, though the father continued to work in Portland. Both children attended Brower School. Mr. Lofstedt served as the Clerk for District 50, which required him to pay teachers, receive tax funds and keep the books. The family has retained copies of school records and correspondence related to these functions.

The Brower School burned in 1902 when a forest fire swept through the area. The Brower Mill and surrounding homes were destroyed. Brower School was rebuilt at a different location, but neither the mill nor most of the homes were replaced. Though only fifteen at the time of the fire, young Charles was working at Palmer Mill, which was also devastated. After the fire, he went to work at the main mill in Bridal Veil, the Bridal Veil Lumber Company. In the fall of 1918, he received a notice from the draft board directing him to report for induction into the U.S. Army, October 12, 1918. Exactly thirty days later, November 11, 1918, the Ar-

Charles Lofstedt

Charles Lofstedt (right) working for the Bridal Veil Lumbering Company. Photo courtesy of Bertha MacKay.

The Lofstedt Family

Rear, From L, Charles and Clara. Front, Gussie, Frieda, Sophia, Carl, Ellen and Clarence. Photo courtesy of Frieda (Lofstedt) O'Neil.

mistice took effect. Charles was discharged from the Army December 17, 1918.

On Christmas Day, 1919, Charles A. Lofstedt married Clara M. Mannthey in Corbett, Oregon. Clara had been born December 21, 1892, in South Dakota. In 1909, her family came to Oregon where her father had located an 80-acre place on what is now Mannthey Road (off Loudon), and which her father purchased later that same year (see "1982 Supplement," *Pioneer History*). Charles and Clara purchased a place on Loudon Road from James C. and Myra I. Wilson. Before the marriage Clara had worked at the Chanticleer Inn, located at what is now the Portland Women's Forum overlook. While working there, President Woodrow Wilson dined at the Inn, and as Clara always maintained, "Enjoyed eating the biscuits I made." Charles and Clara Lofstedt had 6 children, all of whom were given two middle names, customary with the Lofstedts: Carl Allen Christ, b. January 3, 1921, and twin Clarence Walter Martin, b. January 4, 1921; Sophia Elsie May, b. May 27, 1922; Augusta Helen Maude, b. August 12, 1924; Ellen Alma Margaret, b. January 6, 1926; and Frieda Rose Laura, b. October 4, 1927.

Charles worked for the Multnomah County Road Department until World War II, working out of the Corbett shop for a time, and running

298

Lofstedt Home on Loudon

Gussie and Frieda Lofstedt in their front yard at home.

Frieda Lofstedt

Frieda stands beside the car in which she learned to drive. Photos courtesy of Frieda (Lofstedt) O'Neil.

the rock crusher on Larch Mountain when the Larch Mountain Road was under construction during the 30's. During the war, he worked at the Kaiser Oregon Shipyard. After the war, he worked at the Bridal Veil Lumber and Box Company until retiring in 1957. Although Mr. Lofstedt always had a job off the farm, he and his family raised livestock, hay and grain on the place. The children took care of the livestock, putting up hay and performing the other chores associated with caring for and feeding farm animals.

The older Lofstedt children, Carl, Clarence and Sophia, started school at Springfield (Egypt) School on Loudon. When Springfield voters approved the consolidation with Corbett in 1930, the youngsters transferred there. Augusta 'Gussie,' Ellen and Frieda started at Corbett. Each of the Lofstedt children, after graduating from Corbett Grade, attended CHS. Both Carl and Clarence played on the Corbett team that took the Big Nine-Championship in 1940. Other players on the team were James 'Jimmy' Frommelt, Dan Kerslake, Marion Kirkham, Ray O'Neil, Harold 'Harry' Price and Ellis Snodgrass. Carl, at 6 foot 7, played center, and Clarence, at 6 foot 4, played forward. The two tended to dominate both the offensive and defensive boards. Mr. Les Emerson was the coach and Ronald Price served as manager.

The Lofstedt children worked for local farmers planting, caring for, or harvesting crops such as potatoes, bulbs, berries and cucumbers. The boys worked for Bill Woodard picking up potatoes. During the depression Sophia and Gussie worked at various jobs at school, funded by a federal program. They also worked at the Viewpoint Inn for the Moessners. Sophia, Gussie, Ellen and Frieda picked berries for Dick and Ruth Ellis and picked cucumbers for Floyd Watts and the Baumgartners on Loudon Road. One time Gussie and Frieda "camped out" at the Wallin Place on Stark Street (just east of Logan Road) in order to pick berries. Frieda stated: "It's remarkable that our folks let us do it." (However, the fact that they did probably serves to illustrate the contrast between the 30's and the 80's and 90's with regard to safety considerations for youngsters.) These type jobs were rather typical for youngsters in the 30's and 40's. Each of the Lofstedts, except Sophia and Ellen, also worked at the Bridal Veil Mill at various times.

After graduating from Corbett, Carl Lofstedt started college at Pacific University. World War II intervened, and he entered the service as a draftee in 1942. He served as a gunner in the artillery, seeing action in the South Pacific. After the war, December 29, 1945, Carl married Betty R. Bailes, to whom he was introduced by his sister, Gussie. Betty was born in Sumner, Washington July 16, 1924. During World War II she served in the Women's Army Corps. The couple had four children, 3 sons and a daughter. The oldest son, Jackie, died August 3, 1960. Carl attended San Jose State College for a year. He then decided upon a law enforcement career and enrolled in the Oakland Metropolitan Law Enforcement School, from which he graduated with highest honors.

Carl worked for the Oakland Police Department for about a year, then took a job with the Tulare Police Department. Later, he returned to Oregon as Chief of Police at Sandy. His next position took him to Edwards Air Force Base in California, where he worked in the Security Department. When the rocket facility closed, he returned to Oregon, finishing his law enforcement career here. Because of his extensive background of experience and FBI training, he was appointed to the Oregon State Police Executive Security Branch, which provides the personal bodyguards for the Governor and other officials. He retired in 1981, and died August 25, 1989, age 68. Betty passed away August 22, 1995. Both she and Carl are buried at Willamette National Cemetery.

Clarence, after graduating from Columbian High in 1940, also started college at Pacific University. He was drafted into the U.S. Army in 1942, and served three years overseas in the European Theater. He served in the 846th Aviation Engineers Battalion as a demolition technician. After the D-Day invasion, he was stationed in Normandy, and moved forward into the Rhine Valley as U.S. troops advanced. Upon his discharge in November 1945, he returned to Corbett, and started to work at the Bridal Veil Lumber and Box Company. He married Bertha B. Snowley July 28, 1951, in Corbett. Bertha was born October 15, 1924, in Michigan, and was living at home with her parents in Corbett when she met Clarence. The Snowleys had purchased the Riggs place in 1945.

Clarence and Bertha had three daughters: Constance A., Julie K. and Laurie J. For a time, Clarence and Bertha rented housing then decided to buy a home in Wood Village, Oregon. In April 1951, during the Korean War, Clarence was called to active duty with his reserve unit, and served in the 62nd Supply Squadron at Moses Lake Air Force Base until November, 1952. When discharged, he returned to his job at Bridal Veil and worked there until the mill closed in 1960. Later he worked at Reynolds School District as a custodian. Clarence died December 30, 1963, age 42, of kidney failure. The couple's youngest daughter, Laurie, died September 23, 1983. Bertha and her two daughters, Constance and Julie, live at the family home in Wood Village (1997).

Sophia graduated from high school in May 23, 1941. She enjoyed her high school years very much, and was selected to represent the Tri-Y Club at a banquet honoring Principal P.J. Mulkey when he left Corbett in 1939, one of the few sophomores to be so honored. She also was pleased and proud to watch her older brothers play basketball for Columbian High. Sophia is known for the greeting cards she has sent to friends and relatives throughout the years, particularly remembering birthdays. She has corresponded with her former 5th grade teacher, Annabelle Acklen (now Savage), since the mid-30's, and Mrs. Savage came to Sophia's 75th birthday celebration in 1997. Sophia met her future husband, William E. 'Earl' MacKay, at a family gathering. Earl was a brother of her cousin Bertha's husband, Roy MacKay. Sophia married Earl at the Corbett Christian Church shortly after graduating from high school, August 23, 1941. Earl was born in Chicago, Illinois, August 25, 1892. He worked as a carpenter most of his working life, and was employed by Claude Woodle, Corbett Hardware, on many jobs. The couple lived on Larch Mountain Road just beyond the old road to Latourell, and had 9 children: Beverly E., Donald E., Joyce E., Margaret E., William E., Daniel E., Kenneth E., Christina E., and Sharon E., all born in Portland. William died at age 12 from a fall on Larch Mountain when he tried to retrieve a toy airplane that he spotted beyond the fence at the summit. Another son, Daniel, died one day shy of his 23rd birthday at Latourell, Oregon, and a daughter, Margaret, died from complications related to diabetes in May 1985. Earl died January 5, 1986, age 93. Sophia now lives at the Powell Valley Manor in Gresham (1997).

Augusta "Gussie," after graduating from high school, enrolled at the Northwest Christian College in Eugene. While there, she introduced an acquaintance of hers, Betty Bailes, to her brother, Carl. Betty married Carl after the war. Gussie returned home and went to work at the Bridal Veil Mill. Her brother-in-law set up a blind date with a buddy stationed with him at Camp Adair, James "Jim" B. Kendrick. Jim came to the Northwest from Houston, Texas. Gussie said, "I finally found a man tall enough for me to feel comfortable with." Jim and Gussie were married July 8, 1944, in Colorado Springs, from where he was scheduled to be sent overseas.

Jim landed in Cherbourg, France, shortly before Paris fell to the Allies and after a brief period his unit, the 385th Field Artillery Battalion, 104th Infantry Division (Timber Wolves) was sent to the northern sector of the front under the command of the English General, Bernard L. Montgomery. Jim was serving as a radio operator at a forward observation post when his unit came under intense fire from German positions at their front. He was awarded the Silver Star for "gallantry in action" when he and his colleagues moved their observation post to a different position while under constant enemy fire, thus enabling his unit to bring the enemy guns under concentrated counter-fire. He was wounded during the engagement and in addition to the Silver Star, received the Purple Heart.

At home, Gussie continued to work at the Bridal Veil Mill, and did so on a fairly steady basis until 1953. When Jim returned in 1945, he and Gussie moved into the house on the Etling Place that at one time housed the Corbett Post Office, and lived there until 1977. Jim also worked at the mill, and stayed there until it closed in 1960. In 1962 he was hired by the City of Portland's Park Bureau, and worked there until his retirement in 1988. Gussie started working at the W.R. Hicks Company in Gresham October 31, 1960. She started as a clerk, later became Office Manager, and continued to work there until her retirement in January 1989. Many East County residents shopped at Hicks, and Gussie remembers her parents buying clothes for the children there. Started by Mr. W.R. Hicks,

Mr. Ray Bergeron later became a partner. Eventually the partnership went to Bob and Jim Bergeron, sons of Ray. According to Gussie, the Hicks and Bergerons "were wonderful people to work for." The store closed in April 1989, shortly after Gussie retired.

Jim and Gussie have two daughters, Patricia J. Crampton, b. May 22, 1945 and Roxie I. Swanson, b. May 9, 1952. Both attended Corbett Grade and CHS. Jim and Gussie moved to Gresham in March 1977, and continue to reside in the house they purchased at that time. They are neighbors of Lenore (Lampert) Winters. Patricia now lives in Sandy, Oregon, and Roxie lives with her parents in Gresham.

Ellen had completed two years at Columbian High when she married Luther V. Young, of Jacksonville, Florida September 18, 1943. He was soon sent overseas, and served in France. When he returned home after being discharged, he worked at the Bridal Veil Lumber and Box Company. In 1951, Ellen and Luther moved to Jacksonville, Florida. Luther and Ellen had four children: Luther V. Jr., b. October 3, 1948; Lillian V., b. October 2, 1949; Linda V., b. May 23, 1951; and Laura V., b. October 27, 1966. In 1967, Ellen and Luther were divorced, and she married Marion A. Tryon October 9, 1969. Marion worked for the Seaboard Coast Line as a train dispatcher. He adopted Laura, and, according to Ellen, the years she spent with Marion "were the best years of my life." Marion died December 22, 1989. Ellen continues to make her home in Jacksonville where her children have settled.

Frieda, the youngest of the Lofstedts, graduated from Corbett Grade School in 1942. Two students in her class, George Sakurai and Mitzi Uyetake, missed the final weeks of the year because the federal government forced all families of Japanese extraction to leave the area on May 12, 1942. The Japanese were sent to "Relocation Centers" in California, Utah, Idaho or Arizona. Frieda started high school, but had met a young man serving in the CCC's, and they married. Frieda had a daughter, Judy L., from this marriage. On October 12, 1946, Frieda married Eugene 'Gene' V. O'Neil. Gene was born in Portland March 28, 1924, and moved to Dodson with his parents in 1937. (See "John O'Neil").

Gene and Frieda had eight children, and raised nine as a family: Judy L., b. April 20, 1944; Colleen L., b. June 11, 1947; Michael E., b. December 3, 1948; Sam C., b. March 29, 1950; Molly M., b. February 22, 1954; Charles R., b. April 9, 1955; Andrew J., b. October 22, 1956; Leslie S., b. June 23, 1961; and Peggy J., b. September 30, 1964. All of the

A Slight Mishap

Gene O'Neil, courting Frieda, makes a less than perfect landing in the Lofstedt pasture.
Photo courtesy of Frieda (Lofstedt) O'Neil.

children attended Corbett Grade School and CHS. The entire family enjoyed sports and were avid fans of the High School's teams, including football, track, volleyball and baseball, but particularly, basketball. This interest now centers on Gene and Frieda's sixteen grandchildren. Gene served as a Scoutmaster, was a Corbett School Board member four years and a volunteer with the Corbett Fire Department for 40 years. Gene's interest in the latter served as a model for his sons as all four served as firefighters with the Portland Fire Bureau.

After he was discharged from the Army Air Corps, Gene was employed at the Bridal Veil Lumber and Box Company. The family first lived at Coopey Falls, then moved to Bridal Veil when a Company house became available. In 1950, Gene went to work for Pounder Truck Service. He and Frieda purchased the Hicks' place from the Southers. (The place is located across the highway from the Portland Women's Forum Overlook.) When Albert Pounder sold his trucking company to Gresham Transfer in 1956, Gene went to work for that Company. With his large family, Gene found it necessary to work at a second job. First, he fished for Francis and Minnie Reed. Then he purchased their drift right, and fished it until 1968. In 1968, Gene and Frieda purchased the Larch Mountain Label Company from Mick Dunken. It has been operated as a family business since. It provided an opportunity for their youngsters to learn

Charlie Lofstedt and Granddaughter

Charlie's granddaughter, Leslie O'Neil, wants her Grandpa to try some.
Photo courtesy of Frieda (Lofsted) O'Neil.

to work and additional income for the family. In 1982, the business was sold to their son, Charlie, who now operates it.

After retiring from Gresham Transfer, Gene drove truck for Bob Dunken, who owned Portland Sawmill Machinery. He and Frieda enjoyed many trips together picking up or delivering sawmill machinery. He also worked for the Ekstroms at Gresham Sand and Gravel, and was working there when he died November 28, 1988. Frieda said, "Gene really enjoyed working for Roger and Evelyn Ekstrom. They were really nice people." (Evelyn Ekstrom is a daughter of Robert and Madeline Ihrke–see "Frederick and Mary Ihrke and Descendants," *Pioneer History*) Frieda lives at her home in Corbett where she continues to take an active part in community affairs.

Sophia MacKay, Gussie Kendrick and Frieda O'Neil.

Lofstedt Farm

On the load, Mike, Andy, Charlie and Sam O'Neil. Below, Charlie Lofstedt, Don MacKay and Gene O'Neil.   Photos courtesy of Frieda (Lofstedt) O'Neil.

Gene and Frieda's Family

Front, L to R: Leslie, Judy, Mike, Frieda, Gene and Peggy. Rear: Charlie, Colleen, Sam, Molly and Andy.

Verne S. Lucas
Laura M. (Canzler) Lucas

Vern Lucas was born December 18, 1890, in Beloit County, Nebraska. He came to Oregon in 1908 at age 17 to start clearing a place his parents, Thomas and Sarah Lucas, had purchased earlier. (When Vern's son, Clarence, asked his father how he had managed to clear the land without a "Cat," he said, "Dynamite, and I used enough to blow the stumps, roots and all, out of the ground.") The Lucas' interest in moving to Oregon was spurred by their affiliation with the Church of the Brethren, which had a parish in Springdale. The family moved to Springdale sometime around 1910, and built a house near the intersection of what is now Lucas Road with the Columbia River Highway. Thomas Lucas was born in Ampton, England, on March 13, 1853. His wife, Sarah (Walker) Lucas was born May 17, 1855, in Northampton, England. Their first daughter, Ellen May, remained in England when the family immigrated to the United States. The family settled first in Nebraska, hoping the dry climate there would help with Mr. Lucas' respiratory problems, and the family lived there for a time before moving on to Oregon. When they moved, their next three children, Kate, Annie and Alfred remained in Nebraska. The younger Lucas children, Flora, Ruth, Hazel and Eva, accompanied their parents to Oregon to join Vern, who had come earlier. Flora and Ruth moved to Hood River, but Hazel, Vern and Eva remained in East Multnomah County to marry and make their homes.

The Lucas place was located on the West Side of Lucas Road, bounded on the North by Mershon Road and on the south by the Columbia River Highway. As the place was cleared, wood was sold to the Union Pacific Railroad in Troutdale. In addition to helping his father clear the land, Vern worked breaking horses to harness for use in pulling wagons or buggies. He would team a 'new' horse with a trained animal, and work the two together until the prospect tired and became manageable. Vern married Laura May Canzler, daughter of Henry and Kate Canzler, who owned the place east across Lucas Road from the Lucas family. Laura was born May 8, 1888, in Malcolm, Nebraska, coming to Oregon with her family in 1905. The Canzler family was also affiliated with the Brethren Church. Vern and Laura had four children: Alice Wilma, b. May 17, 1917; Clarence William, b. September 29, 1921; Ruby Eleanor, b. Janu-

Clarence Lucas With Classmates at Springdale Grade, 1935

From L, John Kondo, Clarence Lucas, Elaine Collins, George Toyo, Floyd Bates, Harold Shelley and Mrs. Lillian Strachan.   Photo courtesy of Grace Stolin.

ary 25, 1925; and LaVerne Lorraine, b. September 4, 1927. The children all attended Springdale Grade School, and graduated from CHS in Corbett, Wilma in 1935; Clarence in 1939; Ruby in 1943; and LaVerne in 1945.

In the 20's, Vern became interested in electricity, and opened a shop in a building he rented from the Crowstons at the corner of Bell Grade and the Columbia River Highway. He sold radios, light bulbs and electrical supplies to people whose homes were just becoming connected to this new power source (for the area). He also did a good business wiring homes so that people could take advantage of the electric power coming in. Vern also operated a small construction business, putting up telephone and electric lines. Some said that Vern could be "out of his car and up a pole before the car door closed." As he operated his various businesses and worked for the Columbia Telephone Company, Vern started to buy its stock. By the late 20's, he owned a controlling interest and had a telephone business to run. Columbia Telephone Company, organized in 1908 by Tom Evans, Willis Hicks and Fred Reed Sr., gradually placed its lines to various areas in East Multnomah County. In the early days, lines were attached to whatever was handy, including fence posts and

Laverne Lucas

Laverne Lucas, CHS graduate 1945. '45 Cohimore photo courtesy of David Rees

trees. In 1909, R.P. Rasmussen, James Ross, F.N. Lasley, Grant Bell, and S.M. Davis purchased stock in the Company. As early investors sold shares, Vern bought.

Unfortunately, the depression hit in 1929 and many customers had dropped phone service when they could not pay the bill. Though the telephone business was never a great moneymaker, it did require much hard work on Vern's part to keep the lines in service. East Multnomah County, with its sleet storms and east wind, may not be the ideal place for a telephone business requiring poles and lines. And the most difficult time to keep the lines in service came when the wind howled, the snow drifted or a sleet storm brought down the lines.

Nevertheless, Vern kept the business going despite the hard times and the hard work. As World War II hit Europe and Southeast Asia, he had an opportunity to go to work for Alcoa Aluminum Company, and worked there during the war, in addition to maintaining the telephone business. Vern's son, Clarence, learned the telephone business by helping his father while attending high school. When the war came, however, Clarence was drafted into the U.S. Army, and he was no longer available to help. Vern died July 24, 1945, at age 54, before the war in the Pacific was concluded. Mrs. Laura Lucas turned over the operation of Columbia Telephone to her daughter, Wilma, and Wilma's husband, Raymond Smith. The Smiths operated Columbia Telephone until it was sold to Cascade Utilities in 1972.

Clarence Lucas reported to the army July 5, 1942. He was working at Alcoa Aluminum when drafted. On February 28, 1942, he married Dorothy Janet Arrington. Janet Arrington's family lived on Brower (later Larch Mountain) Road. She had attended Corbett Grade School, and graduated from CHS in 1941. Her family had homesteaded land in Multnomah Basin early in the century (see "Edwin A. Arrington"). After training, Clarence was sent overseas in 1943 then to Burma in 1944, where he worked on the famous "Burma Road." Considering his background, it is not too surprising that he found himself in the Signal Corps which had been given the responsibility of placing a telephone line along the Burma Road from India to China. A 1944-45 issue of the *Cardinal*, CHS, contained a description of one of the jobs undertaken by the Signal Corps, which came from a paper published by the Army. The article tells how Lucas, with the help of eleven men, strung wires across the Irrawaddy River. The current was exceptionally strong and every time the wire touched the river it snapped in two. After 20 attempts Lucas finally had the wire strung up to a tower on one side, then men in boats took it across to the other, and the wire was strung at last.

While in this theater, he was under the command of General Joseph Stillwell. American troops had hacked a base area out of the jungle in Burma, and were trying to make it somewhat habitable. One day a P-40 engaged some Japanese aircraft, and it was shot down. The pilot bailed out, and the plane nose-dived into the cleared area. It nearly buried itself in the swampy ground. As the pilot drifted down, some engineer troops shot at him, thinking he was Japanese. The officer in charge got a real chewing out when the parachuting pilot turned out to be a U.S. major with the famous "Flying Tigers."

This wasn't the only problem endured by American troops in this area. An Indian army with English officers was stationed there also. According to Clarence, the troops hated the English officers more than the Japanese, which complicated the situation somewhat. Also, the Chinese army commanders were more interested in getting American supplies and equipment stockpiled for use against the Chinese Communists, rather than "wasting" it for use against the Japanese. All this complicated General Stillwell's life a great deal. One time a few U.S. troops in a vehicle had an accident with a vehicle containing Chinese troops. The Chinese came out of the vehicle with guns blazing, which didn't help matters much. As the American army advanced into Burma, they came across a village abandoned by the Japanese. Three girls came out of a hut, and claimed they were Koreans. It turned out that these girls had been promised good pay for six months "duty" serving as "comfort" girls for the Japanese Army. Of course, the "duty" period was of indeterminate length, and the promised pay was not forthcoming.

The American and Allied troops were up against the famed Japanese 38th Division, which had conquered Hong Kong, Singapore and Burma.

310

It suffered its first defeat at the hands of General Stillwell's forces. Clarence remained in the China Theater until the war was over, and he was discharged from the army in September 1945.

After returning home, Clarence and Janet made their home in Springdale. Clarence went to work for Portland General Electric Company, and worked for the company 38 years until he retired in January 1984. He and Janet had three children; Gregory Wade, b. January 26, 1944; Cheryl A. Stewart, b. July 19, 1946; and Rita H. Clemmons, b. July 23, 1949. Gregory lives in Tacoma, has two children, a son and a daughter, and works for Boeing. Cheryl Ann lives in Portland. Rita Helene was widowed when her husband was killed in a tractor accident. She lives in Fairview. Clarence's mother, Laura, died February 12, 1976, age 86. (For more information about the Lucas family, see: "Raymond Smith" and "Harley Bates.")   *Clarence Lucas*

Latourell Flume c1890's.   Photo courtesy of the Kerslake Family.

Roy MacKay
Bertha (Nelson) MacKay

Roy MacKay was born in Chicago, Illinois, February 22, 1889. He migrated to Canada for a time, and eventually came to East Multnomah County to work as a carpenter. He met Bertha Nelson, daughter of Nels and Ellen (Lofstedt) Nelson while working in the area. Nels Nelson had been a fisherman at Astoria before moving to Latourell, where he worked as a blacksmith. Here he met Ellen Lofstedt, daughter of Charles A. Lofstedt, and the couple married in Portland, Oregon in 1910. Bertha Nelson was born November 12, 1911. Shortly after she was born, her mother and father were divorced, and Bertha and her mother never saw her father again. Bertha's mother lived with her father at the Lofstedt homestead near Brower after the divorce. A great uncle to Bertha, Peter Perrson, also lived with them (see "Charles A. Lofstedt").

Bertha attended grade school at the Brower School, and high school at Columbia High in Corbett. While in high school, Bertha worked for Judge Arthur Languth, who lived in a home off Larch Mountain Road between its intersection with Loudon and Deverell Roads. Bertha married Roy MacKay August 12, 1930. During the depression, he worked as a carpenter when work was available, and also worked for the Workers' Progress Administration (WPA) on various construction projects in the area. Bertha and Roy had six children: Douglas, b. June 29, 1932; Clara, b. October 16, 1934; Charles, b. March 5, 1937; Iona, b. July 15, 1938; Barbara, b. April 29, 1941; and Flora, b. March 8, 1944.

Bertha worked at Johnson's Restaurant at Crown Point before the war and also worked for Ward Evans in bulbs and in the corn cannery. During World War II and into the 50's she worked seasonally for Pete Binn at his Troutdale produce warehouse until it closed (the building was moved across the Union Pacific tracks, and now houses a business dealing in art works.) Later she worked at Bradford Gardens in Portland and continued there as nursery manager after it was sold to Mr. McCarter, who had operated the Swan Island Dahlia Farm previously. She also worked at Multnomah Falls Lodge and at the Cliff House near Bridal Veil. Meanwhile, her husband, Roy, worked as a carpenter for Ray Holtgrieve at Coopey Falls after the war until his retirement.

Logging Camp on Larch Mountain

Logging camp above Palmer on Larch.   Photos courtesy of Bertha MacKay.

Logging Crew

Woods crew who worked at the logging camp above.

Roy MacKay died in April 1969, age 80. Bertha inherited one-half the original Lofstedt homestead from her mother, and she and Roy raised their family on the place. When it was suggested she sell the place, she said: "Why? Where would I go? I got the place for nothing, and I'm staying right here!" Bertha continues to live on the home place now (1999), and must be one of the few daughters of pioneer stock who stayed put. She fully intends to end her days right there.

E. Chester May
Eudora (Harrison) May

Chester 'Chet' May was born in Oklahoma October 1, 1899; Eudora Harrison was born in Oregon February 5, 1914. The couple married June 22, 1932, in North Powder, Oregon. Two of their children, Joretta, b. May 8, 1933 and Zorada, b. July 10, 1934, were born in North Powder before the family moved to East Multnomah County in 1934. The family first rented a home in Howard Canyon before settling on Littlepage Road. Two more children followed, Donford, b. December 11, 1935 and Wymard C., b. December 21, 1937. The youngsters all attended and completed elementary school at Corbett Grade. Three graduated from CHS, Joretta in 1951, Zorada in 1953 and Wymard in 1957.

Chet May died in an automobile accident on Stark Street in 1949. The November 23, 1949 *Cardinal* reported the tragic accident: "Mr. and Mrs. Chester May were injured in an auto wreck, which occurred last Saturday night near the Mountain View Nursery on Baseline. Their two sons, Donford and Wymard, were in the car asleep when a car going west crashed into the side of May's car. Mrs. May, who was driving, suffered a broken ankle, fractured kneecap and face injuries. Mr. May received such severe head and internal injuries that he died yesterday morning. The man in the other car was killed instantly."

While Eudora May recovered, the children stayed with friends for about three months. After Wymard 'Chester' graduated from CHS, Eudora May married Merrill Fox, a minister who did mission work at the Union Gospel Mission for many years. Later, they moved to Halsey, Oregon, where Eudora Fox worked for the US Postal Service. Merrill and Eudora had one child, Esther, b. December 7, 1958. Eudora (May) Fox passed away February 2, 1990.

During their school years, the May children worked for different farmers in the area, working in such crops as berries, daffodils and vegetables, including potatoes. According to Joretta, "Mother worked right along side us kids." During the war years, Chet May worked at the Oregon shipyard. Joretta said, "When I turned eighteen and had graduated I said, no more strawberries and went into Portland to find work." Joretta obtained her first job with Farmers Insurance Company. She stayed with Farmers until after she married Dale Ferrington February 7, 1952, and

Chet and Eudora May Family

From L, Chet, Joretta, Zorada, Donford, Wymard and Eudora May at home.

Eudora May and Daughters

From L, Eudora May with her daughters Zorada and Joretta. Photos courtesy of Joretta (May) Ferrington.

started a family. Joretta and Dale have three children, Louise, Robert and Glenda (also see "Erick Enquist").

June 10, 1954, Zorada married Lotis Hanks. Lotis worked as a caretaker of the Thornfeldt (former Porter) place off Lucas Road for several years. Later Lotis worked for N. Pacific Lumber, then he went into the construction business in Lafayette. Lotis served as Mayor of Lafayette for many years. Zorada and Lotis have two children, John and Lisa.

Donford left CHS before graduating and enlisted in the US Army. He married Marilyn Saling December 12, 1957. The couple moved to Hermiston, Oregon where Donford worked in a manufacturing plant. Marilyn worked for the US Postal Service as a mail carrier. Donford and Marilyn have four children, Ken, Donna, Larry and James.

Chester (Wymard) enlisted in the Army after graduating from CHS. He did not marry, lives in San Diego, California and works for the City in its Department of Public Works.

Alfred D. Mershon
Sarah L. (Jefferson) Mershon

Alfred D. Mershon and Sarah L. Mershon came with their family of four children to Oregon in 1889. Both Alfred and Sarah (Jefferson) were born in Kentucky, he, April 19, 1857 and she, May 18, 1864. According to information submitted by Louis and Ernest Mershon (see "Alfred D. Mershon,' *Pioneer History*), the Mershons settled on the hill in 1891. However, Dorothy Klock, in her book, *Crown Point Country Schools*, includes the Mershon family in the Pleasant View school census of 1890 (p. 41). Alfred and Sarah had eight children, including the older four born in Kentucky. The eight are: Leroy B., b. October 3, 1884, Louis J., b. February 19, 1886, George W., b. October 15, 1887, Lucy J., b. March 16, 1889, Anna G., b. April 29, 1892, Margaret M., b. August 26, 1894, Ernest A., b. November 10, 1901 and Alice C., b. June 1, 1905. All attended Pleasant View grade school. Only the two youngest, Ernest 'Mac' and Alice 'Polly' attended CHS, which opened in 1914. Neither, however, graduated from the school.

The Mershons purchased 5 acres at the NE corner of Chamberlain and Mershon Roads sometime in the 1890's. Later they added 12 acres across Mershon Road and 27 adjacent acres to the east. Seventeen acres of the latter were sold to Harry Uyetake in 1923. Shortly before this, two of the brothers, George W. 'Jum' and Louis J. 'Bill,' purchased parcels from the Corbett Estate in Corbett. Later, Bill sold his place to Frank C. Riggs, but the parcel owned by Jum remains in his family. George W. Mershon Jr. and his family live there now.

At the time the Mershons settled in the area, much of the land was still covered by forest. Jum remarked at one time that the settlers discovered what caused the "whistling sound" one heard in the treetops after the trees were removed. Most of the timber in this area was cut and sold as cordwood. Cordwood was delivered to Lower Corbett for use by steamboats and later, locomotives. Alfred D. Mershon farmed and became known as the "onion king." The Mershon youngsters shared stories about weeding "acres" of onions on their hands and knees. He also grew sufficient tobacco to provide leaves for his cigars, which he rolled himself. During the construction of the Columbia River Highway, Mershon provided a team and worked together with other area farmers on that project.

Mershon Family c1904

Rear, L to R: Leroy, Lucy, George and Louis. Front, Alfred D., Ernest, Anna, Margaret and Sarah L. Mershon.   Photo courtesy of Earl Clare Mershon.

In 1918, Alfred and his youngest son, Ernest, dug a hole alongside a large boulder (likely an erratic) lying in the pasture behind the family home. May 18, 1918, after rain had soaked the ground overnight, the two went to the pasture to continue the task. When Ernest started into the hole, his father told him, "It's too dangerous. I'll dig." After Alfred descended into the hole, the ground beneath the boulder gave way and it slid into the hole, crushing him. Sarah Mershon remained on the farm until her children married, then moved to Portland. She lived with her daughter, Polly Barnard, until her death January 19, 1951.

Leroy Mershon married Myrtle Kennedy before embarking upon a mission to The Netherlands East Indies for the Seventh Day Adventist church. In 1917, while serving in Borneo, Myrtle died of disease. Leroy remained in the Far East for more than 20 years, serving as a missionary in Borneo, Java and The Philippines. Upon his return, he became parson of a church in Vale, Oregon. He passed away in 1974.

Bill Mershon married Idella F. McBride September 14, 1906. After graduating from Oregon Agricultural College, Idella came to Pleasant

Alfred D. Mershon

Alfred D. Mershon stands beside his workhorse, Prince.
Photo courtesy of Earl Clare Mershon.

View to teach school. She was a daughter of a pioneer family that settled in Shedd, Oregon. Bill and Idella first lived in a small house on the 17-acre parcel located to the east of the original 5 acres. During these years, Bill Mershon was farming as well as helping his father on the family farm. He also worked for Multnomah County during the construction of the Columbia River Highway. According to family lore, Bill and Alfred hauled the first two loads of lumber to Crown Point for the Vista House construction. Bill's lumber was unloaded without incident, but a gust of east wind caught Alfred's load and it sailed over the cliff.

Bill and Idella had three children, Clarence 'Earl,' James 'Lyle' and Carroll. After purchasing the property at Corbett, Bill built a home and the family moved there in 1920. However, they lived there only a short time before moving to Sherwood. In the mid-20's, Bill obtained a job with the Oregon State Highway Department. The job took him to various locations throughout the State. When Bill retired, he was bridge tender on the Highway 101 bridge across the Siletz River at Kernville, Oregon. Bill Mershon passed away October 30, 1962.

George W. married Laura A. Wilson December 15, 1915 (see "George W. Mershon"). Lucy Jane married Robert W. Larson (see "Robert W.

318

Mershon Family c1914

Rear, From L: Ernest, George, Jasper Mershon. Middle: Idella (McBride) Mershon, Myrtle (Kennedy) Mershon, Leroy, Margaret and Lucy Jane. Seated: Anna, Louis, C. Earl (on his father's lap), Alfred D. Mershon, Alice 'Polly,' Sarah (Jefferson) Mershon, Robert 'Tood' Larson Jr., Robert W. Larson and Alfred L. Larson.

Photo courtesy of Dorothy Larson.

Larson"). Anna G. married Ralph Rogers (see "William H. Rogers"). Margaret M. 'Marge' married Henry Sumpter. The couple had one son, Henry 'Bucky.' Later she married Nels Lundberg, and had two more children, Louise and James. Marge raised her children in Portland. She passed away July 3, 1989. Ernest 'Mac' married Magdaleine Pulliam (see "Ernest A. Mershon"). Alice C. 'Polly,' married Kenneth Barnard February 19, 1923. The couple purchased a home in NE Portland where they raised three children, Richard, Barbara and David. Alice 'Polly' Barnard passed away January 23, 1987.

Marge (Mershon) Sumpter

Marge (Mershon) Sumpter with her son, Henry 'Bucky.'

The Barnards

Kenneth and Alice 'Polly' Barnard.
Photos courtesy of Dorothy Larson.

Alice 'Polly' Barnard

Polly Barnard visits her sister, Lucy Larson. The Larson barn is in the background. Photos courtesy of Dorothy Larson

Barbara Barnard

Barbara Barnard catches a 'ride' on her cousin Tood Larson's truck loaded with potatoes. The truck is parked along Ogden Road in front of the Larson residence.

320

Ernest A. Mershon
Magdaleine (Pulliam) Mershon

Ernest 'Mac' Mershon marriedMagdaleine Pulliam November 28, 1922. They lived in Portland until 1933, then moved to Maygar, Oregon. In Maygar, Mac farmed, growing strawberries and feed for his dairy cows and other stock. Mac and Magdaleine had six children, Ardis, b. June 2, 1924, Alfred 'Bud,' b. January 3, 1927, William 'Bill,' b. February 3, 1933, Allan 'Pete,' b. April 2, 1935, John, b. January 10, 1937 and Carol, b. April 7, 1944. In 1940, when jobs became more plentiful, Mac returned to the Corbett area, purchasing a place at the intersection of Mershon and Ogden roads. He worked for Woodbury & Company in Portland before obtaining a job at the aluminum plant in Troutdale. He worked at Reynolds Aluminum until he retired in 1970. Mac also farmed the place, which was usually planted to cabbage. Magdaleine worked to provide a home for her six children. Mac Mershon died April 4, 1973. Magdaleine (Pulliam) Mershon passed away January 12, 1990.

Ardis completed her high school years at CHS, graduating in 1942. Similarly to many of her peers, she worked for various farmers before she married Jim Baker June 6, 1944 (see "Louie Baker"). Jim and Ardis' daughters, Pat and Linda Baker, graduated from CHS. Pat Lucas had two sons, Jeff and James, graduate from CHS and Linda Traxler had three, Peter, Robert and Sam. Therefore, four generations in the family have graduated from CHS [1]: Magdaleine Pulliam ('20), [2]: Ardis Mershon ('42), [3]: Pat and Linda Baker ('65 and '69, respectively) and [4]: Jeff and James Lucas ('89 and '91, respectively), and Peter, Robert and Sam Traxler ('95, '96 and '96, respectively).

After completing grade school at Corbett, Alfred attended CHS, graduating in 1945. He too, worked for various farmers, including his uncle, Bob Larson, and Larson and Winters. His mother's family included several commercial fishermen, This gave Alfred an opportunity to learn this trade working with his Uncle Earl Pulliam, while he was still in high school. After graduating in 1945, Alfred served in the Merchant Marine before WW II ended. He then enlisted in the Army and served a tour as a member of the Occupation Army in Japan. Alfred resumed his career as a commercial fisherman upon his return home.

Ernest Mershon   **Ardis and Alfred Mershon**   **Ardis Mershon**

Ernest Mershon in   Ardis and Alfred Mershon c1927.   Ardis Mershon, c1943
his youth.   Photos courtesy of Dorothy Larson.

Alfred Mershon married Norma Kent May 26, 1950. They had four children, Daniel, b. December 14, 1951, Paul, b. September 26, 1953, Philip, b. September 30, 1956 and Karen, b. July 25, 1958. The youngsters attended Corbett schools. Dan graduated from the CHS in 1970 after 'standout' athletic accomplishments, particularly in football and track. Paul graduated from CHS in 1971, Philip in 1974 and Karen in 1976. Karen gave the valedictory at the '76 commencement. Dan, following his father's example, became a commercial fisherman. He attended MHCC for two years before embarking upon his career. He fishes Bristol Bay in Alaska and lives in Hawaii during the 'off' season. Dan married Christy Schaffer (CHS '70) and they have two sons, Josh and Nathan. Paul attended MHCC for two years with plans to enter the law enforcement field. However, placement with a fire department for experience led to a career in that field. He works as a paramedic for the Portland Fire Department. Paul married Susan Dunken (CHS '71) (see "James B. Dunken") and they have three children, Carrie (CHS '95), Laurie (CHS '97) and Travis.

Philip also became a commercial fisherman, following his brother, Dan's example by going to Alaska. Since graduating from high school, Philip has fished Bristol Bay for halibut, crab and salmon. Philip married Sherol Smith and they have three children, Tiffany, Heidi and Sallee. Philip and his family live in Walla Walla where he has a boat-building shop. When he is not fishing, he builds fishing boats. Karen Mershon

Alfred Mershon

Alfred Mershon on Ogden Road c1943.

Mershon Youngsters c1943

Allan, John and Bill Mershon play in their driveway. Photos courtesy of Dorothy Larson.

attended Western Business College for a year. She married Mark Beyer of Tillamook and has two children, Stacy and Christopher. She works for the Oregon State Police and lives in Tillamook.

Though many of the fishermen at Lower Corbett discontinued fishing over the years, Alfred continued to work as a commercial fisherman his entire life. When commercial fishing declined, he persevered. One of the few fishermen left on the Columbia, he contracted with the Oregon Department of Fisheries on occasion to help them gain information about fish runs. When fishing essentially closed on the Columbia, Alfred followed two of his sons, Dan and Philip, to Bristol Bay in Alaska. He acted as boat-puller for Philip for 18 years. Norma started working for Corbett School District in 1964. She first worked at Springdale as a cook, then took a secretarial position at Corbett Grade School. She ended her career as District bookkeeper in 1993. Alfred Mershon passed away March 19, 1994.

Bill Mershon completed elementary school at Corbett. He attended CHS, graduating in 1952. During his high school years he worked for his uncle, Bob Larson, for Larson and Winters and for Owen Emily, at Corbett. He enlisted in the Army and completed a tour in Germany as a member of the Occupation Army. After his discharge, he started working at the Reynolds plant in Troutdale. He married Lee Erb, and they had three children, Terri, Sharon and Lori. Bill and Lee raised their family in NE Portland. After Bill retired from Reynolds, the couple sold their home in Portland and moved to Henderson, Nevada.

323

The Mershon Home

The Mershon home on Ogden Road (now [1999] being remodeled).
Photo courtesy of Dorothy Larson.

Pete Mershon, despite being afflicted with cerebral palsy at birth, lived a productive life for most of his years. Because his mother worried about how he might fare at school, she kept him home for some time. However, Pete demonstrated that he could 'give and take' with his peers, and was widely admired for the courage and determination he displayed in interacting with others. Because of his handicap, he would often take a nasty 'spill,' only to come up laughing at himself. He worked for his father, driving tractor and performing other farm jobs well. He worked for several farmers, including Bob and Tood Larson. Those who know Pete Mershon consider him one of the most courageous individuals one could meet. Pete is now in a rest home, totally incapacitated after an operation intended to help him become more mobile. Needless to say, the operation failed.

John Mershon graduated from CHS in 1955. He married Pat Beatty and they have a daughter, Pamela (CHS '77). John recently retired from the James River Corporation. He and Pat now live in Gresham.

Carol Mershon completed both grade and high school at Corbett, graduating from CHS in 1962. She edited the *Cardinal* and was named class Valedictorian. Carol married Doug Quinn August 3, 1963. Doug worked as a civilian employee for the Oregon Air National Guard for 28 years, and has recently retired. Carol has worked for the Corbett Water District for seventeen years. Carol and Doug have two children, Kelli, b. May 1, 1968 and Mark, b. November 23, 1969. Kelli graduated from CHS in 1986, Mark in 1988. Currently Doug and Carol are building a new home on Trout Creek Road, having sold their residence in Corbett.

324

George W. Mershon
Laura A. (Wilson) Mershon

George W. 'Jum' Mershon was born October 15, 1887, in Cadiz, Kentucky. His father was Alfred D. Mershon and his mother Sarah 'Sallie' (Jefferson) Mershon. The Mershon family came to Oregon by train the winter of 1889-90, when Jum was 2 years old, settling first on Stark Street, about a mile east of 12-Mile corner. In 1890, the family moved to the "hill," and eventually purchased a farm located near what is now the intersection of Mershon Road with Chamberlain Road (see "Alfred D. Mershon" and "Family History of Alfred D. and Sarah Lee Mershon," *Pioneer History*,). Jum and his siblings attended Pleasant View School, located on what is now Wand Road. At some point Jum quit school to work on the farm, a common practice in those days.

Upon reaching adulthood, Jum worked at various jobs, including working on the construction of the old highway. He happened to be with a road crew hauling gravel from the Baker Pit across the Nielson Bridge when it gave way, sending the truck into the Sandy River. Of the crew, Charlie Bramhall suffered a broken arm, Frank Fehrenbacher found a splinter imbedded beneath the skin in his temple when he reached home and Jum's back gave him some problems for a time, though no bones were broken. Louis 'Bill' Mershon plus the driver came away unscathed.

Jum married Laura Anna Wilson December 15, 1915. Laura was born January 2, 1894, to James C. and Myra I. (Miller) Wilson in Tulare, California. In May, 1899, when Laura was 5 years old, her parents moved to the Miller (Myra's parents) place off Loudon on what is now Mannthey Road (see "W.H. Miller," *Pioneer History*). Laura attended Springfield ('Egypt') Grade School eight years, then completed high school in Portland, graduating from Lincoln High School in 1914 (see "James C. Wilson"). On May 18, 1918, an event occurred that was to have a profound effect upon Jum and Laura Mershon. Alfred D. Mershon, Jum's father, was crushed while trying to bury a boulder. As a result of the accident, Jum, who was working in the shipyards at the time, decided it was his place to operate the farm. He and Laura built a small house off Lucas Road near its intersection with Mershon Road and moved to the Mershon place. At the time, the farm included about 44 acres, 34 acres of which was tilled.

George Mershon Family

George Mershon Jr.

George 'Jum' and Laura A. Mershon, Elda and Alfred sit in Jum's lap.

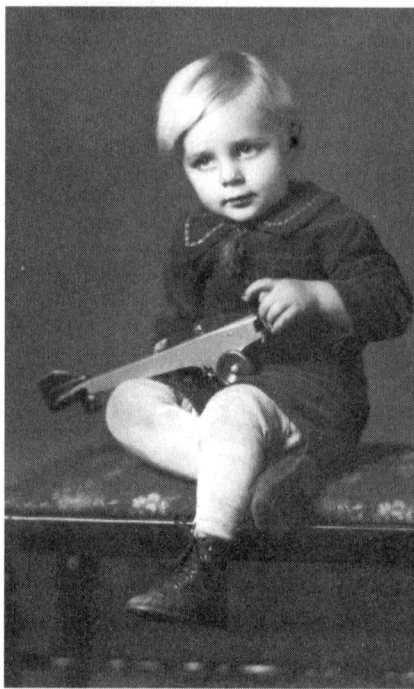

George Jr. with his new, toy airplane. Photos courtesy of Dorothy Larson.

About 12 acres to the south of Mershon Road had been added to the home place, which acreage bordered Louis Berney's property to the east. Jum and Laura built their home on this piece, and the large barn was also located on this parcel. Jum farmed the Mershon place for many years, growing cabbage, lettuce, cauliflower, peas and cucumbers. During the 20's, farm prices held fairly well, but the situation changed dramatically in the late 20's. Many farmers who sold produce through the Troutdale Fruit and Vegetable Growers in 1928 were not paid for the crops delivered. The situation worsened in subsequent years as the depression deepened in the early 30's. Year after year the story was the same: work the ground, plant the crops, cultivate and hoe them, and then plow them under, as there was no market. Libby, McNeil and Libby contracted with farmers to grow cucumbers, which was a crop that provided some income. Though cucumbers brought in some cash, it would not have been a profitable crop to raise if one had to hire much help.

Winters Truck Service picked up the cucumbers in the afternoon, and delivered them to the Libby McNeil and Libby processing plant off

326

Laura and Elda Mershon

Laura and her daughter, Elda, stand in the front yard on the corner where the house was located. The road in the background is Mershon Road.   Photo, the author.

Powell Boulevard in Southeast Portland. When the load arrived at the dock, a sample sack was chosen at random from each grower's shipment and the cucumbers in the sample were graded. Size and shape determined the grade. Number 1's were of a small, uniform size suitable for sweet pickles, number 2's were of medium size for dill pickles, number 3's were large cucumbers suitable for other type pickles and culls were rejects because of size or deformity problems. The "graded" sack set the proportions of each grade for the entire lot, i.e., if the sample contained 10% number 1's, the grower was paid that price for 10% of the shipment.

During the depression, Jum found some part-time work, for example, working at the Rooster Rock seine (see "Harry Kruckman"). In the late 30's, Jum worked for the WPA on construction projects that included building the Larch Mountain Road. He was paid $60.00 per month and was glad to get it. In 1940, when the shipyards started hiring, he went to work at the Kaiser Oregon Shipyard and worked there during World War II. Jum was supposed to buy the Mershon place from his mother, but did not act in a timely manner. In 1943, during the time he worked at the shipyard, his mother sold the place to Robert 'Tood' Larson (her grandson and Jum's nephew). Tood permitted Jum to continue living on the place while Quay Martin built a house on the ten acres at Corbett. The family moved to the Corbett house in 1945. After the war Jum worked at the Woodbury Hardware warehouse as shipping clerk until he was injured. George 'Jum' Mershon died May 10, 1953, age 65, and Laura died September 28, 1984, age 90.

Jum and Laura had five children: Elda May, b. May 27, 1917; Alfred Delos, b. September 3, 1920; George W. Jr., born January 17, 1927; Clarence E., b. April 23, 1931; and Laura Isabelle, b. March 8, 1933. Alfred died of spinal meningitis in the fall of 1922, age two. Each of the surviving Mershon children attended school at Corbett. Elda graduated

Mount Defiance Lookout

From L, George Mershon (holding Clarence), Laura Mershon (holding Belle), George (in front), Elda Mershon, Pearl (Chamberlain) Stephens, and Jim Stephens (holding George). Photo, the author.

from CHS in 1935, and worked as a telephone operator at the Corbett exchange for a time. She met her future husband, Richard 'Dick" Christopher, shortly after World War II started. They were married May 4, 1942, while Dick was stationed in Portland with the U.S. Army Engineers.

Shortly thereafter, he transferred to the Army Air Force, and was sent to Geiger Field in Spokane. From there he was sent to England, then to France, where his unit was among the first Air Force contingents to establish a base on the European mainland after the D-Day landings. During the Korean War, Dick was assigned to a fighter group based near Seoul, his second wartime service. Because of Dick's military career, the couple resided at various duty stations until he retired from the Air Force in 1959. They then moved to Portland, where Dick worked for LeTourneau Sales and Service, and Elda worked as a purchasing agent for Tracey & Company Auto Parts. When Dick retired in 1982, they moved to Carson, Washington. Elda died of heart failure February 9, 1989, and Dick died February 7, 1996. The Christopher's had one daughter, Diane, who now lives in Anchorage, AK (1999).

In his youth, George Mershon spent many hours in the field driving the workhorse, 'Ruby.' Johnson grass grew in profusion in the fields. It may have helped the railroads by keeping the railroad bed from washing out, but the import was a bane to farmers. When the days were hot and dry, George was in the field with Ruby harrowing. The long, intertwined roots pulled from the dry earth by the springtooth harrow were stacked and burned. This reduced the infestation, but it was only a palliative as

George Mershon Jr.

Clarence and Laura Mershon

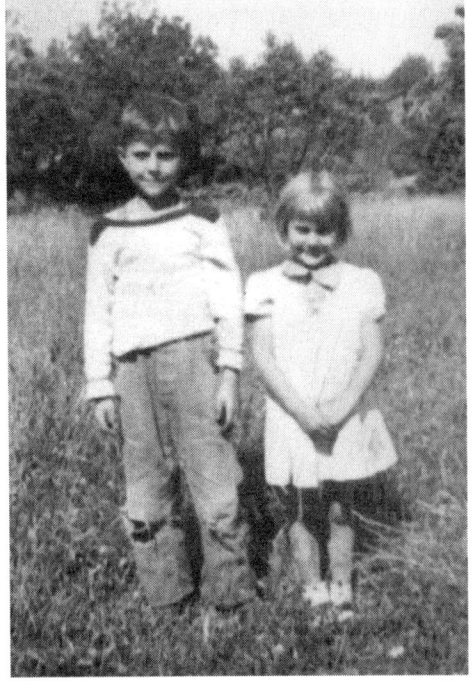

George Mershon ready to ride his new bicycle. Note buildings of the Uyetake place in the background.

Clarence and Laura 'Belle' Mershon stand in their front yard.   Photos, the author.

the damned stuff spread so rapidly. (One can imagine the satisfaction felt by a farmer who applies KERB or a similar herbicide, and the Johnson grass is gone!) When not harrowing, George was kept busy behind Ruby cultivating, spreading manure from a sled or performing other farm work. If not behind a horse, he was planting cabbage (by hand with a shovel), picking cucumbers, milking cows or doing other tasks, such as cleaning the barn.

Of course the days were not all spent at work. George bought a new Columbia bicycle, which he rode all over the country. He had his share of accidents including a head-on encounter with Art Canzler on Lucas Road. He was carrying two passengers on his bike when he cut a sharp corner below the house. Unfortunately, Mr. Canzler was coming up Lucas Road at the time. One of his passengers, Roy Harvey, suffered a gashed leg. The other passenger, Jimmy Benjamin, lost a shoe but was not injured. George was cut badly but had no broken bones.

George and Hank Matsuba were the same age and good friends. Hank was a marvelous athlete who would have contributed much to Columbian

Mershon Place, Winter of 1936-37

The Mershon place from George Mershon's front yard. Note the Uyetake place (left), the Mershon barn (right) and Louie Berney's barn, center (background). Belle, George and Clarence play in the snow (center 'dots'). Photo, the author

The Mershon Barn c1950

Another view of the Mershon barn on Lucas Road.
Photo courtesy of Dorothy Larson.

Hank Matsuba

Hank Matsuba started at CHS in 1941. Photo, the author.

High basketball and baseball teams had he not been sent with his family to a "relocation center" on May 12, 1942. The Matsubas lived just west of the Mershon Place. The closest neighbors to the east were the Uyetakes. Dick and Juanita Berney also lived just east of the Mershon Place and they were frequent playmates. When Ernest 'Mac' Mershon moved his family to the 'hill' from Maygar, the kids, Ardis, Alfred 'Bud,' Bill, Allan 'Pete' and John, were frequent visitors.

330

George started at CHS in 1941. World War II commenced (for the United States) December 7, 1941. That event certainly affected George and others of his generation. Suddenly good paying jobs were available. Teenagers could get such jobs in the shipyards or other plants. When George was sixteen, he started working at the Oregon Shipyard in the summer. Quite unexpectedly one had enough money to buy a car, which gave this age group a measure of freedom unknown a few months earlier. Fortunately, the gas shortage curtailed driving to some extent. Nevertheless, it was quite a change and a "heady time" to be a teenager. The boys faced the possibility of being drafted, which may have caused them to be somewhat less cautious than they might otherwise have been. And some paid the ultimate price (see "Dedication," *Corbett Now and Columbian Then*).

George left high school during his senior year to join the Merchant Marine and served in the Pacific Theater during the latter part of the war. In 1946, he enlisted in the U.S. Army for a two-year hitch and volunteered to become a paratrooper. He spent about a year in Sendai, Japan, on occupation duty. When discharged he returned to a job with Woodbury & Company for whom he had worked prior to going into the Army. On October 9, 1949, he married Viola 'Vi' Heard in Portland. Vi was born December 20, 1928 in Beaverton. The couple had four children: Sandra J., b. February 10, 1953; Cathy A., b. July 12, 1954; Jayne L., b. November 13, 1955; and Jeffery K., b. December 13, 1956.

George worked at the order desk for Woodbury for many years, then went into outside sales, calling on customers in Oregon and Washington. Woodbury was sold to eastern interests, and then acquired by the Schnitzers. George continued in sales and advanced to the position of inside sales manager. When George and Vi acquired Corbett Hardware in September 1967, he resigned his position with the company. In 1970 he was offered a position as inside sales manager with Standard Steel and found himself back in the steel business. He continued with Standard until 1981 when he returned to Metra Steel, owned by the Schnitzers, as sales manager. When George took this job, Vi took over the management of the hardware store. She added a snack shop and video outlet to supplement the hardware business, which was being impacted by competition from chains such as Home Depot and Home Base.

George and Vi moved to the Mershon home in Corbett in 1957. Sandra, Cathy, Jayne and Jeffery 'Jeff' attended Corbett schools. After graduating from Corbett High in 1971, Sandra attended Mt. Hood Community

Mershon Cousins

From L, Cathy, Mike, Chris, Jane, Perry (in front of) Elise, Sandra and Jeff Mershon at the coast.   Photo, the author.

College (MHCC) for two years, then completed her college work at Port-land State University (PSU) as an English major. She is now a high school English teacher. Sandra married Albert 'Al' Brenaman, who is also a teacher, and has a daughter, Katy and a son, Pat. The family lives in Corbett. Cathy also completed two years at MHCC after graduating from Corbett High in 1971 and then attended PSU, majoring in English. She is presently in charge of business publications for ADCT Kentrox Cor-poration in Beaverton. She has not married. After graduating from Corbett High in 1974, Jayne attended MHCC for two years, attended Oregon State University for two years and completed requirements for a degree in chemical engineering at the University of Washington. The Boeing Corporation has employed her since she graduated from college. She has two daughters, Elaine and Emily, and lives in Tacoma. Jeff attended MHCC for two years earning an Associate Degree in Auto Mechanics. He has two children, a son, Sam, who attends Corbett High, and a daugh-ter, Daniele. Jeff lives with his parents at Corbett and works for the Mt. Hood Meadows Ski Resort.

In 1990, the hardware business at Corbett was closed and the stock on hand sold at auction. The building was sold to Dale Burkholder in

Mershon Reunion

From L, Vi Mershon, George Mershon, Pat Brenaman and Katy Brenaman at the
Mershon family reunion, 1998.   Photo, the author.

September 1991. George and Vi also 'retired' that year, but continue the operation of the farm at Corbett, which they have planted to blueberries.

Clarence Mershon started grade school at Corbett in 1937. His first grade teacher was Miss Maude Sherman. A truly outstanding teacher came to Corbett Grade School when Clarence entered the fourth grade, Miss Ruth McCullough (later Mrs. Thomas Sommerville). She had many ideas and activities to encourage students to read, to learn, and to solve problems. According to Clarence, she was the teacher who really inspired him to do well in school. Another teacher he thought most effective was Mrs. Baer, his teacher in both the seventh and eighth grades. She pounded the structure of the English language into her students by constant board work, day after day. One learned to diagram simple, compound and complex sentences with subject, verb, object, clauses, modifiers, qualifiers, prepositions, infinitives, gerunds, participles, adjectives, adverbs, et al. Mrs. Baer was an extraordinarily skilled teacher who had a few personal idiosyncrasies that may have distracted some, but she was most effective in the classroom. Clarence is thankful for the education he gained as a student at both Corbett Grade School and CHS. He says, "Each of us owes the people of this community a debt of gratitude for the fine schools they provided."

Another detail Clarence mentioned about his grade school experiences was the marvelous lunches served in the school cafeteria. Mrs. Alma Bramhall and the other cooks obviously loved children and enjoyed seeing students eat a solid, nutritious lunch. Mrs. Bramhall's hot yeast rolls with butter were exceptional, and she made them nearly every day. And there was no limit on how many one could take. The cooks used fresh vegetables from local farmers, fresh salmon from gill-netters and received surplus commodities from the U.S. Department of Agriculture. As mentioned by others, many of the students experienced grapefruit, bananas and other similar "imported" foods for the first time.

Being born in 1931, Clarence remembers the final years of the 30's depression very well. His father, Jum, planted crops year after year, but had little success in marketing them. Clarence mentioned that relatives often stayed with the Mershon family at various times, including his Uncle Ray Wilson and his cousin, Carlos Anderson. Carlos was rather creative when it came to work. For example, when planting cabbage, Bud and Carlos were expected to plant two or three crates filled with plants. Carlos would tell Clarence and Belle to throw a few extra plants in the hole for "fertilizer." He and Bud would sometimes bury some of the plants and take the rest of the day off, since the day's allotment had been "planted."

When Clarence was six, he had to help George do the cultivating. His job was to keep Ruby (the horse) between the cabbage rows, while George, who was ten, wrestled the single-row cultivator around. Of this experience, he said, "I never rode a horse for fun." The Mershon youngsters performed another annual task, planting cabbage. Jum Mershon planted about 10-15 acres of cabbage each year and it was planted by hand. In late summer, cucumbers had to be picked. Clarence said there were two farm jobs he disliked, picking cucumbers and planting cabbage. He remarked, "The inventor of the 'New Idea' cabbage planter should be accorded a place alongside Thomas Edison!"

Clarence started picking berries for Louis Berney at age seven. He earned two cents per pound and made 74 cents his first day. He also picked berries for the Matsubas and Harry Uyetake. When he was eleven, he started picking berries for Larson and Winters. The following year (1943), he started working summers for the partners. Since Jum was working in the shipyards, not farming, Clarence could work for other farmers. Tood and Howard grew potatoes, cabbage, strawberries, squash, spinach, corn and grain. Later they added daffodils and gladiolas (see

"Howard Winters" and "Robert Larson'). Tood and Howard hired several local youngsters. This help picked berries in season, weeded the cabbage seed bed, planted cabbage (on a 'New Idea' planter), hoed potatoes, cabbage and other crops, picked up, hauled, sorted and sacked potatoes, picked flowers, dug bulbs and cultivated.

Cultivating was a regular job for Clarence. He worked behind Pack (the horse) cultivating various crops day after day. Pack was an excellent cultivating horse, but he could be a little troublesome at times. When Clarence harnessed him in the barn, Pack would sometimes try to "crowd" him against the stall. He would also raise his head to avoid taking the bit. This put off the inevitable for a few moments. One time as Clarence took him out of the barn, Pack bolted and ran through the barnyard. Since Clarence had the reins around his back and under his arms, he was dragged along. Fortunately, the manure-covered ground was soft and Pack went around the rocks. The incident would have been unremarkable in every sense if Clarence had not opened his mouth to holler, "whoa." When cultivating with Pack, one hardly need touch the reins, as the horse would turn the proper way almost on his own at the end of the row. This habit occasioned some problems when a row was missed. When one turned Pack opposite the expected direction, the horse turned his head back seemingly with a look of incredulity.

Since the Mershons did not own an automobile, family members walked everywhere. If items were needed from the store, Laura Mershon sent the kids to Groce's store in Springdale, where they learned to say "charge it." The kids used the lane to Gene Berney's place, then cut over Canzler Hill, coming into Springdale alongside the grade school. When visiting their Uncle Ray on Wand Road, the Mershons would go about a quarter-mile west on Mershon Road and climb through a field north of the road to reach the old "wire trail." Reportedly an old Indian trail, this 'road,' was used for the first telegraph line through East Multnomah County. It ran roughly parallel to Mershon Road and was the travel route in the early days. For the Mershon kids, it was a short cut to Wand Road. Another trail, which was used to reach the Columbia River, took one over the bank from what is now George Perry's place. Jum Mershon used this route when he caught the train home from his job in Portland. The Mershons walked to Corbett to attend church, which was a two-mile hike (one way).

The Mershons also used the "wire trail" to Rooster Rock each year when grapes ripened in the fall. The October 19, 1933 issue of the

Columbian *Cardinal* carried news of the grapes at Rooster Rock: "Grapes are growing wild! Yes, and they are climbing trees, telephone poles and everything in sight. That is what has happened in an old orchard near Rooster Rock. This grape patch has been abandoned for many years and the grapes essentially grow wild." Each year Jum and Laura took the family to this area to harvest grapes by the bucketful. Laura made grape juice and jelly from the bonanza.

One time Clarence was walking with David Wall, and they cut through a field in order to reach the wire trail. Electric fences had recently come into use, and someone had fenced a pasture with an electric fence. David decided to urinate on the electric fence. This had surprising effects (to David), as he let out a holler that stampeded the cows. After David quit jumping around and hollering, he spent several minutes trying to convince Clarence that he should "Just try it." However, David's reaction had already persuaded Clarence to refrain from further experimentation. "I've gone through life without knowing exactly why David hollered so," he remarked.

During his years at CHS, Clarence continued to work for Howard Winters full time during the summer and part-time other months. Howard married Ruth Woodle in 1945 and she soon became an important part of the farm operation. This job was helpful for Clarence since the money earned was used for school clothes, school lunches and other items. In 1945, Clarence started CHS as a freshman fully expecting a "welcome" from the upperclassmen. However, the older students mostly ignored the newcomers. During his first year, Orval Klock coached the boys' freshman basketball team. The frosh team played other freshman teams and some grade school teams, won all their games and had a great time.

According to Clarence, he really enjoyed attending CHS. The Principal his first two years was Mr. Owenby, who, Clarence said, "Would visit our math class and engage the students in a contest to see who could complete a board problem first. Mr. Owenby was hard to beat." Teachers included Mr. William Beck, Mrs. Leora Cheney, Mr. Walt Jackson, Mrs. Johnson, Mrs. Joy Perry, Miss Genevieve Rosen and Miss Marietta Taylor. In 1947, Mr. Les Emerson replaced Mr. Clarence Owenby as Principal. Another great lady was Mrs. Mary Udey, who prepared the noon meal for students and staff. In addition to coaching, Orval Klock served as school custodian and drove school bus. Clarence thought the basketball team of 1948-49, which had a record of 23-5, should have done

Colleen (Innes) Mershon c1951

Colleen Mershon sits in the front yard of her home between the mouth of Buck and Gordon Creeks on Gordon Creek Road. Note the Sandy River in the background.

Clarence Mershon c1951

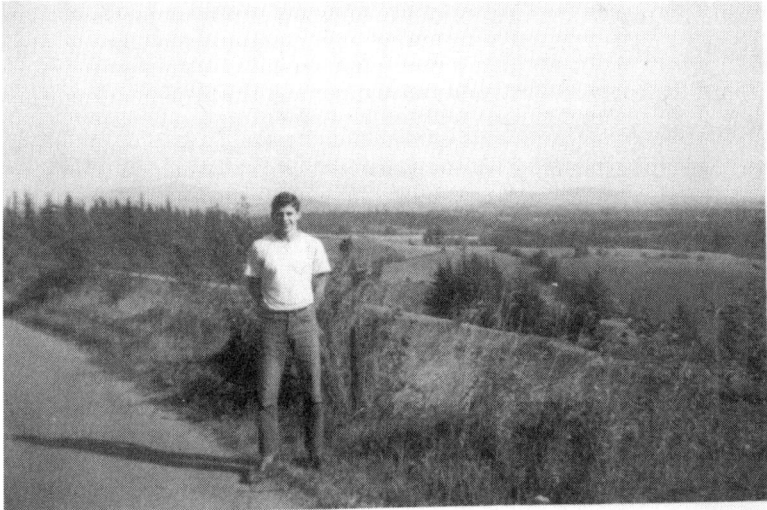

Clarence Mershon stands on Mershon Road above the Amos Porter place. Note Canzler Hill in the background right. This view is now obscured by trees and brush growing on the former Porter farm.   Photos, the author.

better at the B-tournament. He said, "I think we were sort of overwhelmed playing on the college floor at Monmouth, which seemed of gigantic proportions."

After graduating from CHS in 1949, Clarence worked for Howard Winters that summer, then started working for Davidson Baking Company in the fall. He married Colleen Innes, April 28, 1950. He and Jim Rhodes, who had joined the Oregon Air National Guard in 1948, were called to active duty in February 1951. They were assigned with a contingent to O'Hare Field in Chicago, instead of Korea (where many of their comrades in the fighter squadron were sent), as their (extended) enlistment period was nearly up. After Clarence's discharge, he returned to Davidson Baking Company. In 1952 he started college at the University of Portland. He completed three semesters there before "running out of money." In 1954 he started working as a routeman for Marckx Bakery in Gresham. He drove the 'Corbett' route until 1957, when he decided to return to college at Portland State. In 1956, Clarence and his family moved to Wood Village from Colleen's parents' place on Gordon Creek Road, to which they had moved after his discharge.

In 1959, Clarence completed requirements for a degree in education. He started teaching at Heights Junior High in Parkrose that fall. By attending school nights and summers, he completed requirements for a master's degree at the University of Oregon in 1963. That fall (1963), he received a fellowship for a year to study mathematics at the University of Colorado in Boulder, Colorado. When he returned to Parkrose, he taught two more years at the Heights, then transferred to Parkrose High School. He taught in the Mathematics Department at the high school for the next seven years. In 1973 he was appointed to an administrative position with the district, and thereafter worked as an administrator until his retirement in 1989. He completed six years as an elementary school principal.

Clarence and Colleen have four children, Michel C. 'Mike,' b. June 7, 1953, Elise C. (McGuire), b. July 28, 1955, Christopher E. 'Chris,' b. January 9, 1958 and Perry M., b. April 10, 1960. Mike works as a design engineer for Anodizing, Inc. in Portland and lives in Gresham. He is married to Andrea Sprowls and has no children. Elise and her husband, Douglas McGuire, owned Zirca-Tech Machine and Manufacturing, which they recently sold. She is a Certified Public Accountant. She has a daughter, Kara Rohrer, by a previous marriage and a son, Sean. Chris is an urologist with Kaiser Permanente. He is married to Margaret Sung and

Clarence and Colleen Mershon's Children

From left front, Mike, Perry and Chris. Elise stands behind. Photo, the author.

they have a daughter, Jessica. Perry is a full time civilian employee in the Oregon Air National Guard. His wife, Kortney Page, is on active duty with the U.S. Air Force stationed at Portland Airbase. Perry had two sons, Daniel and Micheal, from a previous marriage. In May 1998, Micheal died from a brain tumor. Perry and Kortney have one birth son, Kurtis. Clarence and Colleen have a home in Gresham that they purchased in 1959 and another home in Carson, Washington, which they built in 1991.

Laura Isabelle, called 'Belle' by her siblings during her growing up years, avoided much of the farm work her older brothers and sister experienced because of her age. By the time she was old enough to work in the fields (age seven or eight), World War II had started and her father worked in the shipyards and was not farming. She did pick berries for Louis Berney and other nearby farmers. She attended Corbett Grade School, walking to school her final year after the family moved to the Corbett place.

Laura's early childhood memories include walking to Uncle Jasper 'Jap' Mershon's house every January to celebrate his birthday, with a

339

cake baked for the occasion by her mother. When sent to the store in Springdale, Laura remembers the huge 5-cent ice cream cones dispensed by Mrs. Roy Parsons. Often a group of kids would go swimming at Big Rock or the family would go to the Sandy when the smelt were in. Another annual event kids looked forward to was the Christmas program at Springdale Grade School, where a stocking and candy treats were given to each youngster When the Townsend movement swept the country, Laura's parents attended many meetings. Laura remembers practicing with Mrs. Anna Enquist for a program and singing a duet with her brother, Clarence, at the meeting. She complained that Clarence didn't open his mouth. She also remembers saying goodbye to the Matsuba and Uyetake families when they left for the "relocation centers" in May 1942, and how unhappy everyone was at the parting.

By the time Laura started high school, Jum had resumed farming the Corbett place and she helped with the crops there, principally berries. She also worked for a neighbor, Owen Emily, digging and planting bulbs. During her high school years, she enjoyed going to dances at the Grange Hall, where Charles and Clara Lofstedt, who loved to dance, danced to every tune. She also remembers going to school plays and basketball games, and stopping for hamburgers at St. Claire's Drive-In in Wood Village afterwards. During her junior year, Laura quit school to marry Bill Wynn, who operated the Corbett Café. The couple moved from the area shortly thereafter. Three children resulted from this marriage, Melba (now Melissa), William and Charles 'Chuck.'

Eventually Laura moved to Long Beach, California where she met James 'Stan' Standridge, U.S. Navy. Laura had three more children, Reneé, Stephanie and James Jr. Stan was 'father' to all the children, including Melissa and Chuck. Stan served at various duty stations during his Navy career, including a couple of tours in Vietnam. After retiring from the service, the couple lived in Fairview for a time and Stan worked in Portland. In 1982, Stan joined the U.S. Customs Service and was sent to Alaska to monitor traffic at the border between Alaska and the Yukon. Later he served at the Anchorage airport. Stan retired from the Customs Service in 1994. He and Laura now live in Soldotna, Alaska, where they enjoy the wildlife and fishing. They do travel quite often, traveling through Canada to the lower '48' in their motorhome. Laura and Stan have nine grandchildren and one great grandson.

William Moessner
Clara Moessner

William and Clara Moessner came to Corbett in 1927 when they purchased the View Point Lodge from the Grace H. Palmer Corporation. The 'Lodge' was built in 1924, designed by renowned Oregon architect, Carl Linde. A local builder, George Canzler, was reportedly involved in its construction. The Corporation intended to operate the facility as a teahouse and restaurant, but after approximately two years, the business was sold to the Moessners. William Moessner had been employed as a chef at the old Portland Hotel and at the Benson Hotel previous to his purchase of the 'Lodge.' Prior to immigrating to the United States, he had trained and worked as a chef and innkeeper in Germany. The Moessners changed the name of the establishment to View Point Inn. The Inn is located on Larch Mountain Road about a quarter-mile east of its junction with the Columbia River Highway.

The Moessners operated the Inn from 1927 through the depression and war years and for some time thereafter. It became a popular stopping place for tourists and repeat customers, who savored the impeccable offerings of Chef Moessner. Julius Meier, who owned a nearby estate, was a frequent visitor. European royalty were among a number of distinguished guests and clientele, which included executives, political leaders, business leaders and movie stars. His customers some times went to great lengths to dine at the 'Inn,' including one oil baron who had his chauffeur drive him to the 'Inn' from Southern California on occasion. Moessner prepared the food himself, using an old iron wood range.

William and Clara Moessner had one son, Gearhart, who attended Corbett Grade and CHS, graduating from the latter in 1942. Both he and his mother helped with the operation of the Inn during its heyday, when the old Columbia River Highway was the principal arterial east. In addition to the excellent cuisine presented by Mr. Moessner, the Inn offered stunning westward views of the Columbia River to its guests. With Reed Island visible in the foreground, the cities of Washougal and Camas form a dramatic backdrop with their lights aglow after dark. The I-205 Bridge is clearly visible down river, and the lights of Portland cast a beautiful glow in the western sky at night. The river and the scene below are a never-to-be-forgotten sight when the sun sets in the west.

Gearhart Moessner and Friend

Gearhart Moessner (left) and George Perry at Menucha. Photo courtesy of George Perry Jr.

The Moessners closed the View Point Inn in 1962 after operating the business for approximately 35 years. During that interval, the Moessners employed many local high school students in the business. Included among those who worked there at various times are Sophia Lofstedt, Gussie Lofstedt and June Bates. Gussie remembers that tour busses full of tourists would come to the Inn in the evening to dine. It was a regular stop for this trade during the summer. Local girls waited tables in the glass-enclosed dining area on the West Side of the building. According to Mr. Moessner, he closed the Inn when it became "too much work."

After graduating from high school, Gearhart Moessner attended college and medical school, and practiced in California. He served on the staff of Cedars of Lebanon Hospital in Hollywood, California. Clara Moessner died in 1966. Former employees would often bring their children to the 'Inn' on occasions such as Halloween. Mr. Moessner would invite the youngsters in for cocoa and cookies. Mr. Moessner lived at the 'Inn' until his death in 1979. He took care to maintain the facility, keeping it painted and in good repair while he lived.

The View Point Inn remained closed until recently, when it was acquired by the Lois Thompson Housing Project, a non-profit corporation. It is now open for business and serves its customers with quality meals and excellent service modeled after that provided by the Moessners. As

The Historic View Point Inn

Today's View Point Inn, built in 1924 and recently re-opened after being closed since 1962.   Photo, the author.

the only 'fine' dining experience between Gresham and Multnomah Falls, View Point Inn should have a successful future. As Mr. Moessner said, "Where else could you find a location like this?" (Quoted in *The Oregon Journal,* 11/14/1972.)

In addition to the View Point Inn, four other eating establishments were once found within a half-mile radius: the Morgan's Chanticleer Inn, Mrs. Henderson's Crown Point Chalet, Johnson's Vista Café and Eva Hammer's Summit Tavern.

Recently Multnomah County took the present owners to court alleging that the Inn was not operating within the parameters of their permit. Unfortunately, the owners lost their court battle and the historic landmark has closed. While the present owners seem to place much of the blame for their difficulties on Multnomah County, the situation is more complex. When college students completed a perfunctory "survey" of historic and cultural resources in the Gorge, the Inn was overlooked. According to Sharon Nesbit (*Gresham Outlook*), an Act of Congress would be required if one wished to operate the landmark as an Inn, the purpose for which it was designed and built! If public access to the historic, cultural treasure is the goal, seeking such action may be the only recourse.

Roland C. Morgan
Elizabeth (Benn) Morgan

Roland C. Morgan was born in Iowa July 31, 1881. He married Elizabeth Benn in Wardner, Idaho. Elizabeth Benn was born in Beatrice, South Dakota June 20, 1886. The couple had four children, Dolores, b. September 26, 1908, Roland, b. June 17, 1913, Elizabeth, b. April 21, 1915 and Maxine, b. April 1, 1918. All the children except Elizabeth were born in Wardner. Dr. Hughes delivered Elizabeth at Corbett while her mother was visiting relatives here. (Roland's sister, Jessie K. Morgan, married Roy Emily.) The family moved to the Corbett area sometime in the late teens. All the children attended CHS. Dolores graduated in 1925, Elizabeth and Roland both graduated in 1932, and Maxine graduated in 1936. Upon Mrs. Morgan's death February 2, 1963, Ruth Sommerville wrote:

> "Mrs. Morgan spent 20 years as telephone operator for the Columbia Telephone Company until her retirement in 1957, and stories about her altruistic service repeated often to newcomers by the old-timers will keep her memory always alive. Mrs. Morgan's family held her in great affection and esteem. We hope that they will be comforted in the knowledge that a great many others did also. Hers was the kind of worthwhile life that made knowing her a privilege."

A granddaughter, Ramona (Reeves) Valencia, wrote of a couple of summers spent with her Grandmother Elizabeth Jane Morgan:

> "I remember traveling from home and high school in Klamath Falls without our parents to spend at least 2 summer vacations in Corbett. We stayed with my Grandmother, (I called her Mom), Elizabeth Jane Morgan. She lived mainly in the telephone office located in a small house with a big window that faced the Columbia River Highway in Corbett.
>
> She was the lone switchboard operator. She was "central" to a system that served 300 people. There were a profound number of duties involved. When I think of it now it seems as though she was at the mercy of ringing bells, but there was not a doubt she liked her job and was devoted to the community where she made

Columbia Telephone Switchboard

Elizabeth Morgan stands beside the Columbia Telephone switchboard that she operated for 20 years until 1957.　　　Photo courtesy of Elizabeth (Morgan) Tanner.

her home for so long. She was noted for rendering personal touches with her service. When Sis and I visited in 1942 and 1943 the telephone office was near Settlemier's grocery store.

Sister Ann (Steers) and I relieved her at the tiny switchboard while she cooked dinner and baked delicious pies and cobblers for Uncle

Roland Morgan and us. Every kind of fruit and berry grew in Corbett it seemed. I particularly liked blackberries. The kitchen had a wood stove and was the size of a pantry. To get to the supplies there were stairs, but the dirt basement where they led scared us. She was a very good cook. With such tempting delights we could easily overeat, causing Uncle to dub the desserts "belly ache."

I remember corrupting the resident customer's names and gaining laughs from 'Mom.' No matter how I mispronounced or misspelled a person's name she knew instantly which part I had to connect. Frequently I would actually meet a person whose name was in an index file, which preceded an area directory familiar to us now. I marvel that the wire used to carry messages back and forth in the forties had to be set up as a "party line." Those as young as I was who use today's communications would be amazed to experience such an archaic invention, but what an invention it was. Dials on hand sets took the place of the hand cranked wall telephones. Columbia Telephone disconnected Corbett's switchboard in April 1957.

The Switchboard rang at night, too. 'Mom' emerged from her bed ready to take action whatever the need might be. There was a phone booth attached to the office annex of the house. Occasionally a car would pull up with a customer who used the phone in the booth. 'Mom' conducted business through a counter window, because she had to put a plug in the switchboard for those numbers, also. It was a relief to Sis and I that the window had a security screen on it.

My grandmother had one of the most unusual occupations of anyone I have ever known! She was gentle and soft spoken with us. She used endearing adjectives like 'dear' and 'honey' with out names...I think she started our family tradition of sending picture post cards. I imitated her. Mother did, too. When she could get away from home and work for a holiday she almost never failed to send a card...I particularly remember her sitting at a writing desk in the hotel at Crater Lake National Park. It was an event to go to the Vista House with her. It didn't surprise me to find out later that she saved (the) post cards she received...Post cards aren't so unique, but the older 'Mom's' get the more valuable their preservation becomes... 'Mom' did have a private life,

The Morgan Home

The Morgan home located adjacent to the Corbett Christian Church (note the church in the picture, located to the right).   Photo courtesy of Elizabeth (Morgan) Tanner.

but the public in Corbett knew her as their community telephone operator. Incidentally, she had the post office in her home at one time.

During the summer of 1942 and 1943 we also undertook weeding in Uncle Roland and Owen Emily's 'Staggerweed Bulb and Flower Gardens.' Uncle Roland engaged Sis and I and Pat and Beverly Bramhall in "hoomerous" (Uncle's word) comic reading interludes. I know we didn't appreciate "Li'l Abner" as much as he did. We wish we had our storyteller now. "Staggerweed" was a funny name to us, but I soon learned it was serious to cattle owners, thus its name. It was a truly poisonous weed (larkspur) native to the country."

Ramona said her Uncle Roland took part in the momentous change made at the telephone office in February 1957 when Columbia Telephone Company replaced the old system with a dial system. At the time of the change there were about 300 customers. There was a celebration for Mrs. Morgan, who retired and left for a visit with relatives in Kellogg, Idaho. Roland wrote her a letter telling of the changes taking place:

"They cut the phones over as planned Saturday night, but there were about six complete lines that were not on the dial system

347

yet. Raymond (Smith) was going to leave them on the old system for a few days. Raymond thought he would need Ruth and Wilma (Smith) to keep the old switchboard open, because he thought he would have to cut some of the other lines back. This way he intended to cut the whole works back and forth for a few days. It kept Raymond and Basil (Lampert) and the Portland phone men on the run. Power fed into the old system as well as to the dials; lines and bells were ringing to beat the band. They finally cut the old board off altogether. The Portland installers told Raymond he would have to get the other phones on as he went along. He would not be able to cut back to the old board again.

I stayed at the telephone office for three nights and it was sure dead around there. Sunday morning the old board looked like a black hole in the wall...Less than half the phones were working and most of them would get a wrong number. Several people were into the new office to find out when their phone would be working. They are lined out pretty well now. The fire phones are working and Ferrington has made three test runs on them, getting everybody on the lines and punching buttons. There have been two false alarms, one was turned in by the Portland operator; she dialed the wrong number...We have been having a real storm here for about four days. It started snowing Wednesday and 'blowed' Wednesday through Thursday into Friday morning. Friday afternoon at 2:30 the power went off at Bridal Veil and all the workers went home. About that time it started to sleet and kept up until about noon today...It was the worst snowstorm this winter and the worst sleet storm in over 10 years. Several power and telephone lines went down. Tanner and Taylor's line went down. There were out of juice for about 8 hours. One of the maple trees in back of the house got loaded down with ice and blew over."

Roland went on to tell about how he and Elizabeth (Morgan) Tanner had moved Mrs. Morgan's belongings and the "little old telephone building was vacant."   *(Ramona (Reeves) Valencia)*

Roy Muck
Bessie M. (Knieriem) Muck

Bessie Knieriem was born in Corbett July 16, 1899, daughter of the pioneer George and Emily Knieriem family. After graduating from high school, Bessie Knieriem met Roy Muck when she went to pick up her brothers, who were working on the Columbia River Highway. Roy Muck happened to be employed by a construction company working on the project. Roy's parents lived in St. Johns. His father was formerly the mayor of St. Johns and also became a County Commissioner. Bessie married Roy Muck October 16, 1920. Since Roy was involved in the construction trade, he and Bessie lived at various places in the Northwest. They moved back to Corbett in 1943 and bought out the other heirs of the Knieriem place. After moving to the farm, Roy Muck farmed, though he continued to work in the construction trade. The family raised hay and grain and kept horses. In construction, Roy worked for Tait and Porter-Yett, working on trucks and heavy machinery. Bessie was a member of the Corbett Garden and Needle Club, and enjoyed gardening and sewing.

Roy and Bessie Muck had three children: Virginia, b. July 3, 1922, Bette Jean, b. November 7, 1927 and Roy W. 'Bill,' b. August 30, 1933. Virginia was out of school before the family returned to Corbett. Bette Jean completed high school at Corbett, graduating from CHS in 1945. Bill (ex-'51) completed grade school at Corbett and attended CHS, but left before graduating.

Virginia married Earl Smith, moved to Portland and had two children, Roy and Phyllis. Later she married Frank Krueger and had three more children, Clinton, Laurie and Steve. Virginia is now in a care facility in Vancouver. During the harvest season in 1943, Toot Evans and Harry Rickert came to the Muck place to thrash grain. Bob Dunken, who worked on the thrashing machine, met Bette Jean Muck for the first time. Bette Jean worked for Toot Evans in his daffodils and also worked at the 1st National Bank in Gresham. June 27, 1947, Bette Jean and Bob Dunken married (see "James D. Dunken").

During his early years, Bill Muck worked for Leo Fehrenbacher, Ed Klinski and at the Hill Dairy (former Corbett Estate) on Chamberlain Road. In October 1950, during his senior year at CHS, Bill joined the

Picking Daffodils for Toot Evans

Bette Jean Muck helps Toot and Doris Evans pick their daffodil crop.

Photo courtesy of Bob Dunken.

U.S. Air Force. He spent four years in the service including 11 months in Korea. When he returned home, he drove log truck for Harry Rickert for about four years. Bill then purchased a log truck and did contract hauling for about 10 years. July 12, 1958, Bill Muck married Beverly Coe. They had two children, Tim, b. February 21, 1960, Tina, b. July 7, 1961. Both attended and completed elementary school at Corbett, and both started high school at CHS.

After leasing the Springdale Tavern for about a year, Bill returned to truck driving, working for Gresham Sand and Gravel. He then decided to go into the rock business, purchasing a crusher and setting up in a pit on Brower Road. Difficulties involving Multnomah County and the Gorge Commission caused him to relocate in Howard Canyon. However, Multnomah County officials continued to harass him at that location, so he retired. He continues to live on the original Knieriem place, though a 3-acre parcel including the Knieriem home has been sold. He retains about 25 acres of the original place. Roy Muck passed away February 20, 1979. Bessie M. Muck, a nearly lifelong resident of Corbett, died June 24, 1990.

Tatsuzo Nakashimada
Kisano (Seki) Nakashimada

Tatsuzo Nakashimada came to the United States from Japan in 1907. A railroad company employed him as a laborer in Oregon. His pay was $9.00 per month, $2.00 of which was withheld for subsistence. The hours were sunup to sundown. In 1911, Mr. Dabney of Troutdale offered Tatsuzo a job as gardener at his property located along the Sandy River, which includes the acreage now known as Dabney State Park. With stable employment Mr. Nakashimada sent word to his betrothed, Kisano Seki, in Japan that she should come to America. He met her at the dock in San Francisco and the couple wed November 10, 1911. Mr. Dabney and some of his neighbors had built a house for the couple on his place and they moved in after the ceremony. Mr. Nakashimada worked as a gardener for about two years, and then decided he wanted to farm. He was able to lease a place from Mr. Kendall of Troutdale located on what is now Seidl Road, and they moved in 1913. According to Leke, the "house" was just a shack, but it was a shelter.

Mr. and Mrs. Nakashimada had ten children, all born in Troutdale: Shigeo, b. December 1912; Rosemary, b. November 1913; Thomas, b. January 1915; Elsie, b. April 1918; Leke, b. January 25, 1920; Takey, b. May 5, 1921; George, b. 1923; Mary, b. 1925; Margaret, b. March 1929; and Betty, b. June 1931. Shigeo, Thomas and Mary died in the terrible flu epidemic that struck in the mid-20's. George died of spinal meningitis at age four. In a period of about two years, the couple lost four of their children.

When the family moved to the Kendall property, only about one-half of the twenty acres was cleared. Mr. Nakashimada cleared the remainder "with dynamite, a pick and a shovel," according to Leke. They grew berries, including raspberries, youngberries and strawberries, and also grew cucumbers and cabbage. Mr. Nakashimada soon gave up on raspberries and started planting cauliflower. Soon that became the principal crop on the farm. He joined the "Top of the Hill" cooperative, which was a "big mistake," avers Leke. "Pop didn't get a dime for the crops he delivered there for three years." To compound the problem, the Troutdale Bank, in which Mr. Nakashimada had placed his savings, went belly-up

Tatsuzo and Kisano Nakashimada Family

Front from L, Rosemary, Elsie, Takey, Margaret and Kisano. Rear, Leke and Tatsuzo Nakashimada.   Photo courtesy of Leke Nakashimada.

during the first years of the depression. Leke states his father "had two quarters in his pocket. That was it."

The older youngsters started school at Pleasant View Grade School on Wand Road. When the District consolidated with Corbett, they attended there. Alvin Kinney drove the school bus that transported them to school. Leke said, "Mr. Kinney was a great guy. He was fair to everyone. We used to get salmon from him every year." Rosemary finished grade school at Corbett. She did not attend high school as "she had to help my father on the farm," Leke reported. Leke completed his elementary years at Corbett Grade and graduated from CHS in 1939. He lettered in both baseball and basketball. He said, "Mr. Emerson was a good coach, but he was also a great teacher." Leke had nice things to say about several of his teachers including Mrs. Cheney, whom he had for mathematics, and Miss Rosen, whom he had for typing and English. Margaret and Betty were attending Corbett Grade when the U.S. Government ordered Japanese families to report to the Pacific Livestock Exposition Center May 12, 1942 for evacuation from the West Coast. Takey and the younger Nakashimada youngsters completed high school at the Minidoka camp.

In 1929, Mr. Nakashimada was able to lease the Bramhall Place on Woodard Road. This gave him an additional 54 acres to farm since he continued to lease the Kendall property. In 1931 they moved to a house

Margaret and Takey at the Bramhall Place

Margaret and Takey Nakashimada with Blackie in the barnyard at the Bramhall Place on Woodard Road.
Photo courtesy of Leke Nakashimada.

on the Bramhall place, which gave them much more room for the family. With the additional ground Mr. Nakashimada increased the acreage devoted to cauliflower to about 40 acres each year. The crop was generally sold to Pacific Fruit, which required that the heads be spotless. Since Mr. Nakashimada took great pains with the crop, he sometimes was able to sell cauliflower when other farmers left it in the field. They had three horses to work the ground, Lady, Pete and Pack. Until the mid-thirties horses were used to do the tilling. This included plowing, disking, harrowing and cultivating. Leke remembers cultivating with Pack, who was usually the horse chosen for this work. After Mr. Nakashimada purchased a Massey-Harris tractor in the mid-30's, they did the plowing with it. Later Mr. Nakashimada hired Larson and Winters to plow the entire place with their 'Cat.'

When families of Japanese extraction from the surrounding area gathered at the Pacific Livestock Exposition Center in North Portland, the Nakashimadas were among them. The livestock area was partitioned, forming enclaves for families in the stall areas. Mattresses of straw were furnished and family members used the stalls as further partitions to separate family members. Families spent several months at this facility. Some families volunteered to go to Tulelake, California in August, even though that camp was not yet completed. In September 1942, the Nakashimadas were sent to the Minidoka Camp in Idaho. This is where they spent the war years. Leke was not among them as he had been drafted in July 1941

The Bramhall Place

Margaret (with back to camera), Elsie and Betty (to right) play with a friend.

Nakashimada Brothers

Leke and Takey Nakashimada stand by the family's Buick.

Photos courtesy of Leke Nakashimada.

Nakashimada Siblings, April 1941

From L, Rosemary, Betty, Takey, Margaret and Leke Nakashimada.

into the U.S. Army. Because he was on a farm, he received an extension until January 1942.

Leke Nakashimada reported for basic training at Fort Warren, Wyoming, which took 12 weeks to complete. He also completed training to become a cook at the Baking and Cooking School there. He was then sent to Fort Riley, Kansas. He said, "The Army didn't seem quite sure of what to do with Japanese-Americans in the service." In February 1943, a Nisei unit, the 442nd Regimental Combat Team was formed at Camp

354

Leke at Minidoka Camp

Leke Nakashimada in Italy

Leke Nakashimada visits his family at the Minidoka, Idaho 'relocation' camp where they were interned.

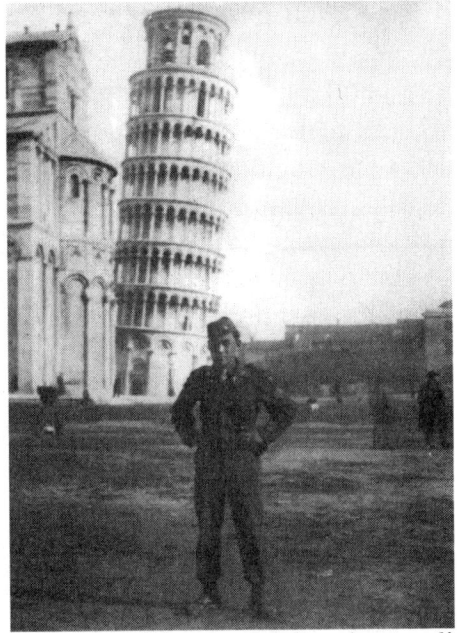

Leke Nakashimada standing 'ram-rod' straight before the Leaning Tower of Pisa (Italy). Photos courtesy of Leke Nakashimada.

Shelby, Mississippi and Leke was transferred there. Part of the Regiment, the 100th Battalion, was sent overseas and other elements quickly followed. The 442nd soon developed a reputation as a fighting unit and it became the most highly decorated unit in the U.S. Army. A cadre of the 1st Battalion was held back to train for replacement purposes, and Leke was assigned to the 171st Replacement Training Unit. It remained in the States until March 1945, when orders were received to proceed to Maryland for overseas duty. The unit landed at Naples, Italy ready to join the 442nd about the time the war ended. His unit then became part of the 3rd Occupational Army that was sent to Gheti, Italy, which involved guarding and feeding 200,000 German prisoners. The unit was sent to Lecco, Italy, where the Alps separating Italy and Switzerland loomed in the background, for a well-deserved period of rest and relaxation (R & R). Next it was sent to Leghorn, Italy, where the unit performed occupational duties at another POW Camp. Leke returned to the U.S. February 2, 1946, landing at Camp Kilburn, New Jersey. He was discharged from the Army in February 1946, having attained the rank of Staff (Mess) Sergeant. When discharged he had completed 49+ months in service to his country.

Rosemary married Eichi Ishida and settled in N. Portland after the war, and still lives there. She has no children. Elsie married Thomas Nakata, who was a veteran of World War II also. They made their home in SE Portland after the war. She and her husband had two sons, both of whom became medical doctors. Leke married Mary Hirata November 10, 1946. She was born December 8, 1923, in Parkdale, Oregon. The couple has four children, John, b. January 13, 1948; Diane, b. January 14, 1950; Debbie, b. March 10, 1957; and Lisa, b. August 1, 1963. John works as an administrator for Kaiser Permanente; Diane lives in Portland and works for Nordstroms; Debbie lives in Portland and operates a beauty shop; and Lisa lives in Lake Oswego and is a pharmacist. Leke Nakashimada operated his own restaurant in N.E. Portland for about ten years, then went to work for Esco Corporation, where he worked until he retired in July 1984. He raised his family in SE Portland and has lived in the same house since 1953.

Takey Nakashimada was also inducted into the Army out of the Minidoka Camp. He underwent basic training in Texas and was assigned to the Third Army. Takey said, "I went wherever Patton went." He served in the European Theater and remembers well the Battle of the Bulge. He married after the war, had three children and worked for the Portland Water Bureau. He supervised the Water Bureau works located at Mt. Tabor. He also worked nights for Franz Bakery. Currently Takey lives with his wife, Mavis (Jacobson) in Portland. Margaret married George Hongo, a veteran who also served in the European Theater. They lived in N.E. Portland and had three daughters. Margaret passed away in 1980. Betty Nakashimada did not marry. She worked in the insurance business and lives in Tigard.

Mr. and Mrs. Nakashimada returned to the Portland area the summer of 1945, and lived with Rosemary and Elsie in a St. John's housing unit, Leke joined them upon his return from the service. As an alien, Mr. Nakashimada was not able to purchase a farm in his name before the war. After the war bitter racial feelings created a situation that made it nearly impossible for citizens of Japanese extraction, including veterans, to buy a home. Tatsuzo Nakashimada died March 5, 1952, in Portland before Leke was able to purchase a home in SE Portland. Thus Tatsuzo died before any member of his family actually purchased a place. His wife, Kisano, passed away January 5, 1969.   *Leke Nakashimada*

John O'Neil
Hilda (Zollner) O'Neil

John and Hilda O'Neil moved to Dodson, Oregon from Portland over the Christmas holiday in 1937. Mr. O'Neil worked as an operating engineer for the Corps of Engineers, which supervised the building of Bonneville Dam. He had been commuting to work there since the start of construction, and "had enough" of traveling back and forth on the old Columbia River Highway. John O'Neil was born February 4, 1898, in Idaho Springs, Colorado, heart of the Colorado mining country. Hilda (Zollner) O'Neil was born July 30, 1899, in Mt. Angel, Oregon. Her grandfather, Robert Zollner, came to Oregon by wagon train in 1867, homesteaded near Mt. Angel, and was instrumental in establishing the first Catholic Church there. On the trip across the country, the party encountered Indians, who offered two of their finest ponies for a young tow-headed boy, Joseph Zollner. His parents declined the offer, and thereafter hid the lad under a large iron kettle when Indians approached. This boy later grew up in Mt. Angel, and was Hilda's father. Hilda met John when she went to Poff-O'Neil Transfer Company to find work. They married August 5, 1919, in Portland.

The O'Neils had five children: Edward "Ed," b. October 14, 1920; Raymond "Ray," b. September 8, 1922; Eugene 'Gene,' b. March 28, 1924; Dorothy, b. November 16, 1927; and John 'Jack,' b. July 5, 1929. At the time of the move, Ed was no longer living at home, Ray was a freshman at Lincoln High School, Gene was in the 8th grade, Dorothy, 4th, and Jack, 2nd. The family rented a small cabin behind and slightly west of the Dodson store. John O'Neil died suddenly December 31, 1938, almost exactly a year after the family moved to Dodson. Mrs. O'Neil kept the family together and got a job with the Corps of Engineers at Bonneville, where she worked for approximately 25 years until her retirement. Hilda continued to live in the Gorge after her children were grown. She never remarried, and died July 29, 1980, one day short of her 81st birthday.

The Gorge area was a marvelous place for kids to grow up. Ray and Gene rode the school bus to Corbett, which picked up other students along the way. Norm and Bob Sherman (Sherman's Inn) rode the bus, as did the Mosso boys (Mr. Mosso was a section boss for Union Pacific

Railroad, and lived near Oneonta Gorge). Lilas Van Orsow, a girl who lived just west of Dodson, rode the same bus. It also picked up students from Bridal Veil, Latourell and points west. Kenneth Ellis was the school bus driver, and did not tolerate bad behavior. One time Ray said he and one of the Sherman boys were wrestling on the bus. Kenneth stopped the bus, picked up an iron bar he carried, called their names and pointed to the door. They walked home from that point. After that, Ray said, "We always behaved ourselves, especially when the weather was bad."

The O'Neils had an Uncle, Chuck Bellarts, who lived in a house on Tanner Creek just upstream from the old highway bridge across Tanner. He maintained a string of traps surrounding the Warrendale Fox Farm, and caught many "escapees" from there. Silver fox pelts brought a good price. He also caught bobcats and an occasional lynx. He taught the O'Neil boys to trap. One time he had a lynx in a trap and told Ray to dispatch it with a rifle, saying, "hit it in the head so it doesn't spoil the pelt." Ray tried. One time the uncle hired Ray to dig a well across the highway from where the O'Neil's lived in Dodson. It was tough digging because of all the rocks, but Ray worked diligently with a pick ax, pry bars and a shovel until the hole was 37 feet deep. There, a huge rock barred the way, which had to be blasted. His uncle said, "There's water right under that rock." Using a hand stone bit, Ray drilled holes for dynamite, stuck dynamite with a blasting cap and fuse attached into the hole and climbed out. Uncle Chuck then lit a rag dipped in kerosene, lowered it by wire and ignited the fuse. That is how they worked to get through the rock, and they did find water. (Note: If one visited Dodson after the unusual flooding during the spring of 1997, one can appreciate "the rocks" of which Ray speaks.)

If their mother wanted a salmon for dinner, and the fish were in, the boys would hike to one of the small creeks near Dodson and spear a fish from the hundreds that swarmed into these small streams to spawn. Ray says Horsetail Creek was probably the best of these streams for fish. He thinks this method of fishing might not have been legal, even then. He and Gene also fished many of the streams that flow into the Columbia, such as Coopey Falls Creek, Bridal Veil Creek and Eagle Creek. Ray, Gene and Dorothy also worked for Joe Bucher at his 'Hollywood Dairy' at various times. All had positive things to say of Joe and his family.

The oldest boy, Ed, who left home before the family moved, worked in Texas for a few years, then went into the U.S. Merchant Marine during

Ray O'Neil on Guam

Ray O'Neil relaxes on a bomb load destined for Japan.

Crew Chief Ray O'Neil

Crew chief Ray O'Neil points with pride to 'his' B-29, The City of Portland.
Photos courtesy of Frieda O'Neil.

World War II. After the war, he returned to Oregon, and worked for St. Johns Motor Express, which was the successor company to his father's business, Poff-O'Neil Transfer. Ed married Peggy Leonard, and they had six children. He and his family lived in St. Johns.

Ray O'Neil started CHS at Corbett during his freshman year. He excelled in sports, and played on two outstanding and long-remembered basketball teams: The 1939-40 Big Nine Championship Team, which included Carl and Clarence Lofstedt, Marion Kirkham, Harold Price, Ellis Snodgrass, Dan Kerslake, Ray O'Neil and Jimmy Frommelt; and the 1940-41 team which was State Runner-up, losing only to Westport in the final after Harry Price fouled out in the third quarter. Players on that team included: Harry Price, Ray and Gene O'Neil, Dan Kerslake, Tadashi Takeuchi, Virgil Kirkham and Jimmy Frommelt. Ray O'Neil and Harry Price were named to the All-State Team.

Judy O'Neil, in the March 28, 1962 *Cardinal* captures the spirit generated by that game, in which her father, Gene O'Neil played: "The guys playing on this team worked together at all times. They had a good ball club because they 'clicked.' …The strangest thing is that there was only one man who played the same position at all times. He was 6' 3" center, Ray O'Neil. …Ray was a player who wouldn't back down from anybody or anything. He would rebound like crazy and when he went up after the ball, 'he wouldn't comeback down until he had it.' Harry Price was one of the fastest players Corbett ever had. "You can't find a better person. He was a real sportsman,' says my father. …Price was also selected as an All-State player that year."

In her article, Judy mentions Dan Kerslake, Jimmie Frommelt, Virgil Kirkham, and her father. "Gene O'Neil is described in the 1942 *Cohimore* as the best player to ever graduate from CHS. He was the only left-handed player on the team. Normally he is right-handed, but while playing basketball, he shot and dribbled with his left hand." Judy goes on to tell of the tournament play, and what the season meant to the players. (There is no question that the CHS basketball teams of this era created a great deal of interest in the sport among young and old alike. And that influence continues to this day as evidenced by the pride that Judy has in her father's team and teammates.)

At the end of the school year, Ray enlisted in the Army Air Force, and was sent to Chanute Field, Illinois. After Japan bombed Pearl Harbor, his outfit was sent to the West Coast, where Ray worked on B-17 bombers. Next he was sent to Puerto Rico with a B-17 anti-sub outfit. He was then sent to Boeing to learn the intricacies of the B-29, and was sent to Guam in 1944 as a B-29 Line Chief with the rank of Master Sergeant. His outfit flew bombing missions to the Islands of Japan. Ray was cited for bravery when he pulled a man out of a burning plane when it returned from a bombing mission. However, the decoration never did "catch up" with him before his discharge.

Ray was discharged December 1, 1945, and returned to Bridal Veil. He fished commercially for Ray Holtgrieve of Coopey Falls out of Dalton Point. There were two drifts at Dalton, the upper "channel" drift, which

Gene O'Neil on Guam

Gene O'Neil lands on Guam and finds his brother, Ray.

Ray O'Neil's Beer Disappears

Visitors Gene O'Neil (right) and an unidentified crewmember (left) help
Ray O'Neil (center) dispose of his beer hoard on Guam.

Photos courtesy of Frieda O'Neil.

ended near Lone Rock on the Washington shore, and the lower "bar" drift, which ended along Sand Island. He also fished for Frank and Francis Reed out of Lower Corbett. He sometimes worked at the Bridal Veil Mill when he wasn't fishing. Ray indicated that the last good fishing year was 1951. During a four-week spring season, he fished from 4:00 a.m. until midnight. During a two-week stretch, he brought in 50 or more salmon per drift of outstanding spring Chinook. Some were sold to Portland Fish and the balance was sold to the Columbia River Packers Association. The gillnet fishermen also fished for shad when they were running in the

Back in the States

Gene O'Neil and a buddy, Omar Olson (L), see the sights.
Photo courtesy of Frieda O'Neil.

spring, and sold them for the roe. Ray had an exceptional shad catch one year, averaging about 400 lbs. of roe each night for two-three weeks. He received $.65 per pound for the egg skeins, and was paid immediately in cash. Since his share was one-half the gross, he thought he was doing very well. Occasionally, there was an incidental catch of blueback salmon, which is excellent eating. Ray liked it as much as anyone did, but the game warden at Camas "was a good one," who, according to Ray, "would hide behind trees and everything" to nail someone. Despite the wardens best efforts, however, Ray said he was able to enjoy a blueback occasionally.

Unfortunately, the salmon catch declined steadily after the '51 season, their numbers affected by the many new dams being built, and Ray quit commercial fishing in 1954. The largest fish he caught on the Columbia was a 9 foot, 6 inch sturgeon that contained 67 lbs. of eggs. He received $1.00 per pound for the roe, and sold the fish to Portland Fish after cutting it into chunks. He worked in construction for about five years, then went to the waterfront one day. Asked if he was looking for a job, he replied affirmatively, and that is how he became a longshoreman. He worked on the waterfront and in the union's offices until he retired. The Union didn't allow its officials to hold office more than a year, so he alternated - a year in office, a year on the waterfront - a year in office, etc. Ray married Pat Allum of Portland September 16, 1951. She had three children by a previous marriage, Joe, Tim, and Steve Martin. Ray and Pat had five birth children, Marilyn, Ed, George, Jim, and John. The O'Neils raised their family in Parkrose, where the youngsters attended Parkrose schools. Pat O'Neil died June 5, 1995, in Parkrose. Ray died this year (1999).

Gene O'Neil also attended CHS, and he too, played on the great championship basketball team of 40-41. After that successful year, the players looked forward to the 41-42 season. Unfortunately, the war, which started December 7, 1941, created a few problems that year. At the end of the school year, Gene enlisted in the Army Air Force, and was accepted for flight training. He completed his basic training at Fresno, California; his pre-flight training at Santa Ana; primary flying school at Santa Maria, California; basic flying school at Lemoore, California; and advanced (multi-engine) flying school at Douglas, Arizona. He was commissioned a 2nd Lieutenant April 15, 1944. He was sent to the South Pacific for duty with the Air Transport Command.

Gene ran into Ray a couple of times during his tour. The first time, he came to Seattle to pick up a B-17 to deliver to the South Pacific. Ray said it was just after payday, and though Gene was only with him a few hours, Ray said he "was flat broke" when Gene left. The second encounter occurred on Guam when Gene flew there on some assignment. Ray was stationed there with a B-29 group. According to Ray, this time Gene cleaned him out of all the beer he had hoarded. Gene was promoted to 1st Lieutenant in November 1944. Gene's duty stations reflect the progress of the war in the Pacific: Oahu, Australia, Christmas Island, Fiji, New Caledonia, New Guinea, Dutch East Indies, Moratais, Leyte, Luzon, Manila, Guam, Saipan and Rabaul. After Japan capitulated, Gene flew the "brass" to Manila to accept the Japanese surrender of the Philippines.

Gene was discharged from the Army Air Corps a 1st Lieutenant and served in a reserve unit until 1950. He started going with Frieda Lofstedt shortly after his return home. One time he was "buzzing" the Lofstedt home on Loudon Road and had to make an emergency landing in their pasture. This didn't dampen the romance however, and the couple married October 12, 1946. Gene and Frieda made their home in this community after the war. Gene worked at the Bridal Veil Mill and the couple lived in company housing when a unit became available. When he started

Picking Up

Gene O'Neil takes up the gillnet after a drift on the Columbia River. The 'observer,' Sam O'Neil, was in exactly this position when Gene brought in a huge sturgeon on one drift. Sam beat a hasty retreat to the cabin!   Photo courtesy of Frieda O'Neil.

working for Albert Pounder in Corbett, the family purchased the Hick's Place, east of Corbett. Gene also fished commercially for a number of years. He had fished for Ray Holtgrieve out of Dalton Point in earlier years. At Corbett, he fished for Francis Reed and eventually purchased his drift right, and fished it until 1968. When Pounder Truck Service was sold to Gresham Transfer, Gene went to work there. He worked for Gresham Transfer until he retired.

After he "retired," Gene continued to work. He worked for Gresham Sand and Gravel and for Bob Dunken, who owned Portland Sawmill Machinery. He also purchased the Larch Mountain Label Company from Mick Dunken, and operated it as a family business. In 1982, the business was sold to a son, Charlie O'Neil, who continues to operate it. Gene and Frieda had eight birth children, and raised nine as a family (see "Charles A. Lofstedt" for more information).

Dorothy O'Neil finished grade school at Bonneville, then decided to attend Stevenson High School, rather than Columbian, because that District had more sports for girls. She graduated from Stevenson High School

Hilda O'Neil and Family Members

Hilda O'Neil plays the piano accompanied by Frieda (Lofstedt) O'Neil (left) and Dorothy. Colleen O'Neil is hidden behind Hilda and Judy O'Neil sits at the end of the bench.

Photo courtesy of Frieda O'Neil.

in 1946. She married Carroll A. Paine who was born May 9, 1924, in Wisconsin. The couple married in Hood River November 12, 1949 and had two sons, Paul and Joe. Dorothy lived at various locations in the Gorge for most of her life. She worked at Tektronix for many years, finally retiring from that company. She is widowed, and now lives in Wood Village.

The youngest of the O'Neil youngsters, John, completed grade school at Bonneville, then attended Cascade Locks High School, graduating in 1948. He worked for the Oregon State Highway Department, and retired from that job. He now lives in Chiloquin, Oregon. He has five children, John, Kathleen, Sandra, Dennis and Richard.

Ray O'Neil, Frieda O'Neil and Dorothy Paine

George H. Perry
Joy (Crockett) Perry

Joy Crockett was born October 12, 1898, in Bellingham, Washington. She attended grade schools in Olympia (Washington), Enterprise (Oregon) and Lostine (Oregon) before finishing in Mesa, Arizona. She attended high school in Alhambra and Los Angeles, California. After graduating from high school, she attended Los Angeles Junior College (later the University of California at Los Angeles) for two years. She completed her undergraduate work at the University of Idaho. Miss Crockett's first teaching job was in Moscow, Idaho, where she taught history in the seventh and eighth grades.

Joy Crockett came to Corbett in 1922 to teach at CHS. Unfortunately, the high school building burned July 3, 1922, when sparks from the burning Knight's grocery adjacent to the school set it afire. Consequently, 1922-23 classes were held in the Columbia Grange Hall building. Miss Crockett held her classes in the 'balcony' room. Other classes were held in sections of the main hall curtained off to form two "classrooms." The new CHS building opened the fall of 1923. Miss Crockett and Miss Pauline Rickli, who started teaching at CHS that fall, became good friends. Miss Crockett continued teaching at CHS through 1927. During this period she met George H. Perry, who came to this area to work for Julius Meier at Menucha (see "George and Joy Perry Family History," *Pioneer History*). George was born July 24, 1890, in Idaho.

Joy Crockett and George Perry were married December 31, 1925. She resigned her teaching position at CHS at the conclusion of the school year in 1927. The couple had two children, George H. Jr., b. August 30, 1928 and Walter C., b. February 23, 1931. Walter Perry died in February 1941, age 10. According to young George, he grew up "with a foot in two different worlds." The first was Menucha, which was owned by the Meier (of Meier & Frank Company) family, and the second was the 'world' beyond the affluence of Menucha. He clearly remembered a visit by President Franklin Roosevelt, who accompanied then Governor Julius Meier on a tour of Menucha in 1934. The President was on his way to celebrate the construction of Bonneville Dam, which had commenced the previous fall. Such occurrences illustrate the difference between his 'life' at Menucha and that experienced visiting friends who lived in quite

CHS at the Grange Hall, 1922-23

Miss Joy Crockett's introduction to CHS where the balcony served as her first classroom. The Grange Hall Hill Road served as a playground.

Photos courtesy of George Perry Jr.

The New CHS c1923

Joy Crockett and Pauline Rickli at the entrance to the new CHS, September 1923.

different circumstances on surrounding farms.

George Perry Sr. started at Menucha in 1923. Julius Meier had acquired the property in 1913, which was located for him by Samuel Lancaster. Lancaster had found the property during his survey work prior to the start of construction of the Columbia River Highway. Meier had a 'rustic' home built on the place, which, in 1923, became George Perry's home for a couple of years. His living quarters were located above the kitchen in the west wing. By 1924, George Sr. had become the manager of the estate. He designed and supervised several construction projects that started in the mid 20's and continued into the 30's, including a new entrance gate (that still stands). A new residence to replace the insect-damaged first home was build in 1926-27; the manager's residence was renovated; and a cottage for the chauffeur was constructed. The grounds were redone with much rockwork, including paths, stairs, ponds and gardens, all designed by Mr. Perry.

367

Rustic Meier Residence, Menucha c1914

Julius Meier's first residence at Menucha faced the Columbia River. The entry road (foreground) came off of Rooster Rock Road.   Photos courtesy of George Perry Jr.

Close-up of the front porch of the Meier residence showing the rustic structural components of the building. Unfortunately, the bark-covered timbers provided an ideal haven for destructive insects, which caused such damage that the structure was removed rather than renovated in 1926.

The estate employed several individuals year round, including Ed Nielson, Ben Bourgeois and Allan Butler (none of whom lived on the estate). During the summer, more than 40 people were employed to maintain the grounds, gardens and facilities. Among other employees, George (Jr.) remembers that Walter Mannthey and Edith Butler worked at the estate quite regularly. In addition, many CHS students held summer jobs

368

Manager's Residence, Menucha c1927

The Manager's residence (background) flanked by the chauffer's cottage left (under construction) and the estate greenhouse.

Photo courtesy of George Perry Jr.

there. In the 20's and 30's, temporary help started at 20¢ per hour; more permanent employees were paid 40¢. George Perry, as estate manager, received $125 per month plus the home provided.

Mrs. Perry resumed her teaching career in 1942 and taught at CHS until she retired in 1964. She taught English, History of Western Civilization, U.S. History and, in earlier days, physical education. A nearly legendary figure in the community, she had an immense influence upon those individuals fortunate enough to be among her students. The Perrys lived at Menucha until 1951. The Meier family used the facility as a summer home until after World War II started. According to George (Jr.), the summer of 1941 was the last year that the Meier family used the estate for a summer residence. After that, the estate was nearly "dormant," used only occasionally by family members until its sale. After Menucha sold to the Presbyterian Church for $65,000, George and Joy Perry moved to an 8-acre parcel carved from the original Chamberlain place on Chamberlain Road. They moved into the home originally built by Elijah Chamberlain on the property in 1904. The Perrys had purchased the home in 1930, renting it in the interim to several families, including the Reynoldsons.

In 1936, George Perry (Sr.) took down the Chamberlain barn and used the lumber to build a new barn closer to Chamberlain Road. After

George Sr. and Joy Perry With Their Son George Jr.

George Perry Sr. with his son, c1930.

Joy Perry with young George, c1935.
Photos courtesy of George Perry Jr.

the move in 1951, he built a new home on the point where the old barn had previously stood. When George (Jr.) returned to the area to teach at Gresham High School, he and his wife, Virginia, moved into the former Chamberlain house and George (Sr.) and Joy Perry moved into the new home. George Perry Sr. died March 2, 1978. Joy (Crockett) Perry passed away April 24, 1991.

George, who completed his elementary and secondary school years at Corbett, graduated from CHS in 1946. That summer he obtained a job at the Bridal Veil mill. His only previous experience working elsewhere (from Menucha) came when CHS dismissed students in 1942 so that they could help with the potato harvest. That fall he attended Oregon State College, where he completed his freshman and sophomore years, majoring in engineering. He then decided to finish at the University of Oregon, to change his major to mathematics and become a teacher. After graduating, he completed a year of graduate work before obtaining a job at The Dalles High School, where he taught science. He taught in there only one year before moving to Gresham High School in 1952. George married Virginia Benda of Gresham October 14, 1950. She and George have six children, Elizabeth, b. October 1, 1951, Susan, b. March 5, 1953, George VII, b. May 12, 1954, Rebecca, b. May 14, 1958, James 'Jim,' b.

George and Virginia Perry With Their Family

Rear from L: Susan, Joy Perry, Elizabeth, George VI and George VII. Front: Virginia's parents, Maurice and Marean Benda, Kevin, Jim, Virginia and Rebecca.   Photo courtesy of George Perry Jr.

July 5, 1960 and John K. 'Kevin,' b. May 28, 1962. George Jr. taught mathematics at Gresham High and at Mt. Hood Community College until he retired in 1983.

Elizabeth Perry attended the University of Oregon including its law school and is now an attorney practicing in Vancouver. Susan attended MHCC, took course work in occupational therapy and now works in that field in Portland. George (VII) graduated from Oregon State College with a degree in engineering and currently works for ESI Corporation in Aloha. He lives in the home adjacent to his parents' home and commutes. He is married to Marguerite (Glassy) and has four children, George (VIII), b. March 5, 1989, Joseph, b. December 25, 1990, Willa, b. December 26, 1992 and Daniel, b. March 27, 1995. Rebecca graduated from OSU, is married to Lynn Gibbons and has a daughter, Anna, b. June 16, 1996. She lives with her family on Larch Mountain Road. Jim graduated from the University of Oregon, lives in Portland and works for the Portland Public Schools. Kevin graduated from Evergreen State College, lives in Seattle and works with handicapped children.

Ernest V. Peterson
Alberta (Pye) Peterson

Ernest 'Chic' Peterson and his wife, Alberta, lived on Woodard Road on a ten-acre farm located between Bill Woodard's place and the Bramhall place (Howard Winters). Chic's father had purchased the place in 1895. Chic was born in Troutdale, September 6, 1895. He attended Pleasant View Grade School on Wand Road. He married Alberta Pye, born in Portland, January 13, 1907, on January 25, 1925. The couple built a house on the family acreage after their marriage.

Initially, Chic farmed with his father. They farmed the home place and sometimes rented additional acreage, such as the Federspiel place, on which they grew vegetables, principally cauliflower. Chic's father was among the founding members of the Troutdale Fruit Vegetable Growers. He was also the person responsible for introducing cauliflower as a crop for growers in this area, importing the seed from Denmark. In the 20's, the Association began to ship cauliflower by rail in cars refrigerated with ice. Later, 'Peterson and Son' obtained the services of Gwinn, White and Prince, vegetable brokers, to establish a market for cauliflower in other regions of the country, shipping it by the carload using ice as a refrigerant.

Chic continued to farm after the death of his father. Starting in the early 40's, he served as an inspector for the U.S. Department of Agriculture, grading the produce of local farmers before it was shipped. After the war, he worked for Multnomah County as its noxious weeds control officer. A passion with Mr. Peterson was his attempt to rid the east Multnomah County area of the imported pest-weed, Tansy Ragwort. He would pull it whenever it appeared, and even hired high school kids to do the same. Since he retired, the weed has become prevalent once again. It is poisonous to cattle, and is dangerous when it grows in a hay field as it ends up in the hay.

Chic and Alberta's daughter, Donna, attended Corbett Grade and CHS, graduating in 1955. During her high school years she worked at the Vista House, meeting people from all over the world. She continues to correspond with some of them some 40 years later. Donna attended the Oregon College of Education in Monmouth for one year. She married Wesley Davis, son of a neighbor family across Woodard Road. They have two

Ernest and Alberta (Pye) Peterson

Ernest 'Chic' Peterson readies cauliflower for sale.

Alberta 'Bertie' Peterson stands in front of their home. Photos courtesy of Donna (Peterson) Davis.

Wes and Donna Davis Family

From L, Donna, Scott, Sheryl and Wes Davis.

children, Scott, age 38, who lives in Lake Oswego and works for Johnstone Supply Co., and Sheryl, who is married, has a son and lives on the home place on Woodard Road. She works as a legal secretary.

Donna (Peterson) Davis

James Pomante
Dorthy (Kerslake) Pomante

James 'Jimmy" or 'Jim' Pomante was born in Penna, Italy December 10, 1902. After World War I, his father came to the United States to establish a home for his family. When he had not been heard from for some time, Jimmy's grandmother sent him, as a teen-ager, to find his father in the States. In the late 20's, Jimmy joined the U.S. Army, and was stationed at Fort Vancouver. Violet Parsons was going with another soldier at the Fort, and introduced her friend, Dorthy Kerslake, to Jimmy. Dorthy was the daughter of Allan B. and Jessie (Hart) Kerslake, of Springdale. She grew up on the family place, and attended Springdale Grade School (see "Allan B. Kerslake"). After graduating from Springdale Grade School in 1926, she enrolled at CHS, member of the Class of 1930.

Three months before school was out, February 28, 1930, Dorthy married Jimmy Pomante. However, Dorthy completed the year and graduated with her class. The depression years were impacting East Multnomah County as much or more than the rest of the country by that year. Dorthy and Jimmy moved in with her parents and lived with them until the mid-30's, when Jimmy got a job with Weatherly Farms. The Pomantes then moved into a house on Hurlburt Road owned by the Weatherlys. The Weatherlys raised turkeys and pheasants at the Springdale operation. Jimmy earned $30.00 per month unless receipts didn't come in, and the employees had to wait for their money. He took an *Oregon Journal* route to supplement his pay.

The Pomantes had three children: Virginia (Elwood), b. February 3, 1931; Thomas "Tom" b. September 11, 1933; and Barbara (Massinger), b. January 19, 1941. The Pomantes also took in Mary Anderson when she was eight years of age, and raised her as one of the family. Mary said of Dorthy: "During the depression, when most families were scraping to feed and take care of you, she willingly took in a homeless girl, welcomed her into the family and treated her as one of her own." She was also there for her nieces, nephews and neighbor children, sponsoring 4-H projects and making certain that the youngsters learned to do things properly, to finish their projects, and to accept responsibility. It was said of her: "Generosity was her middle name." These youngsters also remembered some of her admonitions to them, such as: "A clean conscience

Dorthy Kerslake

James 'Jim' Pomante

Dorthy Kerslake stands in front of a 'classic' automobile at her home.

Jim Pomante in Vancouver, Washington. Photos courtesy of Barbara (Pomante) Massinger.

is more important than a clean house," and, "It doesn't matter what you have, it matters who you have." When times were tough, one just has to work harder. Dorthy picked berries and peas alongside her children to earn extra money, and often divided what she made with her children, as she knew they needed money for school.

When Alcoa opened an aluminum plant in Vancouver, Jimmy got a job there. When a second plant opened in Troutdale, he was the second employee hired, and worked there until he retired. When the big flood of 1948 hit, the employees at the aluminum plant successfully manned the dikes along the river to keep out the floodwaters. The lowlands surrounding the plant were one of the few areas along the river that did not flood. The Pomantes purchased three acres on Christensen Road from Dorthy's brother, Fred, and established their home there. All of the children, including Mary, attended Springdale Grade School. They also attended CHS from which Mary graduated in 1947, Virginia ('48), Tom ('51) and Barbara (ex-'59). Mary (Anderson) Hanson has three children, a son, Jon, in Denver and two daughters, Holly and Phyllis, in Portland. After

375

Dorthy and Barbara Pomante

Dorthy Pomante and her daughter, Barbara, on Christensen (now Stevens) Road, c1947.

Virginia and Dorthy Pomante

Virginia and Dorthy shop in Portland, c1948. Photos courtesy of Barbara (Pomante) Massinger.

Mary Anderson

Mary Anderson, CHS graduate, 1947 '47 Cohimore photo courtesy of David Rees.

Tom Pomante

Tom Pomante, US Army, in France. Photo courtesy of Barbara (Pomante) Massinger.

Pomantes at Tom's Home

Dorothy, Barbara and Jim Pomante share a happy moment
at Tom and Jan Pomante's home.
Photo courtesy of Barbara (Pomante) Massinger.

her husband died, she returned to school and became a registered nurse. She lives in Gresham.

After graduating from CHS in 1948, Virginia attended Western Oregon State College in Monmouth, and earned a teaching certificate. She taught in Corbett before obtaining a position with Gresham Public Schools, where she taught language arts at Gordon Russell Middle School. She recounted standing at the side of the Columbia River Highway during the war years, watching the army convoys roll by. "When the soldiers saw us they would toss out fir cones with their names and addresses rolled around them. We would gather them up and write to them." Virginia married Arthur J. Elwood August 7, 1958. They had two sons, William and Matthew, and two daughters.

After graduating from CHS in 1951, Tom Pomante enlisted in the U.S. Army and served in the United States and France. He married Jan Bevens in July 1956, and they had two daughters, Kim (Snyder), CHS '75 and Angie (Gilmore), CHS '83), and a son, Jeff, CHS '77. Tom worked at the Troutdale aluminum plant as a general supervisor until his death. His son, Jeff, lives in the family home and his widow, Jan, lives in Gresham. Barbara married Bernie Massinger and they had two children, a son, Todd, and a daughter, Jill. They lived in the Reynolds District, where the children attended school. She now lives in Boring.

Dorthy wanted to make certain her grandchildren learned to work, so she made a point of working along side them in the berry fields, and continued the practice of dividing what she earned with them. This gave them a little extra incentive to work. She remembered the days when some of her classmates at school ate the orange peelings that others discarded. It was always her hope that her family would never experience such deprivation. She also believed that strong family ties gave one's life meaning. Jimmy Pomante passed away October 12, 1977. Two of Dorthy's children also preceded her in death: Virginia Elwood died April 16, 1989, at age 58, from Leukemia. Tom died September 27, 1990, at age 57. Dorthy Pomante died October 5, 1997. She cherished her family, and tried her best to convey that love to her children, to her grandchildren and to the entire Kerslake family. *Barbara Massinger*

Columbia High School c1917. Burned July 3, 1922.
Photo courtesy of Ted Berney.

Charles W. Post
Helen (Plog) Post

Charles W. 'Wes' Post was born in Portland, Oregon January 2, 1915. His father, Frank C. Post, born in Minnesota, came from Zion City, Illinois to Oregon in 1907; his mother, Edith (West) Post, born in England in 1883, immigrated to the United States in the 1890's. The couple married in Portland. Though Wes Post carried his grandfather's name, he was told his name came from one of the founders of the Methodist Church, Charles Wesley. Wes was the second child born to his parents, his sister Lillian, b. May 4, 1910, being four and one-half years older. In 1918, Edith Post died during childbirth, leaving Lillian and Wes without a mother. The newborn also did not survive. Frank Post thought it best that the two youngsters live with their grandparents, Charles and Rosa (Cowgill) Post, at their home on ten-acres in the Gorge. His grandfather had found this property when he and his son, Frank, had come to Oregon in advance of the family to look for a place. They acquired the acreage for $500.00 and were told at the time by some local people that "A wind sometimes blows down the river from the east."

Wes' father and grandfather built a home there into which his grandparents had moved in 1912. They named the place "Mayview" to honor their daughter, May, who had died shortly after the family came to Oregon. In 1918, Mayview became home for both Lillian and Wes, and they were destined to spend the balance of their childhood years on the 'hill.' The property provided a viewpoint of the Columbia River Gorge to the East and a panorama of the river to the West. Though the house was plumbed, the family used an outhouse behind the dwelling. The house was wired but they relied on kerosene lamps and candles. However, the builders' foresight paid off in 1937 when the Corbett Water District extended its system to the 'hill,' and Portland General Electric brought in electricity. Prior to those events, water came from a 30-foot, hand-dug well, behind the house, which was equipped with a windlass and bucket.

Wes Post's grandfather was an artist of renown who had completed sculptures of figurines and cornices for the Chicago World's Fair held in 1896. He had a home studio, a studio in the Gorge near Chanticleer Point and traveled the Gorge extensively to make sketches and take pictures

The Gorge From Chanticleer Point

Untitled Charles W. Post painting of the Columbia River Gorge from Chanticleer Point.
Print and cover print courtesy of Wes Post.

for future reference. Unfortunately, his plan to complete a series of etchings of Gorge scenery was cut short with his untimely death in 1922 at the age of 64 (see "Charles W. Post, Artist," *Pioneer History*, 1982 supplement). With the death of their grandfather, Lillian and Wes were now under the care of their grandmother, Rosa Post.

Rosa Post had been a schoolteacher. She had a literary talent displayed in her verse written to complement the various themes of many of her husband's art works. However, she was now faced with the challenge of raising two grandchildren. The family had always kept a number of animals including a cow, a buggy horse (Babe), goats, chickens, turkeys and guinea hens. The goats were registered stock, Toggenbergs and Saanens, and often garnered ribbons when exhibited at the Multnomah County Fair. Lillian and Wes both attended Pleasant View Grade School after they moved to East County, transferring to Corbett Grade School when Pleasant View closed in 1923. Lillian completed her 8th-grade year at

Corbett, which Wes entered as a third grade student. Both attended and graduated from CHS, Lillian in 1928 and Wes in 1932. Lillian must have inherited her grandmother's talent with words, as one of her literary efforts was featured in the 1928 *Cohimore*, "Dedicated to All the World but America." She was most positive about her country, concluding the piece with this line, "World, follow the example of America–successful America." When Wes graduated, the Principal, Mr. P.J. Mulkey, remarked as he handed him his diploma, "Here's a good Post to tie to."

Neighbors of the Posts included Frank and Theresa Wand and their children, Ig, Alex, Louise, George and Julia. The Frank Fehrenbacher family with two children, Jerome and Evelyn, lived across the road. The Henry Fehrenbachers also lived across the road, as did the Masaru Sakurai family. To the West lived the Lamperts, Arnold, Jack, Ferd and Alex and their families. The Riehl and the Stopper families lived close by, also. One of the neighborhood youngsters' favorite pastimes was sledding. The hill at the Wand place was favored, particularly because Theresa Wand always seemed to have popcorn and fudge for the kids. The hill at Jack Lampert's place was another likely place to find the youngsters when snow or ice covered the ground. During his school years, Wes started working for Amos Porter on his farm above Springdale. He worked taking care of cabbage plants, hoed cauliflower and cabbage and remembers one spring when he hauled rotting cabbage from the barn to the fields, spreading it with a manure spreader pulled by a team of horses. Mr. Porter had stockpiled the crop in the barn hoping to sell it, but that year the strategy did not work.

After graduating from high school, Lillian Post married Hervey Ide and moved into the Post family home in Portland. In 1966 Lillian passed away in Portland from Leukemia. The summer after Wes Post graduated his grandmother, Rosa Post, died. Frail in health and physical strength, Wes believes, as he said, "She willed herself to live until I was out of school and able to take care of myself." Graduates during the 30's found this a somewhat difficult task. Jobs were scarce and pay scales low. Picking berries, peas or hops, planting cabbage, tying cauliflower or cutting cabbage earned one twenty or thirty cents per hour. Farm jobs involving working with a team, such as harrowing, disking or cultivating paid slightly more. Wes joined the Oregon National Guard (ONG) at his brother-in-law, Hervey Ide's urging. Hervey, a Master Sergeant in the outfit, belonged to the "President's One Hundred," a select group of the top 100 riflemen in the United States. While in the ONG, under the guidance of Master Sergeant Hervey Ide, Wes advanced in rank to Sergeant and qualified as an expert rifleman.

After grandmother Post's death, Frank Post returned to Oregon from Illinois to live with his son. After his wife's death, he had re-married and had a daughter, Betty, b. May 3, 1921. However, that marriage did not last and Betty remained with her mother. Frank Post lived with Wes for about two years at Mayview. In May 1935, Post was accepted into the U.S. Navy and assigned to the Naval Training Station at San Diego, where he was to spend the next several months. During the training period, Wes applied for the communications school, was selected and therefore remained at the Training Station for further training in radio. After completing this training he was assigned to the USS Ranger, the first carrier in the U.S. Navy built from scratch as a carrier, which was designated CV4 (the USS Langley was CV1, the Lexington, CV2 and the Saratoga, CV3). Because of treaty restrictions, the Ranger was smaller than its predecessors. Post became a radioman on the Ranger and after several attempts, finally gained a transfer to the USS Saratoga for flight duty. He joined Torpedo Squadron Three on the Saratoga as a radioman in September 1937. In 1938, during the period he served on the Saratoga, Wes met and married Helen Plog.

Post's service on the carrier Saratoga was highlighted by two crashes in which his aircraft was involved. Once on November 10, 1939, when the pilot attempted a "go-around," the plane's tail-hook caught on a cable and brought the aircraft down on the portside anti-aircraft batteries, but no injuries ensued. The second incident involved two aircraft (TBD's) flying in formation about 90 miles east of San Diego. The TBD's collided in the air, crashed and burned. Five men bailed out of the two planes, of whom three were injured, including Wes Post, who suffered a sprained wrist. The radioman in the second plane went down with the plane and was killed. On May 9, 1941, Post, an ARM1C, was discharged after six years service. He had completed 1300 hours in the air and had landed on the Saratoga's decks 132 times.

Shortly after Wes Post's discharge from the Navy, World War II commenced for the United States. During the war, Wes obtained a job as an electrical supervisor at Columbia Aircraft Industries in Portland. After the war he joined the Oregon Air National Guard at the Portland Airbase for a couple of years, where he worked for a time as a civilian employee. He served as a Master Sergeant in communications and worked as a recruiter for a time. In 1948, he recruited two CHS students, Clarence

Mershon and Jim Rhodes, into the 142nd Fighter Group. In 1946 Post started an electrical contracting business in Springdale, opening a shop in what had been the local barber shop. He had obtained an electrical supervisor's license from the State of Oregon during his tenure at Columbia Aircraft during the war, which certified him as a qualified electrician.

Shortly thereafter, Ridge Law opened a shop, Ridge's Hardware and Millwork, at the corner of Bell Road and the highway. Some time later, when Ridge closed the shop, Wes Post moved his business to that location. He operated there until about 1960, when he moved his shop to Portland. Meanwhile, Helen Post worked for Corbett School District as an Administrative Secretary. She worked in this position for more than 13 years, resigning in 1966. In 1954, informed that the congregation of the Corbett Christian Church was renovating the parsonage, Wes volunteered to upgrade the wiring. Shortly thereafter he and Helen started attending church there, which continued until they moved to Welches, Oregon in 1966. Once relocated, Wes moved his electrical business to that area as well.

Wes and Helen Post had three children, Wes Jr., b. April 3, 1939, Marilyn, b. January 3, 1942, and Steve, b. August 10, 1944. When Wes returned from the hospital in January 1942, after Marilyn was born, the car ahead of him on the road went into the Sandy River. Wes was able to get one person out of the car, which saved his life. A second person died in the accident. The Post youngsters all attended school at Corbett with Wes graduating from CHS in 1957, Marilyn in 1959, and Steve in 1961. Wes Jr. married Gail, has two children, Laurie and Lisa, and now lives in the Portland area. He is a partner in the Fullerton Insurance Agency. Marilyn married Jim McGetchie and will shortly retire from Portland General Electric after 30 years service. She and her husband plan to move to Central Oregon when she retires. Steve Post married Carolyn and they had two children, Brian and Carmel. Steve has remarried (Wendy), lives in Central Oregon and sells real estate.

Helen and Wes separated in the mid-70's. She continued to live in the log home the couple build on their Mt. Hood property. Helen (Plog) Post passed away in November 1984. November 22, 1976, Wes married Juanita Brown and the couple now lives in Sisters, Oregon. Wes installed a small artificial pond and stream system near their home. Birds and other animals come and go, providing a constantly changing wildlife 'show' for both Wes and Juanita to enjoy.

Albert C. Pounder
Florence (Bowker) Pounder

Albert C. Pounder was born August 3, 1905, at Corbett, son of James 'Jim' and Minnie (Crozier) Pounder. His parents owned an 80-acre farm located at the junction of Knieriem Road with Littlepage Road. Jim Pounder purchased the property from Sam Swinsky and Nathan Weinstein, who had operated a 'notions' store on the place until the building burned. The two peddled their wares throughout the Northwest, using the store as a base. The Pounder family grew hay, grain, corn, rye and vetch, and vegetable crops such as cabbage, cauliflower and potatoes. The Pounders also operated a dairy, and were among the first dairy farmers in the area to use Hinman milking machines. A 70-foot well under the back porch provided water, which had to be carried from the house to the barn to water the stock.

Albert Pounder completed his education at Hurlburt Grade School, graduating in 1919. Thereafter, he worked for his father on the farm until he ventured out on his own starting a freight business in 1926 with Lloyd Bramhall. When Mr. Bramhall withdrew from the business in 1927, Albert continued in the trucking business and started the first scheduled freight service between Corbett and Portland, making daily trips. Albert married Florence Bowker, who was a teacher at Hurlburt Grade School when they met. In 1909, Florence Bowker came to Portland, Oregon with her family from South Dakota (where she was born April 28, 1904). She and Albert Pounder were married on October 12, 1927 (See "Descendants of James and Minnie Crozier Pounder," *Pioneer History* and "Crystal (Pounder) Bayley," this volume).

In 1922, Albert's father had purchased 18 acres along the Columbia River Highway in Corbett, part of the original Corbett Estate. Albert built a warehouse for his freight business at this location and also a home. His wife became a partner in the trucking business, which they operated through the depression era, World War II and the post-war years. His trucking business, Pounder Trucking Service, hauled materials and supplies for businesses and farmers in East Multnomah County and he also included Reynolds Metals Company in Troutdale among his regular customers. A Gresham Outlook story of July 29, 1987, mentioned the difficulties the Pounders had when the depression hit in 1929. Many of the

Pounder Home in Corbett

The Pounder home built in the 20's.

Pounder Truck Service

An early picture of some Pounder trucks parked alongside the house.
The lady in front of the truck (left) may be Florence Pounder.
Photos courtesy of Shirley (Pounder) Foster.

mills for whom he was hauling lumber shut down and, according to Albert, he and Florence "held on by the skin of their teeth and the mercy of a kind banker" until construction started on Bonneville Dam. During the construction of the Dam, Albert hauled five loads a day to the site, working 16 or more hours per day, earning ten dollars per load, or $50.00 per day. According to the *Outlook*, he got the job because of his guts. "I was willing to do anything in those days – I don't know why, but there was nothing I was afraid to tackle." The article also mentioned the difficulties Albert faced in negotiating the old Columbia River Highway between

Pounder Truck Service

Pounder Truck Service after the construction of a warehouse in 1947.
Photo courtesy of Shirley (Pounder) Foster.

Troutdale and Bonneville, particularly when he met a large freight truck on the narrow, winding roadway. "…. We broke a lot a mirrors - Consolidated's and mine, too," he said.

Though he was kept busy running his business, Albert Pounder was active in community affairs. He was among the founding members of Fire District 14, Corbett Fire District. While loading corn at Ward Evans' cannery, Ward told Albert that Corbett School District planned to buy a new school bus and trade in the old one. Albert discussed the situation with Claude Woodle and some others, and made a proposal to the School Board to use the old Dodge bus for a fire truck. The Board decided to lease the bus to the Fire District for a period of 99 years for $1.00. In addition the School District allotted two slots in the bus shed for Fire District use, one for storing the fire truck and the second to provide living space for Ray Lasley, who took the fire calls, drove the truck and was night man on call.

According to Albert, the school bus was stripped to the chassis so that all that was left was the windshield and steering column. Al Woodward was instrumental in securing a pump from Multnomah County. The pump had been used to pump water from a spring near Rooster Rock to water tanks near the Vista House. The pump was mounted in front and connected to the crankshaft by a sliding spline shaft that could be engaged by a lever. Ray Moore, who lived on Knieriem Road at the time, located a 500-gallon tank that was used for water. Bob Knieriem did all the welding and Tom Northway did the blacksmith work required. Holland and Noyes of Palmer Mill gave the District all the fire hose, nozzles and connectors needed to outfit the rig from the stock they had to fight

386

fire in their operations on Larch Mountain. Claude Woodle, Corbett Hardware, donated much of the bolts and other hardware needed to put the truck together. It took several months to complete the project, but said Albert, "It certainly beat the bucket brigade that we had to rely on before, and we saved many houses and the Corbett Church." (Note: The fire in the church started after church services January 20, 1943. The January 23, 1946 issue of the high school paper, the *Cardinal*, contained the following news item: "The Corbett and Springdale fire departments were called out to fight a fire at the Corbett Church Sunday afternoon at 2 PM. Neighbors who saw flames shooting from the roof discovered the blaze. The fire seemed to have originated in the wood box behind the stove, and burned up the wall and into the attic. The damage amounted to $100.00.")

After the war started in 1941, the Fire District installed an air alarm using the School District's air compressor. Every day at noon, the Woodles would sound the alarm to determine if it was working. When the war ended, the Fire District applied to the federal government for a war surplus fire truck. A Chevrolet four-wheel drive 'low pressure' rig was purchased in 1946 for $850.00, which gave the District a 2nd fire truck. A grange hall dance brought in $1100.00, which was more than enough to pay for the truck. A third truck, a Federal, was obtained from Multnomah County and was stationed in Springdale, where George Shelley agreed to man it and take County calls for fire. It finally found a permanent home when the Fire District purchased Bob Scott's garage and converted it to a fire station. In 1949, the volunteer fire district officially became Fire District 14, organized by Albert Pounder, Claude Woodle, Walt Knieriem, Eugene O'Neil and several others.

The Veterans of Foreign Wars had started a building at Corbett, but were not able to complete it because of a shortage of funds. The Fire District made a deal with the VFW to complete a meeting hall and build a fire station alongside, which became the Corbett Station. Later, of course, a new station was built across from Frank Bell's garage at the East End of Corbett. The original fire truck, which was leased from the School District, was sold to Frank Bell, who wanted the pump that had been installed on the vehicle. This always bothered Albert because of all the volunteer work it took to build the District's first fire truck. (The old truck would have made a great exhibit if the Corbett community establishes a historical museum.)

Wedding Anniversaries

From L, Gene O'Neil, Frieda O'Neil, Florence Pounder and Albert Pounder celebrate their wedding anniversaries, which happened to be on the same date.

Photo courtesy of Frieda O'Neil.

Dedication Ceremony, Corbett Post Office

Representative Robert Duncan spoke at the Corbett Post Office dedication in 1975. Photo courtesy of Shirley (Pounder) Foster.

388

Installing Oil Tanks c1950

Gene O'Neil helps bury oil tanks installed for Pounder Oil.

Pounder Truck Service

A special truck ordered by Albert Pounder to haul pot liner from the Troutdale aluminum plant to the Longview plant. Photos courtesy of Frieda O'Neil.

Albert Pounder was active in the Columbia Gorge Kiwanis Club, which undertook many projects to help local communities and families. As Norm Sather said, "Albert was a real people person. He helped the people of this community in so many ways." Albert Pounder helped form the Corbett Water District, which provides water from Gordon Creek to this entire area and which replaced an original source, J. Ward Evans' spring on Pounder Grade. He served on the Corbett Water District Board a number of years. He worked to renovate and restore Sunset Cemetery on Littlepage Road. In 1974, Albert built the Corbett Post Office building, the first time Corbett had its own Post Office building. Previously, it had been located in private homes or a store. He was a member of the Columbia Grange. Besides providing jobs for local residents, he gave of his time and resources to make this community a better place to live.

A truck garage, shop and expanded warehouse were added to the business in 1947. Another job of note that kept Pounder Truck Service busy was the construction of I-80 (now I-84). From 1947 through 1951, Albert hauled materials for the company that dredged sand from the Columbia River bottom to make the road base for the freeway. In 1951, Albert Pounder started Pounder Oil Service, Inc., becoming a distributor of heating oil. He had built storage capacity for 36,000 gallons of fuel oil, and installed an oil plant inside the truck garage. He retained this business when Pounder Truck Service was sold to Gresham Transfer in

1956. He continued in the oil business until 1975 when the business was sold to Leroy Smith.

Albert and Florence Pounder had one daughter, Shirley J., b. December 12, 1934. Shirley attended Corbett schools, graduating in 1953 from CHS. Shirley is married to Jack Foster and has two sons, John C. and Alan D. She lives in Los Altos, California. In 1987, Shirley and Jack attempted to bring their successful business, Linelite Laser, to Corbett. The company manufactured small lasers, a 'clean,' highly technical product for the medical trade. Located in California's 'Silicon Valley,' it is the type of business that many states and locals compete for vigoriously. But the Board of County Commissioners, the Department of Land Use Planning and the Columbia Gorge Commision were not impressed. Linelite could not obtain the required permits in order to locate in Corbett. Consequently, Shirley and Jack continued the business in California. Presently, Jack Foster serves as a consultant to Xros Corporation, which is developing switching technology for fiber optical networks.

Florence Pounder passed away March 26, 1986. Albert Pounder died July 18, 1988. Both he and Florence are interred at Lincoln Memorial Park in Portland. *Crystal Bayley and Shirley (Pounder) Foster*

Corbett Christian Church.   Photo courtesy of Elizabeth (Morgan) Tanner.

Walter H. Quier
Fernie (Davis) Quier

Walter Quier was born in Oklahoma November 25, 1891. He came with his family to Southeast Oregon when he was 16 years of age, settling in the Virginia Valley near the Steens Mountains. He met Fernie Davis, who was born in the Hurlburt District November 12, 1901. Walter served in the Army during World War I, but the war ended before he was sent overseas. The couple married August 31, 1919. They first lived in SE Oregon, where their first child, Sybil, was born June 6, 1920. They moved about considerably the first years of their marriage, alternating between the East Multnomah County area and Eastern Oregon. Their second child, Quinten, was born November 30, 1922, while they were living in Corbett. Their third child, Vivian, was born February 22, 1932, in Crane, Oregon. Shortly after Vivian's birth, the family returned to East Multnomah County to stay.

Both Mr. and Mrs. Quier worked for Ward Evans in his cannery when they finally settled here. He also worked as a carpenter and was often employed by Claude Woodle, Corbett Hardware. After the cannery closed in 1944, he worked for Jack Lampert and Mrs. Quier worked at a cannery in Gresham. Later she worked as a cook at Corbett Grade School, initially with Alma Bramhall, then with Geneva Johnson and eventually with Hazel Venable.

Sybil started school in Eastern Oregon, but the family lived in such an isolated area she sometimes could not attend regularly. She reported, "I finally completed grade school several years late." Both she and Quinten attended grade school at Corbett, and Quinten started high school there. Vivian attended Corbett Grade School eight years, graduating in 1945. She also started high school at Corbett, but did not finish. As with other local youngsters, Vivian remembers picking berries for various farmers, including Harry Uyetake and Cary Kirkham. She worked for John Frommelt weeding carrots and parsnips and for Jack Lampert, in his gladiolas.

Sybil met Eddie Silva, son of Antonia (Silva) Jones, who lived across Chamberlain Road from her parents. The couple married June 12, 1938. They purchased a home from James and Pearl Stephens, which was lo-

Fernie and Walter Quier

Fernie (Davis) and Walter Quier c1919.
Photo courtesy of Vivian (Quier) Jaime.

cated across the creek from the place where her parents lived on Chamberlain Road. Since Eddie worked for the Oregon Humane Society in Portland, they later decided to move to Portland. When they moved, Sybil's parents rented the house from them until it was sold some years later. The Silvas had six children: James, b. August 13, 1940; Frances, b. November 24, 1944; Anthony, b. December 13, 1946; Gerald, b. November 13, 1948; Mary, b. June 5, 1957; and Edward, b. October 31, 1958. Eddie Silva died October 14, 1962. Later Sybil remarried and moved to the Spokane, Washington area, where she now lives.

Quinten married Fannie Kingsbury, with whom he had three sons, Marvin, Richard and Michael. This marriage did not last and his former wife's new husband adopted the three boys. Quinten later married Trudy Potter, and they had two children, Diane and Daniel, and lived in SE Portland. Daniel now lives on Hurt Road on a place adjacent to his grandparents' former home. After Quinten was widowed when his second wife died of cancer, he married a third time to Ernestine Biddle. Quinten and Ernestine lived in Milwaukie, Oregon. Quinten Quier died in December 1996.

Vivian married Everardo C. Gomez April 19, 1947. After the marriage the couple lived in a house owned by Ed Klinski on Chamberlain

Road. Later they moved to Lower Corbett and then to a home on Evans Road. They had seven children: Everardo, b. November 25, 1947; Mark, b. August 20, 1951; Elena, b. January 13, 1953; Alicia, b. July 29, 1954; Marita, b. April 24, 1958; Gabriel 'Gabe,' b. December 1, 1964; and Angelia, b. September 24, 1967. The Gomez children all attended grade school at Corbett. The oldest four graduated from Corbett High School, Everardo in 1966, Mark in 1969, Elena in 1971 and Alicia in 1972. The family moved to Gresham the year Marita was a senior in high school, and she graduated from Gresham High in 1976. Gabe and Angelia also graduated from Gresham High. Everardo Gomez died from a heart attack June 17, 1990, while visiting in Mexico. Vivian now lives near Boring, Oregon.

In the early 50's, Walter and Fernie Quier moved from Chamberlain Road to a place they had purchased from the Seylers on Hurt Road. Mr. Quier cleared the property and built a home. Fernie (Davis) Quier died March 9, 1962 and Walter Quier died August 11, 1969. Both are interrred at the Willamette National Cemetery in SE Portland.

Harding home at the top of Corbett Grade.   Photo courtesy of Pat Paget.

Hugh S. Reeves
Emma (King) Reeves

The Reeves family came to Oregon in 1905 where Mr. Reeves worked at the Booth Kelly Mill in Saginaw. Later they moved to Meldrom, near Oregon City. Before settling in this area, they made another move to Oak Grove, near Hood River and still another to Mosier. They finally settled a mile east of Springdale on a place purchased from Peter Van-de-Kerkhover and Leonardes de-Witte, who had decided to return to Holland where they were born. Part of the family's household goods were lost when the sternwheeler unloading them shifted and the load went into the Columbia River (see "Descendants of Hugh S. Reeves and Emma King Reeves," *Pioneer History*). The couple had four children, Socrates 'Crate,' b. April 17, 1899, Theodore, b. August 7, 1901, Esther, b. 1903 and Raymond, b. March 2, 1907. The first three children were born in Illinois while Raymond was born in Saginaw, Oregon. Granddaughter Ramona (Reeves) Valencia remembers visiting her grandparents after they moved from the farm to Montavilla:

> "We went to Montavilla, suburb of Portland, where Grandma and Grandpa Reeves lived by then. Grandma bought us bacon from the grocer, but she longed for bacon as they used to cure it on their farm located right on the main road between Corbett and Springdale. By the time I was visitor even before 1942 the road was paved. I can't forget her succulent rhubarb sauce or Grandpa's Kentucky Wonder green beans which he continued to grow in the backyard of his modern city (Montavilla) home."

Ray Reeves remembers his father operating a prune dryer, with which he did custom drying for others in the area. Similarly to many others, the Reeves dryer shut down after the prune orchards were destroyed in the ice storm of November 1921. Hugh Reeves farmed until the early 20's.

Crate Reeves attended Springdale Grade and CHS (class of 1919). He married Hattie Atkinson and they had two children, Ila and Tom. Hattie played classical piano and gave lessons to youngsters. He worked for Raleigh True in his Springdale store, farmed the Harley Bates place and then obtained a job driving truck. About this time he moved his family to the Montavilla District in Portland. Crate Reeves went to work for

Socrates Reeves

Socrates 'Crate' Reeves, CHS 1917.

Theodore Reeves

Theodore 'Ted' Reeves, CHS 1917. Photo excerpts courtesy of Ted Reeves Jr.

Consolidated Freightways, where he became a dispatcher, then a salesman in the used equipment division and finally, manager of the heavy hauling division. Crate was very personable, loved food and made a practice of visiting chefs in his favorite restaurants. Naturally he became known and was treated particularly well when he and friends or family dined at these restaurants. He retired from Consolidated in 1964. He continued employment as a consultant to Cummings Diesel for several years afterwards. He passed away December 18, 1971. His wife, Hattie, preceded him in death, January 1969.

Crates' daughter, Ila Reeves, had a beautiful singing voice. She sang solos in church as her mother played the piano. She married Horton V. Ranton and they moved into the "Reeves Neighborhood" in Montavilla. She died young and the couple had no children. Tom Reeves served in the Army during World War II. One job he had during the conflict was guarding Japanese prisoners-of-war. After the war he worked for Consolidated and retired from its management ranks. He married Charlene, and they now live in his parents' former Portland home.

When he left school because of illness, Theodore worked for Harley Bates and George Chamberlain. Then he obtained a job driving truck between Portland and Hood River. World War I was on and he could make $5 per day, which was "better than school." He and Speck Corless would follow each other in their trucks in the winter months. When they came to an icy hill, they spread gas over the highway and set fire to it to melt the ice. Then getting a running start, they would speed up the hill and proceed on their way. If they became stuck, they stayed with their trucks until help arrived. Sometimes Theodore's fiancée, Frances Grimshaw, would bring food to the stranded drivers until they were able to move on. Theodore married Frances in 1922 and they moved to Portland where he worked in a feed store. He started with Safeway Stores in 1928 and retired in 1966 as Manger of Safeway's Distribution Center in Clackamas, Oregon.

The Bramhalls and the Reeves

From L, Lloyd and Doris Bramhall visit Dolores (Morgan) and Ray Reeves in Klamath Falls.
Photo courtesy of Pat (Bramhall) Paget.

Theodore and Frances had two children, twins Theodore and Frederick, born May 5, 1928, in Portland. Fred attended the University of Oregon, Southern Oregon College and graduated from Arizona State University in 1960. He married Peggie E. Frew of Cottonwood, Arizona in 1949, and they had a son, Kent Reeves. Theodore 'Ted' Reeves (Jr.) attended the University of Oregon and the Museum Art School in Portland, Oregon. He married Dolores Ashley of Oregon City, Oregon, and they had four children, Deborah, Krystal, Jason and Adam. Theodore Reeves (Sr.) died September 24, 1993 in Portland. His wife, Frances, preceded him in death, April 12, 1972.

Esther Reeves graduated from CHS in 1921. She married Byron C. Bell of Springdale and they had a daughter, Catherine, b. April 6, 1927. Byron, son of Grant Bell (see "Ulysses G. Bell Family," *Pioneer History*), had a PUC permit and owned a truck, which he used to go into the trucking business. He operated between Portland and The Dalles. Eventually he sold the business to Consolidated Freightways and worked for that company until he retired in 1961. Esther was a homemaker and the family moved to Montavilla shortly before Catherine was born April 6, 1927. Catherine attended Vestal Grade School and graduated from Washington High. She married Floyd L. Whiteman and had two sons, Mark, b. December 28, 1954 and Gary, b. May 5, 1957. Gary died of leukemia at age 8. Currently the Whitemans live in Gresham. Byron C. Bell died April 9, 1965 and Esther (Reeves) Bell died in November 1981.

Raymond 'Ray' H. Reeves graduated from CHS in 1925. He drove truck for Jack Warren, then went to work for his brother, Crate Reeves, in McMinnville. Later Ray drove milk truck for George Atkinson for a couple of years. When the drivers picked up milk they delivered groceries to customers who had phoned orders in to Atkinson's store. Ray also opened a butcher shop in Springdale, which he operated for almost a year before "going broke." On July 14, 1927, he married a classmate, Dolores Morgan. Dolores was born in Wardner, Idaho September 26, 1908. Reeves had an opportunity to go to work for a construction company in Klamath Falls, so he and Dolores moved there. Later he worked for Balsiger Motors and continued working there until the end of World War II. The Reeves had two daughters, Ramona, b. September 17, 1928 and Ann E., b. February 19, 1930, both in Klamath Falls. After the war Reeves went into the garage business, eventually owning three stations and an auto parts store. Dolores (Morgan) Reeves died March 20, 1997 at age 87. Raymond Reeves continues to live independently in Klamath Falls, age 92 (1999).

Daughter Ramona Reeves married Wallace Nordwall and had three children, Arnold, Wallace and Elizabeth, all born in Klamath Falls. Later she married Joe A. Valencia, who was an operating engineer at Alcan near Berkeley, California. Of her children, Arnold now resides in Seattle, Washington and works in yacht electronics and repair; Wallace died of multiple sclerosis is 1992; Elizabeth Hink lives in Monterey, California and has a son, David. Ramona (Reeves) Valencia worked as a school library assistant and currently resides in Pleasanton, California. She remembers visits to her Grandmother Morgan's home in Corbett (see "Roland C. Morgan, Elizabeth (Benn) Morgan").

Ray and Dolores Reeves' daughter, Ann, married Lyle R. Steers in 1951. The Steers now reside in Salem, Oregon.

Ramona (Reeves) Valencia

Jesse C. Rogers
Nettie (Graham) Rogers

Jesse 'Mike' Rogers was born on the family farm at Corbett May 17, 1895. The Rogers place was located on Mershon Road and included the farm now owned by Aldo Rossi (previously owned by MB McKay). Mike Rogers married Anna Robinett of Walla Walla, who died in childbirth in 1916. The child, Margaret, b. February 11, 1916 attended Corbett schools, graduating from CHS in 1934. She married M.J. Kechel, had two children and lives in California. December 9, 1918, Rogers married Nettie Graham, b. May 1899 in Falls City, Oregon. Mike and Nettie Rogers' home sat off Mershon Road at the apex of the long hill east of the Lucas Road intersection. It was located between the Louie Berney and Art Dunklee places. Mike and Nettie Rogers had three birth children, Hazel, b. January 6, 1920, Frances, b. February 11, 1922 and Dorothy, b. August 8, 1923. The three girls each attended Corbett Grade School for eight years, and completed high school at CHS, from which Hazel graduated in 1937, Frances in 1939 and Dorothy in 1941. Mike Rogers worked for the Multnomah County Road Department. He passed away August 30, 1966. Nettie Rogers died within two weeks of Mike's death in September 1966.

Norman 'Norm' Sather, born September 26, 1917, in Idaho, came to Oregon in September 1937 to take a job as a night engineer with Bridal Veil Lumber and Box Company. Besides working in the mill, he also worked in the woods for a time. Shortly after coming to Oregon he met Hazel Rogers. On June 18, 1941, Norm enlisted in the U.S. Army. Two months later (August 17, 1941), he and Hazel married. After Japanese planes bombed Pearl Harbor, Norm was sent to the Aleutian Islands and served in that area most of the war years.

He was discharged September 26, 1945, but stayed in the U.S. Army Reserve. After his return to civilian life, he owned and operated the 'Last Chance Service Station' in Coopey Falls until 1947. He started a wood business, Larch Mountain Fuel Co., first selling mill ends from the Bridal Veil Mill. Leonard Kraft also urged Norm to start a garbage route, which he did, eventually serving the communities of Bridal Veil, Corbett and Springdale. He operated this business for 25 years. In addition to the garbage business, Norm hauled lumber from Seaside to Portland for a couple of years. He also worked for a couple of years building barges for Zidell.

When the Korean War broke out, Norm was called to active duty. His assignment took him to El Paso, Texas, where he was stationed during that conflict. When discharged, he continued in the active Army Reserve, retiring as a Chief Warrant Officer III after 24 years service (Including 5+ years active duty during WW II and the Korean War). Norm helped organize the Corbett Veterans of Foreign Wars Post. He became active in the organization and later served as Commander of the VFW in Oregon.

Norm and Hazel built a home in Springdale in 1947, and that is where they lived while raising their family. They had two sons, Gary L., b. August 7, 1946, and Eric R., b. December 24, 1952. The boys attended grade school at Springdale and high school at Corbett, Gary graduating in 1964 and Eric in 1971. Norm Sather helped start the Corbett Fire Department, and was its first training officer. After the boys graduated, Norm and Hazel moved to Prineville. In 1979, Norm retired. He and Hazel continue to reside in Prineville.

After graduation, Frances Rogers worked for Ward Cook Realty in Portland. She married Robert E. Mills, who was a buyer for Montgomery Ward & Co. They had a daughter, Judy. Dorothy Rogers worked for an insurance agency in Gresham. She married Hienie Ziegler March 17, 1942 at Everett, Washington. He was a Sgt. in the U.S. Army Air Corps at the time. She had been working at the Good Samaritan Hospital as a switchboard operator. After World War II they made their home in Springdale. They had two daughters, Carla, b. September 28, 1949 and Brenda, b. October 28, 1953. Both attended Corbett schools with Carla graduating from CHS in 1967, Brenda in 1971.

William H. Rogers
Hannah L. (Chamberlain) Rogers

William H. Rogers, born in Wisconsin in December of 1864, came to Oregon from Michigan, probably in 1890. Apparently he had married Hannah 'Hattie' (Chamberlain) Enoch that same year. She had five children by a prior marriage to Marshall R. Enoch: George F. Enoch, b. June 10, 1876, Charles Enoch, b. December 1878, Lillian J. Enoch, b. August 20, 1881, Mildred Enoch, b. October 1884 and Lilford Enoch, b. December 4, 1885. Rogers located his newly acquired family on property located on what is now Mershon Road on the 'hill.' Hattie bore three more children, Ralph L., b. September 25, 1891, Ethel, b. July 16, 1893, and Jesse C., b. May 17, 1895. The latter three were all born in Troutdale, Oregon.

William cleared much of the property (which was later sold to M.B. McKay, and is now owned by Aldo Rossi) to farm. Hattie Rogers became a real estate agent and businesswoman, and eventually acquired considerable property in Troutdale and vicinity. She was a talented musician, played and taught piano, and sold musical instruments. Her children also performed, with two, Lilford and Lillian, having featured roles in a Taylor School "Basket Supper" held June 29, 1894, featuring afternoon and evening performances by students.

Since there was no high school for youngsters to attend in the area, the 'Enoch' children were sent to the Seventh Day Adventist School in Walla Walla to complete their schooling. George Enoch graduated from Walla Walla College and taught school for a time in Gresham. Later he became a missionary for the Seventh Day Adventist Church and spent several years abroad, including about ten years in Japan and thirty years in India. He married Bertha M. Graham and had two children, Pearl H. and Gerald. Gerald died in childhood while the family was in India. The 2nd child, Charles Enoch, also attended the church school in Walla Walla and studied medicine. He, too, became a missionary and died of Yellow Fever while on a mission to Trinidad.

Apparently Lillian Enoch also attended school in Walla Walla as she later taught music, piano, organ and guitar, and taught in a church school. She married William A. Ogden October 12, 1903. He also taught school and apparently the family moved from locale to locale as the four chil-

Taylor School Basket Supper

Basket Supper.

TAYLOR SCHOOL HOUSE.

Friday, June 29th, 1894,

At 4 o'Clock P.M.

Order of Exercises.

AFTERNOON PROGRAMME:

Song, ... School.
Recitation, ... Louis Benfield.
Class Recitation, "WISHING,"
Wellie Masterson, Lillie Rasmussen, Zula Bell, Elsie Kincaid,
Martha Leader, Osie Beaumont.
Recitation, ... Edgar Russell.
Recitation, ... Bertha Leader.
"OH DEAR,"
Jessie Benfield, Flora Hughes, May Russell.
Song, ... Class.
Recitation, ... Willie Masterson.
Recitation, ... Lilford Enoch.
"THE INDIGNATION MEETING,"
Glen Russell, Flora Hughes, Jessie Benfield, Bertha Leader,
May Russell.
Recitation, ... John Farlow.
Recitation, ... Martha Leader.
Song, . . .
Recitation, ... Geo. Chamberlain.
Recitation, ... Jessie Benfield.
Recitation, ... Florence Smith.
Recitation, ... May Allard.
Recitation, ... Ida Benfield.
Recitation, ... Lillie Enoch.
Song, ... R. R. Allard.
Recitation, ... Logan Chamberlain.
"MARSHALL MUSIC,"
A. Chamberlain, E. D. Chamberlain.
"CLASS DRILL," School.
SUPPER . . . . FROM 6 TO 8 P.M.

EVENING PROGRAMME:

"Valse des Papillions," . . . (Ludovic),
Nettie Chamberlain.
Song, . . "The Picture That Is Turned Toward the Wall,"
Flora Hughes, Nettie Chamberlain.
Recitation, ... R. R. Allard.
"I'M A MAN,"
Logan Chamberlain, Elsie Kincaid, Saul Fisher.
INSTRUMENTAL MUSIC,
Wm. Reed, Frank Reed.
Recitation, ... Miss Blanch Smith.
"THE SCHOOL MARM'S VISITOR,"
Geo. Chamberlain, Will Masterson, John Farlow, and Class.
Song, . . "YOU'LL MISS ME DARLING CHLOE,"
Nettie Chamberlain, Zula Bell, Flora Hughes.
INSTRUMENTAL MUSIC,
Wm. Reed, Frank Reed.
Recitation, ... Miss Pearl Roper.

"Box and Cox,"
OR
"THE RIVAL LODGERS."

Bert Chamberlain, Miss Essay Buchanan, R. R. Allard.
Cantilena, ... Mrs. Clara Young.
Recitation, ... Alma Smith.
"Manhattan Beach March," . . . (Sousa),
Nettie Chamberlain.
"THE BRIDAL COUPLE,"
Annie Benfield, Frankie Bell.
Tableaux.
TROUTDALE CHAMPION TYPE.

The program consists of afternoon and evening performances, and lists student participants. Program courtesy of Sadie (Rogers) McCormick.

dren resulting from the union, Mae Pearl, Verne, Glen E. and Wilma, were born in Creswell, Knappa, Troutdale and Toledo, respectively. The 4th child, Mildred Enoch, married Jesse A. Allen September 30, 1903. The couple had three children, Winferd, Arlene and Margaret L., all apparently born in Oregon. Arlene died from encephalitis when about 12 years of age. The family moved to California in the late 20's. Later Mildred married Thomas D. Sanford and the couple lived in Sacramento. The 5th child, Lilford Enoch died May 27, 1902, while attending Walla Walla College, of meningitis. He is buried at the Mountain View Cemetery, Corbett.

William and Hattie's first birth child, Ralph L. Rogers, married Anna M. Mershon in 1915. The couple lived on the Rasmussen place on what is now Chamberlain Road. He farmed and during the mid-20's, he and Anna managed the Springdale Hotel and Restaurant. Four children resulted from this marriage: Royce, b. June 14, 1917, Sarah L. 'Sadie,' b. September 18, 1919, Raymond R., b. March 3, 1921 and Raymond's twin, Ruth, who lived only two days. When the couple divorced July 25, 1925, Anna and the three surviving children moved into a house close to Jesse Rogers' home on Mershon Road. Later Anna (Mershon) Rogers married Al G. Patton, who had two children, Ruth and Robert, from a previous marriage. The couple

Anna (Mershon) Rogers

Anna Rogers shortly after her marriage to Ralph Rogers.   Photos courtesy of Dorothy Larson.

Children of Anna (Mershon)

Royce and Sadie, children of Anna and Ralph Rogers.

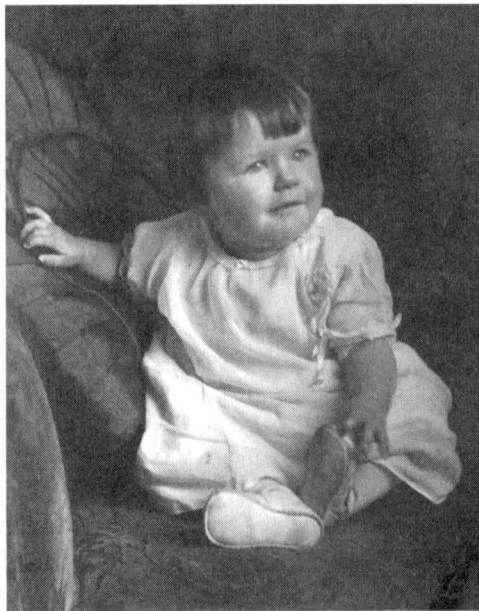

Joan Patton b. January 1927, daughter of Anna and Al Patton.

moved their combined families to the Parkrose area, where the young-sters then attended school. Anna Patton passed away July 20, 1959.

Royce Rogers married Barbara Smith of Hood River, November 14, 1936. Royce worked as a salesman for an automobile dealer in Hood River before starting his own business, 'Rogers Used Cars.' Royce and Barbara had two children, Mildred A., b. April 1, 1937 and William R., b. September 14, 1938. On August 4, 1957, William died in an accident while attending the Naval Aviation School in Norman, Oklahoma. Royce Rogers died October 4, 1990 and Barbara Rogers passed away February 24, 1993.

Sadie Rogers spent many happy hours with her Corbett cousins dur-ing her childhood years. She often stayed at the Mershon place and worked in the fields with her cousin, Elda Mershon. She remembers planting potatoes at her Uncle Jum's place at Corbett, and planting cabbage by hand in the hillside field that bordered the Rogers' place. She married Earle McCormick of Parkrose June 25, 1937. Earle worked in the floor covering business until his retirement. The couple had two daughters, Judy A., b. November 19, 1939 and Carol L., b. July 3, 1944, both born in Portland.

Judy became a registered nurse, served as a medical missionary in New Guinea and worked in the emergency room at Emanuel Hospital until her recent retirement. Carol also became a nurse. She now works at The Dalles Hospital as night supervisor. Carol has a daughter, Mary Beth Stevens, who works as an engineer for the City of Portland. Sadie and Earl now live on the east bank of the Sandy River near Dodge Park.

Raymond Rogers spent four years in the US Navy during World War II. After the war March 22, 1947, he married Viola Merrifield. Raymond went into the grain business as a broker and retired from United Grain Corporation as Senior Vice-President. He and Viola had two children, Roy R., b. February 14, 1945 and Ray R., b. June 26, 1950. Viola and her sister operated a small restaurant on Marine Drive in NE Portland for many years. Raymond and Viola recently sold their home and the restau-rant in NE Portland, and plan to travel.

James Ross
Mae Ross

James "Jim" Ross operated a garage on the north side of the Columbia River Highway just east of its intersection with Knieriem Road. The Ross family sold gas, groceries, lunches and drinks at the business named 'The Summit.' An advertisement in the 1927 *Cohimore* reads: "The Summit - Gas, Oil, Accessories, Expert Repairing, Towing, Lunches, Cigars, Tobacco, Confections, Drinks, Columbia Highway - J.W. Ross." The family lived in the building, which was built by Frank Knieriem. They had a daughter, Laura, who grew up in Oakland, CA. Eva Hammer later operated a tavern and eating establishment at this location.

Latourell & Son Summit Station

Summit Station, J.W. Ross, proprietor.

Summit Tavern

Summit Station after it became the Summit Tavern. Eva 'Ma' Hammer stands in front of the establishment. Photos courtesy of Steve Lehl.

404

Masaru Sakurai
Chiyoko (Takeuchi) Sakurai

Masaru Sakurai was born in Hiroshima, Japan July 20, 1897. His mother died not too long after he was born and his grandparents cared for him. His father left for the United States around the turn of the century, but Masaru remained in Japan. In 1914, after completing school in Japan, he joined his father in the United States. In the interim his father had remarried. Later, Masaru Sakurai met his future bride, Chiyoko Takeuchi, in Portland, where she had been born November 14, 1905. The couple wed in the summer of 1922 and moved to the East Multnomah County area in the late 20's with Mr. Sakurai's father and stepmother. The family first stayed with the Takeuchi family on Wand Road. The Sakurai family purchased a place of approximately 25 acres located just north of the Takeuchi farm on Wand Road. There was a small house on the property, into which the family moved. Much of the place was still covered with timber and brush, so the land had to be cleared for farming. With the use of dynamite and hand tools, the Sakurais accomplished the task with the help of the Takeuchis. Mr. Sakurai's parents decided to return to Japan, and he took over the farm. He planted strawberries, broccoli, cauliflower, cabbage and spinach. Horses did the tilling, which included plowing, disking, harrowing, floating and cultivating. In the early days, Mr. Sakurai often hired itinerant laborers, who lived on the farm while they worked for him.

Mr. and Mrs. Sakurai had six children, Lily, b. July 26, 1924, Richard 'Dick,' b. December 26, 1926, George, b. February 19, 1929, Betty, b. February 21, 1931, Edward, b. May 23, 1936 and Judith, b. July 15, 1938. Lily started at Corbett Grade School in 1930. Her first grade teacher was Miss Maude Sherman and Mr. George Lusby was the Principal. Her younger brothers and sisters, except for Edward and Judith, attended Corbett as well. During the 30's as the children grew older, they were able to help with the farm work. Mr. Sakurai sold much of the farm produce at the Farmers' Market in Portland, which meant everyone was up early to harvest the crops so that Masaru could be at the market when it opened. Lily said they usually started work at 4:30 a.m. On school days, mornings were a busy time at the Sakurai home. According to Lily, the strawberry crop was usually contracted to the Birds Eye Cannery in

Masaru Sakurai Family

From L, Masaru, Dick, Lily, George and Chiyoko Sakurai.
Photo courtesy of Lily (Sakurai) Kajiwara.

Gresham. Spinach was sold to a cannery in St. Johns and broccoli was sold in Hillsboro. Everything was planted by hand, strawberries, broccoli, cauliflower and cabbage. In the late 30's, Mr. Sakurai purchased a Ford Ferguson tractor. Thereafter, the ground was worked by tractor, though some tasks, such as cultivating, continued to be done by horse.

Lily graduated from CHS in 1942. About ten days before her graduation day, the Sakurai family, together with all other families of Japanese extraction in the area, were ordered to leave their homes by the U.S. Government. When this occurred, Dick was completing his sophomore year at CHS and George was in 8th grade. Betty was not in school because she had cerebral palsy. Edward and Judith had not yet started school. When the Sakurai family left home to report to the Pacific Livestock Exposition Center, they were permitted to take only what they could carry. Most of their personal possessions as well as farm implements and household belongings were left at the farm. A neighbor agreed to look after the farm and their belongings for them.

At the Center, they found hundreds of Japanese families crowded together in a facility originally intended for animals. Privacy was not possible, which was particularly difficult for Lily, who was nearly eigh-

406

Sakurai Family, Post-War

Rear, Masaru, Dick, George Kajiwara, Eddie and George. Front, Chiyoko, Betty, Lily, Judy and Janice (George's wife).   Photo courtesy of Lily (Sakurai) Kajiwara.

teen at the time. Since the camps where the Japanese were to be interned were not yet finished, the approximate two thousand people of Japanese extraction located at the Center stayed there until September. According to Lily, the summer was exceptionally warm, which added to their discomfort. In the Sakurai family, seven (of eight) members of the family were U.S. citizens. In September the family was sent to the Minidoka Camp in Idaho.

While in Minidoka, Masaru Sakurai worked on surrounding farms where the principal crops were potatoes and sugar beets. Dick and George also worked as farm laborers during the summer months when school was out. When he was not working as a farm laborer, Sakurai was assigned to janitorial work. All school-age children attended school in camp. Lily worked at the Minidoka Camp School as a teacher. The first year she taught 4th grade, the second, 6th grade and the third, kindergarten. Dick graduated from high school in 1944. His diploma reflects the circumstances as Hunt High School, which was operated by the U.S. Government, awarded the document.

After the war, the Sakurai family returned to Oregon. Mr. Sakurai and Dick drove to the farm to assess the situation. They found their home in deplorable condition. The family's household goods and other belongings had disappeared, taken by parties unknown. Furthermore, Lily said, "Father and Dick felt some animosity toward the Japanese still existed." After a discussion among family members, the decision was made to sell the farm. Consequently, it was sold and the family settled in rental housing at Vanport.

Thereafter, the Sakurai family lived in Portland and Mr. Sakurai became a contract gardener. George completed high school at Roosevelt, graduating in 1946. Edward and Judith attended Failing Grade School. In 1948 the family lost much of what they had accumulated after the war in the Vanport flood. They found a place to rent, which was located at SW 1st and Sherman Street in Portland. Edward and Judith attended Lincoln High School, Edward graduating in 1954 and Judith in 1956. In the mid-50's, the Sakurais purchased a home in Southeast Portland at 84th and Holgate.

Masaru Sakurai took many awards for his gardening activities, particularly with his roses. He was also pleased and proud to pass the test to become an U.S. citizen. Mrs. Sakurai became well known as a poet in the Japanese verse, Haiku. Many of her poems were published locally and in Japan. She received many awards and much recognition for her work. Her daughter, Judith, plans to have her mother's poetry published in book form. Chiyoko Sakurai was also an accomplished singer, performing at many community events. She passed away in March 1986. Masaru Sakurai retired at age 85. He died September 1995, age 98. Mr. and Mrs. Sakurai are interred at the Forest Lawn Cemetery in Gresham.

After the family returned to Oregon, Lily worked for Holman Transfer. In 1952 she decided to travel and see the country. She traveled south through California, across the southern part of the country and up the East Coast. She ended up in New York City and found a job. While there she met George S. Kajiwara, who had settled in New York after being discharged from the U.S. Army. He had served with the 442nd Regimental Combat Team in the European Theater. The couple decided to get married and make Oregon their home. They were wed December 5, 1953. They have one child, Karen, b. October 25, 1961. While Karen was in school, Lily completed requirements for a degree at Portland State University, graduating in 1975. She became a librarian at Portland State, and worked there until she retired in 1994. George Kajiwara was born in Colorado, August 22, 1925. After coming to Oregon, he worked for the Hyster Company, retiring in 1987 when Hyster closed its local plant. He then worked for the American Cancer Society before retiring for good in 1995.

Dick Sakurai worked at various jobs in Portland before deciding to go on to school. He enrolled at Reed College, graduating in 1953 with a degree in Physics. He completed graduate work at Bryn Mawr and taught physics at several colleges in the Midwest. He and his wife, Sandy, have two sons, Saren and Korien. He and his wife now live in Frederick, Maryland (1998).

After graduating from Roosevelt, George enrolled at Oregon State College majoring in biology. He worked in a laboratory for a time, after which he was accepted into the School of Medicine at Oregon Health Sciences University. After completing medical school in 1959, he did his internship at Good Samaritan Hospital. He was accepted into the residency program in psychiatry at the State Hospital in Salem. He practiced as a psychiatrist in Medford, Oregon, for a time before taking a position with the United States Government in Springfield, Missouri. Later, he accepted a position as Psychiatrist for Orange County, south of Los Angeles. He now lives in Westminster, California with his wife, Janice. They have four children, Steven, Larry, Scott and Leslie.

Because of her handicap Betty did not attend school. She lived with her parents until they passed away. She now lives in N.E. Portland with a lady who helps care for her. She did not marry.

After graduating from Lincoln High School, Edward attended Reed College, from which he graduated in 1958 with a degree in mathematics. He then completed graduate work at Washington University in St. Louis. He teaches mathematics at Webster University in St. Louis, a position he has held since completing his graduate work. He is married to Anna, but they have no children.

Judith, after graduating from Lincoln High, attended Reed College and graduated with a major in chemistry. She did graduate work at the University of Oregon, then attended the Stanford Foreign Language Institute. She married Hiroshi Yamauchi, a professor at the University of Hawaii. They undertook several tours to Japan in order to teach there. Judith and her husband have a daughter, Kara, and live in Hawaii.

Lilly (Sakurai) Kajiwara and Dick Sakurai

Raymond L. Schneringer
Blanche (Reid) Schneringer

Raymond L. Schneringer and Blanche (Reid) Schneringer came to Oregon from Wyoming in 1951. Raymond, b. June 1, 1913 and Blanche, b. October 20, 1915, had four children, all born in Nebraska: Nona B., b. March 12, 1936; Dona R., b. August 18, 1937; Phillip R., b. March 10, 1941; and Gladys K. 'Kay,' b. February 3, 1947. The family settled on Larch Mountain Road in a home adjacent to the Walt and Veda Mannthey place. Raymond went to work for the Bridal Veil Lumber and Box Company and remained employed there until it closed in 1960. He then worked as a mechanic at the Gresham Berry Growers plant until it closed. Blanche also worked at the cannery in Gresham. Blanche worked as a clerk at the Vista House gift shop for several years. After Raymond retired, he worked at the Vista House as a custodian for one year.

However, Blanche's primary job was that of a homemaker. Raising four youngsters kept her occupied for several years. The older children started school in Nebraska, continuing in Wyoming after the move there. After the move to Oregon, Nona completed two years at CHS, graduating in 1953. Dona attended CHS four years, graduating in 1955. Phillip finished grade school at Corbett, then completed high school at CHS, graduating in 1958. Kay completed both grade and high school at Corbett, graduating from CHS in 1965. After graduating from high school, Nona attended MHCC and the Providence School of Nursing for two years. Kay attended the Emanuel School of Nursing from 1965-1968.

In 1953, Nona Schneringer met James 'Jim' Layton, who was home on leave from the Marine Corps. Jim came to Oregon in 1946 to stay with his brother, Charles, after his mother died. Charles was married to Margaret Zilm at the time. Family considerations caused Jim to seek another arrangement, and he boarded at the Davis place at the invitation of Anna Davis. When Anna Davis passed away, Lois Dunkin suggested that Jim might make a similar arrangement with her mother, Rae Evans, which he did. Thereafter he lived at the Evans home until he was called to active duty with the US Marines in 1950. Jim had joined a reserve Marine Corps unit with John McCleary and Floyd Kogle. The unit was activated when the Korean War started.

Schneringer Family

L to R: Blanche, Dona, Nona, Phillip and Raymond Schneringer.

The Schneringers at Home

L to R: Phillip, Dona, Nona, Kay and Blanche Schneringer.
Photos courtesy of Nona (Schneringer) Layton.

Jim, John and Floyd were sent to boot camp at Camp Pendleton, then to Korea. Jim, trained as a truck driver, transported troops during his tour in Korea. Discharged in 1953, he re-enlisted and the Corps sent him for a second tour in Korea. After he returned to the States, he drove a bus at Camp Pendleton until discharged in August 1955. After his discharge, he and Nona Schneringer resumed dating. The couple married December 1, 1955. Jim worked at Bridal Veil and held various odd jobs until he went

The Laytons

From L, Helen, Benjamin, Charles, Hiram, Jim, Nona, Dona and Bob Layton.
Photo courtesy of Nona (Schneringer) Layton.

to work for Reynolds aluminum in 1956. In March 1957, Jim and Nona moved to Springdale. When Reynolds had a lay-off, Jim bought the former Bell Garage in Corbett. He and Nona then moved into an adjoining apartment. Jim owned the garage for more than 8 years. In 1961, the Laytons moved into Johnny Dobing's home on Larch Mountain Road, which is where they have lived since.

In 1966 Jim went to work for the Bonneville Power Administration at its Hazel Dell shop. Shortly thereafter, he obtained a job as a truck driver for Bonneville, which he continued until his retirement December 31, 1993. In 1975, Jim and Nona purchased the former Dobing place from the Rickert family after Alvin Rickert died.

Nona quit nurses training when she and Jim married. They have five children: Debra R., b. July 13, 1956, Thomas J., b. September 14, 1957, Pamela K., b. June 11, 1959, Richard K., b. November 8, 1960 and Julie M., b. September 19, 1962. All attended Corbett grade and CHS, from which Debra graduated in 1974, Thomas in 1975, Pamela in 1977, Richard in 1979 and Julie in 1980. Nona remained at home to care for her children until 1969 when she became a teacher's aide at Springdale Primary. She decided to return to school at MHCC for further training (op-

412

Jim Layton's Corbett Garage

A Friendly Neighbor

Jim Layton operated the Corbett (former Bell) Garage from 1959 to 1966. Photos courtesy of Nona (Schneringer) Layton.

Johnny Dobing, neighbor to the Schneringers for many years, sits between Gail Long and Kay Schneringer (left) and Carol Long and Raymond Schneringer (right).

erating room technician program). After completing this program she obtained a job at Providence Medical Center. She continued working at Providence until May 17, 1994, when she took a medical disability because of Parkinson's disease. In October 1996, Jim had open-heart surgery to replace a valve. The surgery was successful, and he has been in good health since.

Both Jim and Nona have been involved in community activities and organizations. Jim volunteered with the Corbett Fire Department until he took the job with BPA. He has been active with the Veterans of Foreign Wars, Northeast Multnomah County Community Association (NEMCA), CHS (sports) and other organizations. He enjoys gardening, sports, fishing and camping. Nona's interests include reading, sewing, crafts, genealogy and Corbett history. She maintains genealogy records of many local families and is a source for much historical data. She, too, has been active in community affairs, serving such organizations as NEMCA, Corbett PTA, Rebekah Lodge, Gresham TOPS and St. Luke's Episcopal Church.

With regard to Jim and Nona's children, Debra graduated from Western Business College and has worked for the First Interstate Bank (now Wells Fargo) for more than 20 years. She married Thomas Granberg and they had two children, David (CHS '97) and Amanda. Jim and Nona's 2nd youngster, Thomas, worked for Owens-Illinois. In 1997, he completed an apprenticeship to become a journeyman electrician. Currently, he serves as Chief of the Corbett Fire Department. He married Gina Erickson and they have four children, Jennifer, Jessica, Jamie and Joshua. Pamela (3rd child) worked for the Portland Police Bureau and the Portland School District before joining American Data Processing about a year ago. She is attending Portland State University to obtain an accounting degree. She has a daughter, Donna. Richard (4th) married Monica Bachand. He worked for Burns Brothers Truck Stops at a number of locations. Presently he is a sanitation engineer at a meat packing plant in Iowa. He and Monica have three children, Briauna, Travis and Kiera. Julie married Donald Dearden and had two children, Christopher (CHS '99) and Donald. After working at Burns Brothers as a waitress for several years, she returned to school and became a nurse. Currently she works at Woodland Park Hospital in the 'short stay' facility.

After high school, Dona worked for Retail Credit Company in Portland. She married Bob Layton June 23, 1956. After Bob's mother died, he lived with relatives for a time, but that did not work out. Church members acquainted with his family sent him to Oregon, where he lived with his brother, Charles, for a time, then lived with the Cramptons. During this period of time he attended Springdale Grade School and CHS. After high school, he worked at the Bridal Veil mill before obtaining a job with the Multnomah County Road Department. He retired from the County December 31, 1996. Bob Layton has been a volunteer with the Corbett Fire Department for more than 40 years and has served as its Chief. Bob and Dona Layton had two sons: Douglas A., b. October 5, 1957 and Daniel A., b. April 29, 1959. Tragically, Douglas was killed in an automobile accident his junior year at CHS. He died December 17, 1974. Daniel was formerly married to Janice Thorud with whom he had two boys, Shawn and Jason. He works for Burbach's garbage service.

When Daniel was born, Dona quit her job to remain at home. In 1964 she took a job at Corbett School District, spending one-half day at the grade school and one-half day at the high school. This evolved into a full time position at the high school. Later she was promoted to the position of Secretary to the Superintendent at the District Office. Dona retired from Corbett School District in December 1996, after more than 30 years service. She has been active in Cub Scouts, Gresham TOPS and St. Luke's Episcopal Church. Bob and Dona live on Larch Mountain Road.

After graduating from CHS, Phillip Schneringer joined the US Navy. He served four years, principally in the Pacific Theater. In 1966, he married Alice J. Scanlan. The couple had two children, Anthony D. and Heidi

414

Bob Layton Family

Bob and Dona Layton with their son, Dan, and grandsons, Shawn and Jason.

Douglas Layton

Doug Layton, killed in an automobile accident in front of his grandparent's home December 1974.

Raymond and Blanche Schneringer in a lovely garden. Photos courtesy of Nona (Schneringer) Layton.

J., and lived in Parkrose. Phillip worked at Owens-Illinois for 25 years until his death October 2, 1994. The Schneringer's fourth child, Kay, has worked at Woodland Park Hospital since completing nurses training at Emanuel. She has three children, Clifton, Michelle and Bradley, from a prior marriage. In November 1993, she married Joe Vetaly. Kay drives to her job at Woodland Park Hospital each day from Grande Ronde.

Raymond Schneringer passed away January 29, 1983 in Portland, Oregon. Blanche Schneringer continues to live independently in the family home on Larch Mountain Road.

415

Perry Settlemier
Esther (Kincaid) Settlemier

Perry Settlemier purchased the store in "East" Corbett in April 1923, from George Chamberlain. He had some experience in the retail trade having owned a dry goods shop in Montavilla previously. In conducting that business, he provided classes that taught women to crochet, knit, sew, or other crafts. Perry was born March 11, 1884, in Sweet Home, Oregon. He married Esther Kincaid of Corbett, in April, 1919. Born October 27, 1898, she was raised on the Kincaid Place off Mershon Road, close to its intersection with the Columbia River Highway. Esther graduated from CHS in 1918, a member of the 3rd graduating class from the newly built CHS (that burned four years later). After the marriage, the couple moved to Woodland, Washington, where Perry worked in a logging business. While living in Woodland, the Settlemiers had a daughter, Blanche E., b. March 8, 1921. From Woodland, the family moved to Corbett.

The Settlemiers operated the store as a "Red and White" general store, and continued in the grocery and dry goods business thereafter. It drew customers from several near-by mills and the Settlemiers delivered groceries to Dodson, Troutdale and other points east of the Sandy River once a week. In 1935, Settlemier modernized his store by taking out part of the storeroom. In 1946, it was expanded along the east and south sides. With this expansion came the "cooling room," or lockers, a first for the area. The store was sold to Aaron Quinn in 1958. The Settlemiers were active members of the Corbett Christian Church, where Mrs. Settlemier was a charter member. Mr. Settlemier was among the founders of the Corbett Fire Department. While the store and community affairs took much of their time, both Perry and Esther loved to hunt and fish, and this was their principal recreational activity. Esther also enjoyed gardening and was a member of the Garden Club.

Blanche Settlemier attended Corbett Grade and CHS, graduating in 1939 as class valedictorian. In 1940 she met a young man from Alabama who had been sent to Oregon in June of that year after joining the Civilian Conservation Corp (CCC's). Jesse E. White was born in Texas, October 24, 1923, moved to Oklahoma at age six, then moved again to Alabama with his parents in 1936. According to Jesse, he "wanted to get out

416

Settlemier Store c1927

Settlemier's store, the Chamberlain home and the Bell garage are visible in this 1927 photo of 'East' Corbett.   Photo courtesy of Pat (Bramhall) Paget.

of Alabama" so took advantage of an opportunity to do so when it came along. Blanche and Jesse were married October 25, 1941.

Jesse White, drafted into the U.S. Army, entered the service in September 1943. After basic training, he volunteered for the paratroopers, and was sent to Fort Benning, Georgia, for training. After qualifying, he was assigned to the 550th Airborne Battalion, which was preparing to embark for the European Theater. His outfit was sent to Italy, and served as a reserve force as the allied armies advanced up the Italian peninsula toward Rome. When the 1st Airborne Task Force was formed for the invasion of Southern France, the 550th was attached along with similar units from Canada, England and France. The 1st landed about 8 miles inland from the invasion beaches near Lamuy, France. Jesse and many troopers in the 550th landed by glider, while other elements landed by parachute. Instead of an expected 90 German troops, the airborne invasion force encountered approximately ten times that number. In the ensuing battle, about three hundred of the opposing German force were killed, and about six hundred were captured. The 550th suffered just one casualty when the battalion's first sergeant was killed. After the initial landing, the 550th moved into the French Alps, conducting patrols and directing artillery fire. In November 1944, the unit was sent to England, supposedly on its way home.

However, the Germans launched a counter-offensive in the Ardennes, which quickly became known as the "Battle of the Bulge." Rather than returning to the States, the 550th Airborne found itself attached to the 17th Airborne Division, which was sent to help the beleaguered Allied Armies stem the German onslaught. Sent into action near the Belgium-France border, the 550th bore the brunt of an attack by a German Panzer division. When the 550th Commander called Division Headquarters for help, the staff officer responding said: "We're pulling out. Goodbye and good luck!" Of Jesse's company of about 90 men, only 30 survived their first (and last) day in combat on that front. When German Panzer tanks approached the building where Jesse and other members of his company sought refuge, an American medic captured earlier was sent forward to extend terms. Using a loudspeaker, the German tank commander said in excellent English: "Surrender or the building will be leveled." The emissary told the members of the company holed up therein, "They have the firepower to do it!" The Company Commander permitted the men to vote, and the outcome favored surrender. The alternative was certain death. During the engagement, Jesse suffered shrapnel wounds to his leg.

When Blanche received word that Jesse was missing in action, she decided to find a steady job. She applied for the position of Postmaster in Corbett, as Louis Arneson was resigning the position. She was appointed to the position in 1945. Meanwhile Jesse was marched into Germany as a prisoner-of-war. On the march, he served his captors in various ways, including doing K.P. for units in the field. When he peeled potatoes, he and his fellow captives were served the peelings – boiled. He was imprisoned in Stalag 13 for a short period of time, then moved to Stalag 14. During his confinement, his leg wounds were never attended to. After 103 days in captivity, he was freed when an English armored division overran the camp April 16, 1945. According to Jesse, the prisoners "scattered." He headed across the road to the headquarters of a Panzer division which had been based nearby, and garnered a few souvenirs, including some small ceramic models of tanks (4 types, including the Tiger, the Panther and two others) and of half-tracks (2 types). Jesse still has these models, which he treasures. He was sent to a hospital in England to have the shrapnel in his leg removed and to regain the 55 pounds he had lost while a prisoner. After Jesse recovered sufficiently, he was flown to the United States in June 1945, and was soon reunited with Blanche and his infant son.

Corbett Post Office Dedication c1975

The CHS chorus performed at the dedication of the new Corbett Post Office in 1975. Postmaster, Blanche (Settlemier) White.   Photo courtesy of the Pounder family.

Blanche continued in her job as Postmaster, and worked in the position for 33 years until she retired in 1978. She was Postmaster when Congressman Robert Duncan dedicated the new Corbett Post Office in 1975. Jesse found employment with Wagner Machinery, transferring to Wagner Mining Equipment after about 7 years. Hired as the first machinist at the firm, he progressed through the managerial ranks until he attained a supervisory position. Jesse retired after 33 years service to the Wagner companies.

Blanche and Jesse White had three children: Jesse T. "Tom", b. July 9, 1943; Jerald D. "Jerry", b. May 3, 1946; and Roger P., b. August 20, 1947. All of them attended Corbett schools. Tom married Carmen Staples, and they had one daughter. Tom passed away in California from complications of rheumatic fever and pneumonia. Jerry lives in Glendale, Arizona, and has two children. Roger is single, and still lives in Corbett.

Jesse White

Robert H. Seyler
Lucretia (Edwards) Seyler

The Seyler family moved from Oklahoma to Oregon in 1937, settling initially in Fairview. Robert Seyler was born in Iowa December 12, 1889. Lucretia 'Myrl' Edwards was born in Missouri, September 27, 1890. The couple married January 11, 1913, in Alva, Oklahoma. In 1941 they rented the Federspiel place on Seidl Road, where they lived until 1946. That year the family moved to a house that Mr. Seyler built at the corner of Hurt and Ogden Roads. He sold a 3-acre parcel to Walter Quier, who had helped him build his first house. The Seylers had four children: Edna H., b. October 7, 1914; Willa S. 'Sue,' b. November 18, 1917; Robert B., b. February 24, 1919; and Nettie L., b. September 3, 1923. All of the children were born in Alva, Oklahoma, which is where all except Nettie completed their education. Nettie completed her secondary school years at Gresham High School from which she graduated in 1942.

Myrl Seyler died February 2, 1956. After her death, Mr. Seyler sub-divided the property and built a 2nd house, which he sold. Eventually he built four houses on the original parcel he had purchased, and sold each of them as they were completed. He sold the family home in the early 60's, and moved to Wood Village. Mr. Seyler passed away in March 1970.

Edna Seyler had left home before her parents settled on the 'hill.' Sue Seyler married Ted Peetz, with whom she had three children, Ted, Penny and Kathy. Sue was widowed when her husband, Ted Peetz, died. After his death, she married Rankin Davis, and had another daughter, Elaine. Rankin and Sue purchased a home in Troutdale, which is where they lived while the children attended school. Robert Seyler was drafted into the U.S. Army, and participated in the D-Day invasion in Normandy. He served as a motorcycle scout, and was killed in action July 27, 1944 when his motorcycle hit a land mine.

Nettie Seyler married Sam Cox Jr., who came to Oregon with his parents in 1939. The Cox family also lived on Hurt Road, where they had located after moving from Springdale. Sam Jr. and Nettie Cox built a home on 2.5 acres on Ogden Road in which they lived for 12 years. They then bought a home on the corner of Woodard Road and the Columbia River Highway, where Nettie now lives. Nettie was working for Pacific Northwest Bell when she married Sam Cox. She retired from the

Rankin Davis and Sue Seyler Marriage

From L: Sam Cox, Rankin Davis, Sue Seyler, Edna (Seyler) Alexander and Nettie (Seyler) Cox.

Seyler Sisters

From L:, Edna Alexander, Nettie Cox and Sue Davis.

Photos courtesy of Nettie (Seyler) Cox.

Telephone Company in 1983 after 36 years with the Company (see "Sam K. Cox").

Nettie Cox

Raymond Smith
Wilma (Lucas) Smith

Raymond Smith, son of George H. and Anna M. Smith grew up in the Brower area (see "Descendants of George H.W. and Anna M. [Telton] Smith," *Pioneer History*). He attended Brower School, completing the 10th grade there but was short some credits, so entered CHS as a sophomore in 1932. Because of the delay, Raymond graduated in 1935 together with his sister, Wilma, and his future wife, Wilma Lucas. In the area in which Raymond grew up, logging and lumbering provided most of the jobs. He remembers taking a handcar belonging to the Bridal Veil Lumbering Company from Brower into Gordon Creek to go fishing. His first job after completing high school was in a logging camp. According to Raymond, he quit that job in order to return to Corbett and his "girl friend." He and Wilma Lucas married August 21, 1936.

Raymond started working at the Bridal Veil Lumbering Company, but a strike closed it down. He then went to work helping to lay water lines for the Corbett Water District from the newly established Gordon Creek source. He set a record when he dug 153 feet of ditch in one day on the line along Mershon Road. The ditch was 14 inches wide and 32 inches deep, so his effort would have filled one 10-yard dump truck and a second more than three-quarters full. Raymond said, "The boss was very particular and measured the ditch with a straight-edge to make certain it met the standard." He also helped carry 3 and 4-inch iron pipe into Gordon Creek for the pipeline coming from the water collection area. "It was hard work. Two men packed the pipe, one on each end. We moved it from shoulder-to-shoulder, then from hip-to-hip, then back to our shoulders until we reached the site. We packed pipe half a mile or more. After this experience I was pleased to get a job walking the picket line at the mill (Bridal Veil)." During the winter of 1936, Raymond worked for the company that salvaged the steel rails from the Bridal Veil Lumbering Company's railway lines. (It was likely sold as scrap iron to Japan.)

After Raymond and Wilma married, they moved into a home located on Hurlburt Road. The couple had three boys, Curtis, b. August 1, 1937, Albert, b. May 15, 1939 and Leroy, b. September 21, 1941. The youngsters completed elementary school at Springdale Grade. Each then enrolled at CHS with Curtis graduating in 1955, Albert in 1958 and Leroy in 1959. When their home burned in 1959, the family moved to a place (Milford Farm) on Littlepage Road, which they leased. Later Raymond bought the former Gebhardt place on Loudon Road and has lived there since.

After working at various jobs in the 30's, Raymond started logging just before World War II commenced. He hired three men and sold logs and cordwood. When the war started, he started working at the shipyard, but the work had not yet been organized well, and he left after about 3 months. "We just stood around. The (contractor) worked on a cost-plus basis, so he didn't mind." He resumed logging and has been involved in that field since. Though the original Smith property in the Brower area did not remain in the family, Raymond began buying property in that general area. He purchased more than a thousand acres from Multnomah County (sold for taxes), bought 160 acres from Bridal Veil Lumbering Company and 143 acres from the Coopey estate. He sold 70 acres of the latter to the State of Oregon, which wanted the property because it included Coopey Falls. He also bought 20 acres from Charlie Sutton and started acquiring land in Howard Canyon.

After Vern Lucas died in July 1945, Wilma and Raymond took over the operation of Columbia Telephone Company. Later they purchased the Company from Laura Lucas. At the time, the business had 138 customers served by 30 lines. Its territory reached from Multnomah Falls to Gordon Creek (south) and to the Stark Street Bridge and Woodard Hill (west). In 1945 Raymond put in a new type of lead-covered overhead line, but the wind whipped it causing the cover to crack, and water shorted the line. He next tried burying war-surplus shipboard cable, which worked fairly well. Soon thereafter, companies began producing underground cable, which was first used by Columbia Telephone in areas subject to the east wind. After the underground wires were installed, customers often times had phone service when the electric lines were down.

Raymond said, "The trouble with the telephone business is the busiest time is always during the worst weather." In 1950, when snowdrifts reached a depth of 25 feet in some areas, Raymond said they walked along drifts to repair lines. When the roads were plowed, sometimes packed snow and ice would hit and sever a line. As lines were placed underground, this type of problem no longer existed. Raymond told of other experiences during the placement (or replacement) of various lines. When a line was laid across Buck Creek to Murray Evans' place, the crew found a huge cottonwood tree about four feet in diameter that had been girdled by beaver. It was still standing, though only about 12 inches of the trunk remained for the animal to remove.

In February 1957, Columbia Telephone converted to a dial system (see "Roland C. Morgan"). Under a government-sponsored 'on-the-job' training program, Basil Lampert had been hired by Raymond to work for the Telephone Company. Raymond remarked, "Hiring Basil helped a lot. Because we were adding customers, it took money from our timber business to keep the Telephone Company going. With Basil taking care of the lines and switches. I could spend more time logging." Basil worked for Columbia Telephone for 17 years. Another employee was Mrs. Elizabeth Morgan, who took care of the office and switchboard until the advent of the dial system.

In 1972, Columbia Telephone merged with Cascade Utilities, Inc. Raymond said, "We were paying 11% interest on a loan from Stromberg-Carlson. Cascade had access to REA (federal government) money at 2%, which gave them a huge advantage." During Raymond and Wilma's ownership, the number of customers increased from 138 to more than 1100 when the merger took place. Because the company that had the right to extend service to Aims did not wish to do so, Columbia Telephone Company extended a line to that area.

Since the sale, Raymond has devoted himself exclusively to taking care of his timberlands and logging. Wilma Smith passed away in 1977. Currently, the Smiths log 1500+ acres of timber located in Hood River County and approximately 800 acres located in Howard Canyon. The former was obtained in a trade with the Forest Service for 1755 acres of timberland located in the scenic area, which Raymond and Rueben Lenske had accumulated after World War II. The latter was accumulated during the same period, starting with 20 acres purchased from Charlie Sutton. Raymond married Ruth Ellis July 27, 1978. Similarly to Raymond, she had lost her spouse of many years.

Of Raymond and Wilma's children, Curtis Smith married Rita Carpenter (see "Dewey Carpenter") and they have two children, Brian and Dana. After graduating from Portland State, Curtis worked in the produce business in Portland. Rita is a physical therapist working for a spinal specialist. Curtis and Rita live on Curtis Road between the Columbia River Highway and Smith Road. Brian and Dana attended Corbett schools, with Brian graduating from CHS in 1978 and Dana in 1980.

Albert Smith worked for the Telephone Company until the merger, when he was forced to go on disability because of eye problems. He married Lynn Houck and the couple had six children, Charles 'Albert,' Teresa, Mike, and triplets, Karl, Kory and Kristin. All attended Corbett schools, graduating from CHS in 1980, 1981, 1983 and 1987, respectively.

Leroy Smith married Sharon Rose and they had three children, Melanie, Jeffrey and Valerie. Melanie graduated from CHS in 1980, Jeffrey in 1981 and Valerie in 1986. Leroy, too, worked for the Telephone Company for a time, then purchased Pounder Oil Company. Later Leroy sold this business and purchased a ranch in Sparta and another place near Medical Springs. When he returned to this area to go into the logging business with his father, he kept 40 acres in Sparta. Presently, Leroy helps his father manage the extensive timber holdings of the family.

'Batch' plant at Corbett, Columbia River Highway construction.   Photo, the author.

Thomas J. Sommerville
Ruth (McCullough) Sommerville

Thomas Sommerville born June 29, 1914, was raised in Harrisburg, Oregon. He obtained a teaching certificate from Oregon Normal School in 1937, and attended the University of Oregon and Portland State University, where he earned a bachelor's and master's degree in education, respectively. He came to Corbett Grade School as a teacher in 1940. Ruth McCullough also came to Corbett Grade School in 1940 as fourth grade teacher. She had three years experience, a year in Eastern Oregon and two years in Hood River County, before coming to Corbett. Mr. Sommerville and Miss McCullough were married May 23, 1942. He was in the Army from 1942 to 1946 and served in the European Theater.

Upon his return, Thomas Sommerville resumed his career in education, teaching at Corbett and Orient before joining the Multnomah County Education Service District in 1954, appointed Assistant Superintendent. He was promoted to Deputy Superintendent, then became Superintendent, in which capacity he served until his retirement in 1979. After retiring, he became active in the Oregon Retired Educators' Association. He also served in a number of appointive positions, including the Governor's Task Force on School Funding Reform, the Governor's Conference on Aging, and the Governor's Commission on Senior Services. He also served in a number of capacities with the American Association of Retired Persons. He was active in the Masonic Order, The American Legion and the Elks Lodge.

Thomas and Ruth Sommerville had three children: H. Christine, b. July 24, 1953, J. Wiley, b. November 10 1952 and Timothy N., b. February 28, 1955. The children attended grade school at Corbett and Christine graduated from CHS in 1968. Both Wiley and Timothy graduated from Barlow High School. Christine has four children, Stephanie, Brian, Jennifer and Kortney. Wiley has two girls, Mary and Laura and timothy has 3 children, Ashley, Micheal and Anthony.

Ruth Sommerville taught at Corbett Grade School until 1946. She did not return to the teaching field until 1966, when she resumed teaching at Corbett. She stayed at Corbett for five years, then taught one-half year in Gresham before going to Cottrell, where she taught an additional 5 years. Thomas Sommerville passed away January 21, 1992. Ruth Sommerville continues to live in Corbett.

Ruth Sommerville, Grade 4

Ruth Sommerville, grade four teacher, and Principal George Lusby with her fourth grade class, 1943. Photos courtesy of Joan (Ellis) Benner.

Ruth Sommerville

Ruth (McCullough)
Sommerville

Latourell Falls footbridge over the Columbia River Highway c1916. Photo, the author.

Juichi Uyetake
Chise Uyetake

Both Juichi 'Harry' Uyetake and Chise Uyetake were born in Hiroshima, Japan, he November 25, 1884 and she, August 31, 1890. The Uyetakes came to East Multnomah County in 1913, first locating in a rental house on Henkle Road. In 1916, they purchased five acres on Mershon Road across the road from the Porter place. About a year later Harry purchased approximately 17 acres located on Mershon Road from the Mershon family. He moved his family into the house on the property in 1918. The main structure of the house (in which Shio Uyetake now lives) was built circa 1890. Harry and Chise Uyetake had five children: Shio, b. March 16, 1915; Kor, b. September 2, 1921; Fujie, b. December 28, 1922; June, b. June 18, 1925; and Mitzi, b. February 26, 1927.

Shio started grade school at Pleasant View on Wand Road, transferring to Corbett Grade School when Pleasant View closed in 1924. The other youngsters attended Corbett Grade School, from which each graduated. Shio, Kor and Fujie graduated from CHS in 1933, 1939 and 1940, respectively (before the Japanese were interred during World War II). The Uyetake children also attended the 'Japanese School,' which was located on the five-acre parcel the Uyetakes owned on Mershon Road, about one-half mile west of the home place. Japanese children living in the area attended this school once or twice a week, including a session on Saturdays. The students learned to read, write and speak the Japanese language. Other families whose children attended the school included the Matusubus, the Takeuchis, the Sakurais, the Nakashimadas, the Kondos and the Toyas. Teachers included Mr. Nakata and Mr. Fukuda, among others. Shio went on to attend the University of Washington, from which he graduated with a degree in Business Administration in 1937.

The Uyetakes grew vegetable crops and berries. During the 30's their berry crops included strawberries and boysenberries.They hired a number of area residents to pick for them including George, Clarence and Isabelle Mershon, Eva Knieriem and Norah Davis. Harry purchased seven acres immediately behind the Mershon residence at the corner of Lucas Road and Mershon Road; he also purchased thirteen acres on Lucas Road where the Baker family lived for a time. Thus, the family had accumulated approximately 42 acres before the war started in 1941. After Japan

428

Juichi 'Harry' Uyetake Family

From L, Fujie, June (in front of), Shio, Harry, Kor (behind), Mitzi and Chise Uyetake.
Photo courtesy of the Uyetake Family.

Uyetake Farm

The Uyetake farm looking east. Notice the Berney and Rogers homes in background.
Photo courtesy of the Uyetake Family.

attacked the United States fleet at Pearl Harbor as well as other outposts in the Pacific, the government required persons of Japanese ancestry (including U.S. citizens) to leave the area. After spending several months in a holding facility at the Pacific Livestock Exposition grounds, the Japanese were sent to 'relocation camps'. Authorities sent the Uyetake family to the Tulelake Camp in California.

Digging Out in 1937

From L, Harry, Fujie, Mitzi and June clear driveway after record snow in 1936-37.

Snowbound, 1937

Snowbound and abandoned automobiles on Mershon Road, 1936-37.

Photos courtesy of the Uyetake Family.

When the family was forced from the farm in 1942, the Uyetakes entrusted Louis Berney to take care of their property. In 1943, the family left Tulelake for a farm in Michigan. Juichi 'Harry' Uyetake died in Michigan in May 1944. Though they had an opportunity to remain in Michigan after the war, Chise Uyetake, Shio, Fujie, June and Mitzi returned to their home in East County. Shio took over the operation of the farm and farmed the place until 1961. During this period he raised berries and

House on the Uyetake Place

From L, Harry Uyetake, Chise Uyetake, Shio Uyetake, Yoshiko Kuwabara, Joe Kuwabara. Note: This home was built c1890.

Uyetake Home After Remodeling c 1940

The Uyetake Home in 1940 after it had been remodeled – view from Mershon Road.
Photos courtesy of the Uyetake Family.

vegetables. Shio sold berries to Snider Farms and then to Scenic Fruit. The other crops, cauliflower, cabbage, lettuce and broccoli, were sold to S.T. Produce and Birds Eye Foods, which had developed a market for frozen vegetables.

Shio Uyetake married Nobuko Mukai (born in Fresno, California July 27, 1921) September 17, 1950. The couple had four children: Arlene,

431

Shio Uyetake Family

Rear, From L, Shio, Arlene and Nobuko. Front,
Donna, Verne and Lyle (on his mother's lap).
Photo courtesy of Shio Uyetake.

b. August 2, 1951; Donna, b. August 22, 1954; Vern, b. December 26, 1956; and Lyle, b. December 1, 1960. All attended Corbett Grade and High School, with Arlene graduating from CHS in 1969, Donna in 1972, Verne in 1975 and Lyle in 1979. Arlene graduated from the Oregon College of Education (now Western Oregon University), but did not teach. She and her former husband, Vance Dunlop, built a home on the 7-acre parcel adjacent (west) of the Mershon place mentioned above, which was later sold. She has two children, Tara and Beth, now lives in Sandy and works for the US Bank. Her daughters attend Sandy High School.

Donna graduated from Portland State University, married Frank McConnell, has a son, Mark, and lives in Issaquah, Washington. Verne graduated from Oregon State University in 1979, has not married, lives at home and works as a journalist and photographer for the *Lake Oswego Review*. He also does free lance photography. Lyle attended Oregon State University from which he graduated in 1983. He married Sue Ireland, works at the Stanford University Laboratory and lives in Redwood City, California.

Kor, who did not return to Oregon after the war, completed college at the Missouri College of Mines and worked in the mining industry in Colorado after the war. He married Mary Hishinuma and had two boys, Sidney and John. Kor passed away several years ago. Fujie married Bill Furumasu and had two boys, Stacey and Russell. She now lives in Green Acres, Washington. June married Kiyo Ogawa and had one son, Steve. She now lives in Altadena, California. Mitzi married Tosh Okada and had two children, Kerrie and Dale. Kerrie Okada graduated from Oregon State University and now lives on Littlepage Road. Mitzi lives in Los Altos, California. Chise Uyetake died February 6, 1958, living her final years at the farm on the 'hill.'

Shio reported that farming became unprofitable in the late 50's, so he decided to take a job with a more certain income. He went to work for Kubla Khan Company, which produced canned and frozen Chinese foods. He worked for the company approximately 20 years, retiring in 1981. He also worked part-time for Kwan Ying's Kitchen as a cashier and deliveryman. Nobuko Uyetake started working at Edgefield after the children were in school, and worked there until the facility closed. She transferred to the Juvenile Justice Center where she worked until her retirement in 1984.

Pleasant View School c1922.   Photo courtesy of Shio Uyetake.

Ivo Van Speybrock
Leona (Neyrinck) Van Speybrock

Ivo Van Speybrock, born in Belgium, April 4, 1858, after immigrating to the United States, moved from Portland to Corbett in 1890. His wife, Leona Neyrinck, a native of Belgium b. May 6, 1864, also immigrated to the US. The couple married in Portland sometime before the turn of the century, exact date unknown. They settled on 30 acres across what is now the Columbia River Highway from the eastern terminus of Mershon Road. The Speybrocks had five children, Frank, b. 1890's, Mary, b. 1890's, Emma, b. July 30, 1900, and twins, Leon 'Johnny' and Leona, b. September 28, 1903, all born at home in Corbett. Theresa Wand served as midwife for the birth of the twins. The children attended Taylor Grade School. The mother, Leona Van Speybrock, passed away February 2, 1919. After the death of his wife, Ivo sold the farm, 15 acres to Cecil Pounder (bordering Smith Road) and 15 acres to John Burbee (bordering the highway). Ivo visited relatives in the place of his birth, Belgium, before he died in 1929.

Of the children, Frank married Jessie Maybee. The couple lived on a farm in Gresham, where they raised vegetables and later, nursery stock. Jessie, one of five children in the Maybee family (Edna, Jessie, William, Albert and Wesley) grew up on the family place located on Bell Grade (nearly directly across from the Bates family place). Frank and Jessie had one child, a son, Ernie, who attended Gresham schools. The oldest Van Speybrock girl, Mary, married Tom Northway. Tom operated a store in Springdale (started by his father) and owned a shop with Roy Parson for a time. An advertisement in the 1926 *Cohimore* reads: "Parsons and Northway, Garage and Blacksmithing, Machine Work of all Kinds." Later Tom Northway worked as a blacksmith for Multnomah County, first at the shop at Corbett, then at Vance Pit, where he was working when he retired. The Northways lived on the family place on Northway Road. Mary and Tom Northway had two children, Juanita A. (Mack) and Gloria J. (Robinson) (see "William W. Northway," *Pioneer History*). Both completed elementary school at Springdale Grade. Juanita graduated from CHS in 1935.

Emma Van Speybrock married Harry C. Rickert in 1918. Harry opened a garage in Aurora and assembled Model-T Fords for sale in the North-

Leona (Neyrinck) and Ivo Van Speybrock

The Van Speybrocks moved from Portland to Corbett in 1890. Both were born in Belgium.

Photos courtesy of Bob Van Speybrock.

Northway Family

From L.: Gloria, Mary (Van Speybrock), Tom and Juanita Northway.

west. In the early 20's, the Rickerts built a home and a garage in Corbett. In 1926, they enlarged the garage and added a restaurant (west of the garage), which Emma operated for many years. Harry Rickert also fished commercially on the Columbia River. The Rickerts purchased the family place on Rickert Road where he farmed a number of years, first milking a small dairy herd and later, raising beef cattle. Harry and Emma purchased the former Ellis place, the Arrington home and Judge Lannguth's place (all on Larch Mountain Road). Harry and Emma had one son, Alvin (see "Elihu Rickert" and "Descendants of Elihu G. Rickert," *Pioneer History*).

Van Speybrock Twins

Leona and Leon 'Johnny' Van Speybrock c1905. Photo courtesy of Bob Van Speybrock.

Alvin went into the service before completing high school. After World War II, he went into the logging business with his father. They logged the family holdings and did contract logging as well. Harry Rickert passed away November 15, 1961. Emma lived at the former Arrington home for many years. She passed away March 1, 1995.

Alvin Rickert married Maxine Nichols, b. May 4, 1922. They had two children, Robert H., b. December 18, 1941 and Sandra, b. June 7, 1944. Maxine (Nichols) Rickert passed away in August 1946. Robert married Sandra Heminger and they had two children, Cindy A., and Robert married Angelina Cerrutti, who graduated from CHS in 1991.

Alvin's daughter, Sandra (Redfern), now lives on the former Ellis place on Larch Mountain Road. Her son, Todd (CHS '86), lives at the Arrington place and her other son, Torey (CHS '90) lives on the Ellis place adjacent to his mother's home. Alvin left Corbett to become a rancher in Paisley, Oregon.

Leona Van Speybrock married Cecil J. Pounder. Cecil went into the construction business and built several structures in the area. His first may have been a home he built for Roy Emily in Corbett (north of the highway). Among the buildings he constructed: a home for he and Leona on 15 acres of the Speybrock place, the "new" Hurlburt School and the Bridal Veil Lodge (now operated as a 'Bed and Breakfast' by Laurel Slater). He also took up flying and operated an aviation school, Pounder Flying Service, at Portland Airport in the early 30's. An advertisement in the 1930 *Cohimore* states: "Learn Flying (from) the Ground Up with Pounder Flying Service, one-half mile East of Parkrose – Passenger and Taxi Flights." Cecil and Leona had three children, June, Kathleen and James. They moved to Spokane, Washington, which is where they raised their family.

Rickert's Garage c1925

Rickert's Garage in Corbett. Albert Soderstrom talks to Si Chamberlain, right.   Photo courtesy of the Pounder family.

Rickert's Garage, the Corbett Café and CHS

This aerial view shows Rickerts garage and café just west of Pounder Truck Service, CHS and other buildings in Corbett.
Photo courtesy of the Pounder family.

Johnny Van Speybrock fished commercially, operating a gillnet boat for the Reeds. (Johnny pointed out to the author a place where he 'hung up' while fishing one time as we proceeded west on I-80 (now I-84). The locale was east of the freeway bridge over the Sandy about one-half mile, at a point where the Columbia must now be nearly a mile farther north. Johnny also worked at the Cameron Hogg Mill in Aims during his earlier days.

Viola M. Pye was born May 27, 1910, in Portland. She and Johnny Van Speybrock married December 22, 1927. They first lived in a small

437

Johnny Van Speybrock

John Van Speybrock, Board Member, Corbett School District. '47 Cohimore Photo courtesy of David Rees.

home across from the former Emily place (now across from the new Corbett Grade School} on the Columbia River Highway. During the depression Johnny managed Frank C. Riggs 'Dutch Bulb Garden,' located just west of George Mershon's place on the highway. The family moved into the home and Johnny took care of the "daffodils, tulips, iris, delphiniums, lilies and field budded roses" advertised in the 1931 *Cohimore*. In 1937, Johnny went to work for the Multnomah County Road Department where he worked for 29 years, principally as a truck driver. Leon 'Johnny' Van Speybrock passed away November 2, 1993. He is interred at the Mountain View Cemetery in Corbett.

Johnny and Viola had two sons, Donald V., b. January 27, 1931, and Robert L., b. May 17, 1933. Both attended grade and high school at Corbett, Donald graduating from CHS in 1948 and Robert 'Bob' in 1952. Donald then attended Oregon State College, graduating with a degree in engineering. He married Shirley Molton, and they had five children, Ron, Don, Rich and twins, Cindy and Becky. He recently retired from Wah Chang metals, where he worked for a number of years as production manager, and lives in Albany.

Bob worked for Toot Evans in bulbs and other crops during summers while he attended CHS. After he graduated, he went to work for Multnomah County, where he spent 34 years before retiring. Bob married Gloria Maybee (daughter of William) and they adopted two children, Lee, b. June 18, 1964, and David, b. June 23, 1967. Bob and Gloria purchased property once owned by Peter Van-de-Kerkhover and Leonardes de-Witte, which lies between Bell Grade and the Columbia River Highway near the eastern end of Bell Grade. The two Dutch natives sold portions of their land to Hugh Reeves (1911), Hattie (Graham) Carter (1911) and William Keppers and Pete Maykoskie (1921). Bob bought his piece from Gertrude Keppers, heir of the latter two. Gloria Van Speybrock passed away in September 1976. Lee Van Speybrock was age 12 and David, age 9.

438

Viola Van Speybrock

Viola Van Speybrock wheels an old Fordson about the Rigg's place. Note the bulb shed in the background. Photos courtesy of Bob Van Speybrock.

Bob Van Speybrock

Bob Van Speybrock displays a fine catch of trout.

Joyce Hanks, born in Corning, Iowa, June 11, 1941 came to East County with her parents in 1943. After graduating from CHS in 1959, she worked for Snider Packing and the Gresham Berry Growers. She then worked for Jantzen Knitting Mills until her marriage in 1977. During the summers of '71, '72 and '73, she managed a kitchen for Arctic Missions (now InterArctic Ministries) in Alaska. Joyce and Bob Van Speybrock married July 4, 1977. Joyce then helped raise the boys, both of whom attended Corbett schools, Lee graduating from CHS in 1983, David in 1985.

439

Auda Venable
Hazel (Hogan) Venable

The Venable family moved from Missouri to Corbett in 1948. Both Auda and Hazel were born in Doniphan, Missouri, he on June 3, 1912, and she on September 25, 1911. At the time of the move, the Venables had four children: Oral, b. January 4, 1931; Lavada, b. July 2, 1932; Juanita, b. June 21, 1934; and Carleton, b. September 1, 1936. Oral had completed school in Missouri and did not attend school in Corbett. Lavada enrolled at CHS as a junior, Juanita as a freshman and Carleton started at Corbett Grade School as a 7th grade student. According to Juanita, the move was a "traumatic experience for us, changing schools, leaving friends and relatives," but "adjusting to our new community was much easier than we had anticipated. We soon had new friends and a great place to finish our school years."

Juanita said she enjoyed "the small school atmosphere, the school plays, the good basketball teams" and even "picking strawberries with all my friends." Auda Venable worked at the Reynolds aluminum plant in Troutdale. Hazel Venable started working for the school district as a cook at Corbett Grade School, then transferred to the high school where she worked until she retired. All the students she served have fond memories of the good food she prepared as well as her pleasant disposition.

Oral Venable married Beverly Noel (CHS Class of 1951) and they had a daughter, Kathleen. Oral and Beverly divorced and he remarried. Oral had a son, Rod, by this second marriage. Lavada graduated from CHS in 1950. She married Jack MacFarland and the couple lived on Hurlburt Road for many years. They had two girls, Glenda and Kelly. Both girls attended Corbett Grade School and Glenda attended Corbett High School, graduating in 1972. The family moved to Gresham where Lavada and her husband now live.

Juanita Venable graduated from CHS in 1952. She married Joseph Mount and they had a daughter, Carla. Juanita's husband died April 12, 1976. She now lives in Vancouver, Washington. Carleton Venable graduated from CHS in 1955. He married Iris Stepper, who was living in Portland at the time. She was born in Yakima, Washington, February 18, 1940 and she also attended school in Yakima. The couple made their

Auda and Hazel Venable

Auda and Hazel Venable celebrate their 50th wedding anniversary.
Photo courtesy of Iris Venable.

The Carlton and Iris Venable Family

From L, Shelly, Iris and Carlton Venable at home.
Photo courtesy of Iris (Stepper) Venable.

home on Henkle Road and had a daughter, Shelly, b. March 26, 1962. Shelly graduated from CHS in 1980. Carleton Venable passed away September 9, 1993. Iris continues to make her home on Henkle Road.

Hazel Venable retired from her job with Corbett School District in 1973. She passed away November 9, 1987. Her husband, Auda Venable, retired from the aluminum plant in 1977. He died December 13, 1993.

Juanita Mount

441

Walter E. Vockert
Marie (Loos) Vockert

Walter E. Vockert was born in Bloicherhode, near Nordhausen in the Hartz Mountain area of central Germany, July 8, 1901. He was educated in Germany, completing an agricultural vocational program of the German educational system, and managed a farm enterprise in Germany in the 1920's. There were several reasons why Mr. Vockert left Germany. He was the youngest child in his family and customs favored the eldest. Germany suffered through a period of horrendous inflation in the early 20's. Finally, the United States encouraged European immigrants with special skills to come to the States. Therefore, Mr. Vockert decided to emigrate in 1928 and came to Portland as his sister had located here previously. His first job in Portland was with a lumber company working on the green chain.

In 1929, Marie Loos, who had grown up on a farm in Heuttengesses, Germany, near Hanau and Frankfurt on the Main, emigrated from Germany to join her fiancée in Portland. Marie was born May 24, 1904. Walter and Marie married December 1, 1929. They lived in Portland until an opportunity arose in 1933 for both to go to work for Fairview Farms in Troutdale. While the job for Mr. Vockert was much more in keeping with his educational background, his employer did little to take advantage of his specialized knowledge. For the next eight years, Walter worked in the dairy's milk house, while Marie cooked for the crew. Mr. Vockert had one day off per month, while Mrs. Vockert worked every day. As Mrs. Vockert remarked concerning the depression era, one "had to be satisfied with little." At least, she said, "We had jobs."

In April 1942, the Vockerts moved to Corbett. They found a farm to their liking, and purchased the Emily Place on Littlepage Road, located between Loudon and Rickert Roads. They quickly established a prize Guernsey dairy herd there, and the farm has been in the family since. The Vockerts raised two sons on the farm, Walter E. Jr., b. February 11, 1931, and Karl, b. January 16, 1936. Walter Jr., who had started grade school at Fairview Elementary, entered Corbett Grade School during his 5th grade year. Karl started at Corbett Grade the next fall and both boys completed their grade and high school years at Corbett. Meanwhile, Walter and Marie continued to improve their dairy herd, and many of their ani-

Walter Vockert

Walter Vockert, CHS sophomore, 1947. Cohimore photo courtesy of David Rees.

Karl Vockert at CHS

Karl Vockert (left) with Don Woodruff and Jackie Beatty at CHS. Photo courtesy of Nona (Schneringer) Layton.

mals set production records, garnering honors at both the Multnomah County and Oregon State Fairs. Both Walter Jr. and Karl were active in 4-H activities, and exhibited their animals at these fairs, also. As the Vockerts built their herd, they remodeled the barn and the milk handling equipment, so that milk went from the cow to the cooling room without being touched by human hands.

Mr. Vockert was renowned for the various sausages he made in the "German" style. His sons' friends tasted (many probably for the first time) Liverwurst, Thuringer, Weinerwurst, Bockwurst, Kochwurst, Bratwurst, Blutwurst, Summerwurst, Kupfkasse and Kupswurst and other delicacies. Any friend of one of their sons was welcome in the Vockert home. They shall always be remembered for their hospitality to these visitors (who were youngsters at the time). A constant admonition to these young people was this: "Go to college – get an education." (The author is grateful for the many things he learned from the Vockerts, but most particularly for this advice.) Mr. Vockert made excellent wines from grapes and berries, which were served to friends and neighbors.

The Vockerts set an outstanding example for others. They worked long hours on the farm, where Mr. Vockert was able to put his specialized knowledge to work in building an exceptional dairy herd. The Vockerts were exceptionally thrifty, nothing being wasted. But most of

Walt Vockert at Washington State University

From L, Colleen Mershon, Walt and Jan Vockert at Pullman, Washington c1960.
Photo, the author.

all, they will be remembered for their interest in and hospitality to their neighbors, friends and, most particularly, to friends of their sons.

After graduating from high school, Walter Jr. attended Oregon State College, graduating in 1953. After spending two years in the Air Force, including a few months in Morocco, he resumed his education at Oregon State, starting a five-year program leading to a doctoral degree in Veterinary Medicine. The requirements led him to complete one year of "pre-DVM" work at Oregon State, followed by four years at Washington State University in Pullman. Walter Jr. married Janet 'Jan' Lee Ireland in Portland, August 24, 1957. Jan was born in Portland March 13, 1936. She accompanied her husband to Pullman where he completed requirements for his Doctor of Veterinary Medicine degree.

After completing his education, Walter worked at the Gresham Animal Clinic with Dr. Powers for several years before starting his own practice in 1969. He and Jan worked diligently to build his practice at the Halsey East Animal Clinic, located near 162nd and N.E. Halsey Street, until her untimely death December 23, 1996. Walter and Jan have two children, Stephen P. "Steve," b. September 17, 1959, and Susan M., b. August 21, 1962. Steve followed in his father's footsteps by becoming a veterinarian, is associated with his father in the clinic, and lives with his father. Susan graduated from the University of Oregon with a degree in geriatrics, and works in that field in Portland, where she lives.

Karl, after graduating from CHS in 1954, also attended Oregon State, graduating in 1958. After graduation, he went directly into the U.S. Air

444

Force. He took flight training and was assigned to intelligence duty in the U-2 overflight program. After four years active duty, he was assigned to the Air Force Active Reserve at the Portland Air Base in 1962. Karl married Mary L. Keptlinger of Seattle, Washington, on April 20, 1973. She had two children, Michael and Patricia Hoyt, from a previous marriage. She and Karl had three birth children, twin boys, J.W. "Hans" and S.K. "Fritz," b. October 29, 1974, and a daughter, M.K. "Trina," b. June 24, 1976. Karl and Mary divorced in 1981, but the children remained with Karl on the farm. Karl worked for Emery Air Freight for a time, then established his own airfreight forwarding business. Following his father's death March 3, 1977, Karl took over the operation of the farm. His mother helped with the rearing of Karl's children, all of whom attended Corbett schools. The dairy herd had been sold in 1964, and the Vockerts raised beef cattle. Karl now raises cattle and hogs. He continued in the Reserves as an intelligence officer until January 16, 1994, when he retired with the rank of Colonel. Mrs. Vockert, after recovering from recent heart surgery (1997), moved to the Heritage Village in Gresham. Unfortunately, she fell and broke her hip, an unfortunate accident from which she never fully recovered. Marie Vockert passed away March 28, 1998. *Marie Vockert*

Toot Evans cultivating his daffodil crop.   Photo courtesy of Sandra Evans.

James C. Wilson
Myra I. (Miller) Wilson

James Clarence Wilson was born October 9, 1871, in Platteville, Wisconsin, son of Erwin Merrick Wilson, a native of New York, and Laura Augusta Powers, also of New York. His mother died when he was about two years of age. Soon thereafter, his father brought James and his older brother, Delos (Del), to California, settling in the Bay area. James met Myra Isabella Miller, from Latourell, Oregon, who had accompanied her parents to California, and the couple married March 22, 1893, in Tulare, CA. Myra was the daughter of William H. and Anna J. (Schermerhorn) Miller of Latourell, Oregon. William was a native of New York, as was his wife, but Myra had been born in Illinois, April 13, 1870. The Miller family had come to Oregon from California in 1881, purchasing a place on what is now Mannthey Road. (see "W.H. Miller," *Pioneer History*). James and Myra remained in Tulare, California, until 1899, where she gave birth to their first four children: Laura A., b. January 2, 1894; Bessie A., b. June 13, 1895; Olive G., b. March 3, 1897; and Delos E., b. March 22, 1899. While in Tulare, James worked as a clerk in a grocery store operated by R.T. McMillan. Mr. McMillan wrote a recommendation for him when the family left for Oregon:

Tulare, California   May 10, 1899

To Whom It May Concern:

    This is to certify that the bearer, Mr. J.C. Wilson, has been known to me for a time of years and I have found him to be both honest and industrious and any confidence reposed in him will not be betrayed.

/s/ R.T. McMillan, Grocer

In 1899, the Wilson family moved to Latourell, Oregon, to live on the Miller Place. They had seven more children after the move: Louis A., b. February 22, 1901; Ethel M., b. November 20, 1903; Florence I., b. February 19, 1906; Raymond L., b. February 3, 1908; Clarence H., b. March 31, 1910; Woodrow M., b. August 6, 1912; and William D., b. October 24, 1913. Each of the children started school at the Springfield 'Egypt' School on Loudon Road, from which the older siblings graduated. The younger children attended there until the family moved to Springdale in 1919. Before the Millers sold their 180-acre place to the

446

Erwin Wilson with his Sons

Erwin Wilson with his two sons, Delos (L) and James.
Photo, the author.

Miller Home

The Miller home on 180 acres, located at the end of (now) Mannthey Road. This home remained until Murray and Stella Evans replaced it in 1949.   Photo courtesy of Stella Evans.

James C. and Myra I. Wilson

James Clarence and Myra Isabelle (Miller) Wilson shortly after their marriage in Tulare, California.   Photos, the author.

Wilson Children c1899

From L, Laura, Olive and Bessie Wilson in 1899, the year Myra (Miller) Wilson returned with her family to Oregon.

James Wilson at Palmer

James Wilson (seated on the log) working with the 'crosscut sawyers,' 'barkers' and yarding crew of Bridal Veil Lumbering Company.
Photo courtesy of Bertha MacKay..

Ihrkes, the Wilsons had moved to an 80-acre place they purchased on Loudon Road across from the Gebhardt family.

When the family came to Oregon, James 'Curly' Wilson worked at the Palmer Mill. In 1902, a fire swept through the Larch Mountain area. When that fire spread, the Wilson children were told, "Get ready, you're going to have to fight fire." Each child old enough was given a bucket of water and a gunny (burlap) sack, and told to put out any spot fires that started. According to Laura Wilson, the fire "roared down Trapper Creek Canyon like a freight train." The Miller house was surrounded by meadow, a factor that gave the firefighters a chance to save it. A stump in the meadow suddenly burst into flames, and the smoke was nearly intolerable, but the family saved the house. At one point a basket of wet clothes sitting on the porch started to burn. One person worked on the roof until the danger passed, wetting it down with buckets of water.

James worked at other mills including the Gebhardt Mill on Trapper (Buck) Creek. He also farmed, did custom work for other farmers, and worked on the Columbia River Highway when it was under construction. The custom work involved baling hay using a horse-powered baler. A team of horses drove a sweep, which powered a plunger to compact the hay into bales. The hay was forked into a hopper from a nearby haystack. 'Boards' were inserted at intervals to form the bales, and a 'tie-er'

449

Latourell Band

The Latourell band, early 1900's. Curly Wilson is second from right, front. Second from left, front, may be one of the Knieriem family.   Photo, the author.

inserted baling wire through the holes provided in the 'boards' to hold the bales together. Each bale was tied, weighed, tagged, tallied and stacked. The going rate was $1.50 to $2.00 per ton, and the daily goal was 10 tons. In addition to James Wilson, the baling crew was composed of his sons, Del, Louis, Ray or Henry, at various times. Wilson's ability to accomplish repairs in the field to get the baler going after it broke down earned him the sobriquet, "Haywire Wilson."

When Wilson worked on the Columbia River Highway, he provided a team of horses, for which he received $2.50 per day, and he was also paid $2.50 per day for his labor. His team pulled a "Fresno," which was a scraper to move dirt. It was equipped with a "Johnson" bar for control. The Fresno required two men to operate it: James drove the team and a second man used the Johnson bar to direct the scraper and dump the dirt. Sometimes the family's income was supplemented by gathering "chitum," the bark of the cascara buckthorn tree. Curly directed his children to strip bark from buckthorn trees. It was sacked and apparently sold, but the children complained that they "never saw any of the money" for their work.

In 1918, Curly and his son, Del, purchased a milk route from Ben Bruger. They bought a new Maxwell truck to haul the milk, which was picked up from local dairy farms in 10-gallon cans (5-gallon cans for cream) and transported to Portland for processing. They purchased a second truck, a Winther, from Wentworth and Irwin early in 1919. Del was the principal driver, though others pitched in to help if needed. Unfortunately, Del drowned while swimming in the Sandy River at Big Bend on July 4, 1919. The following winter, the Wilsons sold the place on Loudon Road to the Charles Lofstedt family. They had purchased the grocery store owned by Tom Northway in Springdale, and the family moved there between Christmas and the New Year (1919-1920). The family's belongings were moved from the place on Loudon to Springdale by horse-drawn sled over ice and snow covered roads. The winter of 1919-20 was quite severe, with the Columbia River Highway through Springdale being closed about two weeks because of drifting snow and cold weather. James had past experience in the grocery business in California, so the move seemed logical at the time.

After the move, the Wilson children still living at home attended Springdale Grade School. The older girls, Laura, Bessie, Olive 'Ollie' and Ethel, had completed or started high school in Portland, earning their board and room working as "family helpers," which made it possible for them to attend high school. Laura had graduated from Lincoln High School, as did her younger sister, Bessie. Ollie graduated from Franklin High School, and Ethel was attending Washington High School at the time the family moved. Ethel enrolled at CHS as a junior. Her younger siblings were still in grade school. Meanwhile, Curly operated the grocery store that was located on the south side of the Columbia River Highway just east of its intersection with Lucas Road. However, the business did not prosper. Ethel and Ray maintained it couldn't have done well "with the kids helping themselves to all the candy they could eat!" Ted Berney said the Wilson kids would give him a candy bar in exchange for a ride on his bicycle. Whatever the cause, Mr. Wilson decided to sell the grocery store and the milk route. Both were sold to George Atkinson, who operated both businesses for many years thereafter.

After the store was sold, the Wilson family rented the Bancroft Place, which was located on the Columbia River Highway about a half- mile east of Springdale. Curly worked for the Multnomah County Road Department under Al Woodward during this period of time. In November 1921, a severe ice storm hit the area, causing much damage. The ice was

Four Generations

From L, Myra (Miller) Wilson, William H. Miller (holding Elda Mershon) and Laura (Wilson) Mershon.

Photo, the author.

6 inches or more thick in many places. Prune orchards were wiped out overnight, fir trees toppled or lost their tops, and deciduous trees split or broke. Ray said the family obtained enough wood from damaged trees to last for the next two years. Florence and Ray were high school students when CHS burned July 3, 1922. Consequently, they and the other students attended school at the Grange Hall, which served as the "high school" the school year of 1922-23. The fall of 1923, students and teachers moved to the new building on the south side of the highway, which building is still in use today (1999).

In 1926, Louis Wilson and his wife, Gladys, purchased a ranch in Idaho. In 1928, an adjacent ranch was for sale, and the Wilsons decided

Myra Wilson and Family

Myra (Miller) Wilson (center) with her surviving children. Rear, from L: Ray, Louis, Woodrow, Henry and Bill; Front, Florence, Bessie, Ethel, Laura and Ollie.

Photo, the author.

to buy it. After the purchase, they moved to the ranch with the two youngest boys, Henry and Bill. Both ranches were located near Council, Idaho. Woodrow (Woody) Wilson had accompanied his older brother, Louis, to Idaho earlier. The purchase came at an inopportune time as the depression hit in 1929 and both ranching and farming became losing propositions, particularly with a debt to repay. By 1934, the Wilsons had no alternative except to get what they could for the ranch. They traded their equity for a Model A Ford and used the vehicle to return to Oregon. Bill accompanied them, but Henry and Woody stayed in Idaho.

The Wilsons lived on the Mershon Place for a short time, moved to the Hanneman Place east of Corbett and finally rented a place from Roy Emily across the highway from CHS. During the 30's, James worked at odd jobs as his health permitted. He worked on the horse seine at Rooster Rock operated by the Kruckmans during fishing season. When Henry and Bill went to work at Weatherly farms the Wilsons moved to the large Weatherly house on Christensen Road.

Weatherly Farm House

Weatherly farm home located on Christensen Road.
Photo courtesy of Carlos Anderson.

James Clarence Wilson died January 9, 1941, in Springdale. All of his life he had enjoyed music and played several instruments. His favorite was the violin, which he played for his own enjoyment as well as for the enjoyment of his neighbors at local dances or other events. After his death, Myra Isabella Wilson lived with her son, Louis, or her daughter, Florence, for much of the remainder of her life. Arlene Marble said Myra Wilson once told her, "During my life I've made enough milk gravy to float a battleship." With a family of 13 hearty eaters, the remark is understandable. She died in Portland August 11, 1949.

Laura Wilson enrolled at Springfield Grade School in 1900 and graduated in 1908. She had vivid memories of the fire that swept down Trapper Creek from the east when she was a young girl. She didn't remember the exact year, but it had to be 1902. Given a pail of water and a gunnysack, she was instructed to put out any small fires that kindled. The experience must have terrified her as she often talked about the experience. Laura did not immediately continue on to high school after completing grade eight. She did enroll at Lincoln High School in Portland when her younger sister, Bessie, started, probably in 1909. She boarded with different families in Portland while attending high school. She stayed with the King family one year and with the Yuan (Dairy) family another. The Yuans owned a fleet of wagons that distributed milk throughout the city. She earned her keep by working as a housekeeper and by taking care of the family's children. Upon her graduation from Lincoln, she received a diploma and a teaching certificate. The family with whom she was stay-

Laura Wilson **Bessie Wilson** **Olive Wilson**

Laura Wilson, Lincoln High School graduate, 1914.

Bessie Wilson, Lincoln High School graduate 1914.

Olive 'Ollie' Wilson, 'mother's helper,' Portland, 1914. Photos, the author.

ing offered to help her obtain a teaching position, but she declined, saying years later that she "was too shy." After graduating she worked for George and Virgie Chamberlain on Evans Road as a housekeeper. She married George 'Jum' Mershon December 15, 1915 (see "George Mershon").

Bessie Wilson attended Springfield 'Egypt' Grade School for 8 years (1901-1909). In order to complete high school, she boarded with families in Portland, exchanging child care and maid service for room, board and expenses. She graduated from Lincoln High School and received a teaching certificate in 1914. In the fall of 1914, she obtained a teaching position at Springfield and found one of her 1st grade pupils was her younger brother, Ray. She taught just one year at 'Egypt,' then moved to Modesto, CA, to stay with relatives. Two aunts, Florence (Miller) Newell and Jessie (Miller) Knieriem lived in Modesto. Her grandmother, Mrs. Miller, was also in Modesto at the time. Bessie continued her teaching career in California. She taught at Livingston, California, among other locales.

Bessie married George A. Warth of Akron, Ohio, in 1917. He was in the U.S. Army, and the couple met in California. They had a son, Raymond, b. July 19, 1918, in San Francisco. Bessie divorced Mr. Warth and resumed her teaching career. She enrolled at San Francisco State

Mignon and Carlos Anderson

Mignon and Carlos Anderson in San Francisco, 1929.
Photos courtesy of Carlos Anderson.

Teachers' College in order to complete requirements for a California Certificate. She married Michael Powers, a Canadian émigré who worked as an automobile mechanic in San Francisco. Later they moved to San Rafael, California, and worked in motel management. After World War II they purchased a combination trailer court/motel in Weott, California. When the Eel River flooded in 1964, they lost the business as well as most of their personal possessions.

Bessie's son, Raymond, often came to Oregon as a teenager, staying with his Aunt Laura Mershon. He also stayed with his grandparents in Idaho for a period of time in the early 30's. In 1940, he enlisted in the Marine Corps. He was sent with the 1st Marine Division to Guadacanal in 1942. As he and three other marines were stringing telephone wire on the battlefield, a mortar round landed among them, killing his three comrades instantly. Raymond was evacuated from the field and lived for about ten days before succumbing to his wounds on Thanksgiving Day, 1942. His death was a severe blow to his mother, and one from which she never truly recovered. Bessie died May 3, 1980, in Portland, Oregon. Her husband, Mike Powers passed away shortly thereafter.

Olive 'Ollie' Wilson attended Springfield 'Egypt' Grade School (1903-1911). Following the example of her two older sisters, she boarded with families in Portland, but attended Franklin High School. After graduating from Franklin she continued working as a housekeeper until her
456

Carlos Anderson

Raymond Warth

Carlos Anderson attended CHS and credits Principal P.J. Mulkey with "straightening him out."

Bessie (Wilson) Warth's only son, Raymond, died Thanksgiving Day, 1942, of wounds suffered on Guadacanal. Photos courtesy of Carlos Anderson.

marriage to Alva P. Anderson, a streetcar conductor. The couple lived in SE Portland, where their first child, Carlos W., was born, June 20, 1918. A daughter, Mignon L., was born November 9, 1920. Mignon was delivered at her grandparents' home in Springdale.

During the summer of 1926 the family moved to San Francisco. Ollie's sister, Florence, accompanied them in order to join her husband, Joe Eber, who was stationed in California in the Navy. About six months later on January 1, 1927, Alva Anderson died suddenly of Typhoid Fever. Ollie found it necessary to seek a job to support herself and her children. She found it at Leighton's Cafeteria. One day she asked her boss what she was to do. He said, "Just keep making biscuits," which she did. The biscuits piled up as the boss forgot the instruction he had given. Ollie worked in the cafeteria about a year then took a job at the "Dairy Lunch" counter on the waterfront as a cashier.

Going through some of the same trials and tribulations visited upon Americans during the late 20's and early 30's, Ollie often sent her children to stay with relatives. Both stayed with their grandparents in Idaho and Carlos stayed with his Aunt Laura Mershon in Corbett. He attended CHS in 1934-35. During one visit, Mignon met Walter Knieriem whom she eventually married.

While working as a cashier Ollie met a longshore walking boss, Ellis E. Johnson. They married in 1936 and had one daughter, Jeannie, b. January 11, 1939. Her children from her first marriage, Carlos and Mignon Anderson, had established ties in the Northwest, and Mignon lived in East Multnomah County many years (see "Frank Knieriem"). Carlos attended CHS his junior year and remarked, "P. J. Mulkey straightened me out." He served in the CCC's and was drafted into the army during World War II. Carlos served in the European Theater. Carlos has three children, Raymond, Walter and Nancy. He now lives in SE Portland with his wife, Crystal (Shiers). Jeannie (Johnson) Linney lives in Pacifica, California, and has two sons, Paul and David. Olive 'Ollie' (Wilson) Johnson died March 28, 1965 in San Francisco. Mignon (Anderson) Knieriem died in Lewiston, Idaho, Thanksgiving Day, 1974.

Delos E. 'Dell' Wilson also attended Springfield Grade School for eight years starting in 1905. He did not attend high school after graduating from 'Egypt.' He helped his father, who did custom work for other farmers, such as baling hay. He also worked as a logger in the Carson, Washington, area. During World War I he worked in a shipyard as a riveter. Before the war ended he went into a partnership with his father operating a milk route, which involved hauling milk and cream from East Multnomah County dairy farms to a creamery in Portland. On July 4, 1919, Dell went swimming in the Sandy River at the Big Bend with Fred Udey. Fred said that Del "just disappeared" in deep water, and did not come up. By the time his parents arrived at the scene his body had been recovered. Del, age 20 at his death, never married.

Louis Wilson was the first of the Wilson children to be born in Oregon. He also attended 'Egypt' Grade School, graduating in 1915. He did not attend high school. During his teen years, he worked for Mr. Luscher on Salzman Road. (Some years later he would purchase this property.) He also worked at the Philippi Ranch near Arlington, boarding there during the summer months. He drove a "four" or a "six," pulling a header machine harvesting grain. (Leora Philippi later taught mathematics at CHS in Corbett. (Of course she was known as Mrs. Cheney to 'Columbian' students.) Louis also helped his father who baled hay on a

458

custom basis for other farmers. After his brother, Dell, purchased the milk route from Ben Bruger, Louis would often help Del load the cans at each stop. After Dell drowned, Louis took Del's place on the milk route. He also drove the horse-drawn sled loaded with the family's belongings to Springdale over the Christmas holiday in 1919 after his father purchased the Springdale Store from Tom Northway.

Ethel Wilson was born November 20, 1903, on the "Old Miller Place," off Loudon Road on Deverell Road. She was the sixth of eleven children born to the Wilsons. Sometime before she entered school, the family moved to a farm they purchased on Loudon Road. This farm was later sold to the Lofstedts. She attended Egypt School along with her brothers and sisters. In the eighth grade, the kids had a substitute teacher they didn't like. Ethel put a note where the 'sub' would find it, stating: "You've got 24 hours to get out of town." All of the kids conspired together and agreed not to go to school the next day. However, the regular teacher returned, and the "strike leaders" had to get the word out to go to school. Ethel finished the eighth grade at "Egypt," then went to Portland as a "mother's helper," which meant she did housework and babysitting in exchange for a place to stay and school expenses.

She attended Franklin High School for two years, working as a "mother's helper" for a lady who was active in the war effort (WW I) selling Liberty Bonds. After her family moved to Springdale in 1919, Ethel returned home. In her junior year, she enrolled at CHS in Corbett. She walked the two miles from Springdale to Corbett to attend high school, using the Bell Grade cut-off. Ethel remembers riding in the milk truck that her father used in the hauling business, and specifically remembered a time when she caused her brother, Ray, to drive off the road. She thought he was driving too close to the bank, and "helped" him, causing him to lose control and go off the opposite side of the road near the Soderstrom place. Ray was twelve years old at the time.

Later, Ethel returned to Portland and worked at a cafeteria on the corner of Broadway and SW Washington, which she said was called the Ernst Café. In 1923, Ethel hitchhiked to San Francisco with a friend, Eva Richards, who left a husband in Portland! The two carried their belongings in backpacks, and Eva carried a gun in hers. By the time they reached San Francisco the gun was gone, no doubt taken by a benefactor who may have been concerned about what they planned to do with it. According to Ethel, the pair had an exciting trip with no unpleasant incidents.

Louis Wilson

Louis Wilson before the family moved to Springdale, 1919. Photo courtesy of Barbara Case.

After their arrival in San Francisco, the two set about finding Joe Eber, sister Florence's husband, who was in the Navy stationed at Mare Island. Ethel approached an officer who took her to his ship, the USS Shoat. He escorted them to the radio room, thinking the operator could help them locate Joe on one of the destroyers in port.

The officer told the radioman, "These ladies are looking for the Percival." The radioman, Bill Hobart, said, "Who do you know there, Eber?" Ethel remarked that Hobart and Joe Eber apparently had a "run-in" concerning a girl. Anyway, that's when and how she met her future husband, William Hobart, who was the radioman. Hobart knew Joe all right, and the ship he was on, but for some reason didn't want to help them get in touch with him. When he discovered that Ethel and Eva were trying to find Joe because he was married to Ethel's sister, he became more helpful. Hobart asked Ethel for a date and the other radioman asked Eva for a date. Both later married the sailors they met that day. (Ethel didn't mention what became of Eva's 'Portland' husband.)

Ethel and Bill Hobart were married at Vallejo, California, on February 18, 1924. He was a native of Kansas. They had one son, William Jr., b. May 31, 1925. Hobart had various duty stations in the Navy, including San Diego, Mare Island, Panama, Hawaii and New London, Connecticut. William 'Bill' Jr. also served in the U.S. Navy. During the war years, Ethel found a job working at a café in Portland. She also worked in the offices of Lipman Wolfe & Company for a period of time. Hobart retired and returned to Portland after World War II. Later Bill and Ethel moved to California, making their home in the San Diego area for many years. Bill Jr. had two daughters, Sandra and Janice. He died May 13, 1988. Ethel (Wilson) Hobart lives in Lemon Grove, California with a niece, Louise (Wilson) May.

Florence Irene Wilson was to be the final girl born to James C. and Myra Isabella (Miller) Wilson, their seventh of eleven children. During her first year in school Florence created quite a stir when she and Lucille Mack were sent to the spring to get water and didn't return in a timely manner. Florence explained that the two "set the bucket by the spring,

Bridge over Big Creek, Hurlburt Road

From L:, Louis Wilson, George Cummings and Florence Wilson linger on the Big Creek Bridge on Hurlburt Road.   Photo courtesy of Ross Johnson.

and started picking lilies." Engrossed in the task, they became confused and lost. Her brother, Dell, sent to search for the wayward adventurers, found the two and returned them to school. Her grandfather, W.H. Miller, served as Chairman of the Board at Springfield School. The Millers lived close by and Florence remembers visiting them at the old home place off Deverell Road (now reached by Mannthey Road). She particularly remembered the tram device that the family used to get water from a spring far below the level of the house. A bucket released from the house dropped to the spring, and was tripped in such a way that it filled with water, then was pulled back to the house by rope.

Bessie Wilson, taught school at Springfield in 1914 and was Florence's third grade teacher. Florence had an acute appendicitis attack when she was nine years of age, which sent her to the hospital with a ruptured appendix. Because of complications, she had a second operation that same year. One time Florence stayed with her sister, Ollie, in Portland for a few days. Her parents came to get her after delivering milk into town, and they were returning to the farm when Edna Parsons came running from Parson's garage in Springdale shouting for them to stop. Florence says she yelled, "Your son, Dell, drowned in the river." The Wilsons immediately went to the 'Big Bend' below Springdale where the incident took place, and sheriff officers were grappling for Dell's body. Florence related two circumstances that shall be etched forever in her memory. The men in the boat "celebrating" when they located the body

461

Florence Wilson c1919

Florence Wilson enjoys the last day of school
at Springfield.   Photo, the author.

and the way Dell's body was secured to a stake driven in the river bank. His body was tied by rope so that it wouldn't drift away while the all concerned waited for the coroner. Florence believes Dell suffered cramps while swimming. According to Fred Udey, who was with Del at the time, "He went down and never came up." His body must have been in the river for some time since the officers had procured a boat and grappling equipment to look for the body by the time the family arrived at the scene. The drowning occurred July 4, 1919.

According to Florence, Dell's drowning precipitated the sale of the farm on Loudon Road to the Lofstedts. Florence started grade eight at Springdale Grade School, became ill during the year, and had to repeat grade eight the next year. She then attended CHS, which burned during the summer of 1922. The Grange Hall housed CHS students her sophomore year. The new high school (in its present location) was built that year, and she attended it her junior year. While attending high school, she worked at the Chanticleer Inn where her mother also worked. She was paid $5.00 per month, plus meals.

During the Rose Festival in 1922, ships of the U.S. Navy visited Portland and Florence went to the waterfront to see the ships. She met a young sailor, Joseph 'Joe' Eber, who was serving on the USS Percival, a destroyer. After the ships left Portland for their homeport of San Diego, Florence corresponded with Joe. This continued throughout the year until Joe returned to Portland with the "fleet" in 1923. He came to see her at the Chanticleer Inn and they decided to get married. There was a problem, since Florence was just 17 years of age. Florence decided to leave home and the two caught a ride on a "soda pop wagon" into Portland. Somehow, her folks got wind of their plans and were waiting for the errant couple at her sister's (Olive) home when the two arrived. After an earnest discussion, the Wilsons gave their permission for Florence to marry, and she and Joe were married July 7, 1923. They spent their honeymoon in Seattle where the Percival was temporarily based. Joe was soon back in San Diego, and Florence back home, waiting for an opportunity (and the money) to get to San Diego.

When Joe was transferred to Mare Island Naval Yard near San Francisco on shore duty, Florence was finally able to join him. Thereafter Joe had duty stations in San Diego and Panama. While living in San Diego the couple had two sons, Joseph 'Sonny,' b. March 22, 1925 and James 'Jim,' b. December 10, 1926. When Joe was sent to Panama, Florence remained in San Diego and worked at the Pullman Cafeteria. While she was employed there, an "old geezer" tried to get fresh and Florence belted him with a large soup ladle. Her boss, whom Florence described as a "nice lady," defended her, telling the manager, "The old boy got what was coming to him," and she kept her job. In 1927, Joe was discharged from the Navy. The Ebers decided to live in Chicago, which is where Joe's parents lived. According to Florence, this was "a big mistake." The depression of the 30's affected urban dwellers particularly hard, as most apartment dwellers had no place to plant a garden. She describes the time spent in Chicago as the "worst years of my life." When World War II started the family immediately moved back to Oregon (January 1942).

The Eber family stayed with relatives near Springdale until they obtained war housing in St. Johns. Joe worked at the Oregon Shipyard and Florence also worked there several months. Florence trained as a welder at the War Production Training School, held at Camp Withycombe in Clackamas, Oregon. She had 134 hours in electric welding, burning and blueprints. Her instructor was Mel Deadmond, and he gave test results as follows: Flat, "passed"; Vertical, "passed"; Overhead, "Fair." She was sufficiently competent to land a job in the shipyard. However, she quit after about 9 months in the yard. She couldn't stand the spit. She related:

Ethel (Wilson) Hobart　　　　　**Florence (Wilson) Eber**

Ethel (Wilson) Hobart c1949.　　　Florence Eber c1949.
Photo excerpts, the author.

"Men are terrible - they spit on everything. They even spat on the plates I had to weld. It made me sick!" Joe and Florence Eber continued to live in Portland after the war. Currently they live in a foster care home in N.E. Portland. On July 7, 1998, they celebrated their 75th wedding anniversary.

Joe 'Sonny' Eber enlisted in the U.S. Navy in 1944, and served in the South Pacific. He survived the Battle of the Philippine Sea, during which a number of U.S. ships were hit by Japanese kamikaze (suicide) aircraft. His ship, the USS Lowry, also took part in the invasion of Luzon in the Lingayen Gulf. The Lowry was in the contingent of U.S. ships that steamed into Tokyo Bay in September, 1945, to take part in the official Japanese surrender, aboard the USS Missouri. After the war, Sonny married Betty Carden of Oregon City. The couple had two children, Jay C. and Cheryl. Joe 'Sonny' Eber died of cancer in 1994.

Jim Eber entered the Merchant Marine in 1945 with a cousin, David Wall. After the war he enlisted in the U.S. Army with George Mershon, but they went their separate ways when George volunteered for the paratroopers. After Jim was discharged in 1948, he married Doris Briggs, whom he had met while both attended CHS. Doris, born July 28, 1929, graduated from Columbian High in 1947.

The couple lived in N.E. Portland when first married, but in 1965 moved to a home on Corbett Grade, which they completely remodeled. Jim and Doris operated their own business, Roth and Miller Autobody and Paint, Inc. They have four surviving children: Joanna, b. May 25, 1954; Sally, b. January 16, 1956; Camille, b. July 21, 1959; and Robert,

Doris Briggs

Doris Briggs, CHS 1947. Photo courtesy of Ross Johnson.

b. November 26, 1963. Each attended grade and high school in Corbett, though Joanna, Sally and Camille started school in Portland. Joanna graduated from Corbett High in 1972, Sally, in 1974, Camille, in 1977 and Robert, in 1982.

Similarly to the other Wilson youngsters, Woodrow 'Woody' started school at Springfield. When the family moved to Springdale in 1919, he finished his second year at Springdale Grade. He completed grade school there, then started attending CHS. After completing his freshman year, he moved to Idaho with Louis in 1927. In Idaho, he worked as a cowpuncher, principally on the Gould Ranch. When the Wilsons returned to Corbett in 1934, Woody remained in Idaho. March 29, 1939, he married Margaret Palmer. She had twin sons, Ronald and Donald, from a previous marriage. A third son, Darrell, was born in Idaho May 15, 1940. After WW II started, Woody returned to Oregon with his family, borrowing $75.00 to make the move.

Woody joined his brother, Bill, working at the Weatherly Bird Farm in Springdale. He got the job because many employees were quitting to go to work in the shipyards. He was soon transferred to the Weatherly (Pig) Farm near Estacada. When Woody's boss found out that he was taking a course in welding, he was immediately fired. However, work was easy to obtain, and Woody got a job working for the King Brothers as a welder, working there until the end of the war. When forced to leave the "pig" farm, the family moved into a house at Eagle Creek. Louise was born August 12, 1943.

After the war, Woody got a job with Fred Leary demolishing houses. Salvaging lumber, he used it to build a house on an eight-acre place in Stafford, which is where Woody and Margaret raised their children. Woody died while fishing the Sandy River February 16, 1987. He had just landed a steelhead, and collapsed on the riverbank. His brother, Ray, was with him at the time. The fish was served to his friends and family after the funeral.

Clarence H. Wilson
Ethel (Stamey) Wilson

Clarence Henry Wilson was born March 31, 1910, at the family farm on Loudon Road. Henry (Heinie) was the ninth child born to Myra Isabella (Miller) Wilson and James Clarence Wilson. Henry entered "Egypt" School after his sixth birthday. He attended Egypt for 3 1/2 years, and when the family moved to Springdale in December 1919, he attended Springdale Grade School. His parents sold the farm to the Lofstedts and purchased the general store in Springdale from Bill Northway. For some reason not all of the Wilson children moved immediately, some staying with the Ihrke family. Henry remembers Bill telling Mrs. Ihrke that her coffee "looked like tea." Bill enjoyed his coffee strong.

Henry remembered working on a baling machine with which his father did custom work for other farmers. Curly Wilson baled for Al Kerslake (where Henry was able to play with Dorthy Kerslake at the end of the day). At Jum Mershon's place the baling crew slept in the barn. Other farms visited included the Jim Pounder place, the Conrads, Mr. Strebins, the Kerslakes (across the Sandy River on Kerslake Road) and the Corbett Estate. The haying season generally lasted from July into September. Henry was just nine years of age when his brother, Del, drowned in the Sandy River. According to Henry, his father "just gave up" when this tragedy occurred, and sold the farm. The baling machine and other farm equipment was sold with the farm later that year.

After the move to Springdale, Henry completed grade school at Springdale. In 1924, he enrolled at CHS, from which he graduated in 1928. He played baseball 3 years, as a pitcher and outfielder, and basketball for two years. He remembers one time when his brother, Ray, had a run-in with the principal, G.N. McKay. Ray parked in the principal's parking spot, and Mr. McKay was livid about it. Ray felt so put upon, he wanted to transfer to another school, but reason prevailed and he continued at CHS. Henry left his algebra book in the lunchroom once, and went to recess. When he came back, the book was gone. He continued in class without the book. In a couple of weeks, Mr. McKay, who taught the class, returned his book to him, remonstrating with him about leaving it in the lunchroom. Henry, who had been getting A's, fell behind and flunked the course. Henry was relatively tall, 6' 1", but was very slender, weigh-

Henry Wilson

Henry 'Heinie' Wilson played first base for Bill Woodard's 'town' team.

Henry Wilson at a family reunion, 1949.   Photos, the author.

ing about 115 pounds. His teeth bothered him constantly, causing him at one point to pull an offending molar himself.

Henry recalled a basketball trip to Odell (South of Hood River) to which the team traveled by automobile. Henry sat on a teacher's lap all the way. Corbett team members stayed with Odell team members overnight, and returned to Corbett the next day. After Henry graduated, the Wilsons left for Idaho to join their sons, Louis and Woody.

As events unfolded, 1928 turned out to be a fateful year to buy a farm in Idaho. The depression affected commodity prices as early as 1928, and by 1930, farm products had dropped precipitously in price, if one could sell them at all. Henry drove the old milk truck to Idaho where his folks had put money down on a 140-acre ranch. The folks had 60 acres, and Louis had 80 acres. The place had two homes, Louis and Gladys living in one and the folks in the second. They also had two barns. Soon after their arrival in Idaho, cousins Carlos Anderson and Raymond Warth came from San Francisco to stay with the Wilsons. Henry said Carlos and Raymond stayed about one year, until they were old enough to sell papers back home. Henry worked as a cowhand on the Charles Lappin Ranch, (brand CL), for four years after arriving in Idaho. The Lappin family consisted of the parents, 3 sons and 2 daughters. Mrs. Lappin noticed Henry's teeth, and offered to have them fixed by the family dentist in Weiser. He had 7 teeth pulled, 27 fillings, 1 crown, and a bridge made. The total cost for the work was $106.00. Of course, Henry paid this back by his work, but he was grateful to get his teeth fixed at last. After his teeth were fixed, his weight went from 115 lbs. to 165 lbs. in two months.

By 1934, the Wilsons had lost the Idaho ranch and moved back to Corbett. After his folks lost the place, Henry enlisted in the CCC's, and spent the first six months in Council. He then was transferred to Horseshoe Bend on the Payette River, and finally was sent to Payette Lake near McCall, Idaho. During this period he worked on a construction crew building roads. In the spring of 1935, Henry took a job back in Council. He got out of his CCC obligation since he had the promise of a job. He went to work as a cowhand on a ranch owned by George Gould, which ran about 700 head, which meant 700 yearlings and 700 two-year olds. It took three teams working constantly to feed the stock during the winter season. Henry was paid $1.00 per day, plus room and board, though he received $1.25 per day thinning apples, and $2.00 per day haying. He spent ten hours in the field, plus chores at both ends of the day. In 1936, he heard from his folks. His father was having some health problems, so Henry decided to return to Oregon to be with them. He had $4.50 coming, and set out for home with that much in his pocket. He obtained a ride to Lewiston, where he caught the train to Portland. Unfortunately, he didn't have enough money for the entire fare, so ended up at Arlington, and had to hitch a ride from there into Portland. The Wilsons were living at the Hanneman Place on the Columbia River Highway close to its intersection with the Larch Mountain Road, at the time. Henry and younger brother, Bill, continued to live with his folks until his father died in 1941.

When Henry first returned to Oregon, he got a job picking apples in the Hood River valley. He didn't do well there, so moved on to the Yakima Valley in Washington. He picked a few days, getting "ticket credits" each day for the boxes he picked. He made friends with a fellow picker, and gave this "friend" his tickets to collect the money due from the orchard owner. The friend disappeared with Henry's money. As he walked dejectedly down the road the following day, a fellow picked him up. It turned out he owned a packing plant, and had an orchard as well. He offered Henry a job picking apples for four cents a box. Henry said the apples were excellent, and he was able to pick around 200 boxes per day. He earned more than enough to buy a ticket home.

Later that year he worked for J. Ward Evans picking corn for $.35 per hour. After the corn was harvested and canned, he planted daffodil bulbs alongside Roy Pulliam. During the winter of 1936-37, a heavy snowfall hit the area, followed by a bad sleet storm. His father fell on the ice, and the east wind pushed him across a field. He had to crawl back to the house on his hands and knees. In 1937, the family moved to the Judd Place, located on the Columbia River Highway just east of Springdale. Henry went to work on the Weatherly Bird Farm as a night watchman.

The Weatherlys raised about 50,000 pheasants and 50,000 turkeys at any one time. He worked nights until the fall. One of his duties as watchman was to make certain that the young pheasants and turkeys were under the brood heaters. Sometimes something spooked them, and the pheasants, particularly, didn't return to the brooders without some urging. One night, after attending a party, Henry fell asleep and didn't wake up until morning. As one might expect, the pheasants had been spooked during the night, and a few hundred died. One of the watchman's duties was to record the deaths each night. Henry added several birds to each night's total for a period of time until one night's losses could be accommodated. Henry received a promotion thereafter, but he had sufficient time to "doctor" the books before this occurred.

In 1938, the Weatherlys purchased a semi-truck, which was used to deliver the birds to market or other destinations. One time, Henry in his new job as truck driver, took a load of Pheasants to Nevada, to deliver to the Nevada State Game Commission. He encountered an overpass which was too low to permit his load to clear, so he had to unload the top layer, drive through, and re-load the top layer on the other side. At least, he didn't plow into it as might have happened. In Nevada, he turned the pheasants loose under the direction of a game management official. His food allowance ($5.00) permitted him to buy a steak in Reno, Nevada, and have enough left to buy his breakfast as well. He remembers the steak as being one of the best he has ever eaten. Additionally, he stuck the quarter he got in change into a slot machine and hit three prunes for sixteen quarters. He felt he had the world by the tail. Shortly thereafter, the United States was to become embroiled in the conflict underway in Europe, Africa and China.

Henry and Ethel Wilson Family

From L:, Henry, Jerry, Renee, Laurel and Robert Wilson. Ethel Wilson in front.
Photo courtesy of Laurel (Wilson) Cookman.

As the conflict expanded, the economic situation in the United States started to improve. Henry got a job as a laborer at Pendleton, working on a construction project at the airport. One day someone mentioned that ironworkers were needed at the hangar and Henry volunteered. In 1942, he moved to a construction project near Umatilla, where an ammunition depot was being built. In 1943, he obtained his union card, and continued in the ironworker trade the remainder of his working career. Thereafter he worked on many different jobs throughout the Northwest.

On April 3, 1943, Henry married Ethel Stamey at Stevenson, WA. Henry and Ethel had five children, Laurel Cookman, b. 1945; Jerome, b. 1947; twins Robert and Mark, 1954 (Mark died at birth); and Renee, b. 1956. Ethel was a beautician and operated her own shop for many years. The Wilsons lived in the west suburbs of Portland near Beaverton. Henry and Ethel separated after their children were grown. Henry now lives in Hillsboro, OR.

Louis A. Wilson
Gladys K. (Haverkamp) Wilson

Louis Andrew Wilson was born in Latourell, February 22, 1901. He was the 5th child born to James C. and Myra Isabella (Miller) Wilson and the first born in Oregon. Louis attended Egypt School through the eighth grade. In his teen years, he worked for the Luscher family on Salzman Road, a place that he would purchase some years later. He also worked on the Philippi Ranch in Eastern Oregon, boarding there during the summer months to earn his 'keep' and a small wage. One Philippi daughter, Leora, later taught at CHS (Mrs. Leora Cheney). At the ranch, Louis drove a 'four' or 'six' pulling the header machine harvesting grain. After his parents purchased the store in Springdale in 1919, Louis drove a horse-drawn sled heaped with the family's belongings to Springdale between Christmas and the New Year.

After the move, he helped in the store and also helped his father and brother, Del, with a milk route, which had been purchased from Ben Bruger. Ten-gallon cans of milk were picked up from local dairy farms and delivered to a creamery in Portland. Louis' older brother Dell, closest in age to him, drowned in the Sandy River below Springdale in 1919. According to Gladys, Louis always regretted the fact that he didn't attend the funeral because he thought his clothes were not suitable. Louis' sister, Olive, had moved into Portland and Louis went to live with her. While living in Portland, Louis secured a job that involved painting railroad boxcars. Also during this period, he met a young neighbor lady, Gladys K. Haverkamp. He and Gladys were married March 2, 1926. Gladys was born in Portland August 22, 1908, and grew up there. Shortly thereafter, Louis quit his job with the railroad because he developed lead poisoning from the paint. At about this time, Louis' parents sold the house in the Lents District, using the money to make a down payment on a ranch located in Idaho. Louis and Gladys had a lot near the Errol Station that they sold and the proceeds applied to the down payment for the ranch.

Louis and Gladys moved to the Idaho ranch in 1927, taking Louis' younger brother, Woodrow (Woody) along. The family acquired some livestock in the exchange, and the ranch included an orchard. They also sold cream from a few milk cows which came with the ranch. Louis'

Louis and Gladys Wilson

Louis and Gladys Wilson, c1926.
Photo courtesy of Barbara (Wilson) Case.

parents moved to Idaho in 1928, bringing Henry, Bill, and a cousin, Raymond Warth. Everything went well for a time, but Gladys used some cream to make butter for home consumption, and Curly Wilson objected. Cream was to be sold, not eaten, since it was one of the few items that brought cash to the family during the depression years. As a result of this episode, Louis and Gladys moved to another house on the ranch and took *their cows* with them. Louis and Gladys' first and only child, a daughter, Barbara, was born August 24, 1930, in Council, Idaho. According to Gladys, Curly Wilson said, "You'd think they could have waited a while."

Because of the depression, both families were having financial difficulties. Curly and his boys, Louis, Henry, Woody and Bill, all took jobs off the farm to help. The situation became so desperate for farmers that the government bought sheep from farmers going broke. The government wanted only the hides for a tally, so people were allowed to take an

Laura Mershon and Gladys Wilson

Laura Mershon and Gladys Wilson in Idaho,
c1929.   Photo, the author.

animal's carcass if they wished. Unfortunately, in many instances the sheep were a bag of bones, as their owners couldn't afford to feed them. During this period, thousands of sheep were slaughtered. The Wilsons worked for other ranchers, pruned fruit trees, put up hay, and performed other farm or ranch work. One time a rancher hired Louis to help load a boxcar. At the end of the day, Louis was paid ten cents. Louis gave the dime back to the rancher, saying: "You must need this more than I do!" About this time he took a job with the Forest Service, cooking for a forest crew which cruised timber, built trail, surveyed, and performed similar tasks. During summers, he worked as an observer in a forest lookout on Indian Mountain. When his parents returned to Oregon in 1934, Louis and Gladys remained in Idaho for about a year since he had a job with the U.S. Forest Service.

In 1935, Louis and Gladys returned to Oregon and moved in with his parents once again, this time on the Hanneman Place, just west of the intersection of Larch Mountain Road with the Columbia River Highway. Shortly thereafter Louis and Gladys found a small house to rent on Larch Mountain Road. This house was owned by Clara Courtney. Later

Louis Stabler bought the place, which was adjacent to Walt and Veda Mannthey's place. Louis could not find a job, and also came down with a severe case of the mumps during the winter of 1936-37. In January 1937, a snowstorm of record setting proportions hit the area, and Louis was in bed with the mumps. Gladys said that Walt Mannthey kept them in firewood and she has always been grateful for the help he extended to them. Barbara started school at Corbett Grade in 1936.

Later that year, Louis was told that the Smith Lumber Company in Coquille, Oregon, was hiring, so the Wilsons moved there in hopes that Louis could get a job. A friend, Buzzy Shoultz, went along to take advantage of the opportunity. Unfortunately, shortly after they arrived and went to work, the mill workers went out on strike, and the job ended. Meanwhile, Louis and Gladys had rented an apartment in Myrtle Point. The landlady required $.50 extra per month if they had a radio, so Louis had to go into the closet to listen to the news. Later they found a house for rent and gratefully moved from the apartment. Louis and Gladys always had a garden, a cow or two and chickens. They sold tomatoes, cream and eggs to get by. Also, Louis worked for Coos County on a "when needed" basis, which helped pay the rent. The strike at Smith Lumber was never settled. Subsequently, the family moved to a farm outside Myrtle Point owned by an elderly gentleman, and Louis and Gladys helped him in return for a place to live and work. In 1940, the Wilsons moved back to East Multnomah County.

When they first returned they rented a house from Eddy Silva located on Chamberlain Road. When James C. Wilson died in January 1941, Louis and Gladys moved to a "company" house on the Weatherly Bird Farm in order to help his mother, Myra Wilson. Next they moved to the Judd Place, above Springdale. Louis got a job clearing right-of-way for power lines, which were being put through to carry electricity from Bonneville Dam. He worked on the line that traversed the countryside south toward Sandy and Estacada. In 1941, Louis and Gladys bought the Garn farm from the land bank. It was located on Hurlburt Road about a mile from Springdale. Louis' mother lived with them there, as did his brother, Henry. Henry slept in a small house across the road from the principal residence. The Wilsons moved on December 7, 1941, the date Japan attacked the Pacific Fleet at Pearl Harbor.

Louis went to work at the Kaiser Oregon shipyard, along with many others from the East County area. The jobs in defense industries created

The Chapman (later Garn) Home

Louis and Gladys Wilson purchased this place from the Land Bank. After WW II broke out, the Garn family reclaimed it.   Photo courtesy of Rosetta (Henkle) Heitzman.

by the war effort changed the fortunes of many family members. Joe and Florence (Wilson) Eber used the opportunity to leave Chicago and head west. Joe and Jim Eber stayed with Louis and Gladys while their parents looked for a place to live. Being from Chicago, they were somewhat apprehensive of living in the "wild west." One day shortly after they arrived, a big shepherd dog trapped Joe, who was 15, while he was using the outdoor privy. He thought it was a wolf. He remained in the privy hollering for help until he was "rescued." Barbara told of another incident that occurred during the winter of 1941-42 when a severe silver thaw hit. She and Henry were across the road in a pasture sliding on the ice. Henry lost his sled and scooted down the hill on his rear end. Unfortunately for him, the thick ice had formed hard nodules around each blade of grass, so he received an unwanted, painful 'massage' and a bloodied rear-end from the trip down the hill.

The previous owner of the Garn Farm had a year to reclaim it, since it was a land bank sale. With improving economic conditions, the previous owner took advantage of the provision, and once more, Louis and Gladys had to find a place to live. In 1942, taking the down payment and payments that were returned to them when the Garn Farm transaction fell through, they bought the Luscher Place on Salzman Road about one-half mile off Larch Mountain Road. This was the same farm Louis had worked on as a boy. It encompassed approximately 160 acres, and they paid $4,000.00 for it.

Barbara had attended either Springdale Grade School or Corbett Grade School, depending on where the family lived, after the move from Myrtle Creek. When they moved to the Luscher Place, she completed grades 7 and 8 at Corbett. Louis worked at the shipyard throughout World War II. On the farm he ran sheep and cattle and raised berries, corn and cabbage. He also separated and sold cream. When the shipyards closed at the conclusion of the war, Louis continued farming, then went to work at the Bridal Veil Lumber and Box Company. He worked with the maintenance crew, which not only took care of the mill itself, but also maintained the residences in the mill town of Bridal Veil. One job performed by the crew, which involved treating the support timbers under structures with the preservative, Penta, may have had unforeseen consequences for the maintenance crew. Barbara continued school at Corbett, and graduated from CHS in 1948. She went to work at the mill as a bookkeeper, staying there for approximately one year. After the war, Louis and Gladys took in foster children from two families, Hawthorn and Pearson.

When Louis' brother, Bill, married Audrey Vandermost in 1960, he sold an acre of land and the house he owned on Salzman Road back to Louis and Gladys. Gladys had taken care of Rick Wilson for a period of time after Bill and Wanda's divorce. Louis and Gladys decided to sell about one-half of the farm in the early 60's. They first moved into the House that Bill had vacated. Shortly, however, they decided to move to a home they had purchased in Troutdale. They had also purchased a house in Corbett, which was rented. Louis went to work for the Multnomah County Parks Department in 1960. After the move to Troutdale, they sold the house that Bill had built to Wilbur 'Bill' Dearixon, and sold the other half of the farm at about the same time.

In 1966, Louis had a health problem that caused him to see a doctor. He was diagnosed with leukemia. While no conclusive connection was made between his contracting the disease and his work at the mill, many of the maintenance crew contracted and died of this or other forms of cancer. Louis continued to work for the Multnomah County Parks Department until his death in September, 1967. Gladys lived in Troutdale until she married Rod Shoultz in February 1973. Rod died from a heart attack while they were traveling in Idaho in September that same year.

The Melody Playboys

From L, Walt Knieriem, Tom Caddy, Bill Wilson, Luther Young, Barbara Wilson, Joe Eber, __?__ and Norman Keller.   Photo courtesy of Barbara (Wilson) Case.

Later, Gladys moved into a trailer located on her daughter and son-in-law's place in SE Portland. Gladys passed away in Gresham, October 2, 1997.

After graduating from CHS in 1948, Barbara Wilson worked at the Bridal Veil Mill for about a year. During her high schools years and for a period thereafter, she performed with a band called the Melody Playboys at various venues, including the Grange Hall. On September 10, 1949, she married Jack Case who had moved to the area from Goldendale. Jack was born in Traverse City, Michigan November 6, 1924. His family moved to Longview, Washington when he was about five and he attended school in Kelso through the eleventh grade. He completed high school at Goldendale. Jack then enlisted in the US Navy and served in the Pacific Theater during WW II in the Seabees. Among his duty stations were Okinawa, Guam and Tinian

After Jack and Barbara married they made their home in Longview for a time before renting a home from the Schneringers on Larch Mountain Road. They then purchased 8+ acres on Hurlburt Road and built a house. Jack and Barbara had two children, Thomas 'Tom' b. July 26, 1950 and Donna, b. March 19, 1954. The youngsters attended school at Corbett with Tom graduating from CHS in '68, Donna in '72. Tom married Vicki Stuart (CHS '69), who lived on Smith Road. Donna married

Vicki's brother, George W. 'Bud' Stuart. Tom and Vicki have two children, Mathew 'Kelly' and Stacy and now live in LaGrande. Donna and Bud have two children, Benjamin and Adam and live in SE Portland.

Jack worked at the aluminum plant in Troutdale for a time, then had an opportunity to get into the logging business with a partner, logging in the Seaside area. Unfortunately a log rolled, pinning Jack, who suffered a severe leg injury. The family returned to their home on Hurlburt Road and Barbara worked at Sears Roebuck & Company until Jack got a job with the Multnomah County Survey Crew. Barbara worked in the school cafeteria at Springdale one year, then became head cook at Corbett Grade, where she worked for five years (1964-69). She also worked for Marion Kirkham at Kaso Plastics. In 1964, the family moved to a 20-acre place off Chamberlain Road, where they built a house. "We lived in the basement while we finished the upstairs," Barbara said.

After Donna completed high school, Jack and Barbara moved to SE Portland. Floyd (CHS '39) and Dorothy (Conn) Bates (CHS '41) live just across the street. Jack transferred to the County Road Department and continued working there until he retired. Jack and Barbara both enjoyed fishing and hunting. They traveled to their favorite places to enjoy these pursuits until Jack's health problems kept them home. Jack Case passed away August 22, 1999.   *Barbara Case*

Corbett Grade School c1934.   Photo courtesy of Carol Daiber.

Raymond L. Wilson
Pearl (Chamberlain) Wilson

Raymond Lester Wilson was born at the family home on Loudon Road February 3, 1908. Dr. Bittner came from Gresham by horse and buggy to attend his mother, Myra Isabella (Miller) Wilson. According to Ray, his father worked at the Gebhardt Mill, which was located on Mannthey Road near the point it crossed Buck (Trapper) Creek. His grandparents, the Millers, lived off Deverell Road, but their place was just across Buck Creek and within walking distance of the Wilson place. Ray, together with his brothers and sisters, attended Springfield Grade School, which was located about a mile east on Loudon Road. His first grade teacher was his sister, Bessie.

Since many of the teachers were just getting started in the profession, and didn't stay at Springfield, he remembers a succession of teachers: Bessie Wilson, first grade; Mary Gebhardt, second grade; Olga Graff, third grade; Louise Sterling, fourth grade; and Mary Gebhardt, fifth grade. The Wilson kids made their own play equipment. Ray reminisced about a sled he put together using vine maple saplings for the runners, which were clad with metal that formerly sheathed a buggy wheel. The runners were tied to the body by a series of sapling stems cut to the proper length, and the body itself was made with thin boards and more sapling lengths. To make a wagon, the youngsters cut rounds from a large tree branch for the wheels (preferably cottonwood). They either bored a hole for the axle or drove a nail through the center of the round to complete the wheels. The bed was made from thin boards, and a 1 by 2 was used for the tongue. The kids also used their imagination to create play opportunities. Ray said they would pile up the mud (which became abundant on Loudon Road when it rained) into great piles, which were hollowed out to form 'igloos.' On a ridge near their home, Ray and his brothers and sisters made a mud slide, using barrel staves for 'sleds.'

In 1913, another big fire swept through the countryside in the Larch Mountain area. Embers from the flames to the east landed near the Wilson's home on Loudon. Everyone pitched in with buckets of water and wet gunnysacks to keep the house from burning. During Ray's sixth grade year, the Wilsons moved from the farm to the Springdale store. It

479

was during this winter that the Columbia River Highway through Springdale was closed for about two weeks because of drifting snow.

Ray completed elementary school at Springdale, graduating in 1922. During his eighth grade year on November 20, 1921, a tremendous sleet storm hit Multnomah County. First, everything was covered with about 2 inches of ice, followed by about an inch and one- half of snow, then capped by more ice, up to 7 inches in places. There wasn't a power line up in East County. This is the storm that ended the Italian Plum (prune) industry in the area, and damaged all the fruit and other types of trees. It took the tops out of thousands of fir trees. The Wilsons got enough wood from the tops of firs and other damaged trees to supply them with enough firewood for two years.

Ray attended Corbett High School, but his freshman year was spent in the Grange Hall because the High School burned during the summer of 1922. The new high school was completed during the 1922-23 school year, and the students moved into the new building Ray's sophomore year. Ray said he and Chester Bell were returning home from school at the Grange and decided to do some rock throwing. They threw rocks at the chimney in the burned-out former high school building until it collapsed. Ray played basketball and baseball during his high school years. In the final basketball game of the 1926 season, Columbian High beat Gresham High for the first time. The team included Ted Berney, Roy Pulliam, John Phipps, Orville Linn, Earl Chamberlain and Ray. Ray graduated from CHS in 1926.

When the family moved to Springdale, they lived in the store. One time Ray, driving the milk truck on its rounds, ran the truck off Hurlburt Road near the Soderstrom Place. Ethel takes the blame for the accident, saying she "helped" Ray because he was getting too close to the edge of the road, but Ray thinks he was just going too fast. He was twelve years of age at the time. Among the dairy farmers Ray remembers were: Jacob Seidl, Sam Hulitt, Ed Woodard, Charlie Bramhall, Franz Frommelt, Julius Wand, Bill Hurt, Charlie Berney, Frank Fehrenbacher, and Martin Nelson. Dell and his father had purchased a second truck, a Winther, from Wentworth and Irwin early in 1919. After Dell drowned, Ray's father, James, continued to operate the milk route business until it and the store were sold to George Atkinson.

One of Ray's first jobs was working for Lorentz Brothers Construction, which had a job on the Meier Estate (Menucha). He worked as a

Mt. Defiance Lookout c1934

Ray Wilson at the Mt. Defiance lookout in 1934. He holds a nephew, Clarence Mershon, while a second nephew, George Mershon, helps with the chores.   Photo, the author.

carpenter's helper. When that job was finished, he continued working at the Estate for the estate manager, George Perry. Ray started college at the Oregon Agricultural College (now Oregon State University) in 1927, attending two terms. He went out for basketball under Slats Gill, but quit at the winter break because Gill seemed to have already selected his team. After he left OAC, he worked for several farmers in East County, and stayed with his sister, Laura Mershon. Once sliding down a hill with Ted Berney on a home made toboggan (a piece of metal plate), Ray sliced off part of his right heel. Another time while backing a car out of the barn, Ray bumped into his nephew, George Mershon, who was about 3. George was running after his Uncle Ray when hit by the car. Ray had to take him to the doctor for stitches. On the return trip home, George said, "That doctor's a son-of-a-bitch." During this period of time, Ray completed two more terms at OAC.

In 1931, Ray got a job to pay his way to Pacific University, planning to play baseball. His foot had healed sufficiently for him to go out for the team. However, during practice as he went to pick up a bat, a line drive hit him in the face and broke his jaw. That ended both baseball and his college days. He returned to the Mershon Place and went to work for the County. His first job involved dynamiting the bluff close to where the Tippy Canoe Restaurant is now located. Ray helped George 'Jum' Mershon, on his farm off and on from 1928 to 1933. In 1933, Ray joined the CCC's. In 1934, the Forest Service called Ray to man the Mt. Defiance lookout. That fall he worked on the Eagle Creek Trail just below

Ray Wilson packing his tent for the fall hunt.
Photos courtesy of Marge (Stephens) Soesbe.

Pearl and Ray Wilson shortly after their marriage. Myra Wilson
(partially hidden).

Wahtum Lake with Nick Anderson and Bill Soderstrom. During the summer of 1935, he was again called by the Forest Service to take the Mount
Defiance lookout. At the close of fire season, he worked on the forest
road being constructed from Larch Mountain to Hood River. One must
remember that the Northwest, similarly to the rest of the country, was
suffering through a severe depression, and jobs were hard to find. The
summer of 1936 found Ray working for the Corbett Water District laying main line pipe to areas to be served by the new district. During the
latter part of the fire season, the Forest Service contacted Ray to again
take the Mt. Defiance lookout. That fall, he was called to fight a forest
fire that broke out in the District.

Ray married Marie (Silva) Wall in April, 1935. She had two children
by a previous marriage, David (7) and Louise (4). They moved into the
old Pleasant View School on Wand Road. Ray bid $219 for the old school
building, which sat on a one-acre parcel. The terms were $100 down and
the balance within a year. He paid for it with his earnings from the Forest
Service. Ray worked for the WPA during 1937 and 1938, helping build
the Larch Mountain Road among other projects. He also worked with Ig
Wand wiring houses. During the period just prior to World War II, he
held several jobs. He worked for the Ridge Lumber Company a couple
of years, rigging one year, and falling and bucking another. He worked
for an interval in Gresham for the company that was building the cold
storage plant; and he worked on construction of the aluminum plant at
Troutdale for several months. It was during this period, also, that his

Pearl and Ray's Family

Rear from L:, Pearl (Chamberlain) and George Stephens. Front: Carol Stephens, Donna Wilson, Del Wilson and Myra Wilson.

From L:, Myra Wilson, Donna Wilson and Marge Stephens. Photos courtesy of Marge (Stephens) Soesbe.

family increased. Myra was born September 15, 1937; Dell was born September 24, 1938; and Donna was born February 21, 1941. Shortly after the war started, he went to work at the Kaiser Swan Island Shipyard as an ironworker. He worked on setting up the Whirleys first, and then did production work in the shipyards until August 1945, when the war ended. Ray and Marie divorced near the end of the war. Ray was given custody of their three birth children, while Louise and David Wall remained with their mother.

Ray started going with his former high school sweetheart, Pearl (Chamberlain) Stephens (see "George Chamberlain"). She had three children by this marriage, George, b. April 1, 1933, Marge, b. March 20, 1936 and Carol, b. October 19, 1937. Ray and Pearl married October 4, 1946, in Grants Pass, Oregon. Pearl was living in Kirby, OR and teaching in Selma at the time. In the spring of 1948, they moved to a farm east of Oregon City in Beavercreek, where they raised their combined family of six children.

Ray Wilson continued working as an ironworker after the war, while Pearl continued in her career as a schoolteacher. She taught at Concord Elementary School for many years before retiring in 1972. Ray eventually was hired by the Ironworkers Union to manage its apprenticeship program. He retired from that position in 1973. Ray and Pearl moved from Beavercreek to a home off 82nd Avenue in SE Portland, and later moved to a home in Milwaukie, OR. Some of their retirement years were spent in a church retirement community located near Mineral, Washington. Later still, they moved to a mobile home park in Gladstone, Oregon. Ray Wilson died at home March 24, 1995. *Ray Wilson*

CHS after the 1922 fire,
Photo courtesy of Ann (Reeves) Steers.

William D. Wilson
Leona (Winegar) Wilson

William D. 'Bill' Wilson was born October 24, 1913, at home (Latourell address). When Bill was born, the Wilsons lived on Loudon Road relatively close to the Miller Place. Bill remembers moving to Springdale during the winter of 1919-20. Bill remembers staying with a neighbor, the Ihrkes, for an interval before moving to Springdale. The Ihrkes had purchased the Miller place from Bill's grandparents. After the move, Bill attended Springdale Grade School, from which he graduated in 1928.

The Wilson family moved to Council, Idaho, in 1928. Henry and Bill were the only children who went with them, but a cousin, Raymond Warth, Bessie (Wilson) Warth's son, also accompanied them. Bill, the other Wilson boys and the cousins worked as ranch hands, helping on cattle drives, branding cattle, haying and similar chores. Despite these jobs and finding other work in the area, such as hauling gravel for the County and picking fruit, the family could not hold onto the ranch. In 1934, they headed for Oregon in a Model A Ford obtained in trade for their equity in the ranch.

When the Wilsons returned to Oregon, they lived in the original Mershon home at the intersection of Lucas Road and Mershon Road for several months. It had been vacant for a number of years and the roof leaked. However, it didn't leak over the beds or over the kitchen stove, which helped some. Eventually the family rented the Hanneman Place, just west of the junction of Larch Mountain Road and the Columbia River Highway. Bill got a job on the Meier Estate (now Menucha). When a co-worker told Bill of PWA (Progress and Works Administration) jobs opening up to build the Corbett Water System, Bill applied for a job. He was hired and worked with the pipe crew, which laid the lines in the previously dug ditches. He worked on the section from the Larch Mountain Road (near the CCC camp) to the reservoir, which was being built on Gordon Creek. His brother, Ray, also worked on the pipe gang.

In 1937 Bill went to work for Mr. G.W. Weatherly at the "bird farm" (off Hurlburt Road). Mr. Weatherly also owned the Weatherly Building in Portland. The principal flocks were turkeys and pheasants. Bill was in charge of the incubators. The hatch each year was between forty and fifty thousand birds, split about evenly between turkeys and pheasants. Bill's brother,Henry, worked at the farm before Bill was hired. Bill worked for the Weatherlys six years. In 1941, with the bombing of Pearl Harbor, World War II commenced for the United States. Since Bill was working for Weatherly Farms, he was exempt from the draft.

Bill married Wanda Preston, whose family resided in Springdale near the junction of Hurlburt Road and the Columbia River Highway. Bill and Wanda's first home was at the bird farm. When Bill went to work for the Colfield Brothers Chicken Ranch in 1943, they moved to Eagle Creek. Bill worked at this ranch for approximately three years, and was involved in all aspects of the chicken business, raising chickens for eggs and fryers. He delivered eggs to the East Moreland Grocery and to the Excel Donuts Company, which used "candled" reject eggs. In 1946, Bill and Wanda moved back to Corbett, renting a house from Art Blanc just off Littlepage Road (near the top of the hill toward the Grange Hall where the Hubbard family later lived). He and Wanda had one son, Rick, born in 1951. Wanda and Rick now live in Sparks, Nevada.

Bill got a job at the Bridal Veil Mill, and worked there for five years. He purchased an acre of land on Salzman Road from his brother, Louis Wilson, where he and Wanda built a house. One day Bill encountered Pat and Bob Kerslake on the road and asked them about a job with the Multnomah County Road Department. Somewhat to his surprise, they hired him, and in 1951 he started with the road department.

Bill married Audrey (Chapman) Vandermost in 1960 and moved to SE Portland. Bill underwent surgery for pancreatic cancer and, beating the odds, survived. After separating from Audrey, Bill met Leona (Winegar) Gilbert. Leona was born in Soldier, Idaho, November 11, 1912. In 1985, Bill and Leona were married in Weiser, Idaho, close to the location of the former Wilson ranch. Bill said the fee was a whole lot cheaper in Weiser, and since they were to be there for the old-time fiddlers' competition anyway, they used the money saved in marriage fees to pay for the trip! Bill has always had an interest in music. His father played the fiddle at community events, and entertained family and friends with his music. Bill learned to play the harmonica while he was in grade school. He took up the fiddle and guitar after the family moved to Idaho, and has enjoyed playing since. He is completely self-taught. Buck Beeman had a group called the Western Pals, and while Bill used to play along with Buck and other friends and relatives, he never played professionally. A niece with whom he and his friends used to "pal" with was Elda Mershon.

She liked to sing and would often sing accompanied by Bill. Another niece who liked to sing with him was Barbara Wilson. She sang professionally with Buck's band among others.

Bill started attending the Grand National Fiddling Contest, an annual event in Weiser, Idaho, in 1966. He participated in the fiddling competition 25 consecutive years, not missing the event until 1991. He amassed a collection of fiddles, but in recent years gave them away. Bill met many celebrities and famous musicians at old time fiddling contests that he attended, and in which he participated.

When the sesquicentennial of the Oregon Trail was celebrated during 1993, Bill had an opportunity to take part because his niece, Laurel Cookman, was one of the organizers of the event. The principal activity to commemorate the anniversary was to be a wagon train following the Old Oregon Trail from Independence, Missouri, to Independence, Oregon. Laurel worked with the Aurora Chamber of Commerce, which sponsored one of the wagons for the trek. The Aurora wagon was to commemorate the story of the founder of the Aurora Colony, "Bringing Willie Home." Willie, the founder's son, had died just before the wagon train left Missouri, and the father, to fulfill a vow, carried his son's body in a coffin to Oregon. The wagon sponsored by the Aurora Chamber was to commemorate this event. Bill contributed the use of his motorhome for the use of Laurel, Henry Wilson and the muleskinner, Earl Leggett. Bill and Henry were called "scouts," and preceded the wagon train each day to the selected camp site to help set it up, and perform some of the advance work.

People at various towns arranged for celebrations as the wagons reached their town. The folks at Hanover, Kansas, had a free barbecue for the "pioneers." Townspeople at Odell, Nebraska, held a barbecue with a beer garden, wagon rides, cloggers and fiddlers. At many stops Bill played his fiddle for the wagon circle. He also played at many of the celebrations held along the way. Bill stayed with the wagon train until it reached Fort Bridger, Wyoming. The wagons followed the Old Oregon Trail through Nebraska and into Wyoming, staying at such famous way stations as Fort Laramie, Cheyenne, Kemmerer (1st J.C. Penney store), Fort Casper (where 10,000+ people visited the train), Chimney Rock, Independence Rock, Devil's Gap, and Pacific Springs (1st camp across the divide). Bill played his fiddle for a wedding celebration held at Rattlesnake Ranch, Wyoming.

Bill left the train July 31 at Fort Bridger to do some advance work in Western Wyoming and Idaho. He met the wagon train several times thereafter, but didn't travel with them. Of course Laurel and Henry continued on with the train as it traveled through Idaho and into Oregon. The wagon train pulled into Independence, Oregon, October, 1993. The trip took weeks and left the participants tired, but grateful to be able to participate in such a commemorative event. They had more comforts than the pioneers, but suffered some of the same problems and personal entanglements that created difficulties for the pioneers.

Leona Wilson died at her home in Milwaukie September 23, 1992. Bill Wilson passed away at home March 24, 1996, age 82. *Bill Wilson*

Weatherly Farms Crew Christmas Party 1941

Rear, (second from left) Vernon Jameson, (far right) Woody Wilson holding Darrell. Middle, Gertrude Jameson, ? , ?, Margaret Wilson, Wanda (Preston) Wilson, ?, ?, ?. Bottom, (second from left) Ronald Wilson, Bill Wilson and Donald Wilson.

Photo, the author.

Howard Winters
Ruth (Woodle) Winters

Howard was born December 13, 1913, in Lawrence, Michigan. His father was Andrew Winters, and his mother was Geneva (Wallings) Winters. The family moved to Oregon in 1915, settling first in Bend, then moving to Astoria, before finally settling in Falls City. Howard has three brothers, Elmer (killed in WW II), Herb (deceased) and Merle, and four sisters, Margaret Pierre (deceased), Genevieve Roseman, Marie Kathleen (deceased) and Gertrude Marie Myers. During the family's early years in Oregon, Howard's father, Andrew, worked as a common laborer, mostly in lumber mills.

According to Howard, he picked berries for Fred Delgen of Falls City when he was just 6 years of age, along with others in his family. The family moved from Falls City to Portland when Howard was eight years of age, where he attended Elliott School. He remembers picking raspberries with his family for a Gresham berry grower, Andy Auglinder, during these years. As fall approached in 1922, the Winters moved to Hood River in order to pick fruit. They remained in Hood River until Howard was eleven. In 1925, the family moved to Corbett, where they stayed at George Chamberlain's campground. The charge for a cabin was $1.00 per night, and for a camping space, $.50 per night. They stayed in a tent initially, but took a cabin when the weather turned cold and wet. Howard and his sister, Margaret, worked for Phil Van Hee in Corbett for $.25 per hour. He also remembers working for Harry Burkholder picking up potatoes, for which he was paid $.05 for a 60 lb. bag. After a few months of "roughing it," the family rented a house from Erik Enquist in Springdale, across the Columbia River Highway from Lige Chamberlain's place. Howard attended Springdale Grade School, graduating from the eighth grade in 1928.

Howard's parents separated in the spring of 1929. Howard stayed a month with Barney and Marian Woodard, who lived on Hurlburt Road in the building which had formerly housed the Woodmen of the World Lodge. In May he went to work for James (Jim) Pounder, who lived on Littlepage Road. Mr. Pounder had married Nettie Kincaid after he lost his first wife several years previously. Pounder grew crops such as cabbage, cauliflower, potatoes, barley, wheat, hay, rye and vetch, corn (for ensilage), and kept dairy cattle. Howard gained some experience operating farm equipment since Mr. Pounder owned a Fordson tractor, a Champion binder and a Case thrashing machine. Howard worked for the Pounders until November 1933, remembering Mr. Pounder as being a good, honest, hardworking man from whom he learned much about farming. He credits this experience with helping him attain his own success in subsequent years.

During the time Howard lived with the Pounders he attended CHS, from which he graduated in 1932. He played baseball for the high school team. He also played baseball for Bill Woodard's team. Other players on the teams included: Francis Benfield, August DePaepe, Clifford Ellis, Bob Ellis, Dick Ellis, Art Grimm, Frank Jackson, Walter Jackson, Carl Lofstedt, Roland Morgan, Charles Pulliam, Wesley Post, Donald Reed, Jimmy Tanner, Alex Wand, George Wand, Henry Wilson, James Wilson and Ray Wilson. Howard remembers his high school teachers, among whom were: P.J. Mulkey, Principal, math and history teacher; Leslie 'Spike' Emerson, science and industrial arts teacher and coach; Sarah A. Poor, literature and Spanish teacher; Miss Genevieve Rosen, English, French and typing teacher; and Miss Pauline Remington, business, home economics and typing teacher. He has positive things to say about his teachers, and thought very highly of Mr. Mulkey.

Howard left the Pounders in the winter of 1933, moving to Portland where he stayed in Lents with the Arnett family. Shortly he moved to Scappoose, where he worked for Walter and Margaret Erickson on their dairy farm. He received $25.00 per month plus room and board. He moved again in 1934, after getting a job at the Martinose Dairy on the Willamette Slough. In October 1934, he returned to Corbett, working for Ed Wilson on his bulb farm for about a month before moving to the Ed Klinski farm. The Klinkis had dairy cattle and raised potatoes, peas, cabbage, cauliflower and lettuce. In addition to room and board, he was paid $15.00 per month and received 10% of the crop. Klinski grew "British Queen" seed potatoes, which were sold to Fred Doss in Portland at $.55 per hundred pounds.

In December 1935, Howard rented the McGill place for $75.00 per year. He paid $40.00 down. This place is located off Woodard Road on Mutch Road. He sublet it to Ed Klinski for a few years. A Mr. Howell owned the property. During 1935 and 1936 Howard continued to work for other farmers, including John Seidl, for whom he drove a team for $2.00 a day. Robert (Tood) Larson hired Howard to do some hauling for

490

Winters Truck Service

Howard Winters with a load of hay hauled from Touchet, Washington.

Andrew Winters

Howard's father, Andrew Winters standing in front of the Bramhall house on Woodard Road. Photos courtesy of Dorothy Larson.

Cultivating Strawberries

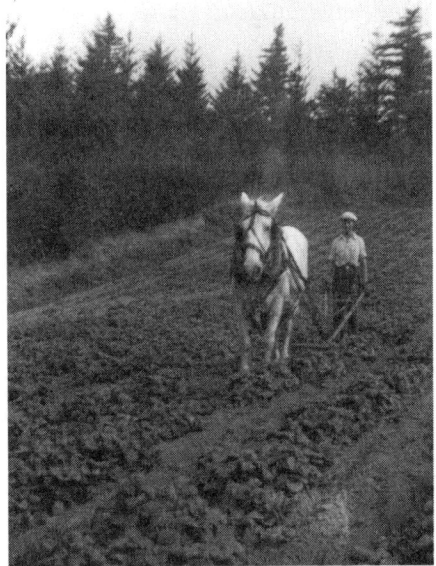

Howard Winters cultivates strawberries on the Bramhall place with Pack, obtained from the Tatsuzo Nakashimada.

him to Touchet, Washington, near Walla Walla, for $5.00 a trip, the round-trip taking two days. He hauled concentrate to the Conser Feed Mill in Walla Walla, carrying wheat on the return trip to Portland for a J.J. Chisholm. Tood was getting $4.00 per ton to haul the concentrate, and $5.00 per ton to transport the wheat. The truck's capacity was nine to eleven tons. During the late summer and fall, Howard also hauled cucumbers from farmers in East Multnomah County to Libby, McNeil and Libby, Knight Packing Company and Kerr Conserving Company. Also in 1936, Howard started working for Tood's father, Bob Larson, at their farm on Ogden Road, for which he received room and board.

Later that year, Tood Larson offered Howard a 25% interest in the trucking enterprise, which Howard accepted. Thereafter the business was called 'Winters Truck Service.' Howard said that he had to accept part of the risk, but that he might also gain from his willingness to work hard. Winters Truck Service purchased a new Diamond T truck in 1936, a new Ford truck in 1937, and a new Ford semi-tractor in 1939. They continued the hauling jobs mentioned earlier, while expanding the operation by hauling produce to Pacific Fruit branches in Bellingham, Mt. Vernon, Kelso, Centralia, The Dalles, Salem, Corvallis, Eugene, Coos Bay, Roseburg, Grants Pass, Medford, Klamath Falls, Bend, LaGrande, Pendleton, Pasco, Yakima, Walla Walla and Spokane. Because both of them worked so hard during these latter years of the depression, their trucking business made money each year during the period. Howard purchased an additional 25%, making him a full partner with Tood.

In 1940, Howard and Tood formed a partnership to farm. Ed Klinski decided not to rent the McGill Place in 1940, so this gave them an extra incentive to start farming. It turned out to be an opportune time because the market for farm produce started to pick up that year. Their first purchase was a new R-2 Caterpillar, with which they did a lot of custom work. In 1941, they purchased a new D-2 Caterpillar, which turned out to be excellent timing, since equipment became very difficult to obtain after the war started December 7, 1941. He also bought an almost new '41 Pontiac from Hiro Takeuchi, which was a great automobile. When the Japanese were sent to "relocation" camps in May 1942, Larson and Winters rented the Bramhall Place on Woodard Road, which the Nakashimada family had been farming. They purchased much of Mr. Nakashimada's equipment. Howard moved into the house located on the Bramhall place in 1942. Larson and Winters continued the trucking business during the war, but farming became much more important to them because there was such a heavy demand for produce. The Federal government purchased heavily for the armed services and for export to our Allies. The partnership raised potatoes, cabbage, strawberries, grain, bulbs, and cauliflower, but because cabbage, potatoes and grain were especially in demand, they planted more acreage to these crops (see "Robert Larson").

492

The '41 Pontiac

Howard stands beside his '41 Pontiac purchased from Hiro Takeuchi. Hiro sold it because of the forced relocation of the Japanese people to internment camps.   Photos courtesy of Dorothy Larson.

Farm Help

From L, Gus McCleary (on the hood), Alfred 'Bud' Mershon, George Mershon, Merle Winters and Bill McCleary worked for Larson & Winters at the Bramhall Place. Photo courtesy of Dorothy Larson.

Howard purchased the McGill Place (33+acres) in 1943, paying $3700 for it. The Bramhall Place (54 acres) was purchased in 1945. On September 18, 1945, Howard married Ruth 236Woodle, daughter of Claude and Gladys Woodle. The Woodles owned and operated Corbett Hardware (across from CHS) for years. Howard and Ruth's first son, Howard, was born August 12, 1946. In 1946, Howard and Tood dissolved their farm partnership. Prior to this, they had sold their PUC hauling permit. Tood took the bulb business; Howard took the farm equipment. He and Ruth continued to farm. A second son, Chris, was born July 16, 1948. In

493

Dusting Cauliflower c1942

Howard fills the duster with rotenone to dust cauliflower.
Photo courtesy of Dorothy Larson.

Working the Bramhall Place

Howard Winters disking the Bramhall Place. Note the barn in the background. Photo courtesy of Dorothy Larson.

1950, Howard bought a 53.75-acre farm on Seidl Road from Leo Fehrenbacher for $22,350. Leo had obtained the place after the Kuwabara family vacated it before the war. Howard, Ruth and family moved into the house on that property after the purchase. In 1949, Howard and Ruth purchased a 4 2/3-acre parcel on the east side of the Mutch Road (where it intersects the Woodard Road) from Martin Nelson for $400. A daughter, Eileen, was born to Howard and Ruth August 18, 1950. In 1951, they purchased the Campbell Place, off Mutch Road for $1650.00, which added 18+ acres to their farm, and In 1952, they added the Crowston Place (49+ acres at the end of Mutch Road) to their holdings at a cost of $8500.00. A third son, Marven, was born June 6, 1954. In 1987, they

494

Ruth (Woodle) Winters

Together Howard and Ruth Winters accumulated approximately 240 acres of farm and timber land on the 'hill.'   Photo courtesy of Chris Winters.

purchased the Federspiel Place (22.45 acres), which is across Ogden Road from their home, for $60,000.

Howard has been associated with the farm economy in East Multnomah County since 1925. From humble beginnings, he has, through hard work, perseverance, an astute business sense and a willingness to take risks, amassed approximately 240 acres of land, about 140 acres of which he and his family farm. His farm is one of a few in the Corbett area that survived the post war years as a functioning economic unit.

The Winter's oldest son, Howard, attended Corbett schools 12 years. After graduating from CHS in 1964, he served 3 1/2 years in the Air Force. Young Howard married Patricia Ann LaTrent in 1968. After his discharge, he attended Oregon State University, graduating with a business degree (accounting). The couple's son, Brian, attends Cal Tech and their daughter, Laura, attends Reynolds High School. Howard and Ruth's second son, Chris, also attended Corbett schools for 12 years. He then worked for Parman & Ellis in Portland, the company that manufactures

Freeman Farm Equipment. Chris married Ingaborg Remun of Switzerland. They have a son, Ian, and a daughter, Sophie. After about 5 years, he was called home to help manage the farm, and has been working there since. Howard and Ruth's daughter, Eileen, attended Corbett schools for 12 years, graduating in 1968. She then attended Mount Hood Community College, where she studied business. She applied for a job with Fireman's Fund Insurance and has been in the insurance business since, though she continues to keep the books for the Winters' farming operations. Howard's youngest son, Marven, attended Corbett schools 10 years before transferring to Barlow High School, from which he graduated in 1972. Marven stayed on the farm, and continues to help manage that enterprise.

Howard lost his beloved wife, Ruth, July 9, 1990. Ruth suffered from cancer, and died from its effects. Howard has been slowed by some health problems, including replacement hip surgery and triple bypass heart surgery, but he has not been sidelined by any means. He serves as an advisor to his sons who operate the farm, and to his daughter, who takes care of the books. Speaking as one who worked for Howard, he could probably still outdo me on a cabbage planter, even at the age of 80+ years. He thoroughly enjoys his four grandchildren, pays close attention to their progress, and delights in rewarding them for their achievements.

Howard Winters

Bramhall Home

Second Bramhall home on Springhill Road.
Photo courtesy of Pat (Bramhall) Paget.

496

Index to Complementary Photographs

498

Front Cover: The picture on the front cover is from an untitled painting by Mr. Charles Wesley Post. At age 16, Post traveled to Europe to study art. A pupil of the Royal Academy in Munich, he also studied in Paris, Florence and Rome. He became interested in engraving and was associated with William Unger, Germany, for two years. After returning to the United States, he established a studio at Chanticleer Point. For Post, the Columbia River Gorge became his passion. He roamed the hills, sketching and filming its wonders. In March 1922, before he could complete the work he had undertaken, Post passed away. *The artist's grandson, Charles W. 'Wes' Post, kindly provided the print reproduced on the front cover.*

Back Cover: The top picture (c 1955) is a planting of Beersheba daffodils on the Murray and Stella Evans farm, Mannthey Road. The cultivar, Beersheba, was used extensively in hybridizing. *Photo courtesy of Stella Evans.*

The center picture (c 1955) is a planting of tulips on the original Van Speybrock place, Columbia River Highway. Planted by the Van Speybrocks, the blooms provide a hint of the beautiful fields of flowers that once flourished in East Multnomah County. The young lad in the picture is Donald Van Speybrock's oldest son, Ronald. *Photo courtesy of Bob Van Speybrock.*

The lower picture (c 1952) is a planting of daffodils on the Vic Ellis place, Evans Road. Again, the picture is a reminder of the glorious panorama that greeted visitors to East Multnomah County when the growing of daffodils, gladiolas and other flowers was a major part of the farm economy. *Photo courtesy of Joan (Evans) Benner.*

Acknowledgments

As mentioned in the Foreword, Alice Wand provided the impetus that started me on this project. Board members of the East Multnomah County Pioneer Association have been most supportive and helpful. In addition to sharing many superb photographs, Frieda O'Neil provided the initial encouragement needed to 'get me going' in earnest. Arlene (Johnson) Marble read a draft copy of the book and corrected several errors. In addition to Frieda, the Bates family, Joan Benner, Mickey Chamberlain, Rosetta Heitzman, the Kerslake family, Dorothy Larson, Steve Lehl, Inga Myers, Pat Paget and many others provided exceptionally useful photographs of historic interest. Acknowledgement of the individual who supplied each photo is found beneath the picture.

The individual(s) from whom information and data were obtained is credited at the conclusion of each family's 'story.' Several individuals deserve special mention. Joan (Ellis) Benner kindly volunteered to do the final edit. She has an acute eye for errors and detail discrepancies that one could easily overlook. She also suggested several changes to eliminate awkward, confusing or ambiguous phrasing. Nona Layton's genealogical records are invaluable. One needs only call her to obtain the data desired. Of course, Bea Graff's original work is an invaluable resource regarding pioneer families. Albert Kimbley's knowledge regarding 'who lived where' has been very helpful. Once again, Denny Hyde provided computer expertise, converting the work from Word, into PageMaker,, scanning and enhancing the photos and getting the book 'camera ready' for publication. His skill in this area is unsurpassed (and individuals with such skills are difficult to find).

Finally, many thanks to my wife, Colleen, who has encouraged me in this endeavor. She has read every sentence, been most supportive and has refrained from criticizing me for the long hours spent at this work.

Index

502

506

507

515

517